# The Medieval World

# The Medieval World

HELEN HOWE
ROBERT T. HOWE

Longman

Authors:
**Helen Howe**
teacher of Ancient and Medieval History and of
Latin at Walnut Hills High School, Cincinnati, Ohio
**Robert Howe**
Professor Emeritus, University of Cincinnati

Executive Editor   **Lyn McLean**
Production Director   **Ed Castillo**
Developmental Editor   **Anne Jensen**
Project Designer   **Gayle Jaeger**
Photo Researcher   **Katherine Rangoon**
Art Studio   **J & R Art Services, Inc.**

ISBN: 0-8013-1100-4

Longman
10 Bank Street
White Plains, New York 10606

*Associated Companies:*
Longman Group Ltd., London
Longman Cheshire Pty., Melbourne
Longman Paul Pty., Auckland
Copp Clark Pitman, Toronto
Pitman Publishing Inc., New York

*Supplementary Materials:*
Teacher's Handbook
Worksheet Masters

7  8  9  10-DOC-96

*Contributing Editor:*
**Dean Moore**
Supervisor of Social Studies
Cincinnati Public Schools

*Consultants:*
**Mildred Alpern**
History Teacher
Spring Valley Senior High School, New York

**Wentworth Clarke**
Professor of Social Science Education
University of Central Florida at Orlando

**William R. Dunnagan**
Social Studies Teacher
Klein Independent School District, Texas

**Roy Erickson**
Program Specialist for Social Studies
San Juan School District, California

**Jean Hutt**
Social Studies Department Chairperson
Saline Area Schools, Michigan

**Mary Lauranne Lifka**
Professor of History
College of Saint Teresa
Winona, Minnesota

**Roy R. Pellicano**
Professor of Education, Social Studies Teacher
Brooklyn, New York

**Denny Schillings**
Western Civilization Teacher
Homewood-Flossmoor High School, Illinois

**William White**
Past Coordinator of Social Sciences
Jefferson County Public Schools, Colorado

*Special thanks to:*
**Grace and Roy Pellicano**
authors of chapters on India, China, Japan, Africa, and Middle America
**Samuel Jenike**
author of the Prologue and Prehistory chapters

# *Contents*

# Maps

# *Acknowledgments/Credits*

**SOURCES OF CHAPTER-OPENING QUOTES**
*Page 2:* George Buttrick, quoted in Huston Smith, *The Religions of An* (New York: Harper & Row, 1965), pp. 301-2. *Page 18:* Fulk of Chartres, as quoted in Philip Sherrard et al., *Byzantium* (New York: Time-Life, 1966), p. 36. *Page 32:* Mohammed, "Unity," in *Koran*, trans. N.J. Dawood (Baltimore: Penguin Books, 1959), p. 257. *Page 66:* Translation of tombstone inscription quoted in Donald Bullough, *The Age of Charlemagne* (New York: G.P. Putnam, 1966), p. 198. *Page 84:* Quoted in J.H. Hexter and Richard Pipes, *Europe Since 1500* (New York: Harper & Row, 1971), p. 39. *Page 144:* Voltaire, *Essai sur les Moeurs*, 1756. *Page 155:* English poem of 1401, quoted in Helen Cam, *England Before Elizabeth* (New York: Harper & Row, 1960), p. viii. *Page 222:* Dino Compagni, "Song on Worthy Conduct," in R.S. Lopez and I.R. Raymond, *Medieval Trade in the Mediterranean World* (New York: Norton), pp. 425-6.

**BLACK-AND-WHITE PHOTOS**
The publisher gratefully acknowledges the contributions of the agencies, institutions and photographers listed below.
*Note:* The following abbreviations have been used for frequently cited sources:
**Art Resource** Art Resource, Inc., New York City; **Barnaby's** Barnaby's Picture Library, London; **Bettmann** Bettmann Archive, New York City; **Frost** Frost Publishing Group, New York City; **Hirmer** Hirmer Fotoarchiv, Munich; **Mansell** Mansell Collection, London; **Metropolitan Museum of Art** Metropolitan Museum of Art, New York City.

**Unit Openers    p. x,** View of Constantinople, Houghton Library, Harvard University; **p. 64,** Man in Armor, Mansell; **p. 142,** View of medieval Florence, Bettmann; **p. 212,** Lorenzo "the Magnificent," Mansell

**Chapter 1    6, 10,** Art Resource; **8,** Frederic Lewis: **11,** Bettmann
**Chapter 2    18** *(bottom),* **21, 22,** Bettmann; **26,** Sonia Halliday, Weston Turville, England; **27,** Frost; **18** *(top),* A.F. Kersting, London
**Chapter 3    51,** Barnaby's; **33,** Bettmann; **46** *(right),* British Library; **50** *(top),* Frost; **34,** Mansell; **37, 44, 46** *(left),* Metropolitan Museum of Art; **50** *(bottom),* Monkmeyer Press Photo Service, New York; **35,** Chester Beatty Library, Dublin
**Japan    54** *(left and right),* **56, 58,** Frost; **57,** Sekai Bunka

**Chapter 4    71,** Art Resource; **72, 74,** Bettmann; **77,** Frost; **76,** Giraudon/Art Resource; **67,** G.E. Kidder Smith, New York City; **75,** Pierpont Morgan Library, New York City
**Chapter 5    97,** Art Resource; **90, 93, 95** *(left),* Bettmann; **95** *(right),* Robert Harding, London; **100,** A.F. Kersting, London
**Chapter 6    109, 111, 113,** Bettmann; **107** *(left),* Frost; **105,** Pierpont Morgan Library, New York City
**Chapter 7    130** *(right),* Art Resource; **118, 119, 122, 124, 125, 126** *(left and right),* **127, 129** *(left),* **130** *(left top and bottom),* **131,** Bettmann; **128,** Huntington Library, San Marino, California
**The Mayas    136,** Frost; **136, 138,** J. Kerr
**Chapter 8    145, 147, 149, 150,** Bettmann; **152,** Houghton Library, Harvard University
**Chapter 9    156, 160, 161, 162** *(left),* **163** *(left),* **164, 167, 169, 173, 179,** Bettmann; **162,** British Tourist Authority; **170** *(right),* Giraudon/Art Resource; **157,** A.F. Kersting; **171, 175,** National Portrait Gallery, London; **158,** Pierpont Morgan Library, New York City; **163** *(right),* Royal Commission on Historial Monuments, England
**Chapter 10    187,** Alinari/Art Resource; **179, 182, 184, 188** *(left and right),* 189, 190 Bettman
**Chapter 11    195, 196, 197, 200, 206** *(left and right),* **208, 209, 210,** Bettmann; **199,** Mansell
**West Africa 213, 215,** Frost; **218,** Newberry Library, Chicago
**Chapter 12    223, 227, 230, 232, 233, 234,** Bettmann
**Chapter 13    242, 250** *(right),* **251** *(top left),* **253,** *(top right),* **255, 256** *(left),* **260** *(bottom),* Alinari/Art Resource; **254, 255, 257, 251** *(bottom left and top right),* **257** *(left and right),* **258, 260** *(top),* Bettmann; **251** *(bottom right),* Foto Enit Roma; **239, 261,** Giraudon/Art Resource; **240** *(right),* **241** *(left and right),* **249, 250** *(left),* **256** *(right),* **259,** Mansell; **243,** Royal Library, Windsor Castle; **240** *(left),* Scala/Art Resource

**COLOR PHOTOS**
*Cover photo:* Duc de Bérry, Trés riches heures (février). **Giraudon/Art Resource**
**Art Resource.** Stained glass windows, Chartres Cathedral (p.4); Facade of Bourges Cathedral (p.5); Ghiberti's bronze doors (p.6); Mona Lisa (p.7); Russian icon (p.7); Raphael's School of Athens (p.8); Titian painting (p.8).
**British Museum.** Manuscript illustration from Lindisfarne (p.1); Anglo-Saxon King and Council (p.3).
**Frederick Lewis,** New York City. Detail of Sistine Chapel ceiling (p.7).

# Glossary

**Arianism**  the doctrine that Jesus was a lesser divinity than God. Arianism was declared to be heretical by a council of bishops in 325.

**chivalry**  the code of honor for medieval knights. It included an obligation to be brave, to help the powerless, and to be courteous to women.

**Dark Ages**  Middle Ages; especially the period from the 5th through the 10th centuries.

**feudalism**  the political and social system of early medieval Europe, in which peasants, or *serfs*, were bound to the land they worked and *vassals* received rights of tenancy in return for homage and allegiance to a lord.

**fief**  the land granted by a lord to a vassal under the system of *feudalism*.

**geocentric**  centering upon the earth. In a *geocentric* world scheme, the heavenly bodies are thought to revolve around the earth.

**gnosticism**  the doctrine that knowledge of good and evil can be grasped through intuition.

**Gothic**  the style of architecture first developed by Abbot Suger of Saint Denis in the 12th century. Characterized by the use of flying buttresses, tall, vaulted ceilings, and stained-glass windows.

**guild**  an association of craftsmen practicing the same trade. Medieval guilds regulated the quality of crafted items and protected the interests of their members.

**heliocentric**  centering upon the sun. In a *heliocentric* world scheme, the planetary bodies revolve around the sun.

**heresy**  a religious belief which has been condemned by an established church as a possible danger to the well-being of the faithful.

**humanism**  the study of the arts and literature, with an emphasis on the works of man rather than religious subjects.

**icon**  an image or picture of a sacred subject which is itself venerated as sacred.

**manorialism**  the method of allotting farm lands under the feudal system. Tenant farmers received the right to work certain fields and in return gave a portion of the crops they harvested to the lord who owned the land.

**medieval**  pertaining to the Middle Ages. Originally, this term referred to the interim period between the Resurrection and the Last Judgment. During the Renaissance, it came to denote the interval from the Classical age to the 15th century.

**monasticism**  the way of life of religious communities who cloister themselves in convents or monasteries.

**monotheism**  the doctrine that there is only one god.

**parochial**  narrow or restricted. A *parochial* outlook or view is one of limited area or scope.

**primogeniture**  the system by which the eldest son inherits his parents' estate.

**schism**  the break or division of an organization due to a doctrinal dispute or other quarrel.

**serf**  a peasant who is bound to the land he works and considered as property.

**simony**  the practice of buying or selling Church offices.

**vassal**  a person or state subject to a higher authority. In the Middle Ages, a person who received protection and rights of land tenancy in return for homage and allegiance.

# The Medieval World

# Forces for Change

● *If all the trees on earth were pens, and if there were seven oceans full of ink, they would not suffice to describe the wonders of the Almighty.*

MOHAMMED

● *If ye have faith as a grain of mustard seed, ye shall say unto this mountain, Remove hence to yonder place; and it shall remove; and nothing shall be impossible unto you.*

JESUS

● *It was given as the chief and most necessary sign of his coming on those who had believed, that every one of them spoke in the tongues of all nations; thus signifying that the unity of the Catholic Church would embrace all nations and would in like manner speak in all tongues.*

AUGUSTINE

● *Nature is nothing else but God and the divine Reason that pervades the whole universe. You may, if you wish, address this creator of the world by different names, such as Jupiter Best and Greatest, the Thunderer, or the Stayer. This last title does not derive from the tale told by historians about the Roman battle-line being stayed from flight in answer to prayers. It simply means that all things are upheld by his benefits....You may also call him Fate; that would be no mistake. For since Fate is only a connected chain of causes, he is the first of the causes on which all succeeding ones depend. Any name that you choose to apply to him will be appropriate if it connotes a power that operates in heaven. His titles are as countless as his benefits.*

SENECA

*Jesus was a little known Jewish carpenter who was born in a stable, died at the age of thirty-three as a criminal rather than a hero, never travelled more than ninety miles from his birthplace, owned nothing, attended no college, marshalled no army, and instead of producing books did his only writing in the sand. Nevertheless, his birthday is kept across the world and his deathday sets a gallows against every sky. Who, then, was he?*

GEORGE BUTTRICK

# Christianity

During the reign of the emperor Augustus, an event occurred in an obscure town in Palestine, an eastern province of the Roman Empire, that would later transform the Roman world. That event was the birth of Jesus of Nazareth. One historian summarized the life of Jesus in the quotation above. The answer to who Jesus was—and how his teachings became the basis for a popular and powerful religion, Christianity—will be explored in this chapter.

At the time of Jesus' birth, many different religions flourished within the Roman Empire. Under the peaceful conditions of the early empire, a number of new religions were carried to Rome from the lands its legions had conquered in the East. The cult of Isis, an Egyptian goddess, and the worship of Mithras, a Persian god, gained followers among the Romans. Along with these great religions were many minor ones. All of them tried to explain the mysteries of the universe. Many spoke of sin and called for fasting and other rituals of purification. Their beliefs included faith in a god who had died and risen again and whose life and death were associated with the spring planting season and the winter season when nothing grew.

As Christianity grew, it gained a foothold amid these countless religious cults, but it drew on a different tradition, the ethical monotheism of the ancient Hebrews.

## THE SETTING FOR CHRISTIANITY

In Chapter 4, you learned that the ancient Hebrews believed that God had made a covenant with Abraham and that they were God's chosen people. As part of that covenant, the Hebrews accepted the belief in one God. Unlike the other peoples of the Middle East, they held firmly to their monotheism.

The religion of the Jews was closely tied to their history. Palestine was conquered many times by the different strong empires that rose in the Middle East. In 536 B.C., the Persian emperor, Cyrus, allowed many Jews who had been taken into exile in Babylon to return to Jerusalem. The Jews rebuilt their Temple at Jerusalem and set up their own state, which enjoyed a measure of independence under its Persian overlord.

In the 4th century B.C., Alexander the Great conquered Palestine, and after his death in 323 B.C., it was ruled first by the Ptolemies and later by the Seleucid kings. Hellenistic culture came to influence the Jews, many of whom began to use the Greek language rather than Hebrew. Around 200 B.C., Hebrew scholars decided to translate their holy writings, or *scriptures*, into Greek. This work came to be known as the *Septuagint* because it was completed by 70 scholars.

During the 2nd century B.C., the Seleucid king Antiochus IV (175–163 B.C.) tried to force the Jews to accept Hellenistic forms of worship. He forbade them to observe their Sabbath or practice the rite of circumcision. He confiscated the wealth of the Temple at Jerusalem and set up a statue of Jupiter within the inner sanctum. Jews were outraged at the violation of their holy place. In 168 B.C., they revolted against the Syrians. Judas Maccabeus became the leader of this revolt and in 165 B.C. succeeded in driving the Syrian army out of Jerusalem. The Jews turned at once to the task of purifying the Temple and rededicating it to Yahweh, or God. This event is still celebrated by Jews each December as the "Feast of Dedication," or *Hanukkah*. Although Judas Maccabeus was killed in 161 B.C., his brothers continued the struggle, and the Maccabeans eventually set up an independent kingdom that lasted until a Roman army under Ptolemy the Great conquered Palestine in 63 B.C.

### RIVAL JEWISH SECTS

During the 2nd and 1st centuries B.C., the Jews were divided into many factions. All Jews believed in the one God, but they differed over how to interpret God's law and therefore over how to conduct certain religious practices. The three main sects were the Sadducees, Pharisees, and Essenes. The Sadducees were wealthy, well-educated people—priests, landowners, and merchants —who controlled the Sanhedrin, the religious council that dealt with civil and criminal cases as well as with violations of Jewish religious laws. The Sadducees had little influence with the common people. While they believed that the Torah was the only source of authority for the Jews, they embraced the Hellenistic culture and were willing to compromise with the Roman rulers of Palestine.

The Pharisees, or "Separated Ones," were scholarly middle-class people who followed very closely the rituals of worship and living which set Jews apart from other people. They put great emphasis on living in accord with God's laws as set forth in the Torah and enforced by centuries of tradition. They believed that if they devoted themselves to the study of the scriptures and strictly observed the Mosaic laws, they would experience life after death.

The Essenes were a group of pious Jews who devoted themselves to the study of the scriptures, prayer, and fasting in preparation for the end of the world, which they believed was imminent. They looked for a Messiah, the "anointed one," to be sent by God to save his people. The Jewish historian Flavius Josephus described the Essenes in these words:

• • • *These last are Jews by birth, and seem to have greater affection for one another than the other sects have. These Essenes reject pleasure as an evil, but esteem continence [self-restraint], and the conquest over our passions, to be virtue . . . These men are despisers of riches, and so very communicative, as raises our admiration. Nor is there any one to be found among them who hath more than another; for it is a law among them, that those who come to them must let what they have be common to the whole order—insomuch that among them there is no appearance of poverty, or excess of riches, but everyone's possessions are mingled with every other's possessions; and so there is, as it were, one patrimony [heritage] among all the brethren.*[1]

Little was known about the Essenes, beyond what Josephus wrote, until 1947. That year, a Bedouin boy was searching for a stray goat when he saw a small, cave-like opening

---

[1] Josephus, *Wars of the Jews* II, 8, 2.

*The Dead Sea Scrolls have provided much information about the culture of the Essenes.*

in a hill near the Dead Sea. He threw some stones into the cave, but became frightened and ran away when it sounded as though one of the stones had smashed against something in the cave. Later, he returned to the site with a friend. Together, they worked their way into the opening, where they found several clay jars filled with scrolls.

At first, the scholars who examined these "Dead Sea scrolls" declared them to be worthless. But in 1951, a team of archaeologists explored the vicinity of Qumran, on the Dead Sea, more carefully and discovered the foundations of a building that they thought was an Essene monastery. They also found fragments of other scrolls dating from the three centuries preceding the birth of Jesus.

Other Essene scrolls referred to a "Teacher of Righteousness," whom the Essenes honored, but scholars have been unable to identify who this may have been. They estimate that the Essene group may have had 4000 members at the time of Jesus' birth. The Es-

senes were popularly known as "Followers of the Way," and they lived by a strict discipline laid out in their "Manual of Discipline." The Essenes believed that a new prophet would appear to help the Jews defeat their enemies and bring in a new age. They valued Jewish law and observed many rites, including a sacred meal of bread and wine.

Scholars have debated the influence of the Essenes on early Christianity. Some have suggested that John the Baptist and some early followers of Jesus were once members of the Essene community.

### ZEALOTS

A fourth group of Jews, known as the Zealots, or people of action, came mostly from the Pharisees. The Zealots interpreted various prophetic writings concerning the coming of a Messiah as forecasting a great military leader who would restore the Jews to the political status they had enjoyed under King David. The success of the Maccabean uprising of 168 B.C. led them to organize local groups, which met in the hills of northern Palestine and plotted to throw off Roman control. They became interested in Jesus' ability to motivate large numbers of people, but when Jesus finally convinced them that his mission was not of a political nature, they ignored him.

**LIFE OF JESUS** Virtually no contemporary sources make any mention of Jesus and his teachings. Flavius Josephus, who was born about the time that Jesus died, mentions him in this description:

• • • *Now there was about this time Jesus, a wise man, if it be lawful to call him a man; for he was a doer of wonderful works, a teacher of such men as receive the truth with pleasure. He drew over to him many of the Jews and many of the Gentiles. He was [the] Christ.*[2]

---

[2]Josephus, *Antiquities of the Jews* XVIII, 3, 3.

## THE GOSPELS

Historians and religious scholars have to rely on the New Testament to learn about the life of Jesus. The first four books of the New Testament—Matthew, Mark, Luke, and John—are believed to have been written shortly after the death of Jesus by his disciples, or followers. These books, often called the *Gospels*, or "good news," include many sayings of Jesus. But the Gospels themselves are the subject of heated debate because there were no scribes to record Jesus' words as he spoke, and the original manuscripts of the Gospels have been lost. In addition, the reports of the four disciples often differ and even contradict each other. The first three of these—Matthew, Mark, and Luke—are often referred to as the "synoptic gospels"[3] because they present similar, but by no means identical, information. The fourth gospel, John, says very little about the life of Jesus, but reports many things that he said. It was probably written about 70 years after the death of Jesus.

Despite the lack of contemporary sources, we can determine the outlines of Jesus' life. According to modern scholarship, Jesus was born in 4 B.C..

The name Jesus is a Greek version of the Hebrew name *Joshua*. Jesus was born to a Jewish family, was educated as a Jew, and taught in Jewish centers of worship. While some Jews accepted his teachings, the vast majority rejected them because they differed from orthodox Jewish teachings. Those who accepted his teachings found their lives so changed that they went through the Hellenistic world proclaiming that they had seen the Messiah.

At the time of Jesus' birth, Palestine was ruled by Herod, who had been put on the throne by the Romans. Herod adopted Jewish practices, married the daughter of the last Maccabean king, and put money into rebuilding the Temple. But he remained un-

[3]Synoptic means "same viewpoint."

In 525 A.D. a Christian abbot and astronomer, Dionysius Exiguus, made calculations that indicated that Jesus had been born 753 years after the founding of Rome. Pope Gregory XIII established a new calendar for dating Church events in 1382, based on the calculations of Exiguus. The new calendar, called the Gregorian calendar, divided time into the years before the birth of Christ (B.C.) and those after the birth of Jesus, anno domini or A.D., meaning "in the year of our Lord." In 1752 A.D., England and its American colonies adopted this Gregorian calendar; today most nations use it. Recent research into the exact year of Jesus' birth has found that the calculations of Exiguus were off by about four years.

popular with most Jewish leaders and the common people; in part because he promoted Hellenistic culture, and in part because he was seen as a puppet of Rome. About the time of Jesus' birth, he ordered the massacre of thousands of Jewish infants—which the Gospels connect to his hearing rumors that a Messiah had been born.

The Gospels reveal very little about Jesus' early life except that his family lived in the town of Nazareth in Galilee, the northern portion of Palestine, and that he was admitted to the Jewish faith in the Temple at Jerusalem at the age of 12. All four of the Gospels report that at the age of about 30 years (26 A.D.) Jesus appeared at the Jordan River, to be baptized by his cousin, a preacher named John the Baptist.

## JOHN THE BAPTIST

John preached against sin and introduced the rite of baptism as an act of purification. This description of John in the Bible has led some scholars to suggest that he was a member of the Essene monastery at Qumran: "John's clothing was a rough coat of camel's hair, with a leather belt round his waist, and his food was locusts and wild honey." (Matthew 3:4). People from all over Palestine came to hear John preach and cry out, "Repent, for the kingdom of heaven is upon you!" (Matthew 3:1.) Many believed him and submitted to being baptized by immersion into the waters of the Jordan River, an act that symbolically washed away their sins. Because John's preaching attracted the attention of the authorities, who feared his success, he was arrested and executed.

### THE TEACHINGS OF JESUS

According to the Gospels, after Jesus was baptized, he had a vision in which the holy spirit spoke to him, and soon after he began to preach. He traveled about Palestine teaching and healing people who came to him with a wide variety of illnesses. Wherever he went in public, he attracted large crowds. He preached a simple message that included these ideas. Because all people are the children of God, they should help one another. People should love God, repent their sins, and accept God's forgiveness. Forgiveness of others and concern for the poor also featured prominently in Jesus' message.

Central to this message was the idea that a new age—the kingdom of heaven—was at hand and that it would be ushered in by a Messiah, the son of God. The meaning of Jesus' teaching on this score has been much debated, especially the question of whether Jesus saw himself as the Messiah. As Richard Cavendish has explained it:

• • • Jesus himself was not a philosopher or theologian and he was not given to precise utterance. His sayings are frequently mysterious and sometimes mutually contradictory. His followers found him both fascinating and puzzling, and what he thought about himself is a mystery. Nowhere is he quoted making a plain and

This early Christian mosaic shows Jesus with two of his apostles.

unambiguous statement that he was divine. The sayings which seem most clearly to imply it—"I and the Father are one," for instance, and "I am the way, the truth and the life"—come from the latest of the gospels, John, and may represent later Christian beliefs rather than Jesus' own belief.[4]

The growing popularity of Jesus and his teachings along with his willingness to associate with persons despised by the Jewish leaders, including Gentiles (non-Jews), tax collectors, and prostitutes, made him increasingly unpopular with the various Jewish sects. The Sadducees feared him because his teachings about the Messiah and a new kingdom could disrupt their good relations with Rome. Moreover, they resented his criticism of the way they operated the Temple at Jerusalem: he said that they were "making it a robber's cave" (Matthew 21:13). The Pharisees despised him because he taught that God was more concerned with love and forgiveness than with the fine points of Jewish law.

---

[4]Richard Cavendish, The Great Religions (New York: Arco Publishing Co., 1980), p. 176.

Soon after Jesus started preaching, he chose 12 assistants known as the *apostles*. The Gospels relate how Jesus and his apostles traveled to Jerusalem to observe Passover, the celebration that commemorated the deliverance of the Jews from slavery in ancient Egypt. The city and Temple were crowded with Jews, for this was a most important religious event. When Jesus was hailed by the crowds as king or Messiah, the Temple authorities grew frightened that the Romans would interpret this outburst as a sign of revolt. So they arrested Jesus and turned him over to Pontius Pilate, the Roman procurator of the region. Pilate ordered Jesus' death by crucifixion, a traditional Roman form of execution. The date of this event was probably 30 A.D.

**THE SPREAD OF CHRISTIANITY** During the next days and weeks, various followers of Jesus reported seeing him, talking to him, and even touching him. Moreover, they announced that Jesus was the long-awaited Messiah of the Jews and that he would soon return to establish the kingdom of heaven. The Temple authorities once more stepped in to prevent possible disturbances. They arrested some disciples and forced others to flee to neighboring cities, where they continued to preach the gospel and spread the teachings of Jesus.

After the death of Jesus, Peter, one of the 12 apostles, became the leader of the *Nazarenes*, as their enemies called them. (They called themselves the *Followers of the Way*.) At first, Jesus' followers continued to worship as Jews in the synagogues and the Temple in Jerusalem and to follow Jewish customs. But they often met together in private homes to pray, read the scriptures, and discuss their memories of Jesus and his teachings. They began to share a simple meal, similar to the one Jesus had shared with the apostles the night before his arrest. At that meal, he had given his followers bread and wine, saying that they were his body and blood. From these simple beginnings, Christianity would spread into a great world religion.

*PAUL*

A key figure in the spread of Christianity was Paul of Tarsus. Tarsus was a Greek city on the southeast coast of Asia Minor. Paul's Hebrew name was Saul. He was a brilliant young man who was educated as a rabbi and once boasted: "My brothers, I am a Pharisee, a Pharisee born and bred" (Acts 23:6). As a Pharisee, Saul despised the followers of Jesus and approved the stoning of one of them, a young man named Stephen. Saul never met Jesus, but a short time after the death of Stephen, Saul was traveling along the road to Damascus when he was confronted by a vision of Jesus asking him, "Saul, Saul, why do you persecute me?" (Acts 9:4). The experience so moved Saul that he changed his name to Paul and dedicated his life to carrying Jesus' message throughout the eastern Mediterranean world.

After his conversion, Paul moved to Antioch, the capital of the Roman province of Syria. There, the followers of Jesus took the name *Christians*, or followers of Christ (the Greek equivalent of Messiah). Paul was a tireless worker who preached the gospel to Jews and Gentiles. From Antioch, he carried the word of Christ throughout the cities of Asia Minor to Greece and eventually to Rome. As Paul moved from place to place, he established small groups of people who accepted Christian teachings. Groups would meet in the home of one of their members to pray and share in the breaking of bread and the cup of wine to commemorate Jesus' last supper. By setting up churches along the great routes of the Roman Empire, Paul laid the foundations for the powerful church organization that would emerge in later centuries.

Since Paul could not be everywhere at the same time and since the Christian groups that he helped to organize came from diverse

The apostles Paul and John made the city of Ephesus in Asia Minor a major center of Christianity. Ephesus was first settled by Greek colonists in the 10th century B.C.

religious backgrounds, many questions arose about Christian beliefs and forms of worship. To answer these questions, Paul wrote a series of letters interpreting Jesus' teachings and resolving disputes. These letters, which Paul wrote in response to Christians in Corinth, Colossi, Ephesus, Galatia, Philippi, Rome, and Thessalonica, were saved by the recipients and became the basis for several books of the New Testament.

A recurring question facing the early followers of Jesus was how to deal with Gentiles who wanted to embrace the teachings of Jesus. Would they have to accept Judaism first? Paul met with Jesus' disciples in Jerusalem and urged them to allow Gentiles to be baptized into the Christian faith without first adopting Judaism. By adopting this policy, the disciples were able to win many more converts than before.

In 58 A.D., Paul returned to Jerusalem, where he was arrested by the Roman authorities as a troublemaker. He exercised his right as a Roman citizen to appeal his case to the emperor. When he arrived in Rome, he was placed under arrest pending a trial. Tradition holds that he was executed in Rome at about the time when the emperor Nero launched a brutal persecution of Christians. Like Paul, the apostle Peter carried the gospel across the Mediterranean world and to Rome, where he was arrested and executed —probably at the same time as Paul.

## PERSECUTIONS
The spread of Christianity created problems for Roman officials ranging from Pontius Pilate, who ordered the execution of Jesus, to the emperors themselves. From the first, Christians were suspect to Roman officials

because they worshiped Jesus, who had been crucified as a rebel. When Christians refused to serve in the Roman army or worship the emperor as a god, they ran into more trouble with the authorities. As a result of the persecutions, Christians met in secret, but this led to persistent rumors that they practiced immoral rites. They were accused of being cannibals (eaters of human flesh) because of their ritual of the bread and wine, which they said represented the body and blood of Jesus.

In 64 A.D., while Nero was emperor, a fire broke out in Rome. It raged for six days, causing tremendous destruction. When a rumor began to circulate that Nero himself had set the fire, the emperor tried to shift the blame onto the Christians. As Tacitus explained, this led to fearful persecutions.

• • • *Nero fastened the guilt and inflicted the most exquisite tortures on a class hated for their abominations, called Christians. . . . Accordingly, an arrest was first made of all who pleaded guilty; then, upon their information, an immense multitude was convicted, not so much of the crime of firing the city, as of hatred against mankind. Mockery of every sort was added to their deaths. Covered with the skins of beasts, they were torn by dogs and perished, or were nailed to crosses, or were doomed to the flames and burnt, to serve as a nightly illumination. . . . Hence, even for criminals who deserved extreme and exemplary punishment, there arose a feeling of compassion; for it was not, as it seemed, for the public good, but to glut one man's cruelty, that they were being destroyed.*[5]

**The Jewish Revolt.** During this same period, the Jews of Palestine suffered as severely as the Christians. In 66 A.D. the Jews rose up in a widespread revolt against Rome. The revolt was finally put down in 70 A.D. by Titus, who captured Jerusalem, looted the Temple, and destroyed the entire city. Only the foundation of the western wall of the

Temple remained intact. Once each year on the anniversary of the destruction of the city, Jews were permitted access to this foundation to offer prayers. Over the centuries, this remnant became known as the "Wailing Wall."

Jews who survived the destruction of the city fled in all directions—some went south into the Arabian desert, some escaped east to Babylon, and some crossed the Mediterranean Sea into Europe and North Africa. Wherever they went in this new diaspora, they established synagogues and schools to maintain their covenant with Yahweh.

A group of Zealots who escaped from Jerusalem fled to Masada, a hilltop fortress overlooking the Dead Sea. There, they resisted the Romans for three more years. When they saw that the Romans were about to overwhelm them, they made a pact with each other, which Josephus described as follows:

• • • *Let us die before we become slaves under our enemies, and let us go out of the world, together with our children and our wives, in a state of freedom . . . God himself hath brought this necessity upon us; while the Romans desire the contrary, and are afraid lest any of us die before we are taken. Let . . . us leave them an example which shall at once cause their astonishment at our death, and their admiration of our hardiness therein.*[6]

When the Romans took the fortress, they found few survivors.

**Laws against Christians.** By the time of the Jewish revolt, Christianity had taken its separate path from Judaism. As you have read, Paul made it possible for Gentiles to embrace the new faith, and during his missionary work, he won large numbers of Gentile converts. As the number of Christians increased, however, they were seen as a greater threat and so were subjected to intermittent persecutions. By tradition, Rome was tolerant of the

---

[5]Tacitus, *Annals* XV, 44.

[6]Josephus, *Wars of the Jews* VII, 8, 6.

*This detail from the arch of Titus shows Roman soldiers looting the Temple of Jerusalem. After the Temple was destroyed, the citizens of Judah were forced to support the temple of Jupiter in Rome.*

diverse religions practiced within its borders. However, Christians (and Jews) posed a special problem because they refused to worship any but their own God.

Even though there were some laws against Christians, Roman governors often overlooked them and tolerated Christians in their provinces. Nonbelievers, however, frequently blamed Christians for such natural disasters as earthquakes and floods and demanded that they be punished.

The dilemma of Roman officials who had to decide between toleration and persecution was evident in the letter Pliny the Younger, governor of Bithynia in Asia Minor, addressed to the emperor Trajan. In it, he asked for advice on how to deal with the Christians. Trajan responded:

• • • *You have taken the right line, my dear Pliny, in examining the cases of those denounced to you as Christians, for no hard and fast rule can be laid down, of universal application. They are not to be sought out; if they are informed against, and the charge is proved, they are to be punished, with this reservation—that if any one denies that he is a Christian, and actually proves it, that is by worshipping our gods, he shall be pardoned as a result of his incantation, however suspect he may have been with respect to the past. Pamphlets published anonymously should carry no weight in any charge whatsoever. They constitute a very bad precedent, and are also out of keeping with this age.[7]*

During the next hundred years, the Christians were alternately tolerated and oppressed, but by 245, as the stability of the Roman government declined, persecution increased. The emperor Decius (245–251) made the worship of *Caesar* (the title of the emperor) compulsory for everyone living in the empire except the Jews. On a certain day,

[7]Trajan to Pliny, *Pliny's Epistles,* X, xcvii, in Henry Bettenson, ed., *Documents of the Christian Church,* 2nd Ed. (London: Oxford University Press, 1963), p. 6.

all people were required to enter the temple of Caesar in their community, burn incense before the emperor's statue in the temple, and proclaim, "Caesar is my Lord." Those who obeyed this decree were given certificates saying that they were loyal citizens of the empire. Anyone who ignored the decree was to be executed. Thousands of Christians died for their faith, but in the end the Roman government was unable to enforce its decree. Moreover, the persecution began to create sympathy for Christians. As one Christian writer pointed out, "the blood of the martyrs was the seed of the church."

The last and bloodiest persecution took place during the reign of the emperor Dio-cletian (284-305), but it failed to crush Christianity and within a few years an edict was issued granting toleration to all religions in the empire.

### OFFICIAL RECOGNITION

The edict of toleration came from the emperor Constantine, who gained control of the Roman Empire in 312. He credited his success against rivals to the imperial throne to a vision of Christ. The following year he issued the Edict of Milan, which said, in part:

. . . *We therefore announce that, notwithstanding any provisions concerning the Christians in our former instructions, all who choose that religion are to be permitted*

The Western or "Wailing" Wall is all that remains of the Temple of Jerusalem.

*to continue therein, without any let or hinderance, and are not to be in any way troubled or molested. . . . Note that at the same time all others are to be allowed the free and unrestricted practice of their religions; for it accords with the good order of the realm and the peacefulness of our times that each should have freedom to worship God after his own choice; and we do not intend to detract from the honour due to any religion or its followers.*[8]

Sometime after this edict, Constantine's mother, Helena, went to Palestine, which Christians now called the Holy Land. On this trip, she attempted to find the places where the important events in Jesus' life had occurred. According to tradition, she even found the cross on which Jesus had died. Constantine then financed the construction of churches on several sites she identified, including the Church of the Nativity in Bethlehem and the Church of the Holy Sepulcher in Jerusalem.

Although Constantine took several other steps to promote Christianity, including the convening of the Council of Nicaea, he did not accept baptism into the faith until shortly before his death in 337. Some historians suggest that he was motivated to support Christianity out of a desire for unity in the empire rather than out of personal conviction. Whatever his motivation, he greatly enhanced the position of Christians in the empire.

In 381, the emperor Theodosius decreed that Christianity would be the official religion of the empire. He closed all non-Christian places of worship and discontinued the Olympic Games, which were seen as a form of "pagan" worship. (*Paganus* in Latin means "country fellow," and pagan came to mean any non-Christian.)

### THE APPEAL OF CHRISTIANITY
Within 400 years of its founding, Christianity had grown from an obscure and persecuted sect in Palestine into the principal religion of the Roman Empire. How did it achieve this success? At first, Christianity appealed strongly to the poor and oppressed because of its promises of immortality and a better life in the world hereafter, and its teaching of the equality of all believers in the sight of God. Its founder, Jesus, was an actual person whose life, teachings, and martyrdom were easily understood. In time, Christianity won converts among the educated classes who accepted its ideas of discipline and moderation, which were reminiscent of the Greek philosophies.

In its early days, the new faith accepted women on a nearly equal basis with men. Christian missionaries worked with enormous dedication, and their work was helped by the *Pax Romana*, the good means of transportation throughout the empire, and a common language. While the persecutions resulted in many deaths, the faith and courage of the Christian martyrs often gained sympathy for a faith that inspired such loyalty. Then, too, as Christianity spread, it developed a strong organization that was modeled in part on that of the Roman Empire. Once recognized as the official religion of the empire, this church organization joined forces—though not always in harmony—with the political institutions of Rome to ensure religious unity.

### THE EARLY CHURCH
The apostles and other early followers of Jesus expected him to reappear within a short time. When this did not happen and the number of Christians continued to grow, they realized the need to set down their beliefs in an orderly fashion and establish some sort of church organization. In the 1st century A.D., the earliest writings of the New Testament were collected. They included the letters that Paul wrote to the various Christian communities in which he dealt with disputes among members and clarified ques-

---

[8]Constantine, "Edict of Milan," in *Documents of the Christian Church*, ed. Henry Bettenson, p. 22.

## THE SPREAD OF CHRISTIANITY TO 400 A.D.
How did Paul help to transform Christianity into a world religion?

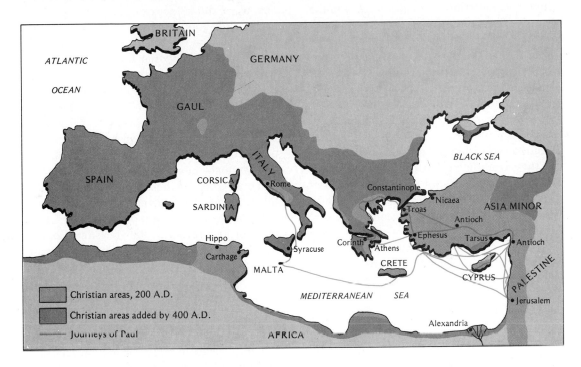

ATLANTIC OCEAN

BRITAIN

GERMANY

GAUL

SPAIN

CORSICA

SARDINIA

ITALY

Rome

BLACK SEA

Constantinople

Nicaea

Troas

ASIA MINOR

Antioch

Hippo

Carthage

MALTA

Syracuse

Corinth

Athens

Ephesus

Tarsus

Antioch

CRETE

CYPRUS

PALESTINE

MEDITERRANEAN SEA

Jerusalem

Alexandria

AFRICA

Christian areas, 200 A.D.

Christian areas added by 400 A.D.

Journeys of Paul

tions of belief. The four Gospels were also written down between about 50 A.D. and 70 A.D. Later, other books were added to and accepted as part of the New Testament.

As you have read, the first Christians met together in small groups in private houses. There was no distinction in rank between the teacher of a local group and the members. In fact, some early groups were led by women although Paul disapproved of the practice. These groups followed ceremonies that were similar to those held in the synagogues, including readings from the scriptures, prayers, and the singing of Psalms. Christians soon added two of their own rites—baptism for all new converts and the ceremony of eating bread and drinking wine to commemorate Jesus' last supper with the apostles.

As the new faith grew, however, many questions of belief and practice were raised. To answer these questions and to meet the other challenges confronting them, Chris-

tians developed a standard organization. A Christian community came to include a "bishop," from the Greek word *episkopos* which means "overseer;" a board of elders, called "presbyters" and eventually "priests;" and several assistants, called "deacons." The bishop was the highest authority on questions of faith and practice. He was helped in religious matters by the priests and in administrative matters by the deacons. By the end of the 1st century A.D., these Church leaders came to be known as the clergy, and the distinction grew between the clergy and the laity, or members of the congregation.

By the 2nd century A.D., the government of the Church had evolved a hierarchy with levels of administration that closely paralleled those of the Roman Empire. Each presbyter, or priest, led a local group, known as a *parish*. A bishop supervised a *diocese*, a region containing several parishes. By about 200 A.D., each city usually had a single bishop

13

and a number of priests. At the next level was a region containing several dioceses, which became known as a *province*, and the bishop of the largest diocese within the province became known as an *archbishop*.

For a time, the bishops of Rome, Constantinople, Antioch, and Alexandria had about equal status. Eventually, however, the Bishop of Rome assumed the title of *pope* and claimed supremacy over the others. The bishops of Constantinople, Antioch, and Alexandria disputed the supreme authority of the pope, but they were accorded the lesser status of *patriarchs*. Struggles for power and jurisdictional disputes within the hierarchy would be only one of the problems facing the early Church.

## CHURCH CONTROVERSIES

Jesus did not establish an organization to carry on his work. Nor did he put his teachings into writing. As long as the apostles lived, they could tell others about Jesus and his teachings, but even before they died, questions arose that Jesus had not discussed directly in his teachings. As the Church evolved, however, the clergy not only took charge of conducting services of worship and administering the Church but also became responsible for clarifying questions of Christian dogma, or doctrine.

Early Church leaders were faced with a large number of controversies. As conflicting points of view emerged, Church leaders attempted to resolve the controversies by meeting together in councils to establish *orthodox* (from the Greek meaning "right in opinion") answers. If Christians disregarded the decision of a Church council, they were guilty of heresy, and a heretic risked punishment such as *excommunication*—being cut off from membership in the Church. In the 2nd and 3rd centuries A.D., a variety of controversies arose. At issue were the nature of Christ, the role of the Church, and the means by which Christians could achieve salvation.

### GNOSTICISM

The people who came to be known as *Gnostics* were dualists, who believed that two forces—of good and of evil—were constantly at war with each other in the universe. They taught that the physical world was evil and that only the world of the spirit was ideal and good. They believed that the God of the Old Testament was an evil force that had created the physical world. To them, Jesus was a messenger sent by the good, all-perfect God to reveal the knowledge (the Greek word *gnosis* means "knowledge") of good and evil. Gnostics denied that Jesus was fully human and emphasized the mystical and miracle-working nature of Jesus. The Gnostics posed a threat to the Christian Church by denying the humanity of Christ and leaning toward a mystical faith, closer to the older mystery religions than to Christian beliefs.

### ARIANISM

A major controversy erupted over the teachings of a priest named Arius (256-336 A.D.) of Alexandria. It centered on the nature of Christ. Arius taught that God existed before Jesus; consequently, Jesus could not have been eternal or equal to God. Other Church leaders, led by Athanasius, the bishop of Alexandria, declared that Jesus was "true God" and even "of the same substance with God." Within a short time, the Arian controversy swept across the Christian world. Not only the clergy but also ordinary citizens debated the various points in the argument. In 325 A.D., the emperor Constantine called for a council of bishops to meet at Nicaea (present-day Iznik), in Asia Minor. After much deliberation, the Council of Nicaea condemned *Arianism* as heresy. The bishops also composed the "Nicene Creed" as a statement of orthodox belief.

● ● ● *We believe in one God the Father Almighty, Maker of heaven and earth, and of all things visible and invisible; and in one Lord Jesus Christ, the only-begotten Son of*

*God, begotten of the Father before all worlds,*
*God of God, Light of Light . . . being of one*
*substance with the Father by whom all*
*things were made; who for us men, and for*
*our salvation, came down from heaven, and*
*was incarnate by the Holy Spirit of the*
*Virgin Mary, and was made man, and was*
*crucified also for us under Pontius Pilate. . . .*
*And we believe in the Holy Spirit, the Lord*
*and Giver of Life, who proceedeth from the*
*Father and the Son, who with the Father and*
*the Son together is worshipped and glorified,*
*who spoke by the prophets. And we believe*
*in one holy catholic and apostolic Church.*
*We acknowledge one baptism for the*
*remission of sins. And we look for the*
*resurrection of the dead, and the life of the*
*world to come. Amen.*[9]

Constantine decreed that the writings of
Arius should be burned and that Arius should
be sent into exile. But Arianism was not so
easily destroyed. Ulfilas, a priest who agreed
with Arius, became a missionary to the Visigoths, Germanic tribes living north of the
Danube River. He converted them to the Arian form of Christianity. The Visigoths spread
Arianism to the Ostrogoths and later to the
Vandals, who in turn carried Arianism into
western Europe. As you will read (Chapter
15), at the end of the 5th century, the Church
found a champion in Clovis, the king of the
Franks, who successfully defended orthodox
Christian teachings in western Europe against
the heresy of Arianism.

Throughout the early centuries of Christianity, the bishops of the largest provinces
met in councils to define matters of faith.
Along with the beliefs expressed in the Nicene Creed, the Church adopted the concept
of "apostolic succession," saying that Jesus
had directed his apostles to carry his message throughout the world and that the apostles had in turn passed this authority on to
the bishops. Because the chief apostle Peter

had gone to Rome, and had been martyred
there, the bishops of Rome claimed that Jesus
had chosen Rome as the site of his church
and claimed authority over the other bishops
and patriarchs.

To fight heresy and ensure orthodoxy, the
Church also decided to establish an official
body of Christian literature. Over a period of
years, Church leaders examined all the existing writings about Jesus and the early
spread of Christianity and decided which to
accept and which to reject. The accepted
writings were combined into the 27 books of
the New Testament, while the Jewish writings of the Septuagint were defined as the
Old Testament. Together, the New and Old
Testaments became the Christian Bible.

*THE CHURCH FATHERS* During the 4th
and 5th centu-
ries, several prominent individuals helped
formulate Christian doctrine. Among them
were Saint Ambrose, a superb preacher, and
Saint Jerome, who translated the Old and
New Testaments into everyday Latin. These
Christian thinkers became known as the
Church fathers because they worked to develop a universal or "catholic" set of principles for the Church.

The most important of the early Church
fathers was Saint Augustine (354-430), who
was born in North Africa to a devoutly Christian mother and a pagan father. Augustine
studied in Carthage to become a professor of
rhetoric. There, he lived a decadent life and
eventually became interested in Manichean-
ism, a Christian heresy similar to Gnosticism. Later, he received an appointment to
teach rhetoric in Milan, where he heard Saint
Ambrose, who was then the bishop of that
city, preach about Jesus, human sinfulness,
and divine forgiveness. Augustine was overcome by a sense of remorse for his past life
and abandoned his old ways.

In his autobiography, *Confessions,* Augustine relates how he was meditating in a
garden when he heard the voice of a child

---

[9]*Book of Confessions,* paragraphs 1.1-.3.

say, "Take up and read!" He picked up the Bible that he had carried into the garden, opened it at random and read "Let Jesus Christ himself be the armor that you wear; give no thought to satisfying the bodily appetites" (Romans 13:13-14). He decided that he must accept Jesus as his spiritual leader. Bishop Ambrose baptized him into the Church, and Augustine returned to North Africa. In 391, he was ordained as a priest, and four years later was named bishop of Hippo.

In this position, Augustine combated many heresies. When the Visigoths sacked Rome in 410, some people charged that Christianity was responsible for the "fall of Rome." This accusation inspired Augustine to write *The City of God*. In it, he set out a Christian philosophy of history that saw all human history as the unfolding of God's will. God, he said, had allowed the Romans to acquire their empire, but the only really worthwhile goal was to achieve the City of God. He compared the two cities—the earthly and the heavenly—in these words:

• • • *Two cities have been formed by two loves: the earthly by the love of self, even to the contempt of God; the heavenly by the love of God, even to the contempt of self. The former, in a word, glories in itself, the latter in the Lord. For the one seeks glory from men; but the greatest glory of the other is God, the witness of conscience. The one lifts up its head in its own glory; the other says to its God, "Thou art my glory, and the lifter up of my head." In the one, the princes and the nations it subdues are ruled by the love of ruling; in the other, the princes and the subjects serve one another in love, the latter obeying, while the former take thought for all. The one delights in its own strength, represented in the persons of its rulers; the other says to its God, "I will love Thee, O Lord, my strength."*[10]

Augustine elaborated other beliefs, in-cluding the concept of original sin—that as a result of the disobedience of Adam and Eve all humans are sinners from birth and that they are destined to eternal punishment. No one could escape from this fate except through the grace of God, but God only granted salvation to a select few. In this belief, he formulated the doctrine of predestination.

Not every Church leader agreed with Augustine. Pelagius, a British monk who arrived in Rome in 385, disagreed strongly with the concept of original sin. Moreover, he believed in a person's free will—that each individual has the ability to choose whether his or her life will be dedicated to good or evil, and that God bestows love and forgiveness on all who repent of evil deeds. Pelagius challenged Augustine's concept of original sin in these words:

• • • *Everything good and everything evil, in respect of which we are either worthy of praise or of blame, is done by us, not born in us. We are not born in our full development, but with a capacity for good or evil; we are begotten as well without virtue as without vice, and before the activity of our own personal will there is nothing in man but what God has stored for him.*[11]

Although Pelagius had many followers, Augustine fought his ideas and eventually triumphed. Pelagius was declared a heretic by the Church and condemned to exile.

Augustine died in 430, a year before the Vandals sacked Hippo. A few decades later in 476, Rome itself "fell" to invading Germanic tribes. With the collapse of the Roman Empire, the only central authority that survived in western Europe was the Church. Christians looked to the Church for leadership and security in a time of uncertainty and despair. From Rome, the pope began to exert authority not only over religious but also increasingly over secular affairs.

---

[10]Augustine, *The City of God* (trans. Marcus Dods, 1881) xiv, 28.

[11]Pelagius, "Concerning Original Sin," quoted in *Documents of the Christian Church*, ed. Bettenson, p. 75.

## SUMMARY

*Jesus was born into a Jewish family in a remote part of the Roman world. During his lifetime, he won a few devoted followers. After his death, his apostles and other missionaries persevered in spreading his teachings, winning converts first in the cities of the eastern Mediterranean and later in the western parts of the Roman Empire. By 200 A.D., a well organized Church had emerged. The early Christian Church faced persecutions from outside and controversies from within, but it continued to grow in size and strength until it succeeded in making Christianity the official religion of the Roman Empire. When Rome fell in 476, Christians throughout western Europe looked to the Church for guidance in political as well as spiritual matters.*

## QUESTIONS

1 What divisions existed within Judaism in the 1st century B.C.? How were the beliefs and practices of the Essenes similar to those of the early Christians?
2 How has archaeology thrown new light on the origins of Christianity?
3 Compare Christian teachings and beliefs to those of other religions within the Roman Empire.
4 How did the organization of the early Church meet its needs? Why did it use the organization of the Roman Empire as its model?
5 What issues were at the heart of the early Christian heresies? Why was the Church so concerned with proclaiming and defending orthodox beliefs?
6 What are the major similarities and differences between Church teachings and organization in the 1st century A.D. and today?

## BIBLIOGRAPHY

**Which book might describe the early Christian heresies?**

MANSCHRECK, CLYDE. *A History of Christianity in the World.* Englewood Cliffs, N.J.: Prentice-Hall, 1974. *A chronological history of the development of Christianity with an emphasis on the forces that shaped current Christian beliefs and trends. Stresses recent developments in Christianity; places current problems in relation to political, social and economic issues; and offers a balanced view of these problems.*

PRITCHARD, JAMES B., ed. *Everyday Life in Bible Times.* Washington, D.C.: National Geographic Society, 1967. *A well-illustrated volume that traces the footsteps of Old and New Testament figures such as Abraham, Moses, David, Solomon, Jesus, and Paul. Increases understanding of the Bible by recreating the world of Biblical times.*

WHITNEY, JOHN R. and SUSAN W. HOWE. *Religious Literature of the West.* Minneapolis, Minnesota: Augsburg Publishing House, 1971. *A survey of the major themes of the three great religions of the West—Judaism, Christianity, and Islam—with selected readings from the Hebrew Bible, the rabbinic writings, the New Testament, and the Koran.*

2

● *O what a splendid city, how stately, how fair, how many monasteries therein, how many palaces raised by sheer labor in its broadways and streets, how many works of art, marvelous to behold; it would be weariness to tell of the abundance of all good things; of gold and of silver, garments of manifold fashion, and such sacred relics. Ships are at all times putting in at this port, so that there is nothing that men want that is not brought hither.*

FULK OF CHARTRES

# The Byzantine Empire

The description above, which was written by an 11th-century visitor from western Europe, refers to Constantinople, the bustling capital of the Byzantine Empire. As the Roman Empire declined in the West, a new civilization emerged in the East and lasted for a thousand years. In 330, the emperor Constantine chose the small Greek trading town of Byzantium as his new capital. This "New Rome" was later called Constantinople, but it gave its ancient name to the Byzantine civilization.

The Byzantine Empire was heir to the Roman Empire; it was also heir to the learning, culture, and traditions of ancient Greece and the Middle East. Byzantine emperors claimed to be the successors of Augustus, but by the 7th century, Greek, and not Latin, was the language of the empire. The Byzantine emperors ruled over a vast territory stretching from the Balkans through Asia Minor, Syria, Egypt, and North Africa. They constantly had to defend their lands from determined invaders—first from the German tribes that overran western Europe, then from the Huns, the Persians, and the Arabs, each of whom seized parts of the empire for a time. Even when they lost territory to invaders, they held firmly to Constantinople, an almost impregnable city which long sustained its reputation as the most marvelous city in the world.

**CONSTANTINOPLE** When Constantine decided to move his capital in 330, he selected Byzantium, which had been founded about 650 B.C. by Greek colonists under the leadership of Byzas.

Byzantium was closer than Rome to the prosperous provinces of the Eastern Roman Empire and to the centers of Christendom at

> The same natural advantages that drew Constantine to the site had influenced Byzas to select it originally. Byzas had been instructed by the oracle at Delphi to establish his colony "opposite the blind." He had been unable to interpret this directive, but later he realized that the Greeks who had settled earlier at Chalcedon, on the Asiatic side of the Bosporus, must have been blind to have overlooked the much more favorable site on the European side.

A stout wall three miles long protected the landward boundary of Constantinople. The city's defenses withstood invaders for more than 10 centuries.

This colossal head of Constantine once stood in the basilica that the emperor built in Rome.

Jerusalem, Antioch, and Alexandria. It was also at the crossroads of the busy trade routes between Europe and Asia and commanded access to the Black and Mediterranean seas.

Just as important, the city could be easily defended because it was bordered by water on three sides: the Sea of Marmara on the south, the landlocked harbor of the Golden Horn on the north, and the Bosporus on the east. During the reign of Theodosius II (408-450), three parallel walls, each 25 feet wide and 3 miles long, were erected across the western, and only landward approach to the city. The walls were built to protect it from the Germanic tribes who were penetrating across the Danube River. Other walls were also built along the Sea of Marmara, and a huge iron chain was forged to stretch across the Golden Horn to protect the harbor against seaborne invasions.

Like Rome, Constantinople was situated on seven low hills, and Constantine set out to make his new capital as beautiful as Rome. He built a forum, several temples, and a magnificent palace. He enlarged the Hippodrome (stadium), which had been built by Septimius Severus in the 3rd century. In time, Constantinople became the commercial and intellectual center of the Mediterranean world, as well as the administrative center of the Eastern Roman Empire.

*JUSTINIAN* In the 4th century, the emperor Theodosius divided the Roman Empire between his two sons, with one ruling the western provinces, the other controlling the eastern provinces. During the 5th century, you will recall, the Roman Empire in the West collapsed under the pressure of successive invasions. In the East, emperors managed to resist attacks from outside and ruled over a prosperous economy.

In 527, Justinian succeeded to the imperial throne and ruled until 565. He was an energetic and ambitious ruler who dreamed of restoring the unity of the Roman Empire. During his long reign, he fought many wars

*19*

to expand the empire, but this policy of re-conquering the West aroused much controversy. So, too, did his marriage to Theodora, an actress and a courtesan. In time, however, Theodora became Justinian's most trusted adviser and proved to be a person of keen political insight and great personal courage.

### THE NIKA REVOLT

Theodora showed her strong determination during an uprising just five years after Justinian took office. In Constantinople, chariot racing was such a popular pastime that it aroused great excitement and fury among the spectators. The two rival teams, the Blues and the Greens, were each supported by a different class. Wealthy aristocrats favored the Blues, while the common people backed the Greens. During the races in 532, fights between factions in the audience exploded into a violent uprising that was soon directed against the emperor who had imposed heavy taxes on the people to pay for his grand schemes for imperial expansion.

During the Nika Revolt—so called because the rallying cry of the people was "Nika!" ("Let us conquer!")—much of Constantinople was burned. At one point, as the mob gathered in the Hippodrome to proclaim a new emperor, Justinian reportedly wanted to flee. But Theodora persuaded him to remain by saying:

. . . My opinion then is that the present time, above all others, is inopportune for flight, even though it bring safety. For while it is impossible for a man who has seen the light not also to die, for one who has been an emperor it is unendurable to be a fugitive. May I never be separated from this purple, and may I not live that day on which those who meet me shall not address me as mistress. If now, it is your wish to save yourself, O Emperor, there is no difficulty. For we have much money, and there is the sea, here the boats. However, consider whether it will not come about after you have been saved that you would gladly exchange that safety for death. As for myself,

I approve a certain ancient saying that royalty is a good burial-shroud.[1]

Emboldened by these words, the emperor held firm, and with the help of his general Belisarius, the rebellion was crushed. About 30,000 people died in this revolt, many of them massacred in the Hippodrome by the army.

### CAMPAIGN IN THE WEST

By the 6th century, the lands once ruled by Rome in the West had been overrun by various Germanic tribes: the Visigoths occupied Spain, the Ostrogoths controlled Italy, and the Vandals held much of North Africa. Justinian longed to restore the power of the Roman Empire in these regions. Before embarking on this venture, however, he attempted to secure his eastern boundary by entering into a treaty with the Sassanids, the rulers of Persia.

Justinian then directed two of his generals, Belisarius and Narses, to lead a large expedition to the western Mediterranean. In 533, Belisarius defeated the Vandals in northern Africa, Corsica, Sardinia, and the Balearic Islands. Three years later, his army recaptured Rome and later Ravenna, from the Ostrogoths. The people of Rome welcomed Justinian's armies because they were unhappy about living under the Arian form of Christianity practiced by the Ostrogoths. Justinian's armies also pushed into southern Spain, overcoming the Visigoths.

During Justinian's reign, the Byzantine Empire reached its greatest territorial extent, and Justinian could claim to rule much of the ancient Roman Empire. But the reconquest of the West drained the empire's resources. Seeing this, the Persians soon renewed their attacks on its eastern borders. Soon after Justinian's death, the empire was besieged on all sides: the Slavs, Avars, and

---

[1]Procopius, History of the Wars I, 24.

*The empress Theodora was an influential advisor to her husband. She is shown here with the members of her court.*

Bulgars threatened from the north; the Lombards pushed into northern Italy; and the Persians moved in from the east.

**JUSTINIAN'S ACHIEVEMENTS** Despite his short-lived military triumphs, Justinian did make changes of lasting significance. Even before launching his campaign in the West, he drew up plans for building a beautiful new cathedral. *Hagia Sophia* (Holy Wisdom), as the cathedral was called, was an architectural triumph that still ranks as one of the world's most impressive buildings. Its relatively shallow dome is 108 feet in diameter and rises to a height of 184 feet. The dome is supported on a complex arrangement of arches and piers.

Originally, the interior of Hagia Sophia was lavishly decorated with mosaics and colored marble. When the cathedral was dedicated in 537, Justinian compared it with the Temple at Jerusalem, as described in the Old Testament, and he is reported to have proclaimed, "O Solomon, I have outdone thee!"

After the capture of Constantinople by the Ottoman Turks in 1453, Hagia Sophia was converted into a mosque. The mosaics of Christian scenes were covered with whitewash, and four towering minarets were added to the exterior. When the nation of Turkey was established in 1922, the whitewash was removed from the mosaics, and the building was made into a museum.

Perhaps the most outstanding achievement of Justinian's reign was his codification of Roman law. In 528, he appointed a commission to compile a new code of law for the empire. The commissioners were instructed

*The Hagia Sophia is the greatest monument of Byzantine architecture. The many windows are made possible by the arches in the walls, which carry the weight of the dome.*

to collect all laws from the existing law codes and eliminate any laws that were obsolete or contradictory. The results of this monumental work came to be known as the *Corpus Juris Civilis* (Body of Civil Law). The code consisted of three parts: the *Institutes*, a textbook of legal principles; the *Digest*, a summary of legal opinions; and the *Code*, a list of laws from the time of Hadrian to the reign of Justinian. The *Corpus Juris Civilis* preserved Roman legal traditions in the Byzantine Empire and later became the foundation of the legal systems of most European nations. Among the principles embodied in the code were rules of evidence such as the requirement that the accuser must prove that a charge is true.

After the fall of Rome, knowledge of Roman law was poorly preserved in western Europe. By the 12th century, however, some scholars in the West began to study Justin-

ian's *Corpus Juris Civilis* and thereby reintroduced these ancient principles. During the 14th and 15th centuries, some European monarchs surrounded themselves with advisers who understood and could apply the code because it stressed the concept that the ruler was the source of all law and that judges were the representatives of the ruler in administering the law.

*CHURCH AND STATE*

Justinian's motto, "One empire, one church, one law," summed up his major goals. Achieving religious unity, however, proved to be difficult. Justinian made membership in the Church a requirement for citizenship. He ordered the university at Athens to close because it was considered a center of pagan teachings. Yet he was unsuccessful in combating *monophysitism*, a heretical movement that claimed Jesus had only a divine nature, rather than a combination of human and divine natures. The problem was complicated by the fact that the empress Theodora was a monophysite. In the end, the emperor himself accepted the heretical teaching, which caused strained relations with the pope.

During his reign, Justinian moved the Byzantine Church along a different path from that taken by the Roman Catholic Church in

| BYZANTINE EMPIRE | |
|---|---|
| 305-337 | *Constantine I* |
| 408-450 | *Theodosius II* |
| 518-527 | *Justin* |
| 527-565 | *Justinian* |
| 610-711 | *Dynasty of Heraclius* |
| 610-641 | *Heraclius* |
| 717-741 | *Leo III* |
| 780-797 | *Constantine VI* |
| 797-802 | *Irene* |
| 867-1025 | *Macedonian Dynasty* |
| 976-1025 | *Basil II* |

the West. The emperor himself acted as head not only of the State but also of the Church. He controlled the election of the patriarch and administered Church affairs. This combining of secular and religious roles is sometimes called *Caesaropapism*. For Justinian, the Church was a rallying point and a symbol of unity, but in the years ahead, Byzantine emperors would become deeply involved in divisive religious controversies, as you will read later in this chapter.

**DYNASTY OF HERACLIUS**

In 610, Heraclius, the military governor of Carthage, seized power and established a new Byzantine dynasty. By this time, the empire that Justinian had expanded was threatened on all sides. The Lombards had conquered much of Italy, leaving the Byzantine Empire in control only of Sicily, southern Italy, and the areas around Venice and Ravenna. However, Heraclius and his successors had no time for Italy; instead, they were forced to concentrate their energies on threats to the empire's eastern provinces.

Early in his reign, Heraclius suffered a series of defeats as Chroeses II, the ambitious ruler of Persia, conquered Syria and Palestine, destroying many Christian churches in Jerusalem. The Persians carried back to their capital many Christian relics, including pieces of wood that supposedly came from the True Cross on which Jesus was crucified. They also invaded Egypt, capturing the fields and storage facilities which provided grain to the empire. Other Persian armies marched through Asia Minor and besieged Constantinople itself.

Heraclius rallied his forces to fight back. With funds confiscated from various churches and provincial treasuries, he bought off the Slavs and the Avars, who were threatening the empire in the north. He also abandoned the Roman system of provincial governments, in which civil power was separated from military power. In its place, he appointed a *strategos* to govern each province.

The *strategos*, who was directly responsible to the emperor, served as both military and civilian governor of the region.

In 627, Heraclius went on the offensive against the Persians. He led his army through Asia Minor into Persia, where he won a decisive victory over the Persians near the site of ancient Nineveh. When Chroeses II was murdered a short time later, Heraclius dictated the terms of a peace treaty to his successor. The Byzantine emperor regained Syria, Palestine, and Egypt and recovered the relics of the True Cross, which he personally returned to Jerusalem.

These long and devastating wars exhausted both Persia and the Byzantine Empire, so that both were ill-prepared to face a new threat—the invasion of the Arab armies who were inspired by the teachings of a new religion, Islam. As you will read in Chapter 14, the teachings of the prophet Mohammed formed the basis for the religion of Islam. Within 20 years of Mohammed's death in 632, Moslem armies had overrun the richest provinces of the Byzantine Empire from North Africa and Egypt to Palestine, Syria, and parts of Asia Minor. In 655, a Moslem fleet inflicted heavy losses on the Byzantine navy in the eastern Mediterranean; between 673 and 678, Constantinople itself was blockaded, and the trade of the empire was crippled. The Moslems were finally repulsed when the Byzantines began to use a powerful new weapon, called "Greek fire." Today, this weapon would be called a "flamethrower." A mixture of naphtha, sulfur, and saltpeter was put into a tube that was closed at one end. When water was added through the open end of the tube, these chemicals underwent combustion and the resulting fire was propelled at enemy ships, causing some damage and much fear.

By the end of the 7th century, the Byzantine Empire faced renewed attacks from the north. Slavs infiltrated the Balkan Peninsula, and Bulgars crossed the Danube in 679, defeating the Byzantine army and demanding tribute to maintain peace. By 700, the empire

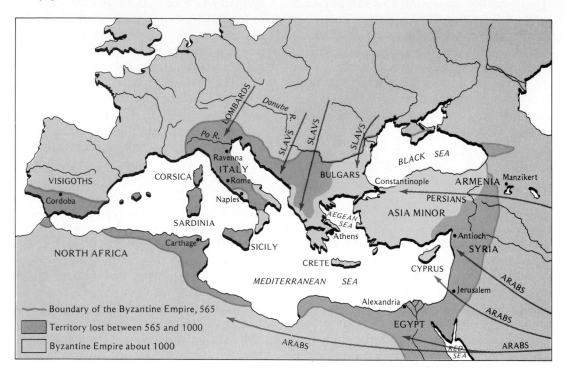

Boundary of the Byzantine Empire, 565

Territory lost between 565 and 1000

Byzantine Empire about 1000

consisted of little more than Asia Minor, the Balkans, southern Italy, and Sicily.

### REIGN OF LEO III

In 718, Leo III, a powerful general from Asia Minor, gained the crown and set about restoring order in the empire. He reorganized its administration, dividing larger districts into smaller ones and making the local commanders responsible for civil and military matters in their own districts. At the same time, he strengthened his authority over them. Leo successfully directed the defense of Constantinople against a renewed Moslem blockade and finally drove the Moslems from Asia Minor. His policies succeeded in freeing the Byzantine Empire from attacks for a few years and restored a stability that enabled it to survive the political and religious controversies of the next few hundred years.

In 780, a 10-year-old boy, Constantine VI, ascended the throne. His mother, the empress Irene, ruled in his name until he reached maturity. With the support of the army, Constantine seized power in his own name in 790 and exiled his mother. After seven years of conspiring to regain the throne, Irene succeeded in overthrowing her son. She then had him blinded and imprisoned. A few years later, after Constantine's death, Irene assumed the title of emperor and ruled for five years (797-802). Her autocratic rule, mismanagement of finances, and unpopular positions on theological issues, which you will read about later in this chapter, created so much controversy that her reign was ended through palace intrigue, and she was again sent into exile.

Irene's rule led to strained relations with Pope Leo III in Rome. The pope declared that the throne of the Byzantine Empire was vacant because a woman was incapable of rul-

24

ing an empire. He then bestowed the title of "Emperor of the Romans" on Charlemagne, the king of the Franks (see Chapter 14) in the hope that Charlemagne would help him exert control over the Church in the East. The Byzantines, who regarded themselves as the sole heirs to Roman power, greatly resented this interference. Their resentment grew in the years ahead as other controversies erupted, deepening the division between the eastern and western branches of Christendom.

*MACEDONIAN DYNASTY* Under the Macedonian dynasty, which lasted from 867 to 1025, the Byzantine Empire enjoyed a new period of expansion and prosperity. Well-equipped and highly trained Byzantine armies recovered Syria, Armenia, Cyprus, and Crete from the Moslems. Finances were handled wisely. The protecting walls of Constantinople were rebuilt, and that city enjoyed a cultural renaissance. The most outstanding emperor of this period was Basil II (976-1025), who earned the title "Slayer of the Bulgars" by crushing the Bulgars in 1004 and annexing their territory to the empire. Basil II maintained friendly relations with Vladimir, the ruler of Kiev in southern Russia, and helped bring about his conversion to Christianity. As a result, Byzantine Christianity and culture were carried into Russia.

*DECLINE OF THE EMPIRE* During the 11th century, the empire again went into a decline, which lasted for 400 years. Emperors faced both internal and external difficulties. In Asia Minor, noble landowners raised their own armies and rebelled against the central government. Faced with this threat, emperors were forced to increase taxes so that they could hire mercenary soldiers. Although Constantinople remained the richest trading city in the Mediterranean region, it faced competition from other centers, especially from Venice, whose merchants were actively trading with the Moslems. The

growing economic rivalry between Venice and Constantinople would have disastrous consequences.

Another threat to the Byzantine Empire came from the advancing armies of the Seljuk Turks, who had converted to Islam and were invading both Arab and Christian lands. In 1071, a Byzantine army under the emperor Romanus IV was defeated at Manzikert in Syria by the Seljuk Turks, and the wealthy eastern provinces fell to the Moslem Turks.

### LATIN EMPIRE

When various Byzantine emperors asked the pope for help against the Turks, the pope finally responded with a call for a *crusade*, or holy war against the "infidel," as Christians called all Moslems. Although the early Crusades were directed toward reconquering the Holy Land (see Chapter 16), the Fourth Crusade (1202-1204) proved costly for the Byzantine Empire. Urged on by Venetian merchants who wanted to eliminate their chief commercial rival, Constantinople, the Crusaders attacked Constantinople. For three days, Crusaders looted and burned the great city. Thousands of citizens were massacred, and much of the treasure of the city was carried to Venice and other parts of Europe.

The Crusaders established a Latin Empire over Constantinople and parts of Greece. It lasted for 60 years until the Byzantine emperor regained Constantinople. However, the city never fully recovered from the devastation caused by the Crusaders. Although the Byzantine Empire survived for almost 200 years more, its rulers presided over only a fragment of its former lands.

### FALL OF CONSTANTINOPLE

In 1451, Mohammed II became ruler of the Ottoman Turks, who had migrated out of Central Asia and conquered the lands held by the Seljuk Turks. Two years later, Mohammed II decided to capture Constantinople. He hired a Hungarian military engineer to design huge cannons, which could project

In 1453, Constantinople was conquered by the Turks, who blockaded the city with a large fleet of ships and besieged its walls.

cannonballs weighing 1200 pounds each, to destroy the walls of the city. Mohammed II lay siege to the city with 100,000 soldiers and blockaded its harbor with a large fleet. For seven weeks, the city's defenders fought by day and repaired their walls by night. When the emperor Constantine XI appealed to Pope Nicholas V at Rome for help, the pope responded that help would be sent if the Church at Constantinople would accept the pope as its head. The division in Christendom was so deep by then that one Byzantine official replied, "It is better to see in this city the power of the Turkish turban than that of the Latin tiara." On May 29, 1453, Constantinople fell to the Moslem Turks. The last Byzantine emperor was killed valiantly fighting on the walls of his capital. Mo-

hammed II then made the city the capital of the new Ottoman Empire and changed its name to Istanbul.

## THEOLOGICAL CONTROVERSIES

By 1453, the Byzantine Empire had endured for more than a thousand years. It enjoyed periods of prosperity and stability along with times of revolt and turmoil. Its rulers established an autocratic and centralized government and were supported by an efficient bureaucracy. The emperor controlled the Church, and the Church in turn was a unifying force. Yet despite the loyalty of the people to the Church, the Byzantine Empire was frequently torn by bitter theological disputes.

One controversy centered around the question of the nature of Christ. Monophysites, as you have read, maintained a belief that Jesus had only a single, divine nature. This belief was held by many Christians in Egypt, Syria, and parts of Asia Minor. However, it ran counter to orthodox Church teachings that Jesus was one person with two natures, human and divine. When the Church tried to fight the heretical belief, disputes arose throughout the East. Eventually, Christians in Egypt renounced the authority of the patriarch and developed their own Coptic Church.

### ICONOCLASTIC CONTROVERSY

Another controversy arose in the 8th century over the use of **icons**, or sacred images. Many common people came to see icons as images to be worshiped rather than as representations of holy scenes or people. They burned incense, lit candles, and prayed to icons. Some Church leaders, and even some Byzantine emperors, claimed that this reverence for icons amounted to idolatry, or the worship of graven images, which was forbidden in the Bible.

In 725, the emperor Leo III issued an edict forbidding reverence for icons and ordering the removal of all religious paintings and

*The Byzantines developed the distinctive iconographic style of art. Sacred figures are represented in a one-dimensional manner, and usually look directly at the viewer.*

statues from churches and public places. This edict led to widespread rioting not only in Constantinople, but elsewhere in Greece and in other Byzantine provinces between *iconoclasts* ("image-breakers"), as those who opposed the use of icons were called, and people who felt that reverence for icons was a legitimate form of worship. During the riots, many icons were destroyed.

The pope soon took a stand on this controversy that was dividing the Byzantines. He decreed that icons could be used (though not worshiped) to help the masses of illiterate Christians to understand their faith, and he denounced the iconoclasts as heretics.

The iconoclastic controversy raged on into the 9th century with some emperors supporting the use of icons and others banning them. It soured relations between the Byzantine Empire and the pope. Although the

quarrel was eventually resolved and icons were restored in the eastern Church, it contributed to the strains between eastern and western Christendom.

### THE FINAL BREAK

Other antagonisms developed between the Byzantine Church and the Roman Catholic Church. Since early in the Christian era, leaders in the eastern and western Churches had been rivals for power and prestige. During the 9th century, several popes felt that they were not getting enough help from the Byzantine emperor in the struggles against the Lombards and Moslems in the West. At the same time, a rivalry developed between Latin- and Greek-speaking missionaries who were trying to convert the Slavs of eastern Europe to Christianity.

Old quarrels between the eastern and western Churches were revived and contributed to the growing split. One involved the Nicene Creed, which a Church council had issued in 325. The Church in Rome and the eastern Church had long disagreed over the wording of the creed. In the 11th century, this disagreement coupled with conflicting claims of the pope and patriarch to rule over the Church in southern Italy led to the final break. In 1054, the pope sent representatives to Constantinople to meet with the patriarch. The meeting quickly led to bitter denunciations, after which the patriarch and the papal representatives excommunicated each other. This event marked the *schism*, or division, between the eastern and western Church.

The Church in the West, which was headed by the pope and used Latin, came to be known as the Roman Catholic Church; the Church in the East, which was headed by the patriarch and used Greek, came to be known as the Orthodox (or sometimes the Eastern Orthodox) Church.

### CONTINUING DIFFERENCES

The Orthodox Church and the Roman Catholic Church had grown apart over the centuries so that the schism in 1054 marked the final break in the unity of Christendom. Today, these differences still remain. For example, the Orthodox Church does not accept two doctrines of the Roman Catholic Church: the infallibility of the pope and the Immaculate Conception of Mary, the mother of Jesus. Roman Catholic priests must take a vow of celibacy, while Orthodox priests are permitted to marry, although a candidate for the office of bishop may not be married. Until 1964, all Roman Catholic services were conducted in Latin, while services in the Orthodox Church were conducted in the language of the people, thereby giving rise to what are known as the Russian, Greek, Serbian, and other Orthodox churches.

In 1964, Pope Paul VI met with Athenagoras, patriarch of Constantinople, at Jerusalem. Each leader rescinded the longstanding excommunication of the leader of the other church. While the churches of the East and West have had more cordial relations since that meeting, they remain widely separated in doctrine and administration.

## BYZANTINE CIVILIZATION

Despite the theological controversies that erupted frequently, the Byzantine emperors presided over a brilliant civilization. At a time when western Europe was in a state of political, social, and economic decline following the invasions of the Germanic tribes, the people of the Byzantine Empire enjoyed the benefits of a stable and diverse economy.

### COMMERCE AND AGRICULTURE

Constantinople was not only the political capital but also the commercial and intellectual center of the empire. With a population of about a half million people from all over the Middle East, it was a beautiful city, with splendid palaces, gardens, and fountains. It had hospitals for the sick, orphan-

ages, and homes for the elderly; and it boasted great public works, including a municipal water-supply system and a sewer system.

Constantinople was the center of Byzantine commerce, with ships and caravans bringing spices, tapestries, leather goods, metalwork, and grain from all parts of the empire. The movement of all these goods was closely monitored by officials appointed by the emperor. Manufacturing was also closely regulated. Craftsmen and merchants were organized into *guilds*, associations formed for mutual aid and protection by people in the same trade or industry. Guilds were under strict government supervision. For example, sons of guild members were required to follow their fathers' occupations, and any infringement of a guild rule was punishable by expulsion from the guild. The government fixed wages and prices, and also controlled working conditions as well as weights and measures.

Byzantine emperors actively encouraged trade and commerce. Constantine introduced the *bezant*, a gold coin that remained the most stable unit of exchange in the Mediterranean world for 700 years. Justinian encouraged several monks who had lived in China to smuggle some silkworms to Constantinople. The smuggled silkworms became the basis for a flourishing silk industry that was made into a profitable government monopoly. Procopius, Justinian's official historian, gives the following account of the beginnings of the silk industry:

● ● ● *While it is impossible to convey the worms thither alive, it was still practical and altogether easy to convey their offspring. Now the offspring of these worms, they said, consisted of innumerable eggs from each one. And men bury these eggs, long after the time when they are produced, in dung, and, after thus heating them for a sufficient time, they bring forth the living creatures. After they had spoken thus, the emperor promised to reward them with large gifts and urged them to confirm their account in action. They then once more went to Serinda and brought back the eggs to Byzantium, and in the manner described caused them to be transformed into worms, which they fed on the leaves of the mulberry; and thus they made possible from that time forth the production of silk in the land of the Romans (i.e., the Eastern Empire).*[2]

The cities of the empire depended on the stable agricultural system. In the early days of the empire, Egypt provided the grain, as it had during the Roman Empire. After the Moslem conquest of Egypt, most food came from Asia Minor. *Serfs*, or peasants tied to the land, worked on huge estates owned by nobles or the Church. Their labor supported the landowners who lived in luxury in the cities.

### LEARNING

Byzantine scholars studied and preserved the heritage of ancient Greece and Rome. They carefully copied the great works of ancient Greek literature. Scholars produced numerous digests of classical Greek works and wrote commentaries on them. During the Byzantine period, manuscripts began to appear in book form rather than as scrolls as they had in the past. These manuscripts became an invaluable source of information for later scholars.

In the early empire, literacy was widespread among people in the upper class. Sons of wealthy parents were educated either by tutors or in private schools. They learned to read the Bible and the writings of classical Greek authors, such as Homer, Sophocles, and Plato. Some boys were educated in monasteries. Wealthier young men often continued their studies in philosophy and rhetoric at the great centers of learning in Athens, Alexandria, and Beirut until the latter two cities fell to the Moslems in the 7th century.

---

[2]Procopius, *History of the Wars* VIII, 17.

Young girls were trained in the household arts by their mothers, while some from wealthy families were tutored in academic subjects as well. A few learned to read and write in convents.

### ARCHITECTURE AND ART

Byzantine architecture and art forms reflected the several traditions that came together in the empire: Greco-Roman, oriental, and Christian. Since most palaces and government buildings were destroyed over the centuries, what remains of Byzantine architecture are the beautiful domed churches with their magnificent, ornate interiors and unadorned exteriors.

From the 9th to 11th centuries, Byzantine architects designed churches using the shape of the Greek cross, which has four arms of equal length. Frequently, they added a narthex (entry space) on one arm and an apse (rounded projection) on the opposite arm for balance. The most striking feature was a large dome arching over the center of the church. The Byzantine style of architecture was adopted by the Venetians when they built St. Mark's Cathedral and by the Russians, who modified the Byzantine dome into the onion-shaped domes seen on churches in Moscow and Kiev.

All forms of art flourished in Constantinople, whose wealthy families supported the finest artists and artisans. Byzantine artists portrayed human forms in a stylized manner: torsos were elongated, and people were almost always depicted in flat, frontal view, with relatively small, almond-shaped faces dominated by large eyes, peering out from under arched eyebrows. The mouths were small, and the noses were long and narrow.

Much art was devoted to portraying holy figures. The apostles and numerous saints were rendered everywhere in frescoes or mosaics. In the churches, these religious figures were always placed in prescribed relationships to one another to show the relative importance of each person. The figure of Jesus, for example, was always in the center of the main dome, with angels arranged in order of importance below him. Major events in the life, death, and resurrection of Jesus were shown below the angels. Representations of the apostles, prophets, and saints were placed at the lowest level.

Byzantine artists also fashioned exquisite secular works of art, such as ivory plaques, intricate gold jewelry set with semiprecious stones, beautifully decorated manuscripts, and small boxes called *reliquaries* that were designed to hold sacred relics. Artists decorated objects using the cloisonné process, in which colorful enamel is laid down between thin wires of gold. Brocade, velvet, and silk fabrics embroidered with gold and silver threads were shipped to all parts of the empire.

### LASTING INFLUENCE

The Byzantine Empire was heir to the civilizations of ancient Greece and Rome. Although it developed its own civilization, its greatest legacy was the preservation of the learning of the ancient world. Through Justinian's code, it preserved the Roman concepts of law. By copying the manuscripts of the ancient Greeks, Byzantine scholars preserved the classical heritage of Greece.

Byzantine emperors developed an efficient bureaucracy that was able to maintain order even during times of dynastic turmoil. For many centuries, the Byzantine Empire fought off determined invaders from the East. In this way, it served as a buffer, absorbing the brunt of invasions that might otherwise have overwhelmed the kingdoms that were emerging in western Europe.

Byzantine monks and missionaries transmitted the ideas and inventions of the Greek and Roman worlds to the Slavic peoples, whom they converted to Christianity. In the 9th century, Saint Cyril and Saint Methodius, who had been educated in Constantinople, were sent as missionaries to the Slavs in Bohemia and Moravia. They created the *Cyrillic alphabet* from Greek letters modified to represent Slavic sounds, and they translated the Bible as well as hymns and rituals of the Christian Church into the Slavic languages. The Cyrillic alphabet is still used in several eastern European countries and in the Soviet Union.

When the split developed between the eastern and western branches of Christendom, the Poles, Bohemians, and Hungarians chose to follow the leadership of the pope at Rome, while the people of the present-day Balkan nations and Russia accepted the leadership of the patriarch at Constantinople. Byzantine culture and traditions profoundly influenced the princes of Kiev and Moscow. When the Ottoman Turks captured Constantinople in 1453, Ivan IV, ruler of an emerging Russian nation, claimed to be the successor of the Byzantine emperors. Russian rulers took the title *czar* meaning "Caesar." Moscow became the seat of the Orthodox Church, and the czars called their city the "third Rome" because it succeeded ancient Rome and Constantinople. They adopted the double-headed eagle, symbol of the Byzantine emperor. In political matters, too, they adopted Byzantine practices by maintaining absolute rule and asserting their authority over the Church.

## SUMMARY

*While Western Europe was plunged into chaos after the fall of Rome, a powerful new civilization emerged in the eastern provinces of the Roman Empire. The foundations of the Byzantine Empire were laid when the emperor Constantine built his new capital at Byzantium, a strategically located site on the Bosporus. In the 6th century, Justinian expanded the empire, regaining much of the lands lost in the West. In the centuries after Justinian's death, the empire experienced periods of strength as well as periods of decline.*

*In its long history, the Byzantine Empire developed a remarkable civilization that preserved the learning of the classical world, and this learning was eventually passed on to the West. Rivalry between the eastern and western branches of Christianity led to a schism and the emergence of two separate Christian churches. At its height, the Byzantine Empire with its splendid capital at Constantinople was the envy of the Western world. However, the riches of Constantinople and its rivalry with Venice led to its devastation during the Fourth Crusade. Although the empire recovered from that blow, it was not strong enough to withstand the onslaught of the Ottoman Turks, who captured Constantinople in 1453.*

## QUESTIONS

1 How did geography shape the development of Constantinople? Of the Byzantine Empire?

2 Describe Justinian's major goals. In what areas did he have the most success? Why? In what areas did he have the least success? Why?

3 Why was the Roman Empire in the East able to survive for a thousand years after the collapse of the Roman Empire in the West? Explain why this survival was so critical to the future of western Europe.

4 What differences developed between the Christian Church in the East and West? What were the causes of the schism? Analyze the immediate and longterm effects of the schism on both the Byzantine Empire and western Europe.

5 What evidence of Byzantine influence can you find in both eastern and western Europe?

## BIBLIOGRAPHY

*Which book might discuss Byzantine influence on the West?*

HEAD, CONSTANCE. *Justinian II of Byzantium.* University of Wisconsin Press, 1972. *A thoroughly researched biography of a colorful Byzantine emperor who ruled from 685-695, was deposed by a usurper, wandered alone for about 10 years among the barbarian tribes before gathering an army of Bulgarian mercenaries and returning in victory to Constantinople. His career spanned a critical time within the Byzantine Empire.*

MANGO, CYRIL. *Byzantium, Empire of New Rome.* New York: Scribner's, 1980. *A study of life in Byzantium from the perspective of its language, society, economy, and religion; based on the point of view of the "average" Byzantine citizen.*

RICE, TAMARA TALBOT. *Everyday Life in Byzantium.* London: B. T. Batsford, 1967. *A discussion of the influence of the Byzantine Empire on Europe through its architecture and religion that examines both the way of life of the common people of Byzantium as well as the rituals of the imperial court and the Church.*

## 3

● *Say: Allah is One, the Eternal God. He begot none, nor was He begotten. None is equal to Him.*

MOHAMMED

# The Islamic World

Islam, the youngest of the major religions of the world, developed in Arabia early in the 7th century. Its followers, who are called Moslems, worship Allah, the same, all-powerful deity worshiped by Jews and Christians. Moslems believe that Allah made his final revelations to his prophet, Mohammed. These revelations were later compiled into the *Koran*, the holy book of Islam. The Arabic word *Islam* means "submit," as Mohammed called on Arabs to submit to the will of Allah, while *Moslem* means "one who submits."[1]

Within ten years of receiving his first revelation, Mohammed had gathered a body of followers dedicated to spreading the message of Allah throughout the world. Within a century of Mohammed's death in 632, Moslem armies had conquered a region stretching from the Atlantic Ocean in the west to the Indus River in the east. Within the vast Islamic Empire, which rivaled that of the Byzantines and Persians, Moslem scholars developed a brilliant civilization incorporating knowledge from the Mediterranean world and eastern Asia.

After the 11th century, a series of invasions fragmented the Islamic Empire, but the religion of Islam continued to unite the various cultural and ethnic groups that had accepted it. As a result, Islam has continued to play an important role in the world to the present day.

**ARABIA BEFORE ISLAM** While the Middle East, especially the Fertile Crescent, has been mentioned earlier in this book, there has been little reference to the vast Arabian peninsula, which forms the southwest corner of the continent of Asia. The inhabitants of this desert region call their land *Jazirat al 'Arab*, "the island of Arabia," because it is a huge peninsula—approximately one-third the size of the continental United States—with the Red Sea to the west, the Mediterranean Sea to the north, the Persian Gulf along most of the east, and the Arabian Sea to the south. Much of the land in the south is called the "Vacant Quarter" because there is no water and few people. In other regions, there are oases which provide water for the sheep, goats, and camels of the Bedouins ("desert dwellers").

---

[1]Mohammed may also be spelled as *Muhammed*, Koran as *Quran*, and Moslem as *Muslim*.

Yemen, which occupies the southwest corner of the peninsula, was called *Felix Arabia* ("pleasant Arabia") by the Romans because it was a source of spices and of aromatic gums, myrrh, and frankincense. Because of its strategic location, Yemen was an important commercial center for caravans carrying goods from India, China, and Africa to the Roman world. With wealth from trade, the people built great cities and beautiful buildings. Many Jews who had fled from Palestine in the 1st and 2nd centuries settled among the Arabs in Yemen.

By 600, Arabs were divided into two groups, Bedouins and city dwellers. The Bedouins were nomads who moved with their herds from oasis to oasis. They were divided into tribes, each headed by a *sheik*, or chief, who was advised by the heads of leading families in the tribe. Each tribe also had its own set of customs, called *sunna*, which served as its code of laws. Strength, courage in battle, and tribal loyalty were the virtues they prized most highly. As in many other primitive societies, sickly infants and unwanted female children were abandoned to die. In the harsh conditions of the desert life, widows and orphans had no protection and were frequently forced to beg for alms to survive. Fighting was the accepted way of resolving disputes, and blood feuds were carried on for generations. Booty from raids on caravans supplemented the meager existence of many Bedouins.

The Bedouins worshiped a variety of nature gods, and each tribe had its own god, often associated with a sacred stone. Poetry was the chief artistic outlet for the Bedouins, and their poems often spoke of the forces of nature that shaped their lives.

City dwellers lived in the busy commercial centers along the eastern shore of the Red Sea. From there, merchants operated caravans that carried goods from Yemen across the desert to cities in Syria and Egypt. The main road ran a few miles inland, where the heat was less intense than along the coast.

Even before Mohammed's lifetime, the Kaaba at Mecca had been a holy shrine. Mohammed removed from it all holy objects except the Black Stone.

Important caravan stops grew up at strategic oases; two of these were Mecca and Yathrib, renamed Medina in the 7th century.

Mecca was the chief Arab city because it housed the *Kaaba* (Arabic for "cube"), a small building erected around a large black stone —probably a meteorite. Arabs believed that the stone had been sent to them from heaven, and they looked on the Kaaba as the holiest of places. Pilgrims flocked to Mecca to worship at this shrine, adding greatly to the prosperity of the city. The powerful Quraysh tribe served as guardians of the Kaaba, which in addition to the Black Stone housed the images of 360 gods and goddesses. The members of this tribe maintained a monopoly on the supply of food and water to the pilgrims who visited the shrine, and they controlled the government and commerce of Mecca.

Yathrib, about 200 miles north of Mecca, had a middle class that included a number of Jews. Although most Arabs remained loyal to their many gods, Judaism won some converts. In addition, the Arabs tended to worship one god—Allah—above the others. Thus, the seeds of monotheism were already planted before the 7th century.

## LIFE OF MOHAMMED

Mohammed (Arabic for "highly praised") was born in 570 in Mecca. Although he was born into the powerful Quraysh tribe, his father died before his birth, and his mother died six years later. He was raised by poor relatives and had few advantages. At an early age, he worked as a camel driver and then led caravans to cities of Syria and Palestine. On these journeys, he probably came into contact with Jews and Christians and learned about their beliefs.

At about the age of 20, Mohammed was hired by Khadija, a wealthy widow 15 years his senior, to manage her caravans. Five years later, they were married. The marriage was a happy one, and his wife's wealth provided Mohammed with the leisure to wander into the desert to meditate on religion.

According to tradition, the angel Gabriel appeared to Mohammed as he was meditating in a cave one day. "O Mohammed," the angel reportedly said, "you are the messenger of Allah." At first, Mohammed told only close relatives of this vision.

Later, inspired by continuing visions which urged him to spread the message of Allah, Mohammed began to preach in public. The two fundamental themes of his teaching were summed up in the Moslem call to prayer: "There is no God but Allah, and Mohammed is his Prophet." Time and again, Mohammed called on people to renounce their faith in other gods and submit to the will of Allah.

### FLIGHT TO MEDINA

At first, Mohammed won few followers. Instead, his preaching angered the powerful Quraysh leaders who saw in his monotheistic teachings a threat to the profitable business of the pilgrimages to the Kaaba. They ridiculed and then persecuted Mohammed and his followers. However, among Mohammed's early converts were several influential men of Mecca, including Abu Bakr, a successful merchant, and Ali, Mohammed's

*According to Islamic tradition, Mohammed was guided by the angel Gabriel through seven heavens, where he met Adam, Moses, Jesus, and finally Allah.*

cousin, who later married Fatima, a daughter of the prophet. As you will read, these men would play important roles in the development of Islam.

According to Islamic tradition, during this difficult period the angel Gabriel miraculously transported Mohammed from Jerusalem to heaven on a winged steed. Moslems celebrate this event as the "Night of Power," and because of it, they consider Jerusalem to be a holy city.

Mohammed's teachings were better received by pilgrims from Yathrib than by the people of Mecca. In 622, some leading citizens of Yathrib invited Mohammed to their city to settle a feud between two local tribes. Continued persecution convinced Mohammed to move from Mecca to Yathrib. Later, Yathrib was renamed Medinat-al-Nabi—"City of the Prophet"—which was shortened to Medina. Mohammed's escape from Mecca to Medina became known as the *Hegira*, or "flight," and the first year of the Moslems' calendar is dated from the year of the Hegira. This means that the year 2000 A.D. of the Christian calendar will be the year 1378 A.H. (after the Hegira) of the Islamic calendar.

Mohammed soon became both the political and the spiritual leader of Medina. He built the first *mosque*, or Moslem place of worship, appointed the first *muezzin* to call the faithful to prayer, and decided that all worshipers should face toward the Kaaba when they prayed or worshiped. He established Friday as the day for Moslems to worship together in a mosque. He also decreed that the faithful should give alms regularly to provide help for the poor and support the work of the mosques.

## RETURN TO MECCA

Mohammed granted his followers in Medina permission to attack caravans originating or terminating in Mecca, and let them keep a portion of the booty. With these raids, he put pressure on the people of Mecca to convert, and at the same time he raised money for Islam.

When a few hundred followers of Mohammed routed a much larger army of Meccans, many Arabs became convinced that Mohammed was truly the prophet of Allah. These early battles in the desert gave rise to the concept of the *jihad*, or "holy war," which held that Moslems who died fighting the infidel, as unbelievers were called, would be immediately transported to heaven. This concept was similar to the Christian idea of a crusade, or holy war against unbelievers.

In 630, Mohammed led an army of converts against Mecca, and the city surrendered without a struggle. Mohammed then destroyed all the idols in the Kaaba except the

The mosque that Mohammed built at Medina had four basic features: a fountain at which the faithful could wash before entering, minarets for the muezzin to summon worshipers, a marker to indicate the direction of Mecca, and a pulpit from which the Koran could be read aloud.

Black Stone. After cleansing the Kaaba, he dedicated it to the worship of Allah. The Kaaba thus became the center of Islam and the holiest site for pilgrims to visit. Mohammed dealt leniently with those who had opposed him, granting them pardons. In the next two years, he sent out missionaries to convert the Bedouin tribes in the desert, and by the time of his death in 632, most of Arabia had accepted the teachings of Islam.

## TEACHINGS OF ISLAM

Within a hundred years of Mohammed's death, Islam had spread from the Arabian peninsula across much of the world. By 750, it had won converts from Spain to India. One reason for the spectacular success of the new faith was its simple, straightforward message.

### THE FIVE PILLARS OF FAITH

Every Moslem is called on to accept five basic duties. First, and foremost, is the reciting of the creed that is the central focus of Islam. The simple but powerful statement of the Moslem faith recalls that "There is no God but Allah, and Mohammed is his Prophet." A person may become a Moslem merely by making this statement. It is whispered into the ears of newborn babies, repeated frequently throughout life, and will, if possible, be the last words spoken before death.

The creed affirms the strict monotheism of Islam. To Mohammed, the Christian belief in the Trinity was equivalent to the worship of three gods and thus amounted to polytheism. To Moslems, the one God is absolute and all powerful, as these words convey:

*Praise be to Allah, the Lord of Creation,*
*The Compassionate, the Merciful,*
*King of the last Judgement!*
*You alone we worship and to you alone we*
    *pray for help.*[2]

---

[2]"Light," in *Koran*, trans. N.J. Dawood (Baltimore: Penguin Books, 1959), p. 15.

Although Mohammed rejected the Christian doctrine of the Trinity, he respected the monotheism of the Jews. He acknowledged that the prophets of the Old Testament and even Jesus were bearers of the word of God, but he saw himself as the final prophet.

The second duty of Moslems is to pray five times each day: at sunrise, noon, mid-afternoon, sunset, and nightfall. Each mosque has at least one minaret from which a muezzin calls the faithful to prayer. In preparation for prayer, worshipers wash head, hands, and feet (at least in symbolic fashion), lay out their prayer mats so that they will be facing toward Mecca, and then bend, kneel, and prostrate themselves in a prescribed way. A believer may pray alone or with others, at home, at work, or in a mosque.

The third duty of Moslems is to give alms, or charity to the poor. Devout Moslems often set aside a portion of their income to help those in need. In modern times, the governments of several Islamic nations have established the *Red Crescent*, an organization similar to the Red Cross that provides help in emergencies.

The fourth duty of Moslems is to observe a fast during the hours of sunlight in the holy month of Ramadan. Ramadan is the ninth month of the Moslem year and was the time when Mohammed received his first revelation. During Ramadan, devout Moslems spend much time in contemplation of the blessings of Allah. They are permitted to eat only after sundown and until the moment at dawn when "one can discern a white thread from a black thread." At the end of Ramadan, a three-day celebration commemorating Mohammed's "Night of Power" is observed with feasting and exchanging gifts.

The fifth duty of Moslems is to make a pilgrimage to Mecca (*hajj*) at least once in their lives. If physically or financially unable to make such a pilgrimage, a believer is expected to contribute to the pilgrimage of another. Over the centuries, this duty has helped to unite Moslems from all parts of the world.

No unbeliever may enter Mecca during the 12th month of the Moslem year when these pilgrimages are made.

In Mecca, all pilgrims wear simple, seamless, white garments to indicate equality within the brotherhood of Islam. Pilgrims may not shave, have their hair or nails trimmed, or engage in sexual relations. They are led to the Kaaba, and move around it three times rapidly and four times slowly, stopping each time to kiss or touch the sacred Black Stone.

On the ninth day of their pilgrimage, the faithful are conducted to the Plain of Arafat, nine miles southeast of Mecca, to worship on the spot where Mohammed delivered his last message. There, they stand in prayer from noon to sundown. On the following day, the pilgrims throw pebbles at three stone pillars to recall how the patriarch Abraham frightened Satan away by throwing stones at him. They then return to Mecca for three days of feasting before walking once more around the Kaaba. Moslems who participate in the pilgrimage, whether in person or by assisting someone else to do so, are referred to respectfully as *hajji*, and believe that they will enter paradise when they die.

### THE KORAN

Like Judaism and Christianity, Islam has a sacred book, the *Koran*, that contains its basic teachings. To Moslems, the Koran is the sacred word of God as it was revealed to Mohammed through the angel Gabriel. It is considered God's final word on every subject, and because it was given to Mohammed in Arabic, Moslems believe that it can be studied only in that language. Since translation into another language might introduce errors, devout Moslems everywhere learn Arabic and memorize parts or all of the 78,000 words of their holy book. This widespread use of Arabic has helped to unite the many different peoples in the Islamic lands.

The Koran consists of 114 messages conveyed to Mohammed by the angel Gabriel. No one knows in what order these messages

A passage from the Koran, written about 1300. Moslem artists developed a highly decorative calligraphy to embellish their sacred literature.

were given, but as Mohammed passed them on to his followers, they were memorized or sometimes written down on paper, stone, dried palm leaves, and even on large bones. About 20 years after Mohammed's death, the sayings were collected in their present form and arranged so that the longest (consisting of several thousand words) would be first and the shortest (consisting of fewer than fifty words) would be last.

### THE SUNNA

As Islam expanded, Moslems found that the Koran did not provide a guide to meet all the new situations that arose. Sometimes, too, passages in the Koran contradicted each other. Early on, Moslem leaders who had been closely associated with Mohammed tried to resolve these difficulties by recalling the Prophet's actions or words on specific occasions. Gradually, a code of detailed rules was put together to deal with situations that were not covered either by the Koran or by traditions associated with Mohammed. These rules came in part from the customs (sunna) that each tribe had developed and that served as their law codes. In time, the *Sunna* were collected and were used along with the Koran as the final authority on all questions. Since Moslems believe that the will of Allah embraces all aspects of life, including political activities, the devout look to the Koran and the Sunna for guidance in all their decisions.

### MORAL AND SOCIAL CODE

Islam set up a strict moral code for Moslems to follow. It called on the faithful to be honest and just in all their dealings. It prohibited blood feuds, which had caused frequent warfare among the Arabs. The drinking of intoxicants and gambling were forbidden. Also, certain foods were considered unclean. For example, one passage in the Koran says:

● ● ● *Eat of the good and lawful things which Allah has bestowed on you and give thanks for His favours if you truly serve Him. He has forbidden you the flesh of beasts that die a natural death, blood, and pig's meat; also any flesh consecrated in the name of any but Allah. But whoever is constrained to eat of it without intending to be a rebel or transgressor, will find Allah forgiving and merciful.*[3]

Infanticide was prohibited, and new inheritance laws were proclaimed to protect the rights of widows and orphans. Although polygamy was permitted, a man could not have more than four wives, and each was to be treated equally. Moreover, a man could not divorce a wife on a mere whim.

● ● ● *If a man accuses his wife but has no witnesses except himself, he shall swear four times by Allah that his charge is true, calling down upon himself the curse of Allah if he be lying. But if his wife swears four times by Allah that his charge is false and calls down His curse upon herself if it be true, she shall receive no punishment.*[4]

The Koran accepted the practice of slavery, but it required that slaves be treated humanely. Slaves were permitted to marry, and could purchase their freedom.

● ● ● *As for those of your slaves who wish to buy their liberty, free them if you find in them any promise and bestow on them a part of the riches which Allah has given you.*[5]

Mohammed taught that there would be a Judgment Day on which Allah would judge all people by the acts they had performed while on earth. For those who obeyed Allah, he promised a joyful afterlife in paradise:

● ● ● *They shall recline on jewelled couches face to face, and there shall wait on them immortal youths with bowls and ewers and cups of purest wine (that will neither pain their heads nor take away their reason); with fruits of their own choice and flesh of fowls that they relish.*[6]

To unbelievers and those who disobeyed, Mohammed described the tortures of hell: "For the unbelievers We have prepared fetters and chains, and a blazing Fire."[7]

### MULLAHS AND IMAMS

There is no priesthood in Islam, and Mohammed did not establish a clergy. Early on, however, the *mullahs*, who taught Islamic law, gained a respected position in Islam similar to that of the clergy in Christian lands. In addition, the religious services in the mosques came to be conducted by an *imam*, who led the prayers and delivered a sermon from an elevated place.

**EXPANSION OF ISLAM** When Mohammed died in 632, he had named no successor, so a council of his closest associates met to decide who would lead the Moslem community. They

---

[3]"The Bee," *Koran*, p. 303. Hebrew Scriptures also forbid the eating of pork (Leviticus 11:7-8).
[4]"Light," *Koran*, p. 208.

[5]"Light," *Koran*, p. 210.
[6]"That Which Is Coming," *Koran*, p. 108.
[7]"Man," *Koran*, p. 18.

soon chose Abu Bakr, an early convert, trusted friend, and father-in-law of Mohammed. Abu Bakr assumed the title of *caliph* (from *khalifa* meaning "successor"). As caliph, he had absolute power.

### THE FIRST FOUR CALIPHS

Between 632 and 661, four caliphs were elected: Abu Bakr (632-634), Omar (634-644), Othman (644-656), and Ali (656-661).

**Abu Bakr.** On assuming the caliphate, Abu Bakr immediately faced a serious problem. Several Arab tribes refused to acknowledge his leadership, claiming that they had pledged allegiance to Mohammed as a person, and not to Islam. Abu Bakr sent troops to put down this rebellion, reportedly saying:

• • •*Mohammed is no more than an apostle, and apostles before him have passed away. If then he dies or is killed, will you turn back upon your heels?*[8]

Although Abu Bakr died after serving only two years as caliph, he succeeded in bringing all of Arabia back under the control of Islam. Before his death, Abu Bakr named Omar, one of Mohammed's most trusted advisers, to be the second caliph.

**Omar.** The Islamic Empire was established under the caliphate of Omar. In 635, an Islamic army under the leadership of Khalid ibn-al-Walid (often referred to as "The Sword of Allah") defeated a much larger Byzantine army in Syria. The victorious army then laid siege to Damascus, which surrendered after six months. In 637, Jerusalem fell to the Moslems. A second army marched against Persia, and by 644, the Persian Empire of the Sassanids had crumbled. At the same time, the Arabs were moving into North Africa. In 639-40, they captured Alexandria and the rest of Egypt.

---

[8]Quoted in *Islam and the Arab World*, ed. Bernard Lewis (New York: American Heritage Publishing Co., 1976), p. 12.

> For many centuries the Arabs were accused of having destroyed the great library at Alexandria by burning the books to heat the public baths. It is now known that Julius Caesar's soldiers destroyed it in 48 B.C.; that it was rebuilt into a great library; and was then destroyed again by the emperor Theodosius in 389 A.D.

**Othman.** After Omar was murdered by a Christian slave in 644, Othman was named the third caliph. During Othman's caliphate, the first official Koran was compiled. However, Othman was unpopular, in part because of his appointment of relatives and friends to important positions. Like his predecessors, Othman tried to consolidate power in the hands of the caliph. This policy outraged many Arabs who were not accustomed to a strong central authority. Also, many Moslems felt that only a member of Mohammed's family should hold the position of caliph. Ultimately, hostility toward Othman resulted in his murder in 656.

**Ali.** Ali, Mohammed's cousin and the husband of the Prophet's daughter Fatima, was chosen to succeed Othman. The election of Ali sparked an immediate dispute. Muawiya, the governor of Syria and a member of Othman's family, challenged Ali's right to be caliph. Ali's refusal to apprehend and punish the murderers of Othman further added to his difficulties. In 661, Ali was assassinated, ending this early period of the first four caliphs.

### REASONS FOR ISLAM'S EARLY SUCCESS

During these early years, the Arabs won a string of smashing victories and conquered most of the Middle East and much of North Africa. The Islamic armies achieved many great military victories in part because they were led by outstanding commanders like Khalid ibn-al-Walid. Arab commanders

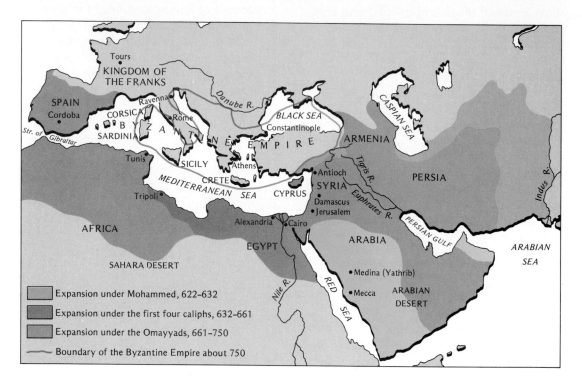

launched attacks with speed and surprise, overwhelming their more numerous enemies. A second reason for the early success of Islam was the disaffection of people in parts of the Byzantine Empire. In Syria and North Africa, people looked on Byzantine officials as alien rulers. In the 7th century, their discontent with Byzantine rule found an outlet in their acceptance of Islam. The new converts soon swelled the armies of Islam and helped them on to new triumphs.

Third, both the Byzantine and Persian empires had exhausted themselves in recent wars against each other (Chapter 13). Fourth, Moslems fought for their cause with enormous zeal. The Koran commanded, "Believers, if you help Allah, Allah will help you and make you strong."[9]

The early caliphs established guidelines for dealing with the conquered peoples. Because the Arabs were relatively few in number, they usually left the existing political structure in place. Moslem soldiers garrisoned the towns, and churches were converted into mosques. In those lands where the people willingly accepted Islam, they were permitted to keep their property as long as they paid tribute. Those people who fought against the Moslems were forced to surrender all of their goods, with one-fifth going to Islam and four-fifths being divided among the Moslem soldiers.

Toward Jews and Christians, Moslems were tolerant. Moslems regarded the Old and New Testaments as the sacred word of God revealed before God's final messenger, Mohammed, had brought them the Koran. Moslems thus called Jews and Christians "the

---

[9]"Mohammed," *Koran*, p. 121.

people of the Book" because they accepted God's word in the Bible. Therefore, Jews and Christians were accorded protection in theory, although this did not always happen in practice. Some Jews and Christians chose to convert, however, and thereby avoid the additional taxes paid by non-Moslems.

## DIVISIONS WITHIN ISLAM

The murder of Ali in 661 brought to the forefront political and religious divisions that had existed in Islam since Mohammed's death. Even before Ali's death, Muawiya had called himself caliph. Muawiya began the Omayyad Dynasty (661-750), which you will read about shortly. His action split Islam into two groups: the Shiites and Sunnites.

**The Shiites.** The Shiites (from the Arabic *shi'i* meaning "follower") were loyal partisans of the murdered Ali. They believed that the caliph should be descended from the family of Mohammed—from Fatima and Ali—and thus they supported Ali's son, Husayn, as caliph. When Husayn was killed in a battle against the followers of Muawiya in 680, the Shiites grew even more adamant in their opposition to the Omayyads. They made the anniversary of Husayn's death a day of mourning that is still observed today.

The Shiites differed from their opponents on another issue. They insisted that the Koran was the only source of guidance for Islam. They rejected the body of traditions that were being accepted as part of the faith.

*Shiites believe that there were 12 divinely appointed leaders of the faith (imams), the last of whom disappeared in 878 A.D. Even today, they await his return to earth as the Mahdi, or "Guided One," who will fill the world with justice.*

**The Sunnites.** The followers of Muawiya and the Omayyad Dynasty were called Sunnites, or traditionalists. They believed that any spiritually qualified man could be elected caliph, not only descendants of Mohammed. The Sunnites accepted both the Koran and commentaries based on the customs, or *Sunna*, as valid parts of the faith.

The Sunnites were always far more numerous than the Shiites. They claimed to represent the orthodox, or correct, beliefs, and most Moslems accepted their point of view. The Shiites split into several sects that have survived until today. Many Moslems in Iran, Iraq, and Pakistan hold to the Shiite tradition.

**OMAYYAD DYNASTY** The Omayyad Dynasty consolidated power in the hands of the Sunnites. To better deal with the growing Islamic Empire, Muawiya moved his capital from Mecca to the more centrally located city of Damascus in Syria. He appointed Syrian and Egyptian officials who had experience in the administration of the Byzantine Empire to positions of authority. He decreed that Arabic would be the official language of the Islamic Empire, and he minted new coins containing quotations from the Koran to replace the Persian and Byzantine coins which had been the money of the Middle East. He set up a postal system modeled on that of the ancient Persians and undertook an extensive program of building, improving transportation, and constructing several beautiful mosques.

During the Omayyad Dynasty, Islamic armies again moved westward, conquering all of North Africa. The Berbers, who lived along the route of the Islamic expansion, resisted strongly. After the Berbers were finally defeated, however, they adopted the teachings of Islam and the Arabic language. Because they were such strong warriors, they were soon recruited into the Islamic army.

In 711, Tarik, the Moslem governor of

North Africa, launched an attack against Spain. As this largely Berber army sailed across the strait separating Africa from Europe, Tarik challenged his men with these words: "The sea is behind you, the enemy is before you: by Allah, there is no escape for you save valor and determination."[10] Tarik landed near the great rock hill that has since borne his name—*Gebel Tarik* ("the hill of Tarik"), or Gibraltar. He defeated a much larger Visigothic army and proceeded to march through Spain.

By 721, the Moslems had won control of most of Spain. Spain yielded easily to the Moslems. The reasons were not hard to find. The harsh rule of the Visigoth rulers, who had conquered Spain in the 5th century, caused some people to look upon the Moslems as liberators. Also, the Goths had tried forcibly to convert the Jews of Spain to Christianity. As a result, the Jews along with many others welcomed the Moslem invaders.

In 732, the Moslem army crossed the Pyrenees Mountains and threatened the kingdom of the Franks. The Moslem advance was stopped, however, by a Frankish army under Charles Martel (see Chapter 15). The year 732 was the centennial of Mohammed's death. By that date, Islam had won a large empire not only in the West but also in the East.

Under the early Omayyads, an Islamic army crossed the Oxus River, the traditional border between the Persians and the Turks, and made Islam the dominant power in Central Asia. In 712, another army reached the Indus River and converted much of northwestern India—the region known today as Pakistan—to Islam.

In 673, a Moslem army had marched through Asia Minor to the eastern shore of the Bosporus, where it threatened Constantinople, the capital of the Byzantine Empire. As you have read, the Moslems continued to attack the city for six years until they were finally forced to retreat by the Byzantines. In 716, the Moslems again reached the Bosporus and prepared to attack Constantinople. The Byzantine emperor Leo III (Chapter 13) ordered the forging of a huge iron-link chain to place across the mouth of the Golden Horn, the harbor of Constantinople. The chain was meant to keep Moslem ships from entering this vital body of water. The plan worked, and the city remained in Christian hands.

## THE ABBASID CALIPHATE

Under the Omayyad rulers, the Arabs received preferential treatment. Non-Arab Moslems were discontent with the policies that required them to pay heavy taxes while the Arabs paid none. Among the dissident groups were Persians, Egyptians, and Syrians, whose cultures were far more advanced than that of the Arabs.

The discontents were attracted to the Shiite sect that had opposed the Omayyads from the outset. They found a leader in Abu'l Abbas, who was not a Shiite but still claimed to be descended from the family of Mohammed. In 750, the rebels, led by Abbas, overthrew the Omayyad caliph and murdered 90 members of his family. Only one member escaped. He fled to Spain, where his descendants established the Omayyad caliphate at Cordoba.

Abbas established the Abbasid caliphate (750-1057). In 762, the Abbasids moved their capital from Damascus to Baghdad, a great new city on the west bank of the Tigris River. The Abbasids ruled with absolute power and established a centralized bureaucracy similar to that of the Byzantine Empire. The caliph was assisted in his work by his vizier, who often exercised as much power as the caliph.

Under the Abbasids, Moslems paid no head tax but did pay a small tax to support Islam. Non-Moslems, however, paid many heavy taxes that were used to support the empire. During the Abbasid caliphate, scholars from the Middle East—and from India—made

[10]Quoted in *Early Islam* by Desmond Stewart et al. (New York: Time, Inc. 1967), p. 62.

*Harun was a contemporary of Charlemagne, the ruler of much of western Europe (see Chapter 15). These two great leaders corresponded with each other in an effort to create an alliance: Harun wanted Charlemagne to help him against the Omayyads, who controlled Spain, and Charlemagne needed Harun's help against the Byzantines.*

Baghdad one of the world's great centers of learning. The reigns of Harun al-Rashid (786-809) and his successor, al-Mamum (813-833), marked the golden age of the Abbasids because of the great advances made in mathematics, science, literature, and the arts.

In spite of the cultural achievements made under the Abbasids, the Islamic Empire entered into a political decline after the reign of al-Mamum. In the 9th and 10th centuries, its territory was fragmented. Separate Moslem kingdoms were established in North Africa, Arabia, and India. In Spain, a descendant of the last Omayyad assumed the title of caliph in 929, thus setting himself up as a rival to the Abbasid caliph in Baghdad. In Egypt, Shiite leaders created the Fatimid caliphate, named after Mohammed's daughter, Fatima. In 969, they established their new capital at *al Qahirai*, which we know today as Cairo. There, they built a university that rivaled Baghdad as a center of Islamic learning.

In the 11th century, the Seljuk Turks from Central Asia invaded the Middle East. They captured Baghdad in 1055 and turned the Abbasid caliphs into puppet rulers. The Seljuks then pushed into Syria and Egypt, where they overthrew the Fatimid caliphate in 1171. As you will read in Chapter 16, it was the conquest of Palestine by the Seljuk Turks that sparked the Crusades, in which the Christian knights of Europe invaded the Holy Land.

The 13th century saw the Mongols sweep out of Central Asia into the Middle East. The Mongols captured and destroyed Baghdad in 1258, killing the last Abbasid ruler.

Later, other rulers assumed the title of caliph, but they were no longer seen as the true successors of Mohammed. Despite the disintegration of the Abbasid empire, Islam remained a unifying force. The brilliant achievements of Moslem culture and loyalty to Islam served to bind peoples from all corners of the Moslem world.

## ISLAMIC CIVILIZATION

From the 8th to the 12th centuries, the Moslem world was a thriving center of scholarship and scientific learning. Islamic civilization reached its zenith under the early Abbasid rulers. During this period, many non-Arabic peoples were merged into the empire, and Islamic civilization synthesized the best elements of all these cultures.

### COMMERCE AND INDUSTRY

The achievements of Islamic civilization were due in part to the prosperous economic conditions that existed throughout much of the empire. Geographically, the Moslems commanded the trade routes of three continents—Asia, Africa, and Europe. Goods from China, India, Russia, Spain, and all parts of Africa passed through the markets of the Middle East. Greek, Jewish, and Armenian traders were allowed access to these markets, from which they carried the luxury goods of the East into western Europe.

In the great cities of Baghdad, Cairo, and Cordoba, industry and commerce thrived. Unlike the towns of western Europe which at this time were small and parochial, the cities of the Moslem world were bustling, cosmopolitan centers, where merchants and artisans enjoyed the benefits of a money economy. The wealth and splendor of Baghdad gave rise to legends such as the stories in the *Arabian Nights*, which you will read about shortly.

The textile industry was especially profitable as traders carried muslins, silks, and cottons across the empire. Crafts such as ironworking and ceramics were also economically vital. Along with commerce and industry, agriculture supported the empire. The fertile soils of Mesopotamia—the ancient Fertile Crescent—as well as the Nile Valley were carefully irrigated and farmed to produce a variety of crops, including wheat, cotton, and citrus fruits.

The movement of people and goods across the Islamic world brought together learning and knowledge from many cultures. The economic prosperity supported an intellectual class with the wealth and leisure to pursue this knowledge. In Baghdad, the caliph al-Mamum established a *House of Wisdom*, or center of learning, in which Greek and Persian works as well as Sanskrit writings from India were translated into Arabic. Under the supervision of Hunayn ibn Ishaq (809-873), a group of 90 scholars worked on these translations. Mamum is reported to have paid Hunayn and his assistants an amount in gold equal in weight to the manuscripts they translated. At first, Moslem scholars used the translations to produce commentaries and encyclopedias, but by the 10th century, they were expanding upon the wisdom of the ancient world to produce new works in the fields of medicine, mathematics, astronomy, and other sciences.

### MEDICINE

Moslem scholars made outstanding advances in the study of anatomy, human illnesses, and other aspects of medicine. Two influential practitioners in this field were the Persian scientists al-Razi (c. 860-925) and ibn Sina (980-1037), better known to the Western world as Rhazes and Avicenna, respectively. Rhazes wrote more than 200 works on many subjects and compiled a huge encyclopedia of medicine that included both his own opinions on a variety of diseases, and Greek, Syrian, Persian, and Indian knowledge on each subject. Translations of Rhazes' mon-

This illustration from an Arabic text shows a pharmacist mixing a medicine. The Arabs learned much of their medicine from the ancient Greeks and also conducted their own experiments.

umental work later reached western Europe, where they influenced medical practice for many centuries.

Rhazes also published a treatise on smallpox and measles, describing their symptoms in careful detail:

● ● ● *The eruption of Small-Pox is preceded by a continued fever, pain in the back, itching of the nose, and terrors in sleep . . . pain and heaviness of the head; inquietude, distress of mind, nausea, and anxiety; (with this difference, that the inquietude, nausea, and anxiety are more frequent in the Measles than in the Small-Pox; while, on the other hand, the pain in the back is more peculiar to the Small-Pox than to the Measles).*[11]

[11]Philip Hitti, *Islam and the West* (New York: Robert E. Krieger Publishing Co., 1979), pp. 118-119.

Rhazes is believed by some to have been the first physician to suture wounds with thread made from animal gut and the first to immobilize fractured limbs using plaster casts. Like many Moslem scholars, Rhazes wrote on a variety of subjects, including mathematics, astronomy, and physics. When he was asked to select a site for a hospital to be built in Baghdad, he hung pieces of raw meat in various places throughout the city and examined the condition of each at regular intervals. He recommended that the hospital be built in the neighborhood in which the meat sample putrified most slowly.

Avicenna, too, was a man of many talents: philosopher, poet, astronomer, and physician, and like Rhazes, he compiled a medical encyclopedia, *Canon of Medicine*. It included descriptions of lockjaw and pleurisy, recommendations for proper diet, and "tender, loving care" in the treatment of disease. He correctly diagnosed tuberculosis as a contagious disease and decided that contaminated soil and water caused a number of illnesses. Avicenna wrote that cancer could be cured if diagnosed early and if the diseased tissue could be completely removed by surgery. He discussed various psychological illnesses, including "love sickness."

Physicians and pharmacists were regulated by the government. Before a physician could practice surgery, he had to pass an examination on his knowledge of anatomy and of the writings of the ancient Greek physician Galen. The dispensing of pharmaceuticals was closely supervised, and there were severe penalties for drug abuse.

Moslem physicians were very skilled surgeons despite the ban—for religious reasons—on dissecting cadavers to learn about human anatomy. Surgeons performed complex cranial and vascular surgery, amputated damaged or diseased limbs, removed soft cataracts from eyes, and inserted drainage tubes into the body to promote recovery from abdominal incisions.

Caliph Harun al-Rashid established the first hospital in Baghdad not only for the care of the ill, but also for the training of physicians. Later, other hospitals were built throughout the Islamic Empire. Each had separate wards for men and women as well as sections for the treatment of eye disease, fractured bones, and mental illness. Outpatient clinics were operated for the treatment of minor injuries. Each hospital had a pharmacy, and medications were prepared from plants, animals, or chemicals. For example, camphor was used in liniments, and copper sulphate was used to speed the healing of wounds.

### MATHEMATICS

Moslem scholars also made important advances in mathematics. As in medicine, they synthesized the learning of the ancient Greeks and Persians and carried it many steps further. Most important, they learned from the Hindus of India to use the nine symbols, or numbers, that we call "Arabic numerals" but which in fact originated in India.

While many mathematical principles were known to the ancient Egyptians, Babylonians, and Greeks, the number systems that they used were not convenient for calculations. The Babylonians devised a very useful system based on the number 60 which is still used in the measurement of time and angles. The Romans used a system (*Roman numerals*) that was convenient for counting, but awkward for calculations. Hindu mathematicians in India devised a system based on the number 10 (*decimal*), which included the concept of zero. By adopting this system of calculation, they made possible advances into higher mathematics.

The mathematician al Khwarizmi (died about 850) wrote the first Arabic treatise on mathematics in which he used the word *al-Jabr*, meaning "bringing together separate parts," from which our word *algebra* is derived. Al Khwarizmi's treatise was later translated into Latin and became the standard textbook in mathematics in European universities until the 16th century.

Another mathematician, Omar Khayyam (d. 1123), is better known today as a poet. However, he devised an accurate calendar and made advances in algebra that led to the development of *analytic geometry*, the branch of mathematics that unites algebra and geometry and underlies calculus.

The Greek mathematicians, especially Euclid and Pythagoras, provided Moslem scholars with the foundations on which to build, but the Greeks had been primarily interested in the philosophy of mathematics. By contrast, the Moslems used mathematics to solve many practical problems and to make important astronomical observations.

### ASTRONOMY AND GEOGRAPHY

As with the ancient religions of the Middle East, the requirements of religious observa-

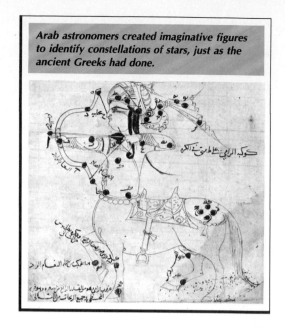

*Arab astronomers created imaginative figures to identify constellations of stars, just as the ancient Greeks had done.*

*The astrolabe, an intrument invented by the ancient Greeks, enabled Arab astronomers to chart the positions of heavenly bodies.*

tions in Islam stimulated the study of astronomy. The five calls to daily prayer required precise knowledge of the time of sunrise, noon, and sunset on each day and in each region of the Islamic world. The need to face toward Mecca while praying required knowledge of astronomical orientation. Prediction of the date of the new moon that marked the beginning of the holy month of Ramadan required knowledge of celestial movements.

In 771, a visitor from India brought a copy of a Hindu treatise on astronomy, *Siddhanta*, to Baghdad. After this work was translated into Arabic, Moslem astronomers used it as the basis for further studies. Harun al-Rashid also ordered that the astronomical works of Ptolemy be translated into Arabic. The Greek astrolabe was adopted to measure the angle of a heavenly body above the horizon. Ptolemy's calculations of the circumference of the earth were then checked and improved to within about one-half mile of the presently accepted value.

Improvements in astronomy allowed Moslem geographers to draw more accurate maps. In addition, the far-reaching scope of Moslem trading ventures gave them an extensive, firsthand knowledge of many regions of the world. Moslem geographers studied climates and developed tables of latitude and longitude. The outstanding Moslem geographer al-Idrisi (1099-1154) was born in Spain but worked in Palermo under the patronage of the Christian king of Sicily. In a landmark volume, he summarized the information submitted to him by assistants whom he had sent to explore the limits of the known world. Al-Idrisi was the first to create maps on spheres representing the shape of the earth. He engraved one such map on silver and presented it to his patron.

## PHYSICS AND CHEMISTRY

Arab investigators made significant contributions to the world's knowledge of physics and chemistry. Al Hasan (965-1039), known to the Western world as Alhazen, is sometimes referred to as "the father of optics" because of his studies on light and vision. Alhazen wrote about the principles of convex and concave mirrors and the refraction of light. Most people of his day believed—like the ancient Greeks—that they could see an object because their eyes sent rays out to an object within their vision, but Alhazen proved that light traveling from an object affected the eye. Alhazen's successor, Kalam ad-Din al-Farisi, was able to explain the optical principles involved in seeing a rainbow.

Moslem scientists made progress in other areas. Like people in many parts of the world, they were interested in finding the *philosophers' stone*, a material that they believed would change common metals, such as iron, tin, or copper, into precious metals such as gold or silver. This notion came to be called *alchemy*, an Arabic word. An outstanding Moslem alchemist was Jabir (b. 721). Like Aristotle, he speculated that all objects were created from combinations of air, fire, earth, and water. However, Jabir experimented with these and other materials. He explored the processes now known as oxidation, crystallization, and filtration, and carefully recorded the steps he took, the equipment he used, and the results he obtained, thereby laying the foundation for the science of chemistry.

One of Jabir's students was the physician Rhazes, who wrote a book on alchemy titled *The Book of the Secret of Secrets*. This book classified all matter as animal, vegetable, or mineral and gave detailed descriptions of the preparation of the known pharmaceuticals of the day. Rhazes also described beakers, vials, distillation dishes, and other laboratory equipment that was used by alchemists and would be essential to the science of chemistry.

## LITERATURE AND HISTORY

Poetry had played a role in pre-Islamic times, and its importance continued to be felt despite Mohammed's disapproval of the pagan poems of the Bedouins. In this early Arabic literature, poets praised their leaders, described the awesome beauties of nature, or extolled their life in the desert. Love was a favorite subject of Moslem poets, and this love poetry came to influence the troubadours of western Europe (Chapter 18).

The best known Moslem poet was the Persian mathematician Omar Khayyam. He wrote in the popular style of quatrains—four-line stanzas, called *rubaiyat* in Arabic. The *Rubaiyat* of Omar Khayyam contains elegant and haunting images, such as the one in this well-known stanza:

*The Moving Finger writes; and having writ,*
*Moves on: nor all thy Piety nor Wit*
*Shall lure it back to cancel half a Line,*
*Nor all thy Tears wash out a Word of it.*[12]

To Moslems, the most important prose work is the Koran, which they consider the

---

[12]Omar Khayyam, "Rubaiyat" (trans. Edward Fitzgerald), Stanza 71.

sacred word of God. Its language is rich in imagery, and certain passages seem as rhythmical as poetry.

To Westerners, the best known prose work is the *Arabian Nights* (also known as *One Thousand and One Nights*). It is a collection of love stories, tales of travel, and fables that came originally from many sources—Persian, Indian, Jewish, Greek, and Egyptian. In the *Arabian Nights* itself, the stories are told by a clever young woman named Scheherazade to outwit the Sultan Schahriar. After several years of blissful marriage, the sultan discovered that his favorite wife was unfaithful to him so he had her executed. As the story continues,

• • • *The blow was so heavy that his mind almost gave way, and he declared that he was quite sure that all women were as wicked as the sultana, if you could only find them out. So every evening he married a fresh wife and had her strangled the next morning before the grand vizir, whose duty it was to provide these unhappy brides for the sultan. . . .*

*The grand vizir himself was the father of two daughters, of whom the elder was called Scheherazade . . . (who told her father) . . . "I am determined to stop this barbarous practice of the sultan's and to deliver the girls and mothers from the truly awful fate that hangs over them."*[13]

Scheherazade marries the sultan but spends her first night with him telling a story that she refuses to finish until the next night. Left in suspense as to the outcome of the story, the sultan did not have her killed. The following night Scheherazade resumes the story but leaves off in the middle of a new one. After 1001 nights, the sultan decides to keep her as his favorite wife.

History was another area of Moslem scholarship. Among the great historians was ibn Khaldun, who compiled a seven-volume

*Universal History.* In it, he wrote not only about history and politics but also about economics, climate, crafts, and other aspects of life in different parts of the world. He developed a comprehensive philosophy of history and made scientific observations of people living in groups, concluding that:

• • • *This science then, like all other sciences, whether based on authority or on reasoning, appears to be independent and has its own subject, viz. human society, and its own problems, viz. the social phenomena and the transformations that succeed each other in the nature of society.*[14]

Ibn Khaldun believed that the power of a state was determined by the depth of loyalty of its citizens, and he characterized an ideal ruler as follows:

• • • *Know then, that the use of the ruler to his subjects lies not in his person, his fine figure or features, his wide knowledge, his excellent penmanship or the sharpness of his intellect, but solely in his relationship to them.*[15]

### ART AND ARCHITECTURE

Islamic architecture and art represented a blend of many traditions—Byzantine, Persian, and even Chinese. However, the overriding influence in this field was the Islamic prohibition against the representation of natural objects or people in a place of worship. As you have read, Mohammed destroyed the idols in the Kaaba and forbade the worship of any but the one God. To him, representations of the human form or natural objects were the equivalent of idols. As a result of this strict prohibition, Moslem artists developed stylized geometric designs to decorate

[13]*Arabian Nights*, collected and edited by Andrew Lang (New York: David McKay Co., 1960), pp. 2-3.

[14]*An Arab Philosophy of History: Selections from the Prolegomena of Ibn Khaldun of Tunis (1332-1406)*, trans. Charles Issawi (London: John Murray, 1950), p. 36.

[15]*An Arab Philosophy of History*, trans. Charles Issawi, pp. 128-129.

mosques. They also enhanced the art of *calligraphy*, or beautiful handwriting, by inscribing the sacred teachings of the Koran in graceful and elegant Arabic script.

In the design of Moslem cities, the mosque was the dominant structure. All mosques have certain features in common: an open courtyard with a large fountain, a covered area with a special niche, and minarets. From the Byzantines, the Moslems learned to use the dome, arch, and columns that feature so prominently in mosques. From the Persians, they adapted many of their decorative patterns. The prohibition against idols came from the Jews, whose scriptures were full of stories of God's anger when people disobeyed this command.

The oldest Islamic building outside of Arabia is the *Dome of the Rock* mosque in Jerusalem. This octagonal structure, with its high domed roof covered in gold leaf, was completed in 691 and still dominates the skyline of Jerusalem. It was built on Mount Moriah, the site of Solomon's Temple: according to Moslem tradition, it was on Mount Moriah that Mohammed had experienced his "Night of Power."

*According to Jewish tradition, Mount Moriah was the place where Abraham had prepared to sacrifice his only son, Isaac, to God (Genesis 22:1:19), and it was also the site of the ancient Temple of Solomon. Christians, too, looked to Jerusalem for inspiration because it was the site of so many events in the life of Jesus. Some scholars have suggested that Omar selected this site either to demonstrate the superiority of Islam over Christianity and Judaism, or to encourage Moslem pilgrims to visit Jerusalem as well as Mecca.*

*One of the great monuments of the Omayyad dynasty is the Dome of the Rock mosque in Jerusalem. Its octagonal plan was adapted from the design of Byzantine churches.*

Another well known example of Islamic architecture is the great Omayyad Mosque in Damascus, built on a site originally occupied by a temple to Jupiter and later by a Christian church. The Moslems razed all elements of these earlier structures except the exterior walls and the Roman watchtowers, which were converted into minarets.

Caliphs often built fortified palaces that were used as administrative centers in remote regions. These palaces with their many rooms and lavish decorations displayed to all the wealth and power of the caliph. Early in the 20th century, archaeologists working in Palestine found the remains of a great palace at Khirbet al Mafjar (Arabic for "place where the water flows"). It had been built by the Omayyad caliph Hisham (724-743) in the valley of the Jordan River east of Jericho. The huge palace was destroyed by an earthquake in 748 and was never rebuilt.

Two more lasting examples of Islamic architecture are the Alhambra Palace in Spain and the Taj Mahal in India. The former is a tribute to grace and beauty. The slender columns, multi-colored, horseshoe arches, and beautiful ceilings are all decorated with intricate calligraphy and fine *arabesque* designs showing acanthus vines interwoven in

The Alhambra palace in Granada was the headquarters of the caliphate in Spain. It was completed in 1391.

The Taj Mahal, built in 1648, was influenced by Persian, Byzantine, and Moslem architectural traditions. The impression of weightlessness that it conveys was achieved, in part, through the use of arches, a reflecting pool, and graceful minarets.

intricate patterns. The Taj Mahal was built by the shah Jahan as a monument to his beloved wife who died while she was still very young. Its design and decorations strongly reflect Persian influences as well as Byzantine and Arabic traditions.

Between 1000 and 1500, Moslem artists excelled in many areas: the making of pottery, glass, ceramic tiles, mosaics, and textiles, including carpets. Potters developed the technique of making lusterware, in which ordinary fired clay was glazed with various metallic oxides to produce metal-like finishes. Glassmakers revived the old Roman art of embedding threads of various colored glass into molten glass to produce intricate designs. Glasscutters produced beautiful bas-relief designs on the surfaces of glass objects. Metalworkers made objects of bronze or brass that were inlaid with designs of gold and silver. Lush fabrics of damask, muslin, and satin and richly-colored "oriental" rugs later became popular among the wealthy people of western Europe.

Despite the limitations on the representation of human forms and natural objects, Moslem painters created magnificent miniatures, or tiny, stylized pictures, which they used to decorate secular manuscripts. Moslem artists also used gold, silver, and other brilliant colors to *illuminate* manuscripts in a highly decorative style.

*ISLAMIC SPAIN*   Aside from Baghdad, one of the greatest centers of Islamic civilization was found in Cordoba, Spain. As you have read, Moslem armies invaded Spain in the 7th and 8th centuries, and they laid the foundations for a civilization that flourished for more than 700 years. In 756, the only surviving member of the Omayyad family, Abd-al-Rahman, reached Spain, where his descendants established an independent caliphate at Cordoba.

Rahman wanted to ensure the survival and economic advancement of his family. He succeeded in winning control of the land and then devoted his attention to peaceful pursuits. He introduced the cultivation of silkworms and the manufacture of paper to Spain. He encouraged the production of fine leather goods and the fashioning of objects made of steel inlaid with gold and silver. He repaired long-neglected Roman walls and aqueducts and developed water power to drive mills. He encouraged the introduction of many edible plants from the Middle East, including citrus fruits, bananas, peaches, rice, sugar cane, almonds, and figs.

From the 9th through the 13th centuries, Cordoba flourished. It was a beautiful city adorned with luxurious palaces, impressive mosques, and attractive gardens and fountains. By the 10th century, it could boast of paved and lighted streets—conditions that were unknown in other parts of western Europe until 700 years later. During these centuries, Cordoba was famous as a center of learning on a par with Constantinople and Baghdad. Among the outstanding scholars of Cordoba was the philosopher, astronomer, and physician, ibn-Rushd (1126-1198), known in western Europe as Averroes. He studied the works of Aristotle and insisted on submitting all truths to the light of reason. Through the use of Aristotelian logic, Averroes sought to reconcile faith and reason. When his writings were introduced into western Europe, they had tremendous impact on Christian scholars.

A contemporary of Averroes, who was also born in Cordoba, was the brilliant Jewish philosopher and physician, Maimonides (1135-1204). Maimonides' family later settled in Cairo, but the work of this great scholar influenced Jewish, Moslem, and Christian thought. Maimonides tried to reconcile religion and science and championed the cause of scientific thought.

The writings of these and other scholars of the Moslem world slowly made their way from Spain across the Pyrenees into western Europe. In English, there are many words that provide evidence of the influence of Ar-

The great mosque at Cordoba, Spain was constructed by the Omayyads and enlarged over a period of several centuries. The columns are oriented in the direction of Mecca.

abic learning. Musical instruments such as the *lute, tambourine,* and *guitar* all entered Europe from Moslem lands. Terms such as *zenith* or *nadir* in astronomy, *cipher* (zero) in mathematics, or *syrup* and *soda* in medicine all have Arabic origins. When Christian Europe finally recovered enough from centuries of invasions to pursue higher scholarship and learning, it found a vast storehouse of knowledge in the Moslem lands beyond its borders.

## SUMMARY

*In the 7th century, a new religion, Islam, burst out of Arabia and swept across much of the world. Inspired by the Koran and the prophet Mohammed, Moslem armies won stunning victories. By the 8th century, Islam was the dominant religion of an area reaching from Spain to India. The primary article of the faith was belief in the one God, Allah. This belief along with the five basic duties of all Moslems helped bind together people from many different cultures.*

*Caliphs ruled over the Islamic Empire and presided over a brilliant civilization that reached its height during the 9th to 11th centuries. Baghdad and Cordoba were the two greatest centers of Moslem learning and culture. In these and other cities, Moslem scholars made important advances in many fields. Like the Byzantines, they helped to preserve the learning of the ancient world and passed it on to the peoples of western Europe.*

## QUESTIONS

1 How did the traditions and beliefs of pre-Islamic Arabs shape Mohammed's ideas?
2 Make a chart comparing the basic teachings and church organization of Judaism, Christianity, and Islam.
3 Why did Islam spread so rapidly after the death of Mohammed? Do you think the Arabs could have achieved these victories if Mohammed had never lived? What conclusions can you draw about the role of great individuals in history?
4 Explain the divisions that developed within Islam after Mohammed's death. Find out how the split between Shiites and Sunnites affects nations in the Middle East today.
5 Why did Islamic civilization flourish from the 8th to 12th centuries? How did Islamic civilization help to shape developments in western Europe?

## BIBLIOGRAPHY

*Which books might compare Judaism, Christianity, and Islam?*

GLUBB, SIR JOHN BAGOT. *The Life and Times of Muhammed.* New York: Stein and Day, 1970. *A classic biography of the founder of the Moslem religion written by an eminent scholar who spent half his life among Moslems. It presents a balanced view of the Prophet's life and teachings and recreates the Arab world in the 7th century.*

LEWIS, BERNARD, ed. *Islam and the Arab World.* New York: Alfred A. Knopf and Co., 1976. *A collection of essays by 13 scholars on subjects ranging from the origins, history, and meaning of Islam, to the achievements of Moslem artists and architects. It explores the splendor of Islamic art; the originality and influence of its science and philosophy; and the range of its political and cultural history. Excellent illustrations.*

LIPPMAN, THOMAS W. *Understanding Islam: An Introduction to the Moslem World.* New York: New American Library, 1982. *A brief account of the founding and growth of Islam, Moslem beliefs, law and government, and the different groups within Islam today. It provides a framework for understanding conflicts within the Islamic world today.*

SEVERY, MERLE. *Great Religions of the World.* Washington, D.C.: National Geographic Society, 1971. *A comparative study of the five major world religions: Hinduism, Buddhism, Judaism, Christianity, and Islam; with fine illustrations and an emphasis on the historical background and rituals of each.*

# JAPAN

*500–1500 A.D.*

Unlike the civilizations of Egypt, Mesopotamia, India, and China, early Japanese civilization is not associated with a river valley. Instead, the ocean played a dominant role in shaping Japanese civilization. The sea that separates the Japanese *archipelago*, or chain of islands, from the northeast coast of Asia has served many purposes. Besides providing an abundant source of food, it has protected Japan from invaders and enabled the Japanese to develop their own distinct culture. Prior to 1945, Japan was never subjected to military conquest and domination. Rather, as Japanese culture emerged, it blended local traditions and values with those it consciously borrowed and adapted from its powerful neighbor, China.

## EARLY HISTORY AND RELIGION

The Japanese trace their earliest history back to a legendary first emperor, Jimmu Tenno, who is said to have ruled in the 7th century B.C. Later Japanese emperors traced their ancestry back to this first emperor. Unlike the nations of Europe, where warring nobles fought to establish their claims to the throne, the Japanese have maintained a single ruling dynasty in an unbroken line to Emperor Hirohito, the 124th ruler in the imperial line.

Also, unlike China, where the emperors were believed to enjoy the Mandate of Heaven as long as the kingdom was ruled with relative peace and justice, the Japanese believed that their emperor had divine origins and was descended from the sun goddess Amartersu.

During this early period, Japanese religious beliefs took shape into a religion that was later called *Shinto*, or the way of the gods. The original Shinto religion glorified nature and focused on the appreciation and awe of nature as a creative, destructive, and renewing force. The Japanese worshiped *kami*, the spirits or elements of nature. For the most part, they looked on these kami as benign.

Shinto was a religion based on ceremony, ritual, and custom, and not on a code of ethics or a concept of sin. Early Shinto beliefs did not contain any ideas about good or evil; instead, its rituals were associated with purification and cleanliness. Furthermore, the worship was individual and not congregational. The worshiper stood outside the shrine to offer prayer and make petition to the kami.

In the early Japanese society, people were organized into *clans*, groups of families who claim descent from a common ancestor. Clans

One of the oldest holy places of the Shinto religion is the Itsukushima shrine. The gateway shown in the background separates the outside world from the sacred precinct.

age in which China enjoyed great prosperity and a high level of cultural achievement. The extraordinary vitality of this period in Chinese history served as an inspiration for the Yamato rulers in Japan as they set about organizing their own government and military system.

*Introduction of Buddhism.* In the mid-6th century, Buddhism reached Japan by way of China and Korea. Around 552, the Yamato emperor eagerly questioned Chinese Buddhist missionaries and learned from them about the achievements of Chinese civilization. Buddhist missionaries of this era have sometimes been compared to the early Christian missionaries: the former transmitted the traditions and cultural heritage of China to Japan and other parts of Asia, just as the latter helped spread the achievements of Greco-Roman civilization to the peoples of western Europe.

At the time of its introduction into Japan, Buddhism was not a monolithic religion. Although the essence of Buddhism was the Four Noble Truths and the Noble Eightfold

in different regions had their own clan and regional gods as well as their own rituals. Also each clan chief had religious as well as secular duties. In the 5th century A.D., the Yamato clan began to extend its control over the large island of Honshu, and eventually it conquered the other Japanese islands. By claiming descent from the first emperor, the chief of the yamato clan won support for his rule, and the present-day emperor of Japan is descended from this clan.

### INFLUENCE OF CHINA

The Yamato clan consolidated its power in Japan at the time of the Sui and T'ang dynasties in China. The Sui dynasty (589–618) was the first ruling house to reunite China after the collapse of the Han empire in 220. During the chaotic centuries between the end of the Han dynasty and the rise of the Sui, Buddhism took root in China. In reunifying China, the Sui and their successors, the T'ang emperors (618–907), revived the glory of the Han period, particularly in the arts and philosophy, and ushered in a golden

The Great Buddha at Kamakura, built in 1252, is Japan's second largest image of the Buddha. Buddhism was introduced into Japan in the mid-6th century.

## JAPAN
*What role did geography play in the development of Japan?*

By the time Buddhism reached Japan, it had absorbed many Confucian ideas, including the emphasis on filial piety. These ideas came to have great influence on Japanese society. The introduction of Buddhism opened the door for further cultural borrowing from China. Early on, the Japanese adapted the Chinese form of writing to their own language, a step that made the Japanese interested in having many classical Chinese texts translated into their own language.

**The Taika Reforms.** Early in the 7th century, Prince Shotoku, a member of the Yamato family, encouraged carefully selected young men to visit China and bring back the best of its offerings. He inaugurated a period of massive cultural borrowing not only in government and military organization but also in philosophy, history, the arts, and literature. In so doing, the Yamato rulers hoped to recreate and surpass the culture of China. They created schools and universities in Japan and encouraged Chinese scholars to settle in Japan. They modeled their court on Chinese lines, dressed in Chinese fashions, and built their new capital at Nara using Chinese styles of art and architecture. In fact, Nara was modeled on the splendid T'ang capital of Changan. It included the Great Buddha Hall, the largest wooden building in the world.

Not everything that the Japanese tried to introduce suited their own traditions, however. For example, they tried to set up a civil service system similar to that in China. But the Japanese were accustomed to the idea of hereditary positions and could not accept the notion of selecting officials based on merit.

Taken together, the changes introduced from China became known as the *Taika Reforms*. The purpose of the reform was to strengthen the power of the central government of Japan by reducing the influence of the various clan leaders. Because of opposition to the civil service system and because of the need to give the nobles vast grants of land to gain their support, the reform movement failed in its primary purpose. It did produce a vital period of cultural activity, however, in which Chinese ideas were incorporated into Japanese traditions.

Path, it had a variety of sects. Belief in the ideas or rituals of one sect, however, did not preclude worshipers from sharing in the beliefs or rituals of another sect. As a result, in India, Hinduism and Buddhism coexisted and eventually merged; in China, Confucianism and related philosophies were adapted to Buddhist beliefs; and in Japan, Shintoism and Buddhism coexisted and blended. The blend suited the emperor, who continued to be seen as a divine being and the chief priest of Shinto, while at the same time adapting many Buddhist beliefs. The style of Buddhism that was introduced to Japan was Mahayana Buddhism. Zen Buddhism did not develop until a later time, and in fact, Zen is based on a blend of Buddhist and Taoist ideas.

**The Heian period.** In 794, the capital again moved to Heian, present-day Kyoto, and the period from 794 to 1185 became known as the Heian period. During this time, the T'ang dynasty declined in China, and contacts between China and Japan were infrequent. Although the Japanese court had adapted an elegant and refined pattern of life based on the Chinese model, it was burdened by endless power struggles. By the 9th century, the emperor was reduced to little more than a figurehead while the powerful Fujiwara family controlled the court and the government. Because of the emperor's semi-divine status, he continued to be treated with respect even though he had become a mere puppet in the hands of others.

## JAPAN'S FEUDAL PERIOD

While powerful families vied for power at court, a new force emerged in the rural areas to threaten the leadership of the Heian court. It was made up of tough warrior-knights, called *samurai*. Many of the samurai were young members of the imperial family or of the lower aristocracy who had not been given the high-ranking positions they felt they deserved. During the 10th century, they began to seize control of territories in the provinces, and developed standing armies to protect their lands. The constant warfare that marked their reigns desolated the provinces and seriously weakened the prestige of the emperor. By the late 12th century, a samurai leader named Minamoto Yoritomo had put

*This castle, built by the first Tokugawa shogun in 1603, symbolizes the samurai life of Japan's feudal period.*

*The tea ceremony, one of the most characteristic aspects of Japanese tradition, was introduced from China. The presentation of the tea is guided by well-defined rituals.*

together a strong enough army to seize power and take the title *shogun*, or military governor. Yoritomo founded the first of three military dynasties that ruled Japan for almost 700 years from 1185 to 1868.

During this long period, feudalism became a way of life in Japan much as it did in Europe during the Middle Ages. Japan's feudal period was marked by frequent warfare as strong lords fought for power. At the head of feudal society was the emperor, who performed important religious functions but otherwise had no political power. The absolute ruler of Japan was the shogun. Below him were the great local lords, called *daimyo*. Like the great feudal lords in western Europe, the daimyo divided their lands among their vassals, the samurai, who were linked to them by ties of loyalty. The daimyo thus controlled private armies made up of their samurai vassals, and they used these armies to challenge one another and the shogun. As in medieval Europe (Chapter 16), towns began to grow up around the castles of feudal lords. As travel became safer and the money economy grew, merchants and artisans gathered in the towns and contributed to their development. Guilds were formed to protect the interests of the artisans, often under the direct control of the daimyo. In time, the leading merchants and tradesmen of the towns threw off the control of the

daimyo and began to take responsibility for the government of their municipalities. When the Europeans made their first appearance in Japan during the 16th century, they found that the free cities of Japan were much like those that had evolved throughout Europe.

***Bushido.*** During the feudal period, the samurai developed a code of conduct called *bushido*, or the way of the warrior. Bushido was similar in some ways to the code of chivalry that developed in medieval Europe. Bushido glorified courage and honor and put obedience to one's lord above all else. A samurai who violated bushido was thought to have brought dishonor not only to himself but also to his family. Unlike the code of chivalry, however, which put noble women on a pedestal and encouraged respect for them, bushido required that the wives of samurai endure whatever hardships they faced meekly and without complaint.

***Patterns of culture.*** During the feudal period, Buddhism gained ground in Japan. Trade with China and Korea kept up a steady flow of new ideas that were adapted to Japanese needs. Although tea was introduced to Japan as early as the 8th century, it did not become widespread for several centuries. By the 15th century, however, tea drinking had become transformed into the graceful and elegant ceremony that was closely associated with Zen Buddhism and its respect for the simple beauty and peaceful ways of nature. Like many other Japanese traditions, the tea ceremony originated in China, but once established in Japan it evolved its own patterns. Like the tea ceremony, *ikebana*, or flower arrangement, was another import from China and reflected Zen influences with its stress on physical and mental discipline as well as a love of nature.

The feudal period saw other cultural developments such as the Noh plays that taught Zen concepts through a combination of poetry and dance. Haiku poetry, a 3-line poem of 5, 7, and 5 syllables respectively, also became popular. Many haiku are about the beauty or simple virtues of nature. In this art form as in many other aspects of Japanese culture, the ancient Shinto respect for nature was combined with Zen ideals to create works of extraordinary and subtle beauty.

At temples of the Zen sect of Buddhism, it is common to encounter scenes of quiet meditation.

## INTRODUCTION TO THE DOCUMENTS

Despite its relatively isolated location on the rim of Asia, Japan has been the heir to both physical and cultural migrations from the mainland.

Between the 6th and 9th centuries A.D., the Japanese eagerly sought out and adopted major elements of Chinese culture. For example, the Taika reforms of the 7th century and the development of Buddhist philosophies were inspired by Prince Shotoku's admiration for Chinese culture. This importation of Chinese culture did not replace Japanese traditions, however. Rather, the new ideas were tested against the old; those that fit were kept while those that did not were cast aside. In the end, the cultural borrowing enabled the Japanese to make their own distinct contributions, especially after they evolved their own system of writing in the 10th century.

In the documents that follow, you will see how the Japanese adapted and transformed what they had borrowed from China in these early centuries.

## DOCUMENT 1   *MAHAYANA BUDDHISM*

*This excerpt is from the* **Vimalakirti Sutra.** *(A sutra is a Buddhist dialogue or sermon.) It is an example of Mahayana Buddhism, also referred to as the "Greater Vehicle," one of the two principal divisions of Buddhism. In contrast to Hinayana Buddhism, or the "Lesser Vehicle," Mahayana Buddhists not only look on Buddha as a god but also believe that all living beings can attain Buddhahood. Implicit in this school of Buddhism is the messianic mission of helping others achieve salvation.*

At that time, there dwelt in the great city of Vaishali a wealthy householder named Vimalakirti. Having done homage to countless Buddhas of the past, doing many good works, attaining to acquiescence in the Eternal Law, he was a man of wonderful eloquence,

Exercising supernatural powers, obtaining all magic formulas, arriving at the state of fearlessness,

Repressing all evil enmities, reaching the gate of profound truth, walking in the way of wisdom. . . .

Residing in Vaishali only for the sake of the necessary means for saving creatures, abundantly rich, ever careful of the poor, pure in self-discipline, obedient to all precepts,

Removing all anger by the practice of patience, removing all sloth by the practice of diligence, removing all distraction of mind by intent meditation, removing all ignorance by fullness of wisdom;

Though he is but a simple layman, yet observing the pure monastic discipline;

Though living at home, yet never desirous of anything;

Though possessing a wife and children, always exercising pure virtues;

Though surrounded by his family, holding aloof from worldly pleasures;

Though using the jewel ornaments of the world, yet adorned with spiritual splendor;

Though eating and drinking, yet enjoying the flavor of the rapture of the meditation;

Though frequenting the gambling house, yet leading the gamblers into the right path;

Though coming into contact with heresy, yet never letting his true faith be impaired;

Though having a profound knowledge of worldly learning yet ever finding pleasure in things of the spirit as thought by Buddha. . . .

Teaching [nobles] patience when among them as the most honorable of their kind;

Removing arrogance when among [priests] as the most honorable of their kind;

Teaching justice to great ministers when among them as the most honorable of their kind;

Teaching loyalty and filial piety to the princes when among them as the most honorable of their kind;

Teaching honesty to the ladies of the court when among them as the most honorable of their kind;

Persuading the masses to cherish the virtue of merits when among them as the most honorable of their kind. . . .

—Thus by such countless means Vimalakirti, the wealthy householder, rendered benefit to all beings.

---

SOURCE: Tsunoda, Ryusaku, W. T. De Bary, and Donald Keene, eds., *Sources of Japanese Tradition*, Vol. 1, pp. 100–103.

**What ethical guidelines does this sutra establish for members of the court? How do these guidelines reflect both Buddhist and Confucian thought?**

## DOCUMENT 2    PRINCE SHOTOKU TEACHES CONFUCIANISM

*Setting an example for the court, Prince Shotoku learned to read and write Chinese and carefully studied Chinese literature, especially Confucian philosophy. Shotoku encouraged the Japanese to adopt Confucianism as the source of political and familial ethics as these excerpts from his writings indicate.*

I.   Harmony should be valued and quarrels should be avoided. Everyone has his biases, and few men are far sighted. Therefore some disobey their lords and fathers and keep up feuds with their neighbors. But when the superiors are in harmony with each other and inferiors are friendly, then affairs are discussed quietly and the right view of matters prevails. Then there is nothing that cannot be accomplished!

III.   Do not fail to obey the commands of your Sovereign. He is like Heaven, which is above the Earth, and the vassal is like the Earth, which bears up Heaven. When Heaven and Earth are properly in place, the four seasons follow their course and all is well in Nature. But if the Earth attempts to take the place of Heaven, Heaven would simply fall in ruin.

IV.   The Ministers and officials of the state should make proper behavior their first principle, for if the superiors do not behave properly, the inferiors are disorderly; if the inferiors behave improperly, offenses will naturally result. . . .

V.   Deal impartially with the legal complaints which are submitted to you. If the man who is to decide suits at law makes gain his motive, and hears cases with a view to receiving bribes, then the suits of the rich man will be like a stone flung into water, meeting no resistance, while the complaints of the poor will be like water thrown upon a stone. In these circumstances the poor man will not know where to go, nor will he behave as he should.

VI.   Punish the evil and reward the good. This was the excellent rule of antiquity. Therefore do not hide the good qualities of others or fail to correct what is wrong when you see it. . . .

XV.   To subordinate private interests to the public good—that is the path of a vassal. Now if a man is influenced by private motives, he will be resentful, and if he is influenced by resentment he will fail to act harmoniously with others. If he fails to act harmoniously with others, the public interest will suffer. Resentment interferes with order and is subversive to law. . . .

SOURCE: Hyman Kublan, *Japan: Selected Readings* (New York: Houghton Mifflin, 1968), pp. 30–34.

**What Confucian values did Prince Shotoku seek to introduce to Japan?**

## DOCUMENT 3  EMBASSY TO SHIRAGI

**The Manyoshu (One Thousand Poems)** *is one of the earliest anthologies of Japanese poetry. Written in 736, after the introduction of Chinese literature as well as Buddhism, these poems reflect Japanese culture during the 7th and 8th centuries. The poem below recalls the sorrow that a Japanese family feels when a loved one leaves on an embassy to China.*

Embassy to Shiragi

When I am parted from you, my dearest,
Who fold me as with wings,
As a water bird its chick on Muko Bay
On the sand-bar of the inlet—
O I shall die of yearning after you.

Could my great ship take you in,
I would keep you, beloved,
Folding you as with wings!

When mist rises on the seashore
Where you put in,
Consider it the breathing
Of my sighs at home.

When autumn comes we shall meet again;
Then how would you raise such sighs
That they would mist the shore!

Wear yourself not out
With yearning after me,
In the month when the autumn wind blows
We shall meet again.

For you, who journey to Shiragi,
I will, in purification, wait,
Longing to see your eyes again,
To-day or to-morrow.

Unaware that the ships must wait
For high tide,
I have parted, to my grief,
From my love so soon.

SOURCE: *The Manyoshu*, Translation of "One Thousand Poems" by The Nippon Gakujutsu Shinkokai (New York: Columbia University Press, 1965), pp. 242–243.

*Why might a young Japanese in the 8th century have chosen to go to China despite the loneliness of leaving family and friends?*

**61**

*About 1000, at the height of the Heian period, several great ladies at court
chronicled the events of the day. These women did not write in Chinese as the men
of the court did; instead, they used the symbols that the Japanese had adapted from
the Chinese to fit their own language. Among the best known works of this period
are* The Pillow Book *by Sei Shonagon and* The Tale of Genji *by Lady Murasaki. The
latter, which has been called the world's first novel, recounts in leisurely fashion the
adventures of Prince Genji, a son of the emperor. Through Murasaki's descriptions,
we gain insight into the ceremonies and rituals of court life.*

Though it seemed a shame to put so lovely a child into man's dress, he was now
twelve years old and the time for his Initiation was come. The emperor directed
the preparations with tireless zeal and insisted upon a magnificence beyond
what was prescribed. . . . The ceremony took place in the eastern wing of the
Emperor's own apartments, and the Throne was placed facing towards the east,
with the seats of the Initiate-to-be and his Sponsor (the Minister of the Left) in
front.

Genji arrived at the hour of the Monkey [3 P.M.]. He looked very handsome
with his long childish locks, and the Sponsor, whose duty it had just been to
bind them with the purple fillet, was sorry to think that all this would soon be
changed and even the Clerk of the Treasury seemed reluctant to sever those
lovely tresses with the ritual knife. The Emperor, as he watched, remembered for
a moment what pride the mother would have taken in the ceremony, but soon
drove the weak thought from his mind.

Duly crowned, Genji went to his chamber and changing into man's dress went
down into the courtyard and performed the Dance of Homage, which he did
with such grace that tears stood in every eye. And now the Emperor, whose grief
had of late grown somewhat less insistent, was again overwhelmed by memories
of the past.

It had been feared that his delicate features would show to less advantage
when he had put aside his childish dress; but on the contrary he looked hand-
somer than ever.

His sponsor, the Minister of the Left, had an only daughter whose beauty the
Heir Apparent had noticed. But now the father began to think he would not encourage that match, but would offer her to Genji. He sounded the Emperor upon
this, and found that he would be very glad to obtain for the boy the advantage of
so powerful a connection.

SOURCE: Lady Murasaki, *The Tale of Genji*, trans. Arthur Waley (New York: Modern Library, 1960),
pp. 18–20.

**How can a novel such as** The Tale of Genji **serve as a historical document? What are
its limitations as a document?**

## TIME LINE FOR JAPAN AND THE WEST

### JAPAN

**400**    Yamato clan begins to extend military control over Honshu, neighboring Japanese islands, and parts of Korea

**552**    Buddhism introduced into Japan

**604– 629**    Prince Shotoku establishes a constitutional monarchy; opens relations with Sui dynasty in China

**645**    Taika reforms instituted—power of central government strengthened; tax-collecting system improved

**794– 1185**    Heian period begins. Capital moved to Heian (Kyoto); contacts with China become infrequent; power of emperor declines

**1000**    World's first novel—Tale of Genji—written by Lady Murasaki

**1185– 1868**    Feudal period. Shogun dynasties rule Japan; emperor becomes merely a ceremonial figure

### THE WEST

**476**    Collapse of the Roman Empire in the West; Germanic invasions

**528– 565**    Justinian briefly reconquers western territories of Roman Empire

**622**    Beginning of expansion of Islam to North Africa and western Europe

**732**    Charles Martel stops Moslem advance at Tours

**800**    Charlemagne crowned Holy Roman emperor

**840**    Carolingian empire declines; feudalism emerges throughout western Europe as Viking, Magyar, and Moslem invasions begin

**1096– 1099**    First Crusade

**1385**    Canterbury Tales written by Geoffrey Chaucer

**1453**    Constantinople falls to Turks; end of Byzantine Empire

# Life in the Middle Ages

● *The universal Church cannot err, since she is governed by the Holy Ghost Who is the Spirit of truth.*
AQUINAS

● *It is impossible for the Christian and true church to subsist without the shedding of blood, for her adversary, the devil, is a liar and a murderer. The church grows and increases through blood; she is sprinkled with blood; she is spoiled and bereaved of her blood.*
LUTHER

● *In form, then, of a white rose displayed itself to me that sacred soldiery which in his blood Christ made his spouse....*
*They had their faces all of living flame, and wings of gold, and the rest so white that never snow reacheth such limit.*
*When they descended into the flower, from rank to rank they proffered of the peace and of the ardor which they acquired as they fanned their sides,*
*nor did the interposing of so great a flying multitude, betwixt the flower and that which was above, impede the vision nor the splendor;*
*for the divine light so penetrateth through the universe, in measure of its worthiness, that naught hath power to oppose it.*
DANTE

● Beneath this burial site has been placed the body of Charles, the Great and Orthodox Emperor who grandly expanded the Kingdom of the Franks, and ruled successfully for forty-seven years.

TOMBSTONE OF CHARLEMAGNE

# *Europe Under Pressure*

The 10 centuries that followed the fall of Rome were once called the Dark Ages because people thought that during those years the "light" of knowledge had been extinguished until it was relit in the Renaissance in the 15th century. Today, however, the idea of the "Dark Ages" has long been discredited. Instead, we refer to these centuries as the Middle Ages, or the medieval period, the age between ancient and modern civilizations.

During the early Middle Ages—the period from the late 4th century to the 10th century—Europe was buffeted by a succession of invasions. The first invaders were Germanic tribes, who were pushing into the western portion of the Roman Empire as they sought refuge from ferocious attacks by the Huns on their eastern settlements. Moving west and south across the old Roman boundary of the Rhine and Danube rivers, the Germanic tribes won control of provinces in western Europe, and, by 450, had established their own kingdoms.

The rulers of these Germanic kingdoms did not destroy what they found; rather, they built on Roman traditions and shaped them to their own ends. When Roman officials abandoned their posts to the invaders, priests, bishops, and monks often stayed with their parishes or monasteries and even assumed control of the local government. The Germanic leaders usually realized that they needed the skills and knowledge of the Christians whom they conquered. The Christians, on the other hand, had no choice but to accept and accommodate themselves to their conquerors.

Late in the 8th century, one of these Germanic rulers—Charlemagne—sought to reunite the fragments of the Roman Empire in the West. Although he briefly succeeded in creating a large empire, it crumbled soon after his death when Europe faced new onslaughts from Moslem, Viking, and Magyar invaders. Ironically, during this time of hardship for the peoples of western Europe, the Byzantine and Islamic empires (Chapters 13 and 14) enjoyed their golden ages.

**GERMANIC MIGRATIONS** The unity and order of the Roman Empire were broken by the influx of successive waves of Germanic tribes, who included the Vandals, Lombards, Alamanni, Goths, Burgundians, Franks, and others. As mentioned above, the Huns, Asiatic nomads from the steppes of Russia, had invaded the territories of these tribes, forcing them to migrate westward across the Danube–Rhine border into the empire.

In 376, the *Visigoths* (western Goths), fleeing the Huns, asked and received permission from the emperor Valens to cross the Danube and settle inside the empire. After they were admitted, they were exploited by local officials who charged them exorbitant prices for food and other supplies. When the newcomers protested, Valens ordered them to leave the empire. Instead of leaving, the Visigoths took up arms against the emperor, whom they defeated and killed at Adrianople in 378. Later, they moved westward to occupy more land. In 410, under the leadership of Alaric, they captured and sacked Rome. Jerome, one of the early Church Fathers (Chapter 12), was stunned by the Visigoth attack on Rome: "Who could believe that Rome, built on the conquest of the whole world, would fall to the ground? that the mother herself would become the tomb of her peoples?"[1]

At about the same time that the Visigoths were attacking Rome, the Vandals crossed the Rhine and moved through Gaul and Spain into North Africa, where they established a kingdom on the site that was once occupied by Carthage. From this base, the Vandals attacked Rome and other parts of the empire by sea. (So terrifying were their raids that to this day one who plunders and destroys is called a *vandal*.)

Meanwhile, the Asiatic Huns continued their push westward. By 450, they were invading northern Italy and Gaul under the leadership of Attila, whom the Romans called the "Scourge of God." The Germanic tribes who had previously settled in Gaul united with the remnants of the Roman army in the region and defeated the Huns at the battle of

*The octagonal church of San Vitale is is an enduring monument of Theodoric's rule at Ravenna. Theodoric planned the church during the last year of his life, and construction was completed by the Byzantines.*

Chalons in 451. The next year, Attila invaded Italy, but Pope Leo, later called "Leo the Great," managed to persuade him not to attack Rome. After Attila's death in 453, the threat of the Huns dwindled.

After the collapse of the Hun threat, the *Ostrogoths* (eastern Goths) moved into Italy, where their leader Odoacer overthrew the last of the Roman emperors in the West. Odoacer's successor was Theodoric, an Ostrogoth who had been educated in Constantinople and had great respect for Greco-Roman civilization. Theodoric established his capital at Ravenna, and during his long reign (489-526), he maintained an uneasy relationship with the Byzantine Empire in the East.

After the death of Theodoric, the Byzantine emperor Justinian sought to reunite the old Roman Empire, and brought most of Italy under his control. As you have read, however, Justinian's success was short-lived. Within a few years of his death, Italy was again invaded. This time, a Germanic tribe known as the Lombards entered Italy, setting up a kingdom in the north—in a region that still bears their name, Lombardy—and conquering other parts of central and southern Italy. The Byzantine Empire held onto Rav-

---

[1] J. H. Robinson, ed., *Readings in European History*, Vol. 1 (New York: Ginn, 1904), p. 45.

enna and some surrounding lands, but Italy was no longer united.

The old Roman province of Gaul suffered a fate similar to that of Italy. The Burgundians gained control of eastern Gaul, while the Alamanni moved into the region to the west of the Burgundians. A short time later, the Franks displaced the Alamanni and eventually gained control of much of what is today France.

**THE MEROVINGIANS**  During the 4th and 5th centuries, Frankish tribes migrated from their homeland along the Rhine River into present-day Belgium and France. In 481, Clovis became the king of the *Salian* ("salty") Franks, a small tribe that lived near the North Sea. He was descended from Merovech, a warrior who reputedly had helped the Romans defeat the Huns at Chalons in 451. Clovis, who ruled until his death in 511, was the founder of the Merovingian dynasty (named after Merovech) and the conqueror of an empire that stretched from the Pyrenees to central Europe.

### CLOVIS

As the young king of the Salian Franks, Clovis forced the general Syagrius, the last Roman commander in central Gaul, to withdraw his troops from Gaul in 486. He then strengthened his army and gained control of the other Frankish tribes of northern France.

In 493, Clovis married a Burgundian princess, Clothilde, who had converted to Christianity. The marriage was significant because it brought Clovis into the Roman Catholic Church. According to Christian sources, on the eve of a battle with the Alamanni, Clovis looked up to the sky and said, "If you give me this victory . . . I will believe . . . and will be baptized." Clovis defeated the Alamanni in 496, and, a short time later, triumphed over the Visigoths at Tours. After these victories, Clovis and 3000 of his warriors were baptized into the Roman Catholic Church. This baptism was important to Clovis and to the development of Europe. Clovis became a Roman Catholic at a time when the other Germanic rulers belonged to a rival Christian sect called Arians (see Chapter 12). Through his conversion, he won the support of the Roman Church. His action strengthened Catholicism and gave the Church a powerful ally against the Arians.

The Church soon made use of its alliance with Clovis by persuading him to attack the Visigoths, who were Arians and thus considered heretics. In 507, Clovis defeated Alaric II, the king of the Visigoths, at Poitiers and extended his control over southern France. The defeated Visigoths then withdrew into Spain. Clovis now ruled much of present-day France. He tried to establish a uniform system of government for the various peoples he ruled by codifying the *Salian Laws*, which were based on the customs of the Germanic tribes, and by encouraging his subjects to adopt Catholicism.

### MAYORS OF THE PALACE

When Clovis died in 511, his kingdom was divided among his four sons, as Frankish custom demanded. This division of power was a basic weakness and prevented a single ruler from establishing effective control. Also, Clovis' sons were weak and frequently quar-

| FRANKISH KINGS | |
|---|---|
| **Merovingian Rulers** | |
| 481-511 | Clovis |
| **Carolingian Rulers** | |
| 714-741 | Charles Martel |
| 741-768 | Pepin |
| 768-814 | Charlemagne |
| 814-840 | Louis the Pious |
| 840-855 | Lothair |
| 840-876 | Louis the German (east) |
| 840-877 | Charles the Bald (west) |
| 899-911 | Louis the Child |

## GERMANIC KINGDOMS IN THE WEST
*Compare this map to the map on page 296. Which Germanic kingdoms did Justinian conquer in the 6th century?*

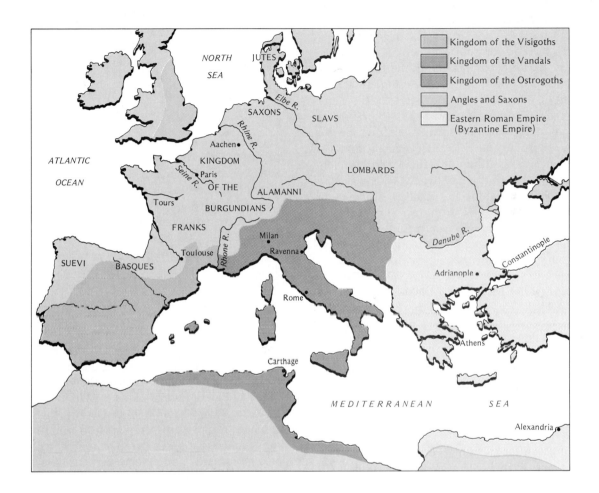

Map legend:
- Kingdom of the Visigoths
- Kingdom of the Vandals
- Kingdom of the Ostrogoths
- Angles and Saxons
- Eastern Roman Empire (Byzantine Empire)

Map labels: NORTH SEA, JUTES, SAXONS, SLAVS, Elbe R., Rhine R., Aachen, KINGDOM, Paris, Seine R., OF THE, ALAMANNI, LOMBARDS, ATLANTIC OCEAN, Tours, BURGUNDIANS, FRANKS, Rhone R., Milan, Ravenna, Danube R., SUEVI, BASQUES, Toulouse, Adrianople, Constantinople, Rome, Athens, Carthage, MEDITERRANEAN SEA, Alexandria

reled among themselves, while their heirs were incompetent. As a result, the rulers who followed Clovis came to be called the "do-nothing kings."

Under the do-nothing kings, local rulers gained control over their own lands and often ignored the commands of their overlord. During the 7th and 8th centuries, the weak Merovingian rulers turned over more and more of their power to officials called the "mayors of the palace." As Einhard, an 8th century chronicler, observed:

• • • Nothing was left to the king. He had to content himself with his royal title, his flowing locks, and long beard. Seated in a chair of state, he was wont to display an appearance of power by receiving foreign ambassadors on their arrival, and on their departure, giving them, as if on his own authority, those answers which he had been taught or commanded to give.[2]

---

[2]Einhard, "Life of the Emperor Charles," in *Readings in European History*, ed. Robinson, p. 120.

**69**

In time, the mayor of the palace became the power behind the throne. By the 8th century, one family had made this position hereditary. They were known as the *Carolingians* (from *Carolus*, the Latin form of Charles). The Carolingians passed the position of mayor from father to son, but always left a Merovingian king on the throne. The most important of these Carolingian mayors of the palace was Charles Martel ("the Hammer") who ruled from 714 to 741. While he exercised all of the powers of a king, he did not assume the title. His greatest achievement was organizing an efficient and reliable cavalry. With this cavalry, Charles was able to defeat the Moslem invaders at Tours in 732 (Chapter 14). Although the Moslems continued to attack western Europe, this battle is often considered a landmark because it marked their furthest advance.

## CAROLINGIAN EMPIRE

After the death of Charles Martel, his heirs ventured along a new course that helped shape the subsequent history of Europe. First, his son, Pepin, gained the title of king; then, Pepin's son, Charlemagne, expanded the Frankish kingdom into an empire that stretched across much of Europe.

### PEPIN

In 741, after his father's death, Pepin became mayor of the palace of King Childeric III. Pepin felt that Childeric was incompetent to serve as king and plotted to gain the title for himself. About 751, he asked the abbot of Saint Denis, a monastery near Paris, to go to Rome and ask for the pope's support.

••• *Pope Zacharias, therefore, in virtue of apostolic authority, told the ambassadors that he judged it better and more advantageous that he should be king and be called king who had the power rather than he who was falsely called king.*

*The said pontiff accordingly enjoined the king and the people of the Franks that Pippin [Pepin], who already exercised the* *regal power, should be called king and raised to the throne.*[3]

The pope's willingness to endorse Pepin's claim was due in large measure to his need for an ally against the Lombards, who were threatening papal lands in Italy. In 752, with the Church to back up his claim, Pepin persuaded the Frankish nobles to name him as their king. Bishop Boniface then anointed Pepin with holy oil and declared him king of the Franks.

A few years later, Pope Stephen traveled to Paris and also anointed Pepin king. In exchange, Pepin led his army into Italy and defeated the Lombards. He then forced the Lombards to give up a strip of territory across central Italy, which he in turn presented to the pope. This gift, known as the *Donation of Pepin*, gave the pope temporal as well as spiritual power over the lands that were later called the *Papal States*. The pope would rule over these lands until the 19th century.

### CHARLEMAGNE

Pepin was succeeded by his son Charles, who so impressed his contemporaries that he was called Charlemagne, or "Charles the Great." During a reign of almost half a century (768-814), Charlemagne conquered an empire that stretched from Spain in the west to central Europe in the east. According to Einhard, his personal friend and biographer, Charlemagne looked like the general and king that he was:

••• *Charles was large and robust, of commanding stature and excellent proportions, for it appears that he measured in height seven times the length of his own foot. The top of his head was round, his eyes large and animated, his nose somewhat long. He had a fine head of gray hair, and his face was bright and pleasant; so that, whether standing or sitting, he showed great presence and dignity. Although his neck was thick*

[3]"The Lesser Annals of Lorsch," in *Readings in European History*, ed. Robinson, p. 121.

*This bronze statuette may be a contemporary portrait of the emperor Charlemagne.*

and rather short, and his belly too prominent, still the good proportions of his limbs concealed these defects. His walk was firm and the whole carriage of his body was manly. His voice was clear, but not so strong as his frame would have led one to expect.[4]

**Conquests.** Charlemagne's goal was to unite all the Germanic tribes into a single Christian kingdom. In pursuit of this goal, he conducted more than 50 military campaigns. In 774, when the Lombards renounced the treaty that they had made with Pepin and renewed their attacks on the papal territory, Charlemagne marched into Italy, defeated the Lombards, and declared himself their king. Then crossing the Pyrenees Mountains, he fought

both the Moslems and the Basques, a native tribe, for control of northern Spain. He then carved out for himself a border kingdom called the Spanish March.[5]

After many campaigns against the Saxon tribes who lived between the Rhine and the Elbe rivers, Charlemagne subdued them and forced them to convert to Christianity. He then moved into Bavaria and drove the Slavs and Avars from the upper reaches of the Danube River. By the time he died, Charlemagne controlled the area of present-day France, Belgium, the Netherlands, West Germany, Austria, Switzerland, and northern Italy.

**Government.** Like his father, Charlemagne allied himself closely with the Church. In 799, when Pope Leo III was driven from the papal throne by a Roman mob and was almost killed in the street, he fled to Charlemagne's court. Charlemagne promptly went to Rome and restored the pope to his office. In gratitude, on Christmas Day in 800, Pope Leo crowned Charlemagne "Emperor of the Romans" and hailed him as *Augustus*, the ancient Roman title.

Charlemagne may have looked on this event as a mixed blessing. Although the Frankish king now carried the title of a Roman emperor and had the prestige of the Church behind him, the coronation implied that the pope had the power to crown (and perhaps remove the crown) of the ruler. When Charlemagne named his son as his successor, he was careful to preside over the ceremony himself without turning to the pope. Yet Charlemagne's coronation that Christmas Day showed that the tradition of a single, united Christian empire—like the one created by the ancient Romans—lingered in the minds of many people.

---

[4]Einhard, "Life of the Emperor Charles," in *Readings in European History*, ed. Robinson, p. 126.

[5]It was during Charlemagne's campaign in Spain that his rear guard was trapped at the pass of Roncesvalles in the Pyrenees Mountains. The heroic last stand of a Frankish noble named Roland later gave rise to the popular medieval epic, *The Song of Roland (Le Chanson de Roland)*.

On Christmas day of 800, Pope Leo III crowned Charlemagne emperor in Rome. This ceremony pronounced Charlemagne as heir of the Roman emperors, but also implied that the pope had the right to consecrate kings. Charlemagne therefore took care to crown his own successor in Aachen.

Charlemagne proved to be an able administrator as well as a successful military leader. He chose capable people to help him; he delegated authority to them; and he insisted that they carry out his wishes. He divided his empire into 300 districts, or counties. In each, a count administered secular business, a duke directed military matters, and a bishop managed religious affairs. In the counties on the frontier, called *marches*, that were threatened by invaders, he appointed special commanders to administer civil and military affairs. A contemporary chronicler praised the quality of Charlemagne's appointments:

● ● ● *The most serene and most holy Christian lord emperor Charles has chosen from his nobles the wisest and most prudent men, archbishops and some of the other bishops also, together with venerable abbots and pious laymen, and has sent them throughout his whole kingdom.*[6]

Charlemagne sent out messengers who acted as royal inspectors, supervising the administrators and punishing those who misbehaved. These inspectors were changed frequently and rotated to different districts to prevent them from cheating the emperor. Each administrator, each inspector, and, indeed, each citizen was required to take an oath of allegiance to Charlemagne.

Charlemagne issued laws based on the

[6]The general capitulary for the *missi*, in *Readings in European History*, ed. Robinson, p. 139.

## THE CAROLINGIAN EMPIRE

**What modern countries include territories that were once part of Lothair's kingdom?**

Kingdom of the Franks, 768

Conquests of Charlemagne, 768–814

principles of Germanic tribal laws. However, these laws were influenced by Christianity in that they condemned pagan practices and promoted Christian practices. Laws dealt with both secular and religious matters. One ordinance, for example, specified in great detail how royal farms should be operated. Each farm manager was required to submit an annual report of assets—such as size of fields, forests, mills, ships, and bridges—under his control. The report was also to include production statistics about everything from "hay, firewood, torches, planks, and other kinds of lumber," to "mulberry wine, coked wine,

73

mead, vinegar, beer, and wine, new and old," and even including "iron, lead, or other substances."

## CAROLINGIAN RENAISSANCE

Charlemagne was concerned not only with creating a strong and efficient government but also with improving learning throughout the empire. He was horrified at the lack of education among the clergy, many of whom did not know Latin or Greek. To improve this sorry state of affairs, he decreed that each cathedral establish a school for the training of the clergy. He even set up a palace school for his own family. Although he himself knew Latin and some Greek, he never mastered the art of reading and writing.

• • • *Charles also tried to learn to write, and used to keep his tablets and writing book under the pillow of his couch, that when he had leisure he might practice his hand in forming letters; but he made little progress in this task, too long deferred and begun too late in life.*[7]

Charlemagne's establishment of learning centers throughout his empire stimulated a rebirth of learning and scholarship that later historians called the *Carolingian Renaissance*. (Renaissance is a French word meaning "rebirth".)

To advance learning, Charlemagne invited to his court at Aachen (or Aix-la-Chapelle) the most renowned scholars of the day, including the famous Anglo-Saxon scholar, Alcuin of York, who set up the palace school for Charlemagne's sons and daughters and for the children of the nobles at court. Charlemagne also encouraged monasteries to establish schools for able boys of all social classes, and he visited these schools to check on the progress of the students.

Charlemagne founded abbeys for the purpose of encouraging monks to make copies

The chapel of Charlemagne at his capital city of Aachen. This design of this church was influenced by two Byzantine monuments that Charlemagne had visited: Constantine's basilica in Rome, and the church of San Vitale at Ravenna.

of the works of Greek and Roman authors, of Jerome's Latin translation of the Old and New Testaments (the *Vulgate*), and of the writings of other early Church leaders. The scribes who did this work often illuminated the first letter of each paragraph with colorful and intricate designs and painted scenes in the margins of events described in the text. These scribes also developed a form of writing in which lower-case letters were used alongside the upper-case, or capital, letters inherited from the Romans.

As Charlemagne's health began to fail, he tried to teach his only surviving son, Louis, the methods that he had used to govern his vast empire. But Charlemagne's gifts as a ruler

[7]Einhard, "the Life of Emperor Charles," in *Readings in European History*, ed. Robinson, p. 128.

could not easily be conveyed to another person. When he died in 814, an unknown monk was moved to write:

Dire sufferings has France endured,
Yet never grief like unto this,
Woe is me for misery;
Now Charles, voice of majesty and power,
To Aachen's soil she has given,
Woe is me for misery.[8]

These words were prophetic in many ways because Charlemagne's brilliant achievements did not survive him for long.

### LOUIS THE PIOUS

Charlemagne's son Louis the Pious (814-840) inherited his father's vast empire, but as his name implies, Louis was more interested in religion than in governing the empire. Within a few years after assuming the throne, Louis lost the support of the clergy and nobles. When these powerful groups recognized his weakness as a ruler, they took more power themselves.

Louis' last years were spent watching the bitter battles among his sons over the spoils of his empire. As provided by German custom, Louis planned to divide the empire among his three sons. He proposed that Lothair, the eldest, succeed to the throne as emperor and supervise the regions inherited

[8]Quoted in E. S. Duckett, Carolingian Portraits, A Study of the Ninth Century (Ann Arbor: University of Michigan Press, 1962), p. 19.

by two other brothers: Louis, called "the German," and Charles, called "the Bald." But the three sons rebelled against their father, and after his death in 840, they quarreled with one another.

### DIVISION OF THE EMPIRE

The empire, which had begun to disintegrate on Charlemagne's death, further declined under his grandsons. In 842, Louis the German and Charles the Bald met at Strasbourg, where they signed the Strasbourg Oath, in which they agreed to work together against their brother, Lothair. The oath was significant because it was written in two languages: one was the language of Charles' kingdom (west of the Rhine River), which was similar to Latin and would eventually become French; the other was the Germanic language of Louis' kingdom (east of the Rhine). Standing before their followers, each brother swore to the alliance in the language of the other. Their oath symbolized the growing split in the Carolingian Empire between the western and eastern lands of the Franks.

In 843, faced with the coalition of his two brothers, Lothair met with them at Verdun and accepted the terms of a treaty that divided Charlemagne's empire into three kingdoms. The western kingdom, which became present-day France, remained with Charles, and the eastern kingdom, which became present-day Germany, with Louis. A middle kingdom consisting of a long strip of land stretching from the North Sea into central Italy went to Lothair. This narrow corridor, known successively as Lotharii Regnum, Lotharginia, and Lorraine, was fought over by the Germans and French for a thousand years. Much reduced in size, Lorraine was taken by the Germans in the 19th century but was reclaimed by the French in 1919.

After the empire was divided, Lothair's central kingdom was soon fragmented. Descendants of Charlemagne ruled the eastern kingdom until 911, when the last Carolingian king died. In the western kingdom, Car-

*The emperor Lothair inherited the central part of Charlemagne's kingdom, while his brothers ruled the eastern and western portions.*

## THE VIKINGS

Scholars are uncertain about the origin of the word *Viking*, which is used to designate the raiders who suddenly appeared from the sea to attack the coast of Britain and northern France shortly before the year 800. Some suggest that it may be derived from the Scandinavian word *vik*, meaning inlet or fjord, where boats could be sheltered; others believe that it may be derived from *vig*, meaning battle. The Vikings came to be known by other names—such as the Northmen or the Norse; their descendants in France were called Normans. Wherever Viking raiders struck, they inspired people to offer the prayer: *A furore Normanorum libera nos, domine.* (From the fury of the Northmen, O Lord deliver us.)

The Vikings were Scandinavians from the region of present-day Denmark, Sweden, and Norway. They were related to the Germanic tribes who moved into Europe during the 4th and 5th centuries. Scholars do not know why the Vikings launched their fearful raids on western Europe in the 9th and 10th centuries. Some theorize that climatic changes lay behind the Viking expansion. Others believe that overpopulation or else the practice of **primogeniture**, in which the eldest son inherited his father's estate, left younger sons without any other means of earning a living.

Because of the geography of Scandinavia, the sea was important to the Viking way of life. By the 9th century, the Vikings had developed technologically advanced sailing ships which carried them on their raids across the seas. Viking ships were propelled by sails and long oars, and could achieve a maximum speed of about ten knots.[9] The largest of these ships could hold up to 100 men, and yet could be maneuvered on the open sea by as few as 15. Since they required a depth of only about three feet, Viking ships could be used on rivers to travel far inland. These remarkable vessels were strong enough to withstand

olingian rule came to an end in 987 when the French nobles elected Hugh Capet, count of Paris, as their king. The Capetians then ruled France for more than 300 years (Chapter 21).

The collapse of Charlemagne's empire was due only in part to the quarrels among his grandsons. At the same time as these internal wars were taking place, the empire was attacked on all sides by new waves of invaders. In the 9th century, the Vikings raided much of northern Europe; Moslems captured Sicily and launched raids on other parts of Italy; and the Magyars swept out of central Asia to terrorize eastern Europe.

---

[9]A speed of one knot is equal to one nautical mile (6080.2 feet) per hour.

The remains of several Viking ships have been discovered. Two ships, the Gokstad and the Oseberg, are on exhibit in the Viking Ship Hall in Oslo, Norway. Both were used for royal burials: the Gokstad for a chieftain and the Oseberg for a queen. The Gokstad, which was discovered in 1880, was an 80-foot-long warship with 16 pairs of oars. In 1893, an exact replica of this ship was built and sailed from Norway to Newfoundland in 28 days. The Oseberg, which was found in 1904, contained the skeletons of a queen, a slave girl, 12 horses, several dogs, and a peacock with feathers. It also contained beautifully carved furniture and a cart, all of which was meant to make life comfortable for the deceased in the afterlife.

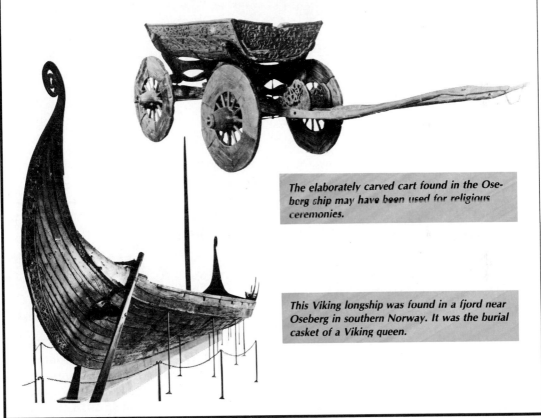

The elaborately carved cart found in the Oseberg ship may have been used for religious ceremonies.

This Viking longship was found in a fjord near Oseberg in southern Norway. It was the burial casket of a Viking queen.

the buffeting of the sea but light enough to be carried around waterfalls, rapids, or fortified bridges.

### ATTACKS ON WESTERN EUROPE

Late in the 8th century, Vikings from Norway occupied islands to the north and west of Scotland. Others created settlements on the coast of Ireland, occupying the ports of Dublin, Waterford, and Limerick. In 793, they attacked the monastery of Lindisfarne, a thriving center of Irish Christian civilization. The Anglo-Saxon scholar, Alcuin, was moved to write about this event.

● ● ● Lo, it is some 350 years that we and our forefathers have inhabited this most lovely land, and never before has such a terror

## INVASIONS OF THE 9TH AND 10TH CENTURIES
**What impact did these invasions have upon Europe?**

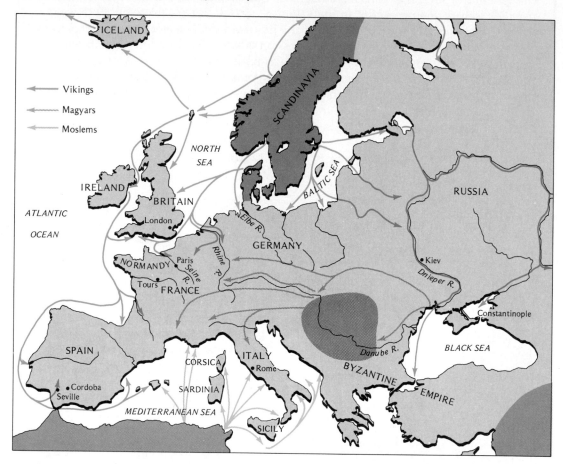

appeared in Britain as we have now suffered from a pagan race, nor was it thought possible that such an inroad from the sea could be made.[10]

In the 9th century, Vikings—whom the English called the Danes—began attacking the northern and eastern coasts of England. In 886, Alfred the Great, the Anglo-Saxon king of Wessex, made a treaty with Guthrum, king of the Danes, by which the Danes gained control of northeastern England. This region

then became known as the *Danelaw*. For the next century, there was almost continuous warfare between Alfred's successors and the Danes. In the 11th century, new waves of Danes attacked England. In 1016, the Danish king, Canute, became king of England, and in 1066, a descendant of the Vikings, William of Normandy, seized the English throne (Chapter 20)

While the Danes were attacking England, other Vikings were raiding the coast of France. Late in 885, a Viking fleet of 700 ships sailed up the Seine River and laid siege to Paris. Under the leadership of Count Odo, the city withstood the siege for several months but was becoming desperate for help when:

---

[10]Alcuin, *Anglo-Saxon Chronicles*, quoted in *Viking, Hammer of the North* by Magnus Magnusson (New York: Galahad Books, 1976), p. 22.

*. . . Odo . . . went forth secretly to seek aid from the nobles of the kingdom, and to send word to the emperor that the city would soon be lost unless help came. When Odo returned to Paris he found the people lamenting his absence. Nor did he reenter the city without a remarkable incident. The Northmen had learned that he was coming back, and they blocked his way to the gate. But Odo, though his horse was killed, struck down his enemies right and left, forced his way into the city, and brought joy to the anxious people.[11]*

Although the siege was eventually lifted, the fear of Viking attacks remained very real. From their base on the lower Seine River, the Vikings raided, looted, and burned rich monasteries, convents, and the few towns that still existed in France. In 911, the Frankish king Charles the Simple, a descendant of Charlemagne, ceded a region on the north coast of France to the Viking leader Rollo, on the condition that Rollo be baptized as a Christian and defend the region against other raiders. This region, the land of the "Northmen," soon became known as Normandy.

### MIGRATIONS INTO RUSSIA
Vikings from Sweden sailed across the Baltic Sea and the Gulf of Finland into present-day Russia. They found their way by water courses and short portages to the headwaters of the Volga River. Following the Volga, they reached the Caspian Sea. They also moved southward from present-day Leningrad to the Dnieper River, which led them to the Black Sea and Constantinople. In 862, they dominated the Slavic peoples along the river valleys and set up their own Viking kingdom centered at Kiev. In time the region came to be known as *Ruotsi*, which was later corrupted to *Russia*.[12]

From Kiev, the Vikings, or *Varangians* as they were called in the east, launched attacks against Constantinople in the 9th and 10th centuries. The Byzantine emperors were impressed with the reckless courage of the attackers. After fending them off, the emperors agreed to use them as an elite corps in the Byzantine army. The Volga and Dnieper rivers became arteries of commerce between the Viking and Byzantine civilizations. Blonde slaves, who were in great demand among the Byzantines, and furs, honey, and amber were carried southward to Constantinople while silk and other luxury goods were carried into Russia and northern Europe.

### OTHER VIKING SETTLEMENTS
In the mid-9th century, Viking warships sailed into the Mediterranean Sea, and Norse raiders attacked settlements along the Iberian coast, invaded North Africa, and possibly roamed as far east as Alexandria, Egypt. Meanwhile, other Vikings sailed westward from Norway and discovered Iceland, where they built settlements. About 980, Eric the Red led settlers from Iceland to the island of Greenland, which he had discovered. The Viking settlements on Greenland lasted until about 1500, by which time, some scholars theorize, the climate of Greenland had become too harsh to support settlers.

Late in the 10th century, Vikings from Greenland explored the seas further to the west. About 1001, Leif Ericson reached the coast of North America, where he established a settlement called *Vinland*, or "Land of the grapes." Archaeologists believe that Vinland was probably on the northern tip of Newfoundland where they have found remains of a Viking longhouse, weapons, and tools. The Vikings fought with the native population, whom they called *Skraelings*, but

---

[11]From the *Annals of St. Vaast*, quoted in *Readings in European History*, ed. Robinson, p. 162-3.

[12]The origin of the word *Russian* is not actually known. The Finns called the Vikings *ruotsi*, mean-

ing "seafarers." By 900, the most powerful branch of the eastern Slavs was known as the *Rus*, and the Vikings may have accepted this designation for themselves.

whom we would probably call *Eskimos*. Within a few years, however, the Vikings abandoned Vinland and returned to Greenland or Iceland.

### VIKING CULTURE

In most contemporary accounts, the Vikings were portrayed as savage pirates intent on loot and destruction. These accounts were written by the people who suffered at the hands of the Vikings. Yet there was another side to these fearless seafaring raiders. They developed their own literature—long narrative poems, called *sagas*, that have been found in Iceland. Like the epic poems of Homer, the Icelandic sagas mix facts with fancy and were sung to audiences by wandering bards. These sagas were not written down until the 13th or 14th centuries, but they memorialize events of several centuries earlier. In fact, our information about the deeds of Eric the Red and his son, Leif, come from these sagas.

The Vikings had a written script known as *runic*, and runic inscriptions on rock and metal have been found in places stretching from North America to the Caspian Sea. The fact that the names of women often appear in the runic inscriptions seems to indicate that women played an important role in Viking society. We know, for example, that women could own property, had the right to consent to their marriages, and could initiate divorces.

In their homelands, the economy of the Vikings was based on agriculture, herding, hunting, and fishing. As you have read, they made the excellent sailing ships that took them on long and dangerous voyages. Artists carved the prow of each ship to resemble a fanciful creature. They also decorated weapons and jewelry with intricate abstract designs and heads of fanciful horses, serpents, and dragons.

The Vikings worshiped a pantheon of gods. Thor, whose symbol was a hammer, was the most important. He was the guardian of humans and the other gods. Odin was the god of wisdom and of war, and Frey was the goddess of fertility. Sacrifices were made to these gods to ensure their protection at home and in battle. Warriors who were slain in battle were called *val*, and they were carried to heaven (*Valhalla*) by handmaidens of the gods (*Valkyries*). Valhalla was a place where heroic battles were fought and celebrations were held with feasts of pork and mead (honeyed ale).

Whenever possible, a Viking chieftain was buried in a ship, with everything he would need in the afterlife: slaves, weapons, armor, food, and furniture. Such a burial is described in the Anglo-Saxon saga *Beowulf*:

*There at the quay, stood a ring-prowed ship—*
*The radiant and eager ship of the lord.*
*They laid down the beloved lord,*
*The giver of rings, in the bosom of the ship,*
*The lord lay by the mast. They brought from afar*
*Many great treasures and costly trappings.*
*I never heard of a ship so richly furnished as this,*
*With weapons of war, armour of battle,*
*Swords and corselets. Many treasures lay*
*Piled on his breast.*[13]

By 1000, the Vikings had settled in many parts of Europe. In France, England, and elsewhere, they converted to Christianity and their culture blended into that of Christian Europe. After the 11th century, their raiding forays ended, but the bold spirit of the Vikings continued in the Norman knights who conquered England in 1066, seized Sicily from the Moslems, and embarked on the Crusades (Chapter 16).

**THE MOSLEMS** While the Viking raids on northern Europe were the most widespread and destructive of the great invasions of the 9th and 10th centuries, the

[13]Quoted in *The Vikings and Their Origins*, by David M. Wilson (New York: McGraw-Hill, 1970), p. 66.

Moslem attacks were equally terrifying to the Christian communities of southern Europe. As you have read, Arab armies conquered the Middle East, the coast of North Africa, and much of Spain in the century after Mohammed's death in 632. By 732, they had crossed the Pyrenees and were turned back by Charles Martel at Tours.

During this same period, the Moslems gradually gained control of the islands in the western Mediterranean, including Sicily, Corsica, and Sardinia. In 827, they virtually completed their conquest of Sicily and soon afterward made Palermo their capital.

### ATTACKS ON SOUTHERN EUROPE

From their strongholds in Sicily and Spain, the Moslems launched frequent raids on Italy and the coast of southern France. Europeans called these invaders *Saracens*, from *sarakenos*, a Byzantine Greek word meaning "easterners." Although Christians in Europe were terrified of the Saracens, they were not above appealing to them on occasion for help in their own quarrels. This was the case in Italy when rivalry among the Lombards and the Byzantine emperor led Naples to ask for Moslem assistance in 838. The Moslems took the opportunity to make new conquests along both the western and eastern coasts of Italy.

They attacked and destroyed the famous monastery founded by Saint Benedict at Monte Cassino and even besieged Rome in 846. Although they did not capture the city, they did plunder the cathedrals of St. Peter and St. Paul outside the walls. A Christian eyewitness described this event:

• • • *At this same time, as no one can mention or hear without great sadness, the mother of all churches, the basilica of the apostle Peter, was taken and plundered by the Moors, or Saracens, who had already occupied the region of Beneventum. The Saracens, moreover, slaughtered all the Christians whom they found outside the walls of Rome, whether within or without this church. They also carried men and women away prisoners. They tore down, among many others, the altar of the blessed Peter, and their crimes from day to day bring sorrow to Christians.*[14]

The Moslems extended their raids into other parts of Europe. They built forts along the south coast of France, which they used as bases to attack merchants carrying goods across the Alps.

In 972, the Moslems captured the abbot of Cluny from a famous monastery in southern France and held him for ransom. Because the abbot was an influential Church leader, French nobles put aside their personal differences to secure his release. Late in the 9th century, Christians began to dislodge the Moslems from their bases on the Italian mainland. However, the Moslems held onto Sicily until the mid-11th century.

### CHRISTIAN-ISLAMIC CULTURE OF SICILY

In Sicily, the Moslems imposed their own culture on the local population. Palermo grew into a thriving commercial center and became a leading Moslem city like Cordoba in Spain or Cairo in Egypt. The impact of the Moslem occupation of Sicily would remain long after the island had been recaptured by Christian Europeans.

The conquest of Sicily was carried out by the Normans between about 1060 and 1091. By the 11th century, these descendants of Viking raiders who had settled in France were looking for new lands to conquer. They were soon expanding their power and influence into the Mediterranean, where they fought and often defeated not only the Moslems but also the Byzantines.

In 1071, the Normans captured Palermo and by 1091 had ended Moslem control of Sicily. The Norman count Roger who then ruled Sicily left much of the Moslem culture in place, and the next two centuries saw Christian and Islamic traditions blended into

---

[14]From the *Annals of Xanten*, quoted in *Readings in European History*, ed. Robinson, p. 160.

a flourishing culture. Roger appointed Moslems to high positions in government and respected the advanced learning of Moslem physicians and philosophers. His son, Roger II, established a brilliant court in which the Moslem geographer al-Idrisi (Chapter 14) wrote his great works based on reports from travelers to distant lands. In the 13th century, Roger's grandson, Frederick II continued the official patronage of Islamic learning. Through trade with the Islamic world as well as his support of Moslem scholars at court, Frederick helped to introduce the more advanced culture of the East into western Europe.

### THE MAGYARS

The third group of invaders to devastate Europe in the 9th and 10th centuries were the Magyars. These ruthless invaders probably came from the region of the Ural Mountains and the Volga River. From there, they migrated southwestward into the steppes of southern Russia. In the 9th century, they descended on the Slavic and Germanic settlements of eastern Europe with unmatched ferocity.

The Magyar warriors were brilliant horsemen. They had learned to use the stirrup—an invention that scholars believe was slowly making its way to the west from its place of origin in India or perhaps China. With the stirrup, an armed rider could stand upright while on horseback and shoot arrows in any direction.

In the 10th century, the Magyars, who had already pushed into present-day Poland and Romania, swept into lands at the base of the Alps. They left a path of destruction across northern Italy, eastern France, and southern Germany. They kept up their devastating raids until 955, when Otto the Great (see Chapter 19) met them at Lechfeld in southern Germany. There, he soundly defeated them. Contemporaries thought Otto's victory at Lechfeld as significant as the victory of Charles Martel at Tours. Certainly, it ended the Magyar threat, for the surviving Magyars

escaped eastward, where they settled along the Danube River in the area that we know today as Hungary.

There are at least two theories about how the land of the Magyars came to be called Hungary. One theory claims that it comes from the Magyar word *onogur*, meaning "ten arrows," which symbolized the confederation of ten tribes that invaded Europe. Another theory says that the destruction of the Magyars reminded people of the Hun invasion of the 5th century, and so they called the new invaders Hungarians.

### RESULTS OF THE INVASIONS

The invasions of the Vikings, Moslems, and Magyars completed the course of destruction that had started several centuries earlier when the Germanic migrations across Europe contributed to the collapse of the Roman Empire in the West. The centuries of invasions transformed western Europe into a land made up of many small kingdoms. The constant warfare had cut off trade. As a result, many towns and cities of Roman times had disappeared; others were much reduced in size.

These and other effects of the invasions will be discussed further in later chapters. Faced with the need to repel invaders, local leaders developed new means to raise armed and mounted horsemen. As early as the 8th century, Charles Martel had seen the importance of having *knights*, or mounted warriors, to resist the Moslem invaders. The upkeep of a horse, the making of armor, and the training of knights required money and time, which the Merovingian mayor of the palace did not have. Instead, he used the one commodity he did have—giving knights the right to certain lands in exchange for military service. The land provided a knight with a means of support. This practice, which was first developed in France, spread to the rest of Europe and became the basis of a new order, called feudalism, which you will study in Chapter 17.

## SUMMARY

*For more than 500 years—from the 5th to the 10th centuries—Europe experienced a succession of invasions. First, the Germanic tribes poured across the borders of the Roman Empire, contributing to its collapse. In the former Roman provinces, German leaders set up small, warring kingdoms.*

*For a brief time, Charlemagne succeeded in reuniting many of the lands once ruled by Rome. During his rule, a revival of learning known as the Carolingian Renaissance brought new life to the fading cultural traditions of the ancient world and helped lay the foundations for medieval civilization. On Charlemagne's death, however, his empire collapsed as his heirs quarreled and divided up his land.*

*The collapse of the Carolingian Empire was hastened by three new waves of invasions: the Vikings from the north, the Moslems from the south, and the Magyars from the east. By the time these threats had ended late in the 10th century, western Europe was devastated and a new way of life based on the need to resist invaders had developed.*

## QUESTIONS

1 What impact did the Germanic migrations of the early Middle Ages have on the Roman Empire in the West?
2 Describe the origins, organization, and decline of the Carolingian Empire. How did Charlemagne reflect both ancient and medieval traditions?
3 How does the Carolingian Renaissance refute the old notion that the period between the fall of Rome and the Renaissance was the "Dark Ages"?
4 Why do you think the Viking invasions were so widespread?
5 On a map of Europe, trace the invasions of the Vikings, Moslems, and Magyars in the 9th and 10th centuries. In what part of Europe would you have chosen to live at that time?
6 Describe how the invasions of the 9th and 10th centuries completed the process of destruction begun in the 5th and 6th centuries.

## BIBLIOGRAPHY

*Which books might discuss the Carolingian Renaissance?*

CABANISS, ALLEN. *The Son of Charlemagne.* Syracuse: Syracuse University Press, 1961. *A reappraisal of Louis the Pious, demonstrating how his achievements have been largely overlooked by historians.*

GORDON, C. D. *The Age of Attila.* Ann Arbor: University of Michigan Press, 1960. *A description of the collapse of classical civilization in the 5th century and the ensuing turmoil that engulfed Europe. Includes contemporary accounts of events such as the siege of Rome by Alaric and the Visigoths.*

HEER, FRIEDRICH. *Charlemagne and His World.* New York: Macmillan, 1975. *An illustrated biography of the great Frankish warrior-king. Examines the social, economic, and cultural developments of Charlemagne's reign along with his political and military successes.*

MAGNUSSON, MAGNUS. *The Vikings!* New York: E. P. Dutton, 1980. *A highly readable, illustrated account of the history, mythology, and society of the Vikings.*

RICE, DAVID TALBOTT, ed. *The Dawn of European Civilization.* New York: McGraw-Hill, Inc., 1965. *A careful reconstruction of Western civilization in the early Middle Ages, focusing on four areas: the Islamic world, the Byzantine Empire, the Germanic kingdoms in the West, and the Carolingian Empire.*

**5**

● *No king can reign rightly unless he devoutly serves Christ's vicar. The priesthood is the sun, and monarchy the moon. Kings rule over their respective kingdoms, but . . . the Lord gave Peter rule not only over the universal church, but also over the whole world.*

POPE INNOCENT III

# The Church in the Middle Ages

The Middle Ages has often been called the Age of Faith because Christianity as a religion shaped the minds of medieval people and the Church as an institution occupied a dominating position in medieval life. At the height of its power in the 13th century, Pope Innocent III could proclaim that the Church was supreme on earth (see quote above). Medieval men and women were deeply concerned with salvation, and the Church alone held the key to salvation. As a result, the Church had enormous power over the minds of individuals. It also ruled their lives, performing the ceremonies that marked their births, marriages, and deaths; and presiding over other services, feasts, and holy days throughout the year.

In the early Middle Ages, the Church was on the defensive. It inherited the mantle of Roman authority at a time when Europe was battered by invasions. Yet it did not falter in its drive to win the invaders over to Christianity. By the 10th century, it had largely succeeded in its missionary goals, converting the "heathen" peoples of the north to Christianity. As the Church consolidated its power and influence, it set off on a new course, one that would put it in conflict with the Islamic world. This chapter focuses on the central role played by the Christian Church in western Europe during the Middle Ages.

**CIVIL ROLE OF THE CHURCH** When the Roman Empire collapsed, the people of western Europe were forced to look to new leaders for security and guidance. The Church and the leaders of the local Germanic kingdoms took control of the land, but there was no longer a single, central civil authority to whom everyone was responsible. With the disappearance of Roman officials and administrative structure, the Church authorities assumed civil responsibilities along with their spiritual leadership. Thus, the Church operated the only schools, hospitals, and orphanages in Europe. Churches and monasteries became *sanctuaries*, or places of refuge where people could find at least temporary protection from a violent world.

The Church also gradually became the largest landowner in western Europe as the secular rulers gave it vast tracts of land as acts of charity or repentance. These land grants enabled the Church to fulfill its spiritual and temporal duties, and they also made it rich and powerful. In the Middle Ages, both wealth and power were based on land ownership. Thus, bishops and abbots were often more powerful than secular nobles or even rulers, and they were frequently in conflict with these secular rulers. The Church has always been a primarily spiritual institution, but in the Middle Ages it was also the most powerful political organization in Europe.

*SACRAMENTS*   The basis of the Church's spiritual role was its claim, accepted by all Christians during the Middle Ages, to be the sole channel through which people could approach God. Divine worship took the form of prayer, attendance at services, and participation in sacred rituals, called *sacraments*, that only priests could perform. The seven sacraments were related to the most important aspects of life from birth to death, and are still fundamental to the Catholic Church. They are baptism, confirmation, matrimony, penance, extreme unction, Holy Orders, and the *Holy Eucharist* (also known as "Holy Communion"), a commemoration of the last supper that Jesus had with his 12 apostles.

Medieval people believed that all people were sinners by nature and that only through the sacraments could they achieve salvation in the next life. Those who were denied the sacraments by the Church were shunned in this life and condemned to eternal damnation in the next. People could be denied the sacraments by the clergy for wickedness or for disobeying Church law. The threat of *excommunication*, of being put outside the sacramental life of the Church, was a powerful weapon in the hands of the Church leadership. Fear of excommunication undoubtedly helped maintain social order and public morality. However, the threat of excommunication was also used by the Church in its political struggles. For centuries, powerful lords and even monarchs were forced to yield to the Church when faced with the penalty of excommunication or of the *interdict*, which

meant that no one living in their territory could participate in the sacraments. Almost invariably, this latter threat forced a lord to yield to the Church.

Through its hierarchical organization, the Church reached all levels of medieval society. At the lowest level were the parishes. Local parish priests were the people on whom medieval Christians depended, for it was the priest who officiated over the sacraments so necessary to salvation. Most ordinary people knew little of the bishops and archbishops who held the higher offices in the Church.

*CANON LAW*   In addition to administering the sacred rituals, the Church fulfilled many functions of a secular state. Among the most important were the functions performed by Church courts. The Church courts tried both civil and criminal cases involving the clergy, and made their decisions based on canon law. *Canon law* was a mixture of Roman law and of the regulations that had been issued over the years by Church authorities and councils.

Decisions of Church courts related to many subjects including marriage, divorce, and wills. On these matters, Church decisions were accepted as having the force of law by Christian rulers and were enforced by public officials. In other areas, however, secular rulers claimed a jurisdiction that the Church fiercely resisted. One of the most disputed issues was whether secular or Church courts could try members of the clergy who were charged with criminal offenses. In some places, this issue created bitter struggles between Church and state which were not resolved until the end of the Middle Ages.

In the first centuries after the fall of Rome, when the states of western Europe were weak and much of Roman law had been forgotten, canon law and the Church courts had no rivals in most of Europe. However, civil law and civil courts eventually developed as secular power grew in the later Middle Ages. Inevitably, there arose conflicts of jurisdiction between civil and Church courts, especially since the fines levied by the courts provided a substantial income.

*MONASTICISM*   During the early years of Christianity, some Christians chose to isolate themselves from society and devote their lives to the contemplation of God and the salvation of their souls. Some lived in solitude and were called *hermits* (from the Greek *eremos*, meaning "desolate"). Others lived together in religious communities called *monasteries*. Both men and women entered into this monastic movement, which spread from Egypt, where it began, across the Mediterranean into Europe. Early leaders of these monasteries established rules by which *monks* (from the Greek *monos*, meaning "alone") lived. Late in the 4th century, a Greek monk named Saint Basil (329-379) drew up a rule, or code of behav-

ior, that was adopted by monasteries in the Byzantine world. Later, another monk, Saint Benedict (480-547), wrote a rule that was adopted by monasteries in the West.

### THE BENEDICTINES

Benedict was born into a patrician family in Rome after the city had fallen to the Goths. When he reached maturity, Benedict decided to remove himself from the moral decadence of Rome, and went to live in a cave near the ruins of Nero's palace. After three years in solitude, he came to the realization that it would be more useful to live with a group of devout men who could pray and work together. In 529, he established a monastery at Monte Cassino, midway between Rome and Naples. There, he put into practice the code of conduct that he had prepared and that became known as the *Benedictine Rule*.

Each man who applied for admission to

*The monastic movement founded by Benedict at Monte Cassino had great influence on the subsequent history of the Church. Through the efforts of Pope Gregory, Saint Augustine, and other reformers, Benedict's rules became the accepted standard of conduct for Church officials as well as for monks.*

Monte Cassino underwent a period of training called a *novitiate*. If he was then approved for membership in the Benedictine Order, he was required to take a vow that he would live a life of poverty, chastity, and obedience to the Benedictine Rule. The rule governed every activity of a monk's daily life. Each day was spent in specified periods of prayer, manual labor, study, and rest.

The monastery was a self-governing body, led by an abbot who was elected to the position for life by the monks and was thereafter answerable only to the pope. It served as a hospice for travelers, the ill, and the lonely. Some monks worked as scribes, copying ancient manuscripts in Greek and Latin; others recorded current events. These records now provide us with valuable information about the life of the times. The monastery was economically self-sufficient and pioneered in a variety of farming techniques. Monte Cassino wine, for example, has been on the world market for centuries.

### CONTRIBUTIONS OF MONASTERIES

Many Benedictine monasteries were established throughout Europe, and the Benedictine Rule became the model for other orders of monks. The monasteries played several important roles. First, they collected and copied valuable manuscripts at a time when the scholarship of the ancient world was being lost. By doing so, they made monasteries into centers of learning. To ensure that monks would be able to read and write Greek and Latin, monasteries operated schools.

Besides protecting learning and promoting education, monasteries were frequently the training ground for missionaries who dedicated their lives to converting the pagan peoples of northern and eastern Europe. Many Benedictines as well as monks from other orders went out to distant places—including Ireland, Scotland, and Germany. Among the most renowned missionaries were Columban and Boniface. Like Saint Benedict, they were later canonized by the Church.

### AUGUSTINE'S MISSION TO ENGLAND

One of the most influential popes of the medieval period, Gregory the Great (pope from 590-604), began his religious life as a Benedictine monk. In 599, Gregory sent Augustine and several other monks as missionaries to England, where Christianity had been largely wiped out by the Germanic invasions of the 5th and 6th centuries. The Venerable Bede (672-735), an English Benedictine monk and chronicler, reported on the mission of Augustine and his companions. Soon after setting out:

● ● ● *they were seized with sudden fear and began to think of returning home, rather than proceed to a barbarous, fierce, and unbelieving nation, to whose very language they were strangers. . . . In short, they sent back Augustine, who was to be consecrated bishop in case they were received by the English, that he might persuade the holy Gregory to relieve them from undertaking so dangerous, toilsome and uncertain a journey.*[1]

Gregory responded to their fears and urged them to fulfill their mission:

● ● ● *Let not, therefore, the toil of the journey nor the tongues of evil-speaking men deter you; but with all possible earnestness and zeal perform that which, by God's direction, you have undertaken; being assured that much labor is followed by an eternal reward.*[2]

Augustine returned to his mission and led the group to England. There, they established themselves at Canterbury and began their work of converting the Anglo-Saxon people of England to Christianity.

The work of Christian missionaries like Augustine was often dangerous, and many lost their lives. Gradually, however, they achieved success, bringing the outlying parts of Europe into the Christian fold.

---

[1]Venerable Bede, *Ecclesiastical History of the English Nation*, trans. J. A. Giles (1843), I, 23.
[2]*Ibid.*

## CONVENTS

In the Middle Ages, women, too, joined religious communities. Benedict's twin sister, Scholastica, was so impressed by her brother's work that she established a convent for women near Monte Cassino. The nuns' duties in prayer and worship as well as in study and labor were the same as those of the monks. In addition, they were encouraged to spin and weave cloth.

In time, many convents were established throughout Europe. Although they usually were less well endowed with land and wealth than monasteries, some convents became very prosperous. Like monks, nuns provided shelter for travelers and cared for the sick. Some convents became famous for their herbs and knowledge of medical matters. Others set up schools, although these schools usually admitted only the children of nobles.

## MONASTIC REFORMS

By the 10th century, monasteries had gained great wealth and power. Their material success, however, led to abuses. Many monasteries ignored the austere rules set down by their founders. Abbots sought to amass more wealth and power. Monks and nuns broke their vows. Similar abuses also existed in other parts of the Church. It was possible for people of wealth to buy Church offices, a practice known as **simony**, regardless of their spiritual characters. Moreover, priests were often uneducated, paid little attention to their duties, and ignored their vows of celibacy. In the 10th and 11th centuries, a great religious revival led both lay and Church leaders to recognize the need for reform and to work toward this end.

### CLUNIACS

The reform movement that swept across Europe received much of its impetus from a newly-established monastic order of Cluny, in east-central France. In 910, Cluny was set up as a disciplined, spiritual center, divorced from the secular world. Unlike many other monasteries that owed allegiance to lords and rulers, the Cluniac monks were direct subjects of the pope and were thus free from any lay influence. The order adopted the high moral standards that Saint Benedict had advocated almost 400 years earlier, but the Cluniacs spent less energy on physical labor than the Benedictines and devoted more time to religious and intellectual pursuits. Above all, the Cluniacs practiced rigid adherence to their vows.

In time, the abbey at Cluny became a model for reforming other monasteries and for establishing new ones. At its peak, the Cluniac order had 2000 monasteries in France alone. By 1150, there were 314 Cluniac houses, with 110,000 monks, scattered throughout France, Germany, Spain, and Italy. Besides enforcing a strict rule in their own monasteries, the Cluniacs in their reforming zeal called on the Church to abolish simony and to stop other abuses.

### CISTERCIANS

Another reform movement that sought to recover the strict monastic discipline of earlier days was directed by the Cistercians, whose order was founded in 1090 at Cîteaux in northeastern France. The best known Cistercian was Bernard of Clairvaux (1090-1153). He believed that all Christians should devote their lives to the study and contemplation of God's goodness and should attempt in every way to follow God's guidance. Bernard believed that God's love was so great that even the most miserable sinner could achieve salvation by turning to God with unquestioning faith.

Bernard insisted that the Cistercian monasteries be built in rural areas where the monks could lead simple, austere lives far from the temptations of towns and cities. The only worldly possession that a monk was permitted to own was a small amount of clothing. Bernard also opposed the ornamentation of churches and monasteries, for he wanted to avoid any distractions.

As a symbol of humility, the Benedictines and other monks adopted the tonsure, in which the top of the head was shaved. In Roman times, this haircut had been a mark of slavery.

● ● ● And in the cloisters, under the eyes of the brethren engaged in reading, what business have those ridiculous monstrosities, that misshapen shapeliness and shapely misshapeness? Those unclean monkeys, those fierce lions, those monstrous centaurs, those semi-human beings. Here we see a quadruped with the tail of a serpent, there a fish with the head of a goat. In short there appears on all sides so rich and amazing a variety of forms that it is more delightful to read the marble than the manuscripts and to spend the whole day in admiring these things, piece by piece, rather than in meditating on the Divine Law.[3]

By the time Bernard died in 1153, there were 353 Cistercian monasteries, tied together by the General Chapter, a governing body made up of the abbots of all the monasteries. By 1300, the number had grown to more than 700 monasteries, plus several con-vents for women who desired to practice the high ideals of the Cistercian order.

Each monastery included a library and a *scriptorium*, a room in which monks copied and illuminated manuscripts. The scribes vowed to "fight the devil by pen and ink" and hoped that "every letter, line or point is a sin forgiven."[4]

Because of their devotion and hard work, the Cistercians converted swamps and wastelands into productive farms. In England, they were so successful at raising sheep that they controlled a large part of the English wool trade and became very wealthy.

***MENDICANT FRIARS*** After the year 1000, the tempo of life in Europe changed. In the next few centuries, the Church reached its greatest triumphs. In the 13th century, Pope Innocent III (1198-1216) presided over the papacy at its highest level of influence and prestige. During this time, he sanctioned the establishment of two new orders, the Dominicans and the Franciscans. The members of both orders chose to be called *friars* (from the Latin *frater*, meaning "brother"). They dedicated their lives to working among needy people, especially those living in towns and cities, rather than isolating themselves in monasteries. It was said that "the world was their cloister." To finance their good works, they went about begging for alms, which led people to refer to them as *mendicants*, or beggars.

Besides caring for the needy, the Dominicans and Franciscans preached and defended the teachings of the Church and fought heresy wherever they encountered it. Both orders attracted members who became outstanding thinkers and whose writings are studied today. The teachings of the Dominican theologian Thomas Aquinas (c. 1225-1374) are still considered the definitive statement of Roman Catholicism (Chapter 18).

[3]Quoted in Kenneth Clark, *Civilisation* (New York: Harper & Row, 1969), p. 40.

[4]Quoted in Ann Freemantle, *Age of Faith* (New York: Time-Life Books, 1965), p. 48.

## DOMINICANS

The Dominican Order was founded in 1216 by Saint Dominic (1170-1221), a well-educated Spaniard. Dominic gained fame by joining the crusade against the Albigensian heresy, which Pope Innocent III was trying to eliminate. The Albigensians were centered in southern France. They believed that the world was a battleground for the forces of good and evil, and they looked on the Church as an evil force because of its wealth and power. Because they challenged Church authority, they at first suffered the full force of its punishment.

Dominic felt that the way to fight heresy was to return to the simple ways of the apostles. Clad in simple clothing, he went among the poor, preaching and teaching. He assembled a group of followers who pledged themselves to preaching, teaching, conducting missionary activities, and combating heresies. In 1216, Pope Honorius III blessed the Order of Friar Preachers, the official name of the Dominicans.

The order won many followers. By 1277, there were 394 Dominican houses throughout Europe and in the Holy Land, where young men prepared for lives of service. Over succeeding centuries, Dominicans established schools and universities around the world, including the United States. Convents for Dominican nuns were also established. Because of their dedication to eliminating heresies, Dominicans were often chosen to staff Church courts. The Dominican order is still one of the largest and most influential in the Roman Catholic Church.

## FRANCISCANS

Francis (1182-1226) was the son of a wealthy wool merchant from Assisi, a town in northeastern Italy. Francis dreamed of becoming a knight but was captured during his first military venture in 1202 and spent a year in prison. After returning home, he was ill for a long time. During this illness, he became convinced that he should renounce his

Through preaching and the example of their own lives, Francis and his friars hoped to revitalize Christian faith, especially among the poor. This Church painting shows Francis in an audience with Pope Honorius.

worldly possessions and dedicate the rest of his life to spreading the gospel to the poor.

After recovering his health, Francis wandered throughout Italy and was appalled at what he saw as the hypocrisy of Christians making pilgrimages to Rome. He was struck by the contrast between the living conditions of the rich and the poor. After returning to Assisi, Francis had a dream in which he was directed to repair several ruined churches near the city. Without asking permission, he used some of his father's money to carry out these instructions, but he was flogged and imprisoned for his efforts.

Francis then pledged himself to a life of poverty and to helping the poor and the sick, so that he could demonstrate the teachings of Jesus. Before long, a small group of like-minded people joined him. Pope Innocent III was so impressed with what Francis was doing that he sanctioned the establishment of the Order of Friars Minor (or Little Brothers). Its name derives from the vows of extreme poverty and humility taken by the members and to Francis' teaching that all people are brothers in Christ.

The Franciscan order became immensely popular and influential. In part, this was the result of Francis' personality—his kindliness and sanctity. In part, it was also the result of the simple life of the Franciscans and their fervor, which was said to be as ardent as that of the early apostles. The Franciscans thus became a major outlet for popular piety. By 1282, there were 1583 houses of the order scattered throughout Europe.

In 1212, Francis so impressed a young noblewoman named Clare that she renounced her inheritance and, with help from Francis, founded an order of nuns, known popularly as the Poor Clares. Clare's sister and mother also joined the order. The Poor Clares lived in poverty, cared for the sick and poor, and provided shelter to travelers. In time, they expanded their work into France, England, and Germany.

**THE CRUSADES** During the early Middle Ages, the Church focused its energies on carrying Christianity to the pagan peoples of western Europe. In the later Middle Ages, its power assured, the Church launched another drive, this time to recapture the Holy Land that had fallen to the Seljuk Turks. For many centuries, Christians from Europe had been making pilgrimages to the Holy Land and to places in Europe that were associated with the lives of various saints. These pilgrimages were acts of penance or manifestations of piety. Of all the pilgrimages, the journey to Jerusalem was the most difficult because of the great distance. But the Moslems who controlled the city that was holy to Moslems, Jews, and Christians alike usually allowed Christian pilgrims to come and go freely.

In the mid-11th century, however, the Seljuk Turks,[5] who came out of central Asia, gained control of much of the Middle East. After moving through present-day Afghanistan and converting to Islam, they migrated westward and sacked Baghdad in 1055. They then pushed further to the west, encroaching on the Byzantine Empire. In 1071, they defeated a Byzantine army at Manzikert, near Lake Van in the eastern part of present-day Turkey.

Gradually, the Turks extended their control over much of Asia Minor, Syria, and Palestine. In 1085, they captured Jerusalem. The Turks were much less tolerant of Christian pilgrims than the Arabs had been. Tales of harassment and persecution of pilgrims filtered into Europe. The Byzantine Empire, which had protected Christians in the East, could no longer do so. Indeed, the Byzantines wanted Western help to recover their lost provinces from the Turks.

### FIRST CRUSADE (1096-1099)

In 1091, the Byzantine emperor, Alexius Comnenus I, sent envoys to Pope Urban II requesting military support, both to protect his own domains and to safeguard Christian pilgrims to the Holy Land from attack by the Turks. Four years later, Urban traveled to Clermont (now Clermont-Ferrand), in central France, to address a Church council. Urban II dreamed of reuniting the Eastern Orthodox Church (Chapter 13) with the Roman Catholic Church. To achieve this dream, the pope called on the assembled clergy and nobles to unite and embark on a holy crusade (from the Latin crux, meaning "cross"). The purpose of the crusade, he said, was to aid the Christians of the East and to liberate the Holy Land from the infidels—as Christians called all Moslems. Years later, Robert the Monk recalled Urban's words:

● ● ● *Let hatred therefore depart from among you, let your quarrels end, let wars cease,*

---

[5]Seljuk was an early leader of these Turkic people.

and let all dissensions and controversies slumber. Enter upon the road to the Holy Sepulcher; wrest that land from the wicked race, and subject it to yourselves. That land which, as the Scripture says, "floweth with milk and honey" was given by God into the power of the children of Israel. Jerusalem is the center of the earth; the land is fruitful above all others, like another paradise of delights.[6]

To this impassioned plea, his listeners responded with enthusiasm: "God wills it!" As soon as Urban finished speaking, hundreds of people volunteered: the First Crusade had begun; there would be many more. The Crusades were a series of expeditions and wars that continued off and on for 200 years. They involved tens of thousands of European Christians from peasants to monarchs.

From Clermont, the call for a crusade spread throughout Europe, but the people who rallied to this first call were primarily from France, southern Italy, and Sicily. The Normans who had recently conquered England were still consolidating their control of that land; the Christian knights of Spain were fighting their own crusade against the Moslems there; and only a few nobles from Germany responded to this call. Yet thousands of others did respond and sewed crosses to their clothes to announce themselves as Crusaders. Historians estimate that the First Crusade included between 5,000 and 10,000 mounted knights, between 25,000 and 50,000 foot soldiers and an equal number of noncombatants. The response was so great that the pope forbade women to go without their husbands and barred the elderly or the very young from taking up the cross.

**Motives.** People became crusaders for a variety of reasons. Some looked on the Crusades as a Christian obligation and believed that they were obeying God's will. Some

*Before departing on the Crusades, knights swore a solemn oath of fealty to God and sewed crosses onto their clothing to symbolize their mission.*

hoped to gain wealth or land and improve their status in life. Others dreamed of adventure or an opportunity to escape from the hardship of their lives as peasants. Still others went as penance for their sins or in hopes of achieving salvation.

The pope had his own motives, hoping to extend his influence over the Eastern Orthodox Church, while sending quarrelsome feudal nobles to fight their wars in a distant land. To encourage nobles to go on the Crusades, the pope promised that the Church would protect their property while they were away. He also excused them from some taxes

---

[6]Urban's speech at Clermont, as reported by Robert the Monk, in *Readings in European History*, Vol. 1, ed. J. H. Robinson (New York: Ginn, 1904), p. 314.

and forgave their debts. To many of these nobles, the chance to fight for the glory of God—combined with the lure of winning kingdoms in the Holy Land—was enough to overcome all hesitation.

**Peter the Hermit.** Since there was far more enthusiasm than organizational planning at the time of the First Crusade, certain unforeseen and tragic events occurred. One of the saddest of these resulted from the religious zeal of Peter the Hermit, a monk from Amiens in France. While the French nobles were still assembling their forces, Peter rode about the countryside recruiting peasants and poor townspeople as Crusaders. After assembling over 30,000 volunteers, Peter refused to wait for the nobles and set forth to the Holy Land by an overland route through eastern Europe to Constantinople.

As these peasant Crusaders passed through the Rhineland, they massacred the Jews whom they encountered and burned their homes. Local rulers promised to protect the Jews living in their lands, but more often than not they ignored their promises. As a result, thousands of Jews were slaughtered.

By the time the straggling peasant mobs reached present-day Bulgaria, they were so desperate for food that they decided that the Christian Bulgars were in fact infidels and their grain could be appropriated. In response, the enraged Bulgars slipped into the Crusader camps at night and murdered many of the peasants. When the remnants of this peasant army reached Constantinople, the emperor Alexius Comnenus I commanded that they be transported across the Bosporus as quickly as possible. Once landed in Asia Minor, they were at the mercy of the Turks who attacked them; those who were not massacred were sold into slavery.

**Departure.** Several months after this disaster, the second contingent of Crusaders, made up of knights and soldiers under the command of nobles such as Godfrey of Bouillon, his brother Baldwin, and Raymond of Toulouse began to reach Constantinople by the same overland route. Unlike Peter's motley followers, these were organized armies. As each leader arrived in the Byzantine capital, the emperor Alexius exacted a promise that if the Crusaders captured a city the Turks had seized from the Byzantine Empire, the city would be returned to Byzantine control. In exchange for these promises, the emperor agreed to supply the Crusaders with ships, guides, money, and provisions for the march to Jerusalem.

The first city the Crusaders reached was Nicaea, about 50 miles southeast of Constantinople. They began their siege only to awake one morning and find the Byzantine flag flying from the ramparts. Alexius had secretly negotiated with the defenders of Nicaea to surrender the city to the Byzantines. William of Tyre reported the Crusaders' anger at this deception.

● ● ●To the commanders the monarch [Alexius] sent immense gifts in the hope of gaining their good will. Moreover, he

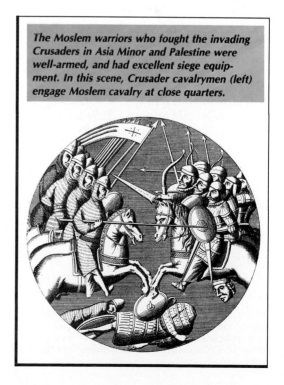

The Moslem warriors who fought the invading Crusaders in Asia Minor and Palestine were well-armed, and had excellent siege equipment. In this scene, Crusader cavalrymen (left) engage Moslem cavalry at close quarters.

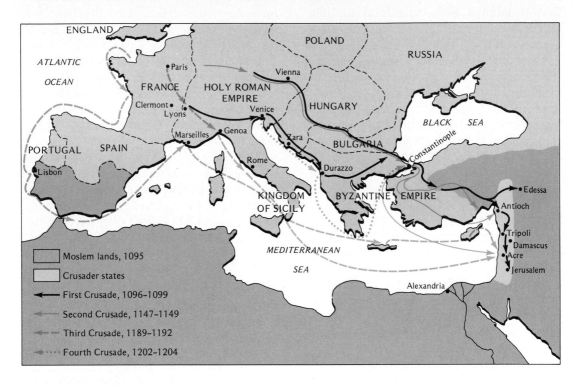

thanked them heartily, both by dispatches and verbal messages, for their honorable service and the great increase that had come to the empire through their efforts.

But the people and the men of second rank were greatly incensed. They too had worked valiantly in the siege of the city and had expected to repair the loss of their own property by the spoils taken from the prisoners and the rich store of goods found in the city itself. They now saw that their labors were not to receive a satisfactory reward.[7]

After a difficult, bloody march through Asia Minor, the Crusaders laid siege to Antioch,

in northern Syria. Betrayed from within, the city fell to the Crusaders, but the Crusaders in turn were soon besieged by a Turkish army. One Crusader, Stephen of Blois, escaped from Antioch and headed for Constantinople. En route, he met Alexius, who was moving southward with an army to attack Antioch. Informed that the Crusaders' cause appeared to be hopeless, Alexius returned to Constantinople. Ever afterward, the Crusaders considered that Alexius had betrayed them.

But the cause was not lost. According to tradition, although exhausted by disease and lack of food, the Crusaders received what they considered to be divine aid. A peasant soldier named Peter Bartholomew had a vision which told him to dig beneath the wall of a church in Antioch. There, Peter found a rusty lance that had supposedly been used by the Roman soldier who stabbed Jesus while he was nailed to the cross. The discovery of

---

[7]William (Guilelmas), archbishop of Tyre, *A History of the Deeds Done Beyond the Sea*, trans. E. A. Babcock and A. C. Krey, ed. A. P. Evans (New York: Columbia University Press, 1943), p. 197.

the lance inspired the Crusaders to return to the battle, and the next day they routed the Turkish army outside the walls of Antioch. From Syria, they moved south and made plans to attack Jerusalem.

***Capture of Jerusalem.*** The Crusaders reached Jerusalem in the spring of 1099 and laid siege to the city. On July 5, 1099, Godfrey of Bouillon and his soldiers broke through the walls and entered the holy city. A terrible massacre ensued. Thousands of Moslems and Jews were killed. So, too, were Christians who lived in the city and were dressed in eastern clothing. Contemporary accounts tell of the Crusaders riding in blood up to their knees. The massacre in Jerusalem was repeated elsewhere as the Crusaders extended their control over Syria and Palestine.

The majority of the Crusaders had left their homes to free the Holy Land. Now, after almost four years of bloody campaigning and with victory in their grasp, most wanted to return home. But their successes had left them with a strip of land stretching over 500 miles along the eastern Mediterranean coast and no means of protecting it from the surrounding Moslems. To strengthen their control over this territory, they divided it into four states: Godfrey of Bouillon was named king of the Latin Kingdom of Jerusalem, which he and his successors ruled until 1187; Baldwin of Lorraine was given charge of the County of Edessa; Bohemond of Italy was made head of the Principality of Antioch; and Raymond of Toulouse was given authority over the County of Tripoli.

*The Church of the Holy Sepulcher was first built by Constantine to mark the place where Jesus was crucified, and was one of the holy sites that the Crusaders were fighting to control. After they captured Jerusalem, the Crusaders rebuilt the church.*

Since the Church had sponsored the Crusades and had the most effective and far-reaching organization in Europe, the pope assumed responsibility for encouraging nobles and peasants to garrison the Christian strongholds in the Middle East. In each of the Crusader states, they built fortified castles, the remains of which can still be seen at Acre, Sidon, and Tripoli.

In time, the Crusaders who remained in the Holy Land came to respect and develop better relationships with the Moslems of the region. Many adopted local customs in clothing and food, sought help from Moslem physicians, and even married Moslem women. Fulk of Chartres, who took part in the First Crusade and remained in the Holy Land, wrote:

• • • *We men of the West have become Orientals. He who was a Roman or a Frank is now a Galilean or Palestinian. He who was from Rheims or Chartres is now a Tyrian or Antiochian. We have already forgotten the places of our birth; to most they are either unknown or unheeded. Some possess already their own houses and servants as if they had inherited them from ancestors; others have already married, and not, indeed, a woman*

*of their own country, but a Syrian or an Armenian, sometimes even a baptized Saracen.*[8]

## RELIGIOUS-MILITARY ORDERS

To help move pilgrims to and from the Holy Land and to maintain Christian troops there, the Crusaders founded three religious-military orders that would later influence events in Europe.

About 1118, a group of knights stationed in Jerusalem organized the *Knights of the Temple.* They chose this name because their headquarters was on the site of the ancient Temple of Solomon. The knights took vows of poverty, chastity, and obedience and took on the responsibility of helping pilgrims. In time, the Templars became so wealthy and powerful that they ignored their original purpose. By the 13th century, for example, the Templars served as a large-scale banking organization.

A second order, the *Knights of Saint John,* or Hospitalers, had been founded about 1083 in the Benedictine abbey at Amalfi in Italy. The original purpose of this order was to provide shelter and food (hospitality) for pilgrims to the Holy Land. In 1201, the Hospitalers expanded their activities to include fighting the Moslems in the Holy Land. After the last Crusader stronghold at Acre fell to the Moslems in 1291, the Hospitalers moved their headquarters from Palestine to Cyprus, Rhodes, and then Malta. Like the Templars, they also became wealthy and entered into power struggles with secular rulers.

A third order, the *Order of Saint Mary of the Teutons,* or Teutonic Knights, was organized in 1127 in Jerusalem by Crusaders from Germany. It later moved to Acre after Jerusalem fell to the Moslems in 1187. Although originally founded as a charitable order, it became involved in military and

---

[8]Quoted in D. C. Munro, "Christian and Infidel in the Holy Land," in *Readings in Medieval History,* ed. Hutton Webster (New York: Crofts, 1946), p. 284.

The Crusaders built fortified castles in sites throughout the Middle East. This is the Castle of the Knights in Syria, which the Hospitalers occupied until 1271.

political ventures. In the 13th century, the Teutonic Knights embarked on crusades against the pagan peoples in the Baltic region. They conquered the eastern Baltic coast as far north as the Gulf of Finland.

### SECOND CRUSADE (1147-1149)

The Crusader states were plagued by rivalry and disunity. They were never more than Christian outposts in an overwhelmingly Moslem Middle East. Once the initial shock of the invasion from the West wore off, the Moslems set out to drive the Crusaders into the sea. Their first victory was the recapture of Edessa in 1144. In response, Pope Eugenius III (1145-1153) ordered Bernard of Clairvaux to call a Second Crusade aimed at the reconquest of Edessa. Bernard spoke to a large group of knights in 1146 and offered the following benefits to volunteers:

● ● ● [W]e decree that their wives and their sons, their goods also and their possessions, shall remain under protection of Holy Church. . . .

Moreover, all they that are burdened by debt and have, with pure heart, undertaken so holy a journey need not pay the interest past due. . . .

Forgiveness of sins and absolution we grant . . . so that he who has devoutly undertaken so holy a journey and finished it or died there shall obtain absolution for all his sins. . . . [9]

---

[9]Quoted in Otto of Freising, *The Deeds of Frederick Barbarossa*, trans. C. C. Mierow and Richard Emery (New York: Columbia University Press, 1953), pp. 72-73.

King Louis VII of France and the Holy Roman Emperor Conrad III responded to the call for the Second Crusade, and both raised large armies. The two monarchs first considered attacking Constantinople but then settled on attacking Damascus. The siege failed, and both Louis and Conrad returned to Europe without ever visiting Jerusalem. The Second Crusade did not achieve its original goal, and Edessa remained in Moslem hands.

### SALADIN

In the next decades, the Moslems found a courageous and gifted leader in Saladin, who embodied the virtues they most admired. Saladin conquered Iraq, Syria, and Egypt, and thus his armies surrounded the Crusader states on three sides. In 1185, he declared his intention to lead a holy war to reclaim Jerusalem from the infidel Christians. Two years later he took advantage of quarrels among the Crusaders to invade the Latin Kingdom of Jerusalem. Saladin defeated the main Crusader army, capturing the king, Guy of Lusignan, and many of his nobles. Many of the Crusader strongholds, including Jerusalem, then fell to the Moslems without a struggle. Saladin's conquest of Jerusalem led a Moslem chronicler to write:

● ● ● *THE DAY OF CONQUEST, 17 RAJAB. By a striking coincidence, the date of the conquest of Jerusalem was the anniversary of the Prophet's ascension to heaven. Great joy reigned for the brilliant victory won, and words of prayer and invocation to God were on every tongue.*[10]

### THIRD CRUSADE (1189-1192)

The loss of Jerusalem to the Moslems left Christians holding only the port of Tyre. However the disaster inspired the three most powerful rulers in Europe—Frederick Barbarossa of the Holy Roman Empire, Philip Augustus of France, and Richard the Lion-Hearted of England—to join together for the Third Crusade. With the encouragement of Pope Innocent III, Richard and Philip Augustus levied new taxes on their subjects to finance the crusade. These taxes came to be called the *Saladin tithe* and set a precedent for the levying of other taxes.

Frederick Barbarossa marched his followers overland, through Hungary and the Byzantine Empire. He drowned in a river in Asia Minor, and most of his army returned home. Philip Augustus and Richard met in Sicily on their way to the Holy Land. There, they quarreled bitterly before embarking. Once in Palestine, they again argued, and Philip Augustus decided to return to France to pursue his own ambitious plans at home.

Richard stayed on to fight Saladin alone. Richard's role on the Third Crusade captured the imagination of many people, and a French admirer described him as follows:

● ● ● *He had the courage of Hector, the magnanimity of Achilles, and was equal to Alexander and not inferior to Roland in valor; nay, he outshone many illustrious characters of our own times. The liberality of a Titus was his, and, which is so rarely found in a soldier, he was gifted with the eloquence of Nestor and the prudence of Ulysses; and he showed himself preeminent in the conclusion and transaction of business, as one whose knowledge was not without active goodwill to aid it, nor his goodwill wanting knowledge.*[11]

Richard laid siege to Acre, the most important port in Palestine, and took it 21 months later. Yet Richard could not recapture Jerusalem, and in 1192 he and Saladin agreed to a treaty which guaranteed Christian pilgrims free access to the city. The Third Crusade accomplished little and highlighted the rivalries that divided the strongest Chris-

---

[10]Quoted in Francesco Gabrieli, *Arab Historians of the Crusades* (Los Angeles: University of California Press, 1969), p. 160.

[11]Richard de Templo, *Itinerarium Regis Ricardi*, Book 2, ch. 5, in *Readings in Medieval and Modern History*, ed. Webster, pp. 100-101.

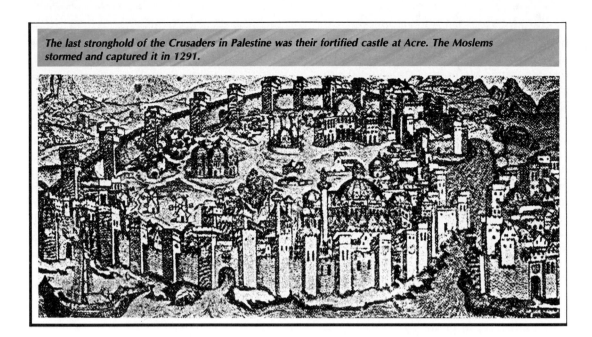

tian rulers in Europe. On his journey back to England, Richard was taken prisoner by Leopold, duke of Austria, whom Richard had insulted during the siege of Acre. Leopold held Richard captive until the English paid a huge ransom for his release.

### FOURTH CRUSADE (1202-1204)

The failure of the Third Crusade meant that Jerusalem remained in Moslem hands. Early in the 13th century, Pope Innocent III called for a new crusade to regain the Holy Land. Several thousand French knights and armed men responded to the call and assembled in Venice to embark for the Holy Land. However, the Crusaders did not have money to pay for their passage. The *doge*, or ruler of Venice, told the Crusaders that they could pay for their transportation by capturing the city of Zara, a trade rival of the Venetians located on the eastern Adriatic. The Crusaders took the city but then found themselves in deep trouble with the pope because Zara was a Catholic city.

In a confused series of events, the Crusaders became involved in a power struggle among the various claimants to the Byzantine throne. Urged on by the Venetians, they then attacked Constantinople, which fell after fierce fighting. Constantinople had never fallen before, and the booty was immense. A contemporary described the looting of the Byzantine capital by the Christian crusaders.

● ● ● *That [booty] which was brought to the churches was divided, in equal parts, between the Franks and the Venetians, according to the sworn covenant. And you must know further that the pilgrims, after the division had been made, paid out of their share fifty thousand marks of silver to the Venetians, and then divided at least one hundred thousand marks between themselves, among their own people.*[12]

In spite of these prizes, the attack of Constantinople in 1204 was a major disaster for all concerned. The Latin Kingdom of Constantinople lasted only until 1261, when the

---

[12]Geoffroy de Villehardouin, *La conquette de Constantinople*, chap. 46, in *Readings in Medieval and Modern History*, ed. Webster, pp. 116-117.

Byzantines regained control of Constantinople, but the Byzantine Empire was unable to recover its former wealth and power. Further weakened by internal struggles, the Byzantines later succumbed to the Ottoman Turks in 1453.

The Crusader attack on Constantinople further embittered relations between the Latin and Greek churches. Although the pope condemned the attack, he replaced the Greek orthodox clergy of Constantinople with priests loyal to the Roman Catholic tradition. As long as Latin rule lasted, the orthodox church was persecuted.

### LATER CRUSADES

The dream of freeing the Holy Land persisted throughout much of the 13th century, but after the shocking events of the Fourth Crusade, there was little interest in a new crusade. In 1212, a 12-year-old French farm boy, Stephen of Cloyes, had a vision urging him to organize a crusade of children to rescue the Holy Land. Stephen's preaching inspired thousands of French children to leave home and travel to Marseilles. Many believed that the waters of the Mediterranean would part so that they could walk to the Holy Land. Thousands of German children also made their way across the Alps to the ports of Genoa and Pisa in Italy. The Children's Crusade ended in tragedy when the children were taken by unscrupulous traders and sold into slavery in North Africa.

By 1217, several Italian city-states were in bitter competition to dominate the trade routes that were thriving on the commerce generated by the Crusades; therefore, they promoted the Fifth Crusade. This crusade adopted the strategy of invading Egypt, the richest and strongest Moslem state. After landing in Egypt, the Crusaders made little progress and were forced to return to Europe in 1221.

In 1228, Emperor Frederick II undertook the Sixth Crusade. Frederick, who knew and respected Moslem culture, decided to try negotiation instead of war. He visited Egypt and through diplomacy won privileges for Christian pilgrims in Jerusalem, Bethlehem, and Nazareth. He himself controlled these holy cities until 1244, when a new Moslem dynasty retook the cities.

In 1248, the 25-year-old king of France, Louis IX, undertook the leadership of the Seventh Crusade, but his religious fervor was not shared by his fellow monarchs. He gained control of Damietta (now Dumyat) in Egypt, at the mouth of the Nile River, but disease and famine forced him to surrender his army in 1254. The Moslems took Louis captive and held him for ransom. After the ransom was paid, Louis returned to France. In 1270, he again attempted to lead a crusade to Tunis, but he died before reaching his goal.

*The Street of the Knights in Rhodes. After losing Jerusalem and Acre, the Knights Hospitalers moved to Rhodes. From their stronghold on this island, they challenged Turkish control of Mediterranean sea routes.*

No more crusades were organized to the Holy Land. In 1291, the Moslems captured Acre, the last Christian stronghold. After 200 years of warfare and countless deaths, the Holy Land remained in Moslem control.

### RESULTS OF THE CRUSADES

While the Crusades failed in their original purpose of bringing the Holy Land under Christian control, they had far-reaching consequences for western Europe. First, by introducing thousands of Europeans to the larger world beyond their borders, the Crusades shattered the parochialism of medieval Europe.

Second, they greatly increased trade between Europe and the eastern Mediterranean. Crusading knights were awestruck at the more advanced civilizations of the Byzantine and Moslem worlds, and soon developed a desire to enjoy the luxuries of the East. As a result, silks, perfumes, rugs, jewelry, fruits, and spices once again moved from the eastern Mediterranean into Europe, as they had under the Roman Empire. Third, the Crusades increased the pace of economic changes that were already underway. For example, the increase in commerce heightened the need for new systems of money, banking, and credit to replace the barter economy that had emerged in most of western Europe after the fall of Rome.

Fourth, the need to move Crusaders and pilgrims back and forth across the Mediterranean spurred the growth of shipping and enabled several ports in Italy, particularly Venice, Genoa, and Pisa, to become powerful and wealthy city-states. Finally, the taste for luxuries, particularly the spices of the East, and the new knowledge of navigation would eventually lead to the exploration of Africa, Asia, and the New World.

Even before the Crusades, Europeans had begun to acquire the learning of the Byzantine and Islamic worlds. The knowledge continued to filter into Europe in the 200 years of the Crusades, but the process went on largely independent of the Crusades. As a result, not only Moslem learning in mathematics, philosophy, science, and medicine, but also Middle Eastern technologies such as manufacturing and dying cloth were transferred to Europe.

Although the Crusades brought many benefits to the peoples of western Europe, they also resulted in a growing religious intolerance. Relations between Latin and Greek Christians, between Christians and Moslems, and between Christians and Jews all deteriorated in this period. Thousands of Moslems and Christians were massacred in the two centuries of struggle for control of the Holy Land. The greatest tragedy was the persecution of Jews in Europe. When organized mobs of Christians issued ultimatums to Jews to convert or die, whole communities of Jews chose to remain loyal to their faith and were slaughtered. During this period, too, laws were passed forcing Jews to wear yellow patches on their clothes and live apart from Christians. Although some Christians protested, these attacks on Jews persisted.

## SUMMARY

*During the Middle Ages, the Roman Catholic Church had enormous power and influence. Its power rested not only on its control of religious life but also on its secular role. During this period, thousands of devout Christians came together to live in religious communities called monasteries. The most influential monastic rule was established by Saint Benedict. New monastic orders continued to be founded, especially when abuses in the older orders led to calls for reform. In the 13th century, two non-monastic orders, the Dominicans and the Franciscans, were founded to work and live among the people.*

*Late in the 11th century, the Church launched the Crusades to rescue the Holy Land from the Turks. The Crusades lasted for two centuries. Although in the end the Moslems regained possession of the Holy Land, the Crusades had far-reaching effects on western Europe.*

## QUESTIONS

1 Compare the role of the Church in the early Middle Ages to that of the Roman emperor at the time of Augustus. How were they similar? How were they different?

2 Why has the Middle Ages often been called the "age of faith"?

3 What contributions did monasteries make to medieval civilization?

4 Why was the reform movement in the Church so necessary in the 10th and 11th centuries?

5 What motivated people to go on the Crusades? How was the Fourth Crusade different from the earlier Crusades? Describe a cause that might motivate people today to join a crusade.

6 Why are the Crusades often called a "successful failure"?

## BIBLIOGRAPHY

### Which books might describe the growth of monasteries?

DUBY, GEORGES. *The Knight, the Lady and the Priest.* Translated by Barbara Bray. New York: Pantheon Books, 1983. *A fascinating survey of how the laws created by the Church during the Middle Ages influenced society and still effect our lives today. Contemporary chronicles explain the status of women in medieval times and the appeal of convents and monasteries.*

KNOWLES, DAVID. *Saints and Scholars.* Cambridge University Press, 1962. *A portrayal of monastic life from the 6th to 16th centuries. Examines outstanding spiritual leaders, writers, artists, and politicians; provides insights into the medieval mind.*

OAKLEY, FRANCIS. *The Medieval Experience.* New York: Scribner's, 1974. *A review of the medieval world that shows how much the Church dominated society. Provides insights into the important changes in religion, economy, and politics that occurred during this long period.*

PRAWER, JOSHUA. *The World of the Crusaders.* New York: Quadrangle Books, 1972. *An examination of this period through the eyes of the Crusaders, Byzantines, and Jews. Details the chivalry as well as the barbarism of the age; the military strategies and weapons used; and the culture of the Crusaders' world.*

THEIS, DAN. *The Crescent and the Cross.* New York: Thomas Nelson, 1978. *An account of the struggle for the possession of the Holy Land from the Crusades to today. Examines the careers of medieval heroes such as Bohemond, Raymond of Toulouse, Richard the Lion-Hearted, and Frederick Barbarossa.*

**6**

*The work of the priest is to pray to God,*
*And of the knight to do justice.*
*The farm worker finds bread for them.*
*One toils in the fields, one prays, and one defends.*
*In the fields, in the town, in the church,*
*These three help each other*
*Through their skills, in a nicely regulated scheme.*
ANONYMOUS

# *Medieval Society*

A 13th century poet wrote the lines quoted above to describe the structure of medieval society. In these few lines, he captures an essential element of medieval life: everyone had a well-defined place in society that carried with it certain duties and responsibilities. This social order did not suddenly emerge; rather, it evolved slowly during the early Middle Ages and, once established, supported the flowering of medieval civilization.

The collapse of Rome in the 5th century had profound effects on European life. Without Roman legions to guard the boundaries of the empire, without the Roman legal system to ensure justice, and without the Roman administrative system to maintain the roads and water supplies, life became much more precarious. Trade and the money economy declined. The only food available was what could be grown or hunted locally. Towns and cities decayed as people abandoned them to seek the protection offered by monasteries or large landholders.

For most people, life became much poorer as the economy of trade and commerce gave way in the early Middle Ages to an economy of small, self-sufficient agricultural units.

Perhaps most importantly, the disappearance of the Roman state created a power vacuum which other forces moved to fill. As you read in the last chapter, one of these forces was the Church. In the early Middle Ages, its power and influence grew enormously. So, too, did the power and influence of the large landowners who developed ways to protect their holdings.

**FEUDALISM** During the centuries of chaos and invasions that followed the collapse of Rome, a new social, economic, and political system slowly emerged that we know today as **feudalism** (from the latin *feudum*, meaning "estate"). As you will read, feudalism was the way of life that governed medieval Europe for hundreds of years. At the center of feudalism were the ties of loyalty that bound local lords to a king. However, feudalism was not a uniform system, and it did not develop in the same way in all parts of Europe.

### ORIGINS OF FEUDALISM

Feudalism grew out of both Roman and German customs. It developed first in France and later emerged in other parts of Europe.

As Rome's power crumbled in the provinces, local nobles acquired vast tracts of land, parts of which they granted to others in exchange for help in defending the land. The granting of land to individuals in exchange for military service would become an essential element in the feudal system.

Feudalism also had its roots in German customs. Among the German tribes, individual warriors swore an oath of loyalty to a chief, and in return, the chief supplied them with food, armor, and weapons. The personal ties between warriors and their chief were another feature of the feudal system.

As the German rulers established their kingdoms in western Europe, these elements of feudalism continued to develop. In the 8th century, the use of the stirrup enabled knights, or mounted warriors, to wear armor while wielding larger weapons. As you read in Chapter 15, the Merovingian mayor of the palace, Charles Martel, saw the need for well-trained and well-armed warriors, so he expanded the practice of granting land in exchange for military service. During the centuries of invasions that followed the collapse of the Carolingian Empire in the 9th century, feudalism emerged as the basic system of government in western Europe.

### LORDS AND VASSALS

Feudalism was based on a system of unwritten rules between lords and **vassals** (from the Celtic *vassus*, meaning "servant"). In theory, everyone in medieval society had a lord and owed him something, and the feudal order was like a pyramid. At the highest point stood the king or emperor who was regarded as the vassal of God. Beneath him were the great nobles who controlled extensive holdings. Next came the lesser nobles, vassals of greater nobles, and so on down to the lowest knights, each of whom was a vassal of the noble who granted him land. The grantor of land was known as the *liege lord* of the person to whom he granted land. As feudalism developed, it became a complex interrelationship of privileges and responsibilities. Gradually, too, a hierarchy of titles of nobility evolved. The greatest nobles were called *dukes* (from the Latin *dux*, meaning "leader"). Below dukes were ranks such as *marquis*, *count* (called "earls" in England), *viscount*, and *baron*.

The mutual exchange of promises between a lord and his vassal was sanctified by a solemn ritual known as *investiture*, in which the vassal knelt before his lord and placed both hands between the lord's hands. He then pledged homage and agreed to obey the lord's commands in words such as these:

• • • *I will always be a faithful vassal to thee and to thy successors . . . and I will defend thee . . . and all your men and their possessions against all malefactors and invaders . . . and I will give to thee power over all the castles and manors . . . whenever they shall be claimed by thee or by thy successors.*[1]

In return for his vassal's homage, the liege lord agreed to provide his vassal with a **fief**, or estate; help protect him; hear his complaints in open courts; and ensure that he and his dependents received justice. During the investiture ceremony, the lord gave his vassal a charter, or deed, and a blade of grass or a clump of earth as symbol of the fief.

Fiefs could vary in size from a small parcel of land to a vast estate. The vassal had complete control over the land and all the houses, villages, and people on the land. As a feudal lord, he could wage war, coin money, collect tolls, make alliances, or engage in any other activity that he was strong enough to achieve, as long as he supported his liege lord with the required military assistance when called upon to do so. He could pass his fief on to his heirs, but in theory, at least, the liege lord still owned the land.

The system of mutual obligations re-

---

[1]Quoted in Hutton Webster, ed., *Historical Selections* (Boston: Heath, 1969), pp. 468-9.

quired a vassal to perform certain services for his lord in return for his fief, but feudal obligations varied greatly from region to region. In northern France, for example, a vassal was expected to serve for 40 days and nights each year on military campaigns or on garrison duty at the castle of his lord. During this time, he might also help his lord hold court and dispense justice. A vassal could refuse to serve longer than the fixed time unless he was compensated in some way. In the late Middle Ages, when money became more common, knights were permitted to pay "shield money" (*scutage*) in place of performing military service. Such payments became an important source of revenue to great lords and permitted them to hire mercenaries rather than depending on their vassals.

The vassal was also obliged to contribute to certain expenses of his lord, such as the knighting of the lord's eldest son or the wedding of his eldest daughter. The vassal had to contribute to the ransom that might be demanded by an enemy who captured his lord.

A liege lord could seize a vassal's fief if the latter failed to fulfill his obligations or died without heirs. By the same token, a vassal was absolved of all obligations to his lord if the lord tried to kill him, enslave him, steal his property, or seduce his wife.

### FEUDAL WARFARE

Feudalism emerged in western Europe during a time of invasion. It developed in part as a means of providing security and protection. The wealth and power of feudal nobles was derived from the ownership of land, and even after the invasions abated, feudal nobles frequently fought with one another over land, family honor, and other rights. As a result, warfare was the most widespread activity of the feudal nobility.

In the early Middle Ages, knights wore padded leather or linen coats and helmets. Later, small iron rings were sewn to the padding to prevent weapons from cutting through

The flexible chain mail that protected medieval knights could be difficult to remove as well as uncomfortable to wear.

the material. Still later, flexible chain mail was developed to protect the body against blows and cuts. Ultimately, every knight wore armor and frequently used specially designed armor to protect his horse. Armor was made of thin sheets of steel joined in such a way that the knight was covered from head to toe but could still walk, mount a horse, and ride. Since a knight needed to distinguish between friend and foe, he carried a shield inscribed with a symbol or design that came to be called his "coat of arms." A noble family's coat of arms was handed down from generation to generation, and this use of distinctive family symbols became known as "heraldry."

Each knight was armed with a lance, which he used to unhorse an enemy; a two-edged sword, which hung from a belt around his waist; a dagger tucked into his belt; and a heavy club, mace, or battle ax. The armor and weapons carried by a knight could weigh as much as 100 pounds.

In the 11th century, the Church took steps to try to reduce feudal warfare. It issued two pronouncements: the "Peace of God" and the "Truce of God." In the "Peace of God," the Church announced that the sacraments would be withheld from anyone who pillaged churches, monasteries, and other holy places. The sacraments were also denied to those who killed women, children, or elderly people not involved in combat.

The "Truce of God" forbade fighting between sunset of any Wednesday evening and sunrise of the following Monday morning, the period of time that Christians believed Jesus had suffered and died on the cross. The truce was also applied to all holy seasons, such as Advent, the four weeks before Christmas, and Lent, the seven weeks before Easter. While these truces were frequently ignored, any knight found to be violating them faced the threat of excommunication.

In the late Middle Ages, feudal warfare did decline due in part to these efforts of the Church and in part to the rise of powerful medieval monarchs who made great efforts to end the constant fighting among their vassals.

### CASTLES

During the early Middle Ages, local lords designed their houses for defense. These fortified houses came to be called "castles" (from the Latin *castellum*, meaning "small military camp"). At first, these fortified houses were made of wood and surrounded by thick wooden walls. Later, feudal lords began to build stone castles on hilltops, in bends of rivers, and at other defensible positions. A castle often was surrounded by a *moat*, or wide, deep ditch that could be filled with water. A bridge that could be raised or lowered gave the only access to the castle.

In time, castles were made quite large; they were designed to house the lord, his household, and, in an emergency, the peasants who lived in the village near the castle walls. Just inside the castle walls was the central court-yard. In peacetime and when the weather was good, the lord held his court in the court-yard. The courtyard also housed the work-shops and kitchen necessary to maintain the castle's armaments and feed its defenders. In addition, the castle had stables for horses, storehouses for food and weapons, and dungeons for prisoners. Each castle kept an ample supply of food and water on hand, so that the inhabitants could survive a siege lasting several weeks or even months.

The lord of the castle and his family lived in the innermost defensible structure, a stone tower called the keep or donjon. But the most frequently used room of the castle was the great hall, which was large enough to house all the knights who might be called to defend the castle. There, the lord and his guests drank, sang, played chess or backgammon, and were entertained by wandering minstrels or jesters.

The nobles ate fish, fowl, wild game, and white bread, accompanied by locally produced wines. The peasants ate porridge, cabbage, turnips, and dark bread, which they washed down with home-brewed beer or ale. Meat was a rarity in the peasants' diet, but nobles enjoyed it more regularly since they were free to hunt the game on their preserves. One medieval cookbook describes how to prepare a tasty meat pastry.

● ● ● *Take a pheasant, a hare, a capon, two partridges, two pigeons and two conies; chop them up, take out as many bones as you can, and add the livers and meats, two kidneys of sheep, force meat into balls with eggs, pickled mushrooms, salt, pepper, spice, vinegar. Boil the bones in a pot to make a good broth; put the meat into a crust of good paste, made craftly into the likeness of a bird's body; pour in the broth, close it up and bake well. Serve it with the head of one of the birds at one end, and the tail at the other, and divers of his long feathers set cunningly all about him.*[2]

---

[2]Quoted in Gertrude Hartman, *Medieval Days and Ways* (New York: Macmillan, 1937), pp. 43-4.

*Medieval castles were designed primarily as fortresses, and offered few amenities to their inhabitants.*

The great hall had one or more large fireplaces, but the castle was still damp and drafty. Food was prepared in a separate building and often arrived cold or half cooked. By today's standards, a castle was an unpleasant place in which to live. Besides the cold and drafts, it had only primitive sanitation facilities and little light.

*EDUCATION*

During the early Middle Ages, there was little formal education. Most children learned at home the skills they needed to survive. A few noble children might attend a monastery school where they would learn Christian duties and perhaps be taught to read and write: Charlemagne, you will recall, brought the scholar Alcuin to Aachen to teach his children and those of the nobles at his court. For much of the medieval period, however, education centered not on learning to read and write but on training for warfare.

**Training for Knighthood.** The sons of nobles were expected to become knights. Usually they were sent, at the age of seven, to another lord's castle for training. There, a young noble served as a page for the lord while the lady of the house taught him Christian values and the manners he must know —respect for women, as well as the arts of singing, dancing, and playing a musical instrument. She might also teach him to read, write, and do arithmetic. At the age of 14, the boy became a squire to the lord, serving him in the castle and on the battlefield, caring for his arms and armor, guarding prisoners, and taking on other noncombatant duties. During this time, the squire learned to handle various weapons and to ride well.

After successfully completing this long training at the age of 21, the squire became a knight. Before being knighted, the young man had to spend a night in a chapel praying for guidance. The next morning, he took the sacrament of Holy Communion, and then after this spiritual preparation, was knighted by his liege lord. In England, this ceremony was accomplished when the lord touched the would-be knight on the back of his neck with the broad side of a sword and declared, "In the name of God, Saint Michael and Saint George, I dub thee knight. Be gallant, be courteous, be loyal." The young knight's parents then provided a great feast to celebrate the occasion.

Young knights trained for real battle at jousts and tournaments. Jousts were mock battles involving two knights in armor riding

*In England, a lord performed the ceremony of knighting by touching the candidate on the back with his sword. Sometimes a soldier was knighted on the battlefield in recognition of his valor, as illustrated here.*

**107**

toward each other at full speed. Each attempted to knock the other from his horse. Tournaments involved teams of knights who engaged in mock fights with blunted lances. In peacetime, a lord and his knights also practiced their skills on horseback as they hunted wild game.

**Daughters of Nobles.** Like her brothers, the daughter of a noble learned to play the role expected of someone in her position. She learned to supervise the servants in the house, to do needlework, and to see that the household ran smoothly, which meant keeping track of food supplies and other necessities. Often, she knew some simple medicine and tended her own family as well as the people on the estate.

Throughout her life, a woman was legally subject first to her parents and then to the husband that her parents chose for her. Yet once she was married, a noble woman could often achieve a certain measure of responsibility and independence, for she was left in charge of her husband's estate whenever he was absent. As Christine de Pisan, an outstanding scholar and writer of this period, explained:

• • • *Because that knights, esquires and gentlemen go upon journeys and follow the wars, it beseemeth wives to be wise and of great governance and to see clear, in all that they do, for that most often they dwell at home without their husbands who are at court or in divers lands.*[3]

**The Code of Chivalry.** In the later Middle Ages, the lives of noblewomen improved with the development of the concepts of chivalry and romantic love. These ideas arose first in southern France during the 11th century and by the 14th century had spread throughout Europe. They were based on the code of conduct for knights known as "chivalry."

Chivalry was supposed to govern the behavior of knights; it blended Christian virtues with the conduct required of knights—bravery, loyalty, and courage. The correct behavior toward women was a focal point of chivalry. Under this code, women were idealized and placed on a pedestal. They were praised for their beauty, goodness, and other virtues. In reality, however, women's lives were filled with many hardships, from the dangers of frequent childbirth to those of disease and warfare.

Rules were drawn up describing the proper conduct of knights. Below is a selection of rules taken from a 12th-century work:

• • • *I. Marriage is no real excuse for not loving.*
*II. He who is not jealous cannot love.*
*III. No one can be bound by a double love.*
*IV. It is well known that love is always increasing or decreasing.*
*VIII. No one should be deprived of love without the very best reasons.*
*IX. No one can love unless he is impelled by the persuasion of love.*
*XIV. The easy attainment of love makes it of little value; difficulty of attainment makes it prized.*
*XV. Every lover regularly turns pale in the presence of his beloved.*
*XVI. When a lover suddenly catches sight of his beloved his heart palpitates.*
*XVII. A new love puts to flight an old one.*[4]

The behavior of knights often fell far short of the ideal, and there were customary remedies for such a case. A knight who failed to live by the code of chivalry could be publicly disgraced. His shield would be hung upside down in a public place; his armor stripped from him; his weapons broken; and he himself placed in a coffin and carried to a church, where a priest held a funeral service, declaring him "dead to honor."

---

[3]Christine de Pisan, *Le Livre des Trois Vertus* (ca. 1406), quoted in Eileen Power, *Medieval Women*, ed. M. M. Postan (Cambridge: Cambridge University Press, 1975), p. 43.

[4]Andreas Capellanus, "The Rules of Courtly Love," in J. B. Ross and M. M. McLaughlin, eds., *The Portable Medieval Reader* (New York: Viking Press, 1940), pp. 115-6.

**MANORIALISM**  Feudalism established the relationship between lords and vassals, but at most feudal nobles numbered only 10 percent of the population. Underlying and supporting the feudal order was the remaining 90 percent of the population made up of peasants who worked the land. They were essential to the economic system known as **manorialism** that emerged in the Middle Ages. Manorialism had its origins in the great estates acquired by Roman nobles in Gaul. During the Germanic invasions, smaller landowners often turned over their holdings to these nobles or to monasteries or churches in exchange for protection and a portion of the crops they raised. They thus became tenant farmers. In time, these estates became known as *manors* and developed as

*In the early Middle Ages, peasants were granted the use of farmland in return for their labor on the lord's estate. In time, peasants became bound to the land they worked.*

the centers of early medieval communities. Under the system of manorialism, the owner of the manor, agreed to protect the people living on the land in exchange for their work in the fields and other services.

During the early Middle Ages, the condition of the peasants who farmed the manor lands changed from what it had been in late Roman times. Instead of being tenant farmers who paid rent in crops and were free to come and go, they became *serfs*. As serfs, they and their descendants were bound to the land and to the service of the lord of the manor. Neither they nor their children could leave the manor. Besides serfs, there were two other kinds of peasants who worked on a manor: slaves who could be bought and sold; and *villeins* (from the Latin *villa*, meaning "farm") who were tenant farmers. Gradually, however, the distinctions among peasants became blurred, and the vast majority of European peasants were serfs.

*PLAN OF THE MANOR*

A manor consisted of the manor house, the peasant village, and the church plus fields, pastures, forests, and wastelands. The manor house, which belonged to the lord, was by far the largest building on the estate. In the early Middle Ages, it was usually a two-story building made of wood. By the late Middle Ages, many manor houses had been turned into castles. Some were well furnished and decorated with works of art.

A small manor might consist of 350 acres of land and perhaps 10 to 15 peasant families, while a larger manor might have 5000 acres and 50 families. The peasants' houses were irregularly arranged near the manor house, and were known as the village. They were small, one-room cottages built of packed earth with thatched roofs. Smoke from the fires used for heat and cooking escaped through a hole in the roof. The floors were of earth; the windows, if they existed, were unglazed; and the furniture consisted of perhaps a plank table, a few stools, and a bed.

*109*

The manor lands were used to sustain the lord and his family as well as all the people and animals on the manor. As the source of water, there was a well, a spring, or perhaps a stream dammed to form a pool. Forests provided wild game for the lord's table and trees for firewood. If there was a pond, fish would be stocked for the lord's pleasure. Open land was used as pasture for animals or was cultivated as orchards and vineyards.

All the arable land on a manor was divided into the lord's portion, called the *demesne*, and the peasants' portion. The peasants' land was divided by footpaths into small strips. By the 8th century, peasants were using a system of planting known as the "three-field system" in which each peasant had three strips of land. In the autumn, one strip was planted with wheat or rye; in the spring, the second strip was planted with oats or barley; the third strip was left fallow, or unplanted, each year. Some of the strips were in good soil and some in poor. Besides working their own strips, peasants had to work on the lord's demesne for at least three days a week and sometimes more during harvest time.

The peasants' tools—which included hoes, plows, scythes, and sickles—were primitive. Most were made by hand from pieces of wood, with iron placed along the cutting edge. Serfs did not use fertilizer and had few animals to use to plow or haul heavy loads. Because there was not enough surplus food to feed large animals such as horses or oxen, the manor tended to have only geese, sheep, or goats. The loss of a harvest to drought, insects, flood, or marauders spelled famine, disease, and death for people on the manor.

As you will read in Chapter 23, in the later Middle Ages, improvements in farming techniques and technology greatly increased output. As the heavy plow, the horse collar, horseshoes, and wind and water mills were introduced into western Europe, they helped peasants produce surpluses of food and supported a growing population. New lands were cleared and drained, creating even more agricultural output.

*LIFE ON THE MANOR*
During the early Middle Ages, the absence of trade meant that most manors had to be self-sufficient. The people on the manor produced not only all the food they consumed but also all the other goods they needed. If the harvest was good, they preserved the food so that they would have enough to eat until the next harvest. Some vegetables and fruits were stored in root cellars; others were pickled. Meat was smoked or salted. Wine and beer were made from the fruits and grains. Bread, the mainstay of the peasant's diet, was baked in the oven of the manor house.

Peasants made all the clothing for themselves, their lord, and his family. They raised sheep for wool and planted flax, which was used to make linen. Linsey-woolsey, a coarse cloth made from linen and wool, was the basic clothing fabric. Women and children were kept busy spinning thread or yarn on small hand bobbins and weaving cloth. Peasants also made leather shoes and harnesses, and fashioned the tools they needed. While some serfs labored on the manor lands, others became skilled workers such as carpenters, leather workers, blacksmiths, or bakers. During the late Middle Ages, as the economic life of Europe was quickening and towns were reviving, manors no longer had to be self-sufficient. Townspeople produced many specialized goods and exchanged them for food grown on the manor.

In the early medieval period, the constant struggle to grow enough food took much of the peasants' time and energy. Still, there were many occasions to celebrate, including births and weddings, saint days, and other holy occasions. On important holy days, pageants and feasts were held at the manor house. Peasants joined in wrestling matches, competed in archery contests, watched dog fights, danced, and gossiped. Wandering poets moved from manor to manor and earned their

*The lord of the manor dispensed justice to the peasants who lived under his protection. In this scene, the lord and a village priest look on as a culprit is tortured on a wheel.*

lodging and food by entertaining the people and spreading the news of the day. Occasionally, a pedlar passed through with strange wares from distant lands.

For much of the Middle Ages, the peasants' life was one of hardship. Peasants had to serve their lord, fighting at his side if he required. They faced harsh punishments if they were caught poaching his fish or game. They were forced to pay whatever fee he set to grind their grain in his mill and bake their bread in his oven. They could do nothing if the lord's huntsmen rode over their fields, destroying their crops. They faced the constant fear of warfare, disease, and starvation. In the 14th century, the English poet William Langland wrote "The Peasant's Life," in which he described these hardships.

*The needy are our neighbours, if we note*
  *rightly;*
*As prisoners in cells, or poor folk in hovels,*

*Charged with children and overcharged by*
  *landlords.*
*What they may spare in spinning they spend*
  *on rental,*
*On milk, or on meal to make porridge*
*To still the sobbing of the children at meal*
  *time.*
*Also they themselves suffer much hunger.*
*They have woe in winter time, and wake at*
  *midnight*
*To rise and to rock the cradle at the bedside,*
*To card and to comb, to darn clouts and to*
  *wash them,*
*To rub and to reel and to put rushes on paving.*
*The woe of these women who dwell in hovels*
*Is too sad to speak of or to say a rhyme.*[5]

### LORDS OF THE MANOR

For much of the Middle Ages, the lord's word

---

[5]William Langland, "The Peasant's Life," in *The Portable Medieval Reader*, ed. Ross and McLaughlin, p. 137.

was the law of the manor. He owned the water, forests, the mill, and the baking ovens, and he could charge his serfs what he pleased in the way of labor or crops for the use of these assets. When the lord's eldest daughter was to be married or his eldest son was to be knighted, he could charge extra levies, called "customary taxes," on the peasants to cover the expense of these ceremonies. The lord could demand payment to permit a peasant to marry someone from another village or exact a portion of the meager belongings of a peasant who died.

Although the lord enjoyed great power over his peasants, he also had responsibilities toward them. The lord was responsible for defending the manor and dispensing justice. He gave out punishments according to custom, and in theory all punishments had to be approved by the parish priest. A person accused of a crime could admit guilt or face a form of trial—"trial by fire" or "trial by water." In trial by fire, the accused person was required to grasp a red-hot piece of metal, to walk across a bed of hot coals, or face some other physical test. If the burned flesh healed, the accused was assumed to be innocent because God had protected him or her. In trial by water, the accused was thrown into a pool of water. A person who sank was judged innocent because the water "accepted" him or her, but a person who floated was judged guilty because the water rejected him or her. Those who were found guilty of lesser crimes were subjected to public humiliation such as flogging, dunking in a pond, or being put in the stocks or a pillory.

If the manor was very large, or if the lord owned several manors, he might appoint a steward to supervise his lands. The steward carried out the functions of the lord, collecting the fees due to him and judging disputes among peasants.

## GROWTH OF TOWNS

As you have read, the towns and cities of the Roman Empire declined during the early Middle Ages. Although cities continued to flourish in the Byzantine Empire and in the Islamic world, they virtually disappeared in western Europe. After the great invasions of the 9th and 10th centuries ended, towns and cities began to revive. The pace of the revival picked up during and after the Crusades.

By the later Middle Ages, conditions in Europe had changed from the uncertainties of earlier centuries. As feudal warfare declined, trade increased. In northern Italy, cities such as Venice, Genoa, and Pisa took the

*The fortification system of the medieval town of Carcassone in France. The outer walls of the town are lined with ditches, which are crossed by means of drawbridges. The round structure at bottom allows soldiers to obtain water from the town's river without exposing themselves to enemy fire.*

and bridges were repaired, allowing merchants to move their goods more easily. Towns grew up along the trade routes: Basel, Mainz, and Strasbourg were important trading centers along the Rhine River; Antwerp, Hamburg, Calais, and London developed as major port cities.

By the 11th century, towns began to form around some strongly fortified castles, or "burgs" (from the Latin *burgus*, meaning "fortified place"). The people who lived in these towns were called "burgers" in Germany, "the bourgeoisie" in France, and "burgesses" in England. Since the towns offered opportunities for advancement, many serfs escaped to them in search of jobs and freedom. According to custom, serfs who lived for a year and a day in a town became free, thus giving rise to the medieval saying, "Town air makes a man free." Other townspeople were former serfs who had bought their freedom, or resident merchants and artisans.

### PLAN OF THE TOWN

Most villages that grew up around a manor or castle were a collection of cottages. As some of these villages evolved into towns, homes were crowded into a small area because a lord usually limited the amount of land devoted to housing. As the population of a village increased, two changes took place: the village was enclosed by a wall for protection; and new houses, often two or three stories high, were built. While the walls provided protection, they also limited the size of the town and further increased the crowding. In time, the narrow paths between the houses of the village became the streets of the town. As multistory houses were built, it was common practice to project each new story out over the streets. In some towns, people living on opposite sides of a street could reach out their windows and touch one another.

The largest single building in the town was the church, and the largest open space was the marketplace, usually adjacent to the

lead in carrying goods from the eastern Mediterranean to western Europe. Other cities such as Antwerp, Bruges, Milan, and Florence prospered from the wool trade.

The renewed interest in travel and trade led to improvements in transportation; roads

church. Merchants and artisans built their shops close to the marketplace. The town's water supply usually came from a well, which was often located in the marketplace. Here, merchants, artisans, visitors, and others gathered to exchange news and gossip.

The fastest growing towns were those that were strategically located—perhaps at a river crossing, or at a site associated with a holy person—or boasted a school that could attract students from a wide area. Because of the overcrowding, newcomers were often forced to settle outside the town walls. When they eventually demanded protection, a new wall would be built to enclose the town, and a wide street would take the place of the old wall. Much later, in the 18th and 19th centuries, town walls were torn down and wide boulevards were built in their place.

### LIFE IN THE TOWNS

In the towns, the living space for each family was not much larger than the cottage of a peasant. Sanitary conditions were poor, and people simply threw their wastes into the streets. Disease spread rapidly in the overcrowded towns. So, too, did fire, which often destroyed many houses. Despite these disadvantages, more and more people settled in the towns. While some townspeople were merchants and artisans, many others were peasants who worked in the fields outside the town by day but lived inside the town walls at night.

Town life centered on the marketplace, where farmers exchanged their produce and traveling merchants set up booths to display their wares. Like the peasants, townspeople worked from dawn to dusk and usually went to bed at sunset. Only the rich could afford to buy candles to light their homes at night. On Sundays and holy days, people attended church services and enjoyed watching contests or other diversions.

Since few people could read, the life of a town was governed by symbols and sounds. Monks and priests kept track of time by means of marked candles, waterclocks, or sundials. They informed the people of the hour by tolling the church bell. The bell was also used to sound an alarm, mark deaths, and announce happy occasions. Merchants and artisans announced their wares by hanging signs with symbols of their goods over their shops. For example, a gilded boot signaled a shoemaker; a twisted pretzel symbolized a baker; an anvil marked a blacksmith. Street names came from the activities pursued there: the Shambles was the street where animals were slaughtered; the Spicery was the place where spices were sold; Goldsmiths Lane was the location of jewelers.

As towns grew in importance, town leaders gained power and could negotiate with the feudal lords who owned the towns. During the 12th century, nobles who went on the Crusades sometimes tried to raise money by levying extra taxes on the towns under their control. The merchants and artisans of these towns responded by demanding new charters guaranteeing them certain rights and privileges. In 1279, the earl of Chester granted a charter to the city of Chester, in England. Like other feudal lords, he had to promise certain rights to the townspeople:

• • • *Let it be known to all of you that I have given and conceded, and by this my present charter confirmed to all my citizens of Chester, their guild merchant, with all liberties and free customs which they have had in the aforesaid guild, best, most freely and most peacefully in the times of my predecessors.*[6]

With the growth of towns, the medieval landscape underwent a change. No longer were people scattered in isolated, self-sufficient communities. Instead, the commerce engendered by the towns greatly expanded their opportunities and supported the emerging late medieval culture (Chapter 23).

---

[6]Quoted in J. H. Robinson, ed., *Readings in European History*, vol. 1 (New York: Ginn, 1904), pp. 408-9.

## SUMMARY

*After the fall of Rome, urban and economic life decayed. After the centuries of chaos and disorder, a new political, social, and economic system emerged in which wealth, power, and social standing were derived from the ownership of land. Under feudalism, a lord gave his vassals land in return for specific duties. The main occupation of the medieval nobles was warfare. In the later Middle Ages, feudal warfare declined, and knights were supposed to conduct their lives according to the code of chivalry.*

*During the Middle Ages, the vast majority of people were peasants who lived on self-sufficient estates called manors. In return for protection, the lord of the manor exacted labor and a share of the crops from those who lived on the manor. Gradually, most of these peasants became serfs, and neither they nor their descendants could legally leave the manor.*

*After the year 1000, economic life in Europe quickened, and towns again became important. Medieval towns were crowded, dirty places surrounded by walls to protect them from attack, but in time they became important centers of medieval culture.*

## QUESTIONS

1 Describe how warfare and preparing for warfare dominated the lives of feudal nobles. How did the Church seek to curb feudal warfare in the later Middle Ages?
2 What role was a noble woman expected to play in the Middle Ages?
3 Why did manors have to be self sufficient in the early Middle Ages? How did peasants on the manor provide for their basic needs?
4 Describe the structure of medieval society. Explain how each person had his or her place in that society. What is one major difference between medieval society and our society today?
5 Compare life on the manor to life in the towns.
6 How did developments in the later Middle Ages affect the lives of both nobles and peasants?

## BIBLIOGRAPHY

*Which books might describe how peasants farmed the land in 1250?*

BARRACLOUGH, GEOFFREY. *The Crucible of Europe.* Berkeley: University of California Press, 1976. *A portrayal of medieval Europe, from the collapse of Charlemagne's empire to the rise of the early nation-states. Describes how people in various parts of Europe defended themselves against invasions and recounts the recovery between 955-1051 that culminated in the "12th century Renaissance."*

DAVIS, WILLIAM STEARNS. *Life on a Medieval Barony.* New York: Harper & Row, 1951. *A detailed description drawn from primary sources of a typical feudal community in the 13th century. It portrays every walk of medieval life, from peasants and villeins to merchants, artisans, knights, and lords.*

SETTON, KENNETH M. *The Age of Chivalry.* Washington, D.C.: National Geographic Society, 1969. *A well-illustrated survey of the period from 500 to 1350 which captures the spirit of the medieval world.*

WILLIAMS, JAY. *Life in the Middle Ages.* New York: Random House, 1966. *A fascinating recreation of the life of this period with explanations of how the people worked, played, fought, and worshiped. Through colorful contemporary drawings, it shows life on the manor and in castles, the role of the Church, and the importance of pilgrimages.*

The light of faith that is freely infused into us does not destroy the light of natural knowledge [reason] implanted in us naturally. For although the natural light of the human mind is insufficient to show us these things made manifest by faith, it is nevertheless impossible that these things which the divine principle gives us by faith are contrary to those implanted in us by nature [reason]. Indeed, were that the case, one or the other would have to be false, and, since both are given to us by God, God would have to be the author of untruth, which is impossible. . . . it is impossible that those things which are of philosophy can be contrary to those things which are of faith.

THOMAS AQUINAS

# The Flowering of Medieval Civilization

During the early Middle Ages, education and learning fell to such a low point that barely literate monks noted in the margins of ancient manuscripts "Greek! It can't be read." This situation so shocked Charlemagne that he took strong measures to ensure a revival in education. Slowly, the seeds planted by Charlemagne took root, and during the 11th century the renaissance in learning began to flower.

In the later Middle Ages, medieval civilization burst forth in a productive outpouring of energy. A central issue in the medieval intellectual revival was the debate over the roles of faith and reason. Saint Thomas Aquinas, quoted above, declared that there was no conflict between faith and reason, and his arguments on the issue have shaped Christian thought to the present. The intellectual debate among scholars was only one of the many signs that marked the vitality of medieval civilization.

## LEARNING AND EDUCATION

During much of the Middle Ages, education was associated with the Church. Monastic schools educated young boys to work in the monastery, although not every student joined the order. Cathedral schools were established to prepare young men to serve as priests. There were few other opportunities for education. Some parish priests taught boys to read; some churches, and especially the cathedrals, conducted "song schools" to train singers for religious services.

Orders of nuns often provided instruction in reading, writing, account keeping, needlework, surgery, and first aid to prepare noble girls to be ladies on a manor. Most other children remained illiterate. As you have read, sons of nobles were trained as pages and squires in preparation for knighthood. Many boys in towns became apprenticed to artisans in various trades. Peasants taught their children how to farm or perform other work on the manor. But very few learned to read and write before the late 13th century, when literacy became more common among the nobility and the wealthier inhabitants of the towns.

### SCHOOLS IN THE EARLY MIDDLE AGES

The curriculum of every cathedral and monastery school consisted of the study of the Bible, the writings of the Church fathers, and the decrees of Church councils. In the 11th century, this curriculum was gradually broadened to include the "liberal arts" (from the Latin *ars*, meaning "knowledge of a subject," and *liber*, meaning "befitting a freeman"). The subject matter was divided into the *trivium* and the *quadrivium*. The *trivium* comprised grammar, the ability to read and write Latin; rhetoric, the ability to express ideas clearly; and logic, the ability to think and reason accurately. The *quadrivium* was composed of arithmetic, geometry, astronomy, and music. Latin was the language of instruction because it was the language of the Church.

In the early Middle Ages, books were rare and expensive, for each was copied by hand on vellum or parchment. Many original works were written in poor Latin and contained numerous errors, but there were a few notable exceptions. Among them was the work of the Venerable Bede, an 8th century Benedictine monk, who wrote the *Ecclesiastical History of the English People*. This famous book is considered by some scholars to be the best history of the early Middle Ages.

One of the most widely read books in the Middle Ages was a textbook on Latin grammar, *Ars Minor*, written by Donatus, who lived in Rome in the 4th century. It was used for 1000 years, wherever Latin was taught. The following is an excerpt from this popular book:

● ● ● *Concerning the Parts of Speech*
*How many parts of speech are there? Eight. What? Noun, pronoun, verb, adverb, participle, conjunction, preposition, interjection.*

*Concerning the Noun*
*What is a noun? A part of speech which signifies with the case a person or a thing specifically or generally. How many attributes has a noun? Six. What? Quality, comparison, gender, number, form, case. In what does the quality of a noun consist? It is two-fold, for either it is the name of one and is called proper, or it is the name of many*

*and is called common. How many degrees of comparison are there? Three. What? Positive, as learned; comparative, as more learned; superlative, as most learned. What nouns are compared? Only common nouns signifying quality or quantity.*[1]

Other texts commonly used for instruction were: *A Handbook of Sacred and Secular Learning* by Cassiodorus, a 6th-century interpretation of the Bible; *The Consolation of Philosophy* by Boethius, a 6th-century view of the misfortunes of man and the love of God; and *Etymologies* by Isadore of Seville, a 7th-century discussion of the real and imagined roots of words.

After the year 1000, religious schools expanded. The sons of nobles began to apply for admission to these schools, even though they did not intend to join the clergy. Occasionally, even the intelligent son of a serf might be admitted. One serf's son, Gerbert, became an outstanding scholar and teacher. Gerbert originally enrolled in a monastery school to become a monk. His brilliant academic record prompted the abbot to send him to Spain for further education. There, he studied under Moslem and Jewish scholars whose learning far surpassed that of teachers in Christian Europe. Gerbert's knowledge of science and mathematics led people to regard him as a magician.

After completing his education, Gerbert was made master of the cathedral school at Aurillac, in south-central France. In this capacity, he revolutionized the curriculum of the school by declaring that henceforth, he would not accept the works of the Church fathers as the only source of enlightenment. His students also had to read the classical authors and were encouraged to use an abacus to solve problems in arithmetic. In 999, Gerbert was elected pope under the name Sylvester II and ruled until his death in 1003.

---

[1]*The Ars Minor of Donatus*, trans. W. J. Chase, in *Readings in Medieval History*, ed. Scott, Hyma, and Noyes (New York: Crofts, 1946), p. 334.

*Beginning in the 12th century, students from Italy and throughout northern Europe traveled to Bologna to study at the city's famous university. The university first specialized in rhetoric, a branch of the* trivium, *and later became a center for law studies.*

### GROWTH OF UNIVERSITIES

During the 12th century, the cathedral schools of France and Italy developed into universities. In part, this was the result of the increased economic activity and the need for people trained in law, medicine, and other subjects not directly associated with religion. Since few people were qualified to teach such subjects, students who wanted to continue their education had to move to the places where the teachers lived. Thus, students of different backgrounds began to meet one another and to exchange ideas, which in turn encouraged intellectual growth and the demand for learning. As students and scholars came together in increasing numbers, the schools that they formed gradually became separated from the existing religious schools.

Unfortunately, some people who called themselves scholars were poorly educated, and sometimes the towns where schools were established were inhospitable to the influx of students from elsewhere. To counter these problems, early in the 12th century, students in Bologna, Italy, organized themselves into a *universitas*, an association to protect their interests. In time, the *universitas* of students at Bologna came to manage the living arrangements of its members, establish the course of study, and force teachers to follow strict regulations such as the ones described below.

● ● ● *We decree also that no Doctor [teacher] shall hereafter exceed one section [part of a book] in one lecture. And if the contrary be done by any one he shall be charged with perjury and punished to the extent of three pounds. . . . [w]e have decreed that no Doctor shall omit from his sections any chapter, decretal, law, or paragraph. If he does this he shall be obliged to read it within the following section. We have also decreed that no decretal or decree or law or difficult paragraph shall be reserved to be read at the end of the lecture if, through such*

At the university of Paris, professors were organized into a guild, or professional society, and maintained firm control over classroom proceedings.

*reservation, promptness of exit at the sound of the appointed bell is likely to be prevented.*[2]

The arrangements created by the students at Bologna provided a model for universities in southern Europe. In northern Europe, however, the University of Paris took the lead. It developed in the late 12th century, although little is known about its origins. It probably evolved from the cathedral school of Notre Dame, which was famous through-

[2]A. O. Norton, ed., "Readings in the History of Education: Medieval Universities," in *Readings in Medieval History*, ed. Scott, Hyma, and Noyes, pp. 353–4.

out Europe for its instruction in the Latin authors, logic, and theology.

When enrollment exceeded the capacity of the cathedral school, the bishop of Paris may have granted the teachers permission to hold classes at other locations in the city, but he retained the power to hire teachers and supervise examinations. The university became so large, however, that it became impossible for the bishop to control it. In 1200, King Philip Augustus of France recognized the University of Paris as a separate institution, independent of the bishop and his cathedral school. When the university moved to the south bank of the Seine, the neighborhood around it came to be known as the "Latin Quarter" because Latin was the language of scholarship.

As universities developed, some became known for the study of a certain subject. Bologna, for example, began as a center of study of law, and Paris was famed as a center of theological study. In the 12th and 13th centuries, other universities were established at Oxford, Montpellier, and Naples, and their number soon multiplied. When the university at Oxford was closed because of student riots in 1209, many students moved to Cambridge, forming the nucleus of a new university.

### STUDENT LIFE

To outsiders and even to the townspeople, the university was often seen as a dangerous place where unruly young men gathered and scholars taught about worldly subjects. Women were not permitted to attend the universities, although a few women were able to study with scholars who tutored them in advanced subjects. Townspeople resented the fact that the university operated as a separate and independent organization within the community. The separation was made more visible in the academic robes, or gowns, worn by the students and faculty. These robes, which were worn partly for warmth and partly to disguise differences of wealth among stu-

**119**

dents and teachers, set members of the university apart from townspeople. Throughout the Middle Ages and even today, the tension between members of universities and townspeople have been called "town and gown" disputes.

Some disputes arose from the behavior of students who often spent more time playing dice and pursuing other amusements than studying. In letters like the one below, students wrote home to their parents asking for money.

••• *Well-beloved father, I have not a penny, nor can I get any save through you, for all things at the University are so dear: nor can I study my Code or my Digest, for they are all tattered.... Moreover, I owe ten crowns.... I send you word of greetings and money.*[3]

Students did have a regular course of study. Although textbooks were few and expensive as they had been in the early Middle Ages, students attended lectures and were expected to memorize the words of the teachers. A typical day might include these activities.

••• *At five or six o'clock each morning the great cathedral bell would ring out the summons to work. From the neighboring houses of the canons, from the cottages of the townsfolk, from the taverns, and hospices, and boarding houses, the streams of the industrious would pour into the enclosure beside the cathedral. The master's beadle, who levied a precarious tax on the mob, would strew the floor of the lecture hall with hay or straw, according to the season, bring the master's text-book, with the notes of the lecture between lines or on the margin, to the solitary desk, and then retire to secure silence in the adjoining street. Sitting on their haunches in the hay, the right knee raised to serve as a desk for the waxed tablets, the scholars would take notes during the long hours of lecture (about six or seven),*

*then hurry home—if they were industrious— to commit them to parchment while the light lasted.*[4]

### DEGREES

The courses of study led to the granting of degrees. After completing from three to five years of study, a student was eligible to take a comprehensive examination. If he successfully completed this examination, he was given the designation *baccalaureatus*, or bachelor, indicating that he had completed the requirements for this first degree. But the bachelor's degree carried little status, and a bachelor could only teach under the guidance of a master teacher.

If a bachelor continued to study for several more years, he became eligible to submit a "masterpiece" on his studies. If he defended this "masterpiece" successfully in an oral examination, he was named a "master." With this title he could become a teacher himself. Today, a student's "masterpiece" is known as a master's thesis.

Masters who continued their studies could earn the degree of *doctus*, or learned. The scholar who took his degree in a specialized field such as law, medicine, or theology was known as a doctor of philosophy (Ph.D.).

### SCHOLASTICISM

The growth in education in the late 11th and 12th centuries fostered an interest in applying logic to Christian faith. During the early Middle Ages, the Church fathers had provided official answers (called *dogma*) for all important questions, but the new scholars, or *scholastics*, challenged these teachings. Increasingly, they sought to prove that Christian principles could be known by reason and logic as well as divine revelation. They based their approach on Latin translations of ancient Greek philosophers, whose texts had entered Europe from Moslem Spain. The most

---

[3]Hutton Webster, *Historical Selections* (Boston: Heath, 1929), pp. 586–7.

[4]Joseph McCabe, *Peter Abelard* (New York: Putnam, 1901), p. 79.

*The discovery of Plato's accounts of Socrates' teaching method had a great impact on medieval scholars. This 13th-century drawing misinterprets the relationship between the two, for Socrates is shown transcribing Plato's words.*

plato.

Socrates.

important philosopher for the scholastics was Aristotle, who had taught that theory must be based on facts and that to know a thing one had to know its causes. The scholastics also adopted the teaching methods of Socrates: instead of making statements, teachers would pose a series of questions intended to reveal their students' ignorance and resolve contradictory beliefs. The Socratic method came to be central to scholasticism.

Anselm (1034-1109), a teacher in the monastic school at Bec, in France, was one of the first theologians to attempt to prove his faith by logic. His guiding principle was "I must believe in order that I might understand" (*credo ut intelligam*). Although Anselm put faith above reason, he still emphasized the importance of studying "to understand what we believe." Anselm later became archbishop of Canterbury, the high-

est Church position in England, and was declared a saint by the Church after his death.

**Peter Abelard.** Anselm's concept was challenged by the French scholastic, Peter Abelard (1079-1142), who reversed Anselm's principle, saying "I must understand in order that I may believe" (*intelligo ut credam*). In doing so, he put reason before faith. Although Abelard never directly challenged the authority or teachings of the Church, he enjoyed raising philosophical and logical questions about Church doctrine to stimulate discussion among his students. In his best known work *Sic et Non* (*Yes and No*), he examined over 150 statements on theology and ethics and included the opinions of Church authorities for and against each statement. He then urged his students to use reason to reconcile the apparent contradictions.

Many Church officials disapproved of Abelard's approach, believing that it was dangerous to apply the principles of logic to matters that should be accepted on faith. In 1112, one of Abelard's books aroused the hostility of these officials, and he was ordered to stay in a monastery for a year. When he was finally permitted to leave the monastery, Abelard moved to a cottage in a forest outside Paris. In his autobiography, he said of this time:

• • • *No sooner had scholars learned of my retreat than they began to flock thither from all sides, leaving their towns and castles to dwell in the wilderness. In place of their spacious houses they built themselves huts; instead of dainty fare they lived on the herbs of the field and coarse bread; their soft beds they exchanged for heaps of straw and rushes, and their tables were piles of turf.*[5]

When Abelard persisted in raising questions about Church doctrine, he was forced to stand trial for heresy. Condemned by a Church court, Abelard took refuge in the

[5]Peter Abelard, *The Story of My Misfortunes*, trans. H. A. Bellows (Glencoe, Ill.: Free Press, 1958), p. 52.

monastery at Cluny, where he spent his last years. Although his own voice was silenced, Abelard's students continued his work.

**Thomas Aquinas.** The greatest of the medieval scholastics was Thomas Aquinas (1222-1274). Born into a noble family near Naples, he became a Dominican friar and later taught in the universities of Naples, Rome, and Paris. Aquinas was convinced that both human learning, which is gained through the process of reasoning, and supernatural truth, which is achieved only through faith, are gifts from God. Because of his conviction, he decided that there could be no conflict between reasoning and faith.

Aquinas used Abelard's technique of posing questions, but unlike Abelard, he attempted to arrive at an answer that accorded with Church teaching for each question he raised. Aquinas' most influential work was the *Summa Theologica*, an encyclopedia of Christian theology that is still regarded as the highest expression of Roman Catholic theology. In addition to the teaching of Christian scholars, Aquinas drew on the ideas of Greek, Jewish, and Moslem thinkers. To Aquinas, Aristotle was the greatest thinker of all time, but he was also familiar with the writings of Averroes (Chapter 14), who had struggled with the problem of reconciling faith and reason.

## MEDIEVAL SCIENCE

In the early Middle Ages, science was based on the few surviving works of classical thinkers, but these often contained many errors, mixing superstition and observed facts. As in other areas of learning, the Church and its teachings had the final authority. In the 12th century, European scholars became familiar with the scientific writings of Moslem thinkers, who themselves owed much to the Greeks. The works of Moslem scholars reached Europe in the form of Latin translations, mostly from Spain and Sicily. Moslem learning about the natural world, especially in optics, mathematics, and med-

icine, was far more advanced than anything known to Christian thinkers, and this "new learning" came as a great revelation to them. Because Moslem and Greek scholarship seldom clashed with Christian principles, Western scholars were able to use it as a foundation for their own scientific work.

### NEW APPROACHES

Among the most influential medieval scientists was Robert Grosseteste (1168-1253), who served as bishop of Lincoln and chancellor of Oxford University. Grosseteste has been called the "founder of modern science" because he urged the objective study of natural phenomena and emphasized the importance of mathematics in scientific study. Through his reading of Aristotle and others, he developed a concern for observation and experimentation to verify all findings. Like all medieval scholars, however, Grosseteste sought to reconcile his scientific discoveries with Christian theology. In his most important work, *De Luce* ("Concerning Light"), he argued that since God is the source of all

*Roger Bacon, English philosopher and scientist, did experimental work in optics, astronomy, and other subjects. Many of his writings contradicted accepted beliefs and were banned by the Church.*

light, knowledge of the properties of light will help a person to know God.

Grosseteste's most famous pupil was Roger Bacon (1214-1292), a Franciscan monk who studied at Paris and Oxford. Bacon is often credited with establishing the foundations for modern scientific inquiry. He believed that all aspects of knowledge are interrelated; therefore, the study of natural sciences is as important as the study of religion and philosophy. Bacon urged scholars to put their beliefs to the test of experimentation:

● ● ● *What others strive to see dimly and blindly, like bats blinking at the sun in the twilight, he gazes at in the full light of day, because he is a master of experiment. Through experiment he gains knowledge of natural things, medical, chemical, indeed of everything in the heavens and on earth.*[6]

After studying Arabic treatises on optics and light, Bacon experimented with various phenomena of light and concluded like Grosseteste that the person who understands the principles of light and optics will understand the divine plan of the universe. Bacon's work led to the development of eyeglasses, and this great medieval thinker also predicted the invention of flying machines and horseless carriages.

### MEDICINE

The field of medicine in medieval Europe was greatly affected by the discovery of Greek and Arabic texts. Medicine was not considered a science, as we understand that term today, but rather a branch of philosophy. Medieval physicians did not experiment, and they only rarely performed surgical operations. Surgery was the domain of barbers, who were organized into guilds of barber-surgeons. The role of physicians was to prescribe for patients on the basis of their knowledge of ancient medical texts.

Medieval medicine was thus based on the medical writings of the ancient Greeks and Romans. The most important of these was the ancient Greek medical writer, Galen (130-200 A.D.). A Latin translation of his medical encyclopedia reached western Europe from the Moslems in the 12th century. For the rest of the Middle Ages and beyond, Galen became the definitive medical authority.

In particular, medieval physicians accepted Galen's theory that health depended on a balance among four bodily fluids: blood, mucus, black bile, and yellow bile. Illness resulted if a person had too much or too little of one of these fluids. The art of medicine lay in diagnosing which fluid was out of proportion and then acting to correct the balance. Treatment could take the form of drugs, diet, rest, or, very commonly, bleeding the patient. Medieval physicians believed that diminishing a person's blood supply would bring all the humors into balance.

*According to the type of illness, a physician would determine how much blood was to be taken from the patient. It could be as little as an ounce, or as much as a pint for serious illness. A barber-surgeon would then make an incision, draw out the prescribed amount of blood, and bind up the wound. Based as it was on a totally mistaken theory of human physiology, bleeding was useless as a remedy for illness. In fact, it weakened patients and exposed them to infection because medieval surgeons did not sterilize their razors. The practice of bleeding continued for centuries, until medicine ceased to rely on the authority of ancient texts and became an experimental science.*

---

[6]Roger Bacon, "Eulogy of One Who Devoted Himself to Experimental Science," in J. H. Robinson, ed., *Readings in European History*, vol. 1 (New York: Ginn, 1904), p. 460.

*Medieval physicians treated many illnesses by letting blood, a practice which often worsened the patient's condition.*

Despite the reliance on inaccurate theories, medicine did make some progress in the later Middle Ages. At the universities of Salerno and Montpellier, medicine was studied as a science, and students learned to dissect animals and human cadavers. Such studies gradually led to better skills in surgery.

Epidemics that swept through Europe taking huge death tolls resulted in efforts to control diseases. Some towns appointed doctors to oversee public health. To combat epidemics, Venice set up a system of quarantines for newcomers. A physician examined people arriving by ship and required that ill passengers remain on board for 40 days to prevent their carrying the illness into the city. Some towns and cities did have hospitals set up by monasteries outside the city walls, but these were often little more than places where the sick could die.

In the Middle Ages, most people who lived in rural areas never saw a doctor. They relied on folk medicine that combined magic charms and chants to prevent illness with traditional remedies such as herbs and roots. Because illness was connected to beliefs in devils and evil spirits, people also used prayer and pilgrimages to seek cures.

**LITERATURE** When the Romans conquered western Europe, they brought the Latin language with them. Latin thus became the language of educated people throughout the West, and kept that position even when Rome collapsed as a political power. Thus, the Church used Latin in its religious services and for its business affairs. Gradually, however, the regions of western Europe that had been influenced by Rome developed their own languages that interwove Latin with the language of the local common people. In each region, the language of the common people became known as the *vernacular*.

The literature of the early Middle Ages was of two varieties. One included the written works in Latin such as poetry and essays on theology. The other consisted of the many traditions and legends that were passed orally from generation to generation until they were eventually written down in Latin or, by the 11th century, in the vernacular.

Before this early vernacular literature was written down, it was carried from town to castle to monastery by wandering minstrels. The stories they told or sang provided entertainment, spread news of events such as battles or plagues, and perpetuated the legends of a particular region. In France, these minstrels were called *jongleurs*, and their songs (*chansons*) evolved into long narrative poems relating the deeds of heroes, both past and present. While based on historic events, these minstrels' accounts were frequently embellished for the greater enjoyment of the audience. Many stories concerned the reign of Charlemagne, which the medieval French regarded as the "golden age" of their nation's history.

Four languages in western Europe —Spanish, Portuguese, French, and Italian—and one in eastern Europe—Romanian—were strongly influenced by Latin and are known as Romance languages. Although the languages of northern Europe included some Latin words, they were most strongly influenced by German and are called Germanic languages. The languages of eastern Europe are known as Slavic languages.

During the Middle Ages, wandering minstrels created and embroidered the legends that were later turned into such epics as the Song of Roland and the Poem of El Cid.

The oldest and most famous of these tales is the *Song of Roland*. Roland was the nephew of Charlemagne and an officer in the army that Charlemagne led into Spain in an unsuccessful effort to drive out the Moslems. While withdrawing to France, the expedition was attacked by fierce Basque tribes in the Pyrenees Mountains. Roland, the commander of Charlemagne's rear guard, led a delaying action in which he and all his soldiers were killed. According to legend, Charlemagne was so moved by this bravery that he marched back into Spain and captured the city of Saragossa from the Moslems. The victory is described in these words:

● ● ● *The pagans are dead. Many of them . . . . And Charles has won his battle. He has beaten down the gate of Saragossa and he knows beyond any doubt that it will not be defended. He occupies the city. His army enters its walls. His men lodge there that night by right of conquest. The white-bearded King is filled with pride. For Barmimunde [the queen of the city] has surrendered her towers to him—the ten enormous ones and the fifty smaller ones.*

*He whom the Lord God helps will triumph.*[7]

The *Song of Roland* was probably told at monasteries along the pilgrimage route to the shrine of Saint James at Compostela, in northwestern Spain, because the events had taken place near there. The long epic became very popular because it glorified the role of Christian knights in conflict with the infidels, thereby symbolizing the victory of good over evil. Pope Urban II referred to the "golden age" of France when he preached his call for the First Crusade at Clermont (Chapter 16): "Let the deeds of your ancestors encourage you and incite your minds to manly achievements—the glory and greatness of King Charlemagne."[8]

[7]*Song of Roland*, in *Medieval Epics*, trans. Helen M. Mustard and W. S. Merwin (New York: Modern Library, 1963), p. 193.

[8]Urban's speech at Clermont, as reported by Robert the Monk, in *Readings in European History*, ed. Robinson, p. 313.

The great Spanish epic, *Poem of the Cid* (*Poema del Cid*), was written down between 1150 and 1250. It recounted the adventures of the Cid ("lord") Rodrigo Díaz de Bivar, who led crusades against the Moslems in Spain (Chapter 22). The German epic, *Song of the Nibelungs* (*Nibelungenlied*), is a composite of several legends relating to the slaughter of a Burgundian tribe by the Huns during the 5th century. In the 19th century, the German composer Richard Wagner used this story as the basis for his cycle of four operas, *The Ring of the Nibelungs*. The earliest epic in English is *Beowulf*, dating from the 8th century, which recounts the heroic deeds of the warrior Beowulf.

In addition to the epics, songs of love and romance became extremely popular during the 11th century. These songs originated in southern France, where those who sang them were called troubadours. William, duke of Aquitaine, and his daughter Eleanor introduced troubadours to the royal courts of France and England. From there, they spread across Europe. The troubadours and their love songs were closely associated with the knightly code of chivalry.

## DANTE ALIGHIERI

One of the most significant works of medieval vernacular literature is the *Divine Comedy* of Dante Alighieri (1265-1321). Dante was born into a wealthy family in Florence and received an excellent education in theology, philosophy, and rhetoric. Around 1300, he was appointed one of the six magistrates in Florence. Two years later, he became involved in a dispute between two political factions and was sentenced to exile. Only the influence of friends saved him from execution, and he never returned to Florence.

*Like Roland, the legendary Spanish hero El Cid won fame in fighting the Moslems. In this illustration, he kneels before his king.*

*Dante was one of the most influential writers of the medieval world. In this illustration, his vision of purgatory is shown at left; the city of Florence at right.*

Dante was familiar with the writings of Aristotle and Saint Thomas Aquinas. His experience in politics made him sensitive to human nature and the ways of the world. Although he became interested in mysticism, he remained a devout member of the Church.

While in exile, Dante wrote his most famous work, *Divine Comedy*, in the vernacular of his home region, Tuscany, completing it just before his death. It is the story of Dante's journey through hell, purgatory, and heaven, the three levels to which souls could be assigned by God after death. Dante peopled each level with the souls of his contemporaries and of people from history, according to his opinion of whether the person was wicked or virtuous. In vivid images, Dante describes the endless torments and sufferings of hell or the blessed joys of heaven.

### GEOFFREY CHAUCER

Another outstanding work is *Canterbury Tales*, written by Geoffrey Chaucer (1340-1400). Chaucer was born into a family of prosperous wine merchants in London. He received a good education and entered into the service of King Edward III. Chaucer was later an envoy to the Italian states, where he came into contact with the writings of Dante. Although Chaucer was fluent in both Latin—the language of the Church—and French—

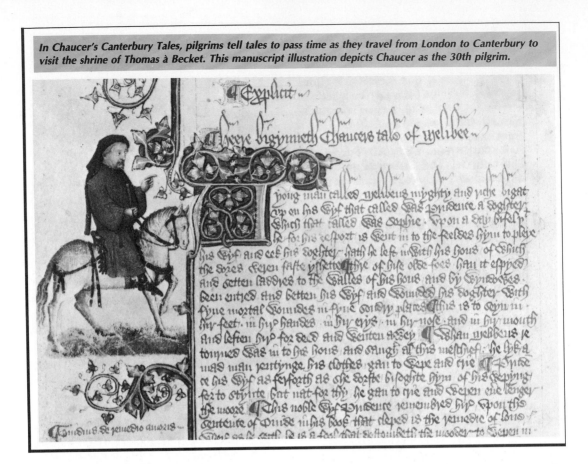

In Chaucer's *Canterbury Tales*, pilgrims tell tales to pass time as they travel from London to Canterbury to visit the shrine of Thomas à Becket. This manuscript illustration depicts Chaucer as the 30th pilgrim.

the language of the English court—he decided to write in English.

Chaucer worked on his *Canterbury Tales* from 1385 until his death 15 years later. While the individual tales probably came from a variety of sources, Chaucer presented them as the stories of 29 pilgrims traveling from London to Canterbury, to pray at the tomb of Saint Thomas à Becket. To pass the time along the road, each pilgrim was to tell two stories on the way to Canterbury and two on the return. Of the 120 projected stories, Chaucer completed only 24 before his death.

Chaucer's descriptions of the pilgrims and the stories each pilgrim tells present a vivid picture of life in medieval England.

### DRAMA

In the Middle Ages, drama grew out of plays performed in the churches. Late in the 10th century, the clergy began to dramatize sacred stories from the Bible to instruct their parishioners, most of whom could not read. At first, members of the clergy acted out the stories on holy days. The presentations were given in Latin within the church buildings.

These dramatizations became very popular, and the performances were moved to the marketplace to accommodate a larger audience. The casts were also expanded to include laypeople, and the local language was used in place of Latin, so that more people could understand the play. These performances came to be called *mystery plays* because they dealt with unusual events in the Bible and in the life of Jesus.

Later, dramatizations of events in the lives of some saints were presented. These came

*Medieval drama evolved from morality plays that were created to teach the lessons of the Church.*

the new buildings, new styles of architecture were developed.

### ROMANESQUE

In the early Middle Ages, large churches were built as modifications of the style of the Roman basilicas, or courts of law. This style of architecture was later called *Romanesque*. The basic plan of a Romanesque church was a large rectangle surrounded by thick walls of brick or stone. A wooden roof was supported by the outside walls and two rows of columns running the length of the building. Between the rows of columns was a wide central space, called the nave, and a narrower space, or aisle, lay between each column and the outside wall. The columns were taller than the walls. As a result, the central part of the roof, supported by the columns, was higher than the sides. This allowed win-

to be called *miracle plays* after the miracles associated with each saint. Finally, the programs were expanded to include *morality plays*, in which the plot presented a particular moral instruction that the audience could easily understand.

### MEDIEVAL ARCHITECTURE

In the early Middle Ages, very little construction was done in western Europe aside from fortified manors for defense and religious buildings such as churches and monasteries. By the 12th century, however, there was a resurgence of construction because of improved economic conditions. The Crusaders, who had seen the beautiful palaces of the Byzantine Empire, returned home with dreams of transforming their own drafty castles into comfortable homes. But the Church with its vast wealth was the greatest builder of the time, spending huge sums on new cathedrals and abbeys. Along with the outpouring of money and faith that went into

*A few of the specialized trades involved in building a Gothic cathedral are shown here: a master stonecutter (bottom left) creates delicate ornaments for the columns; masons (top) test the level of each row of stone blocks; and other workmen (bottom center) operate the winch that raises the blocks to the work site.*

dows to be placed between the two levels of the roof, and light from the windows to illuminate the interior of the building.

Bishops and abbots vied with one another to build the most impressive and grand churches. Thus, further modifications were made in the basic plan. The columns were arranged so that the floor resembled the shape of a cross. A *transept*, or aisle, perpendicular to the nave and longer than the width of the church, was added on each side, to make the cross. When the churches became so wide that wooden beams could no longer support the roofs, barrel vaulting was used. Also the central part of the church was made higher, forcing builders to use buttresses, or brick structures outside the walls, to carry the weight of the roof.

Church leaders also sought to have the most beautiful and elaborate ornamentation on their buildings. The church was decorated both inside and out with sculpture, mosaic, and paintings that showed scenes from the Bible or recounted events in the lives of the saints. A standard stylized form was adopted for each holy person, so that a worshiper entering any church would immediately recognize the person or event shown. For example;

> God, angels, and the apostles go barefoot; other saints are shod. St. Paul must be bald and long-bearded. St. Peter always wears [shaved head], curly hair, and a short beard. The Christ child must lie on the altar. The three Magi represent youth, maturity and old age. In the Crucifixion Mary appears to the right of the cross, St. John to the left. A scene depicting the Resurrection always shows Jesus emerging from an open tomb, cross in hand. Jews invariably wear cone-shaped hats.[9]

### GOTHIC

The abbey of Saint Denis near Paris was an important church in the Middle Ages because it not only housed the remains of Charles Martel but also boasted a relic of Saint Denis, who had brought Christianity to northern France in the 3rd century. In the 12th century, Suger, the powerful abbot of Saint Denis, set out to make the abbey the most beautiful building in Europe. For the rebuilding of the abbey, Suger adopted principles of design that had been used in the Middle East. The new style of architecture soon became popular and was at first called the French style. During the Renaissance, however, when everything medieval was disdained, this style of architecture was called *Gothic*, meaning barbaric.

The Gothic style differed from the Romanesque in several ways. The main differ-

In addition to religious scenes, cathedral sculpture sometimes included gargoyles and scenes from everyday life. This sculpture of a peasant sharpening his scythe is part of a sequence illustrating the seasons of the year.

ence was height—Gothic churches were hundreds of feet higher. This great height was achieved through the use of ribbed, criss-crossed vaulting and "flying" buttresses, which projected outside the building and helped support the high walls. Because of these supports, the walls did not have to hold all the weight of the building. Thus, the walls

[9]Merle Severy, *The Age of Chivalry* (Washington, D.C.: National Geographic, 1969), p. 170.

**In Gothic architecture, the immense weight of high, vaulted ceilings is carried by flying buttresses on the outside of the structure.**

*same width, by means of geometrical and arithmetical instruments, as the central nave of the old [Carolingian] church; and, likewise, that the dimensions of the old side aisles, except for that elegant and praiseworthy extension . . . a circular string of chapels, by virtue of which the whole [church] would shine with the wonderful uninterrupted light of the most luminous windows, pervading the interior beauty.*[10]

Suger's achievement inspired the building of hundreds of Gothic churches and cathedrals throughout Europe: Notre Dame in Paris (begun in 1163), Chartres (begun in 1194), and Amiens (begun in 1220) in France; Canterbury (begun in 1174) and Salisbury (begun in 1220) in England; Cologne (begun in 1322) in Germany and Milan (begun in 1386) in Italy are just a few examples. Workers toiled for several generations to complete each great cathedral. Each remains as a tribute to the ingenuity of the artisans who designed and built them. The master stonemason, who was usually also the architect, was exempted from taxation, given the right to wear fur-trimmed robes (a right usually reserved for the nobles), and provided with a lifetime pension. Wealthy nobles and merchants gave large sums of money for buildings and decorations such as stained-glass windows. Poorer Christians contributed their labor.

The great cathedrals built during the Middle Ages symbolized the solid security offered by the Church. These monuments, which Christians saw as a tribute to "the greater glory of God," dominated the medieval landscape much as the Church ruled their lives. Yet the building of churches and cathedrals was also good business for the towns and cities where they were located because they attracted pilgrims from far and wide even as they do today.

could be hollowed out to make room for huge stained-glass windows that allowed light into the church.

While only the choir of the abbey was completed in his lifetime, Suger described it as follows:

● ● ● *Moreover, it was cunningly provided that—through the upper columns and central arches which were to be placed upon the lower ones built in the crypt—the central nave of the new addition should be made the*

[10]Erwin Panofsky, trans., *Abbot Suger on the Abbey Church of St. Denis and Its Art Treasures* (Princeton, N.J.: Princeton University Press, 1951), p. 101.

## SUMMARY

*In the early Middle Ages, the only schools were in monasteries and cathedrals. In the 12th century, the expanding European economy and increased contact with the Byzantine and the Moslem worlds created a climate in which more people were interested in education and the exchange of ideas. As a result, some cathedral schools in France and Italy evolved into universities that taught a variety of subjects to students from all over Europe.*

*Through contact with the Moslems, European scholars acquired Latin translations of ancient Greek and Moslem works of philosophy, science, and medicine. These texts had an enormous influence on European thought. In theology, the scholastics used the methods of Greek philosophy to reconcile reason with the Christian faith. Moslem writings in science became the foundation of European scientific speculation. Greek medical theory dominated medieval medicine.*

*During the Middle Ages, Latin was blended into the local languages to produce vernacular languages such as French, Italian, and Spanish. Eventually, a written vernacular literature began to appear. The two most significant works of medieval literature are Dante's* Divine Comedy *and Chaucer's* Canterbury Tales. *Throughout the Middle Ages, the building of churches and cathedrals confirmed the strength and importance of the Church.*

## QUESTIONS

1  How did universities develop in the Middle Ages? What brought about disputes between "town" and "gown" factions in the Middle Ages? Why do these disputes occur even today?
2  What questions were the scholastics trying to answer? How were they influenced by Greek thinkers like Aristotle?
3  Describe how the work of Robert Grosseteste and Roger Bacon prepared the way for later scientific advances.
4  Why was the development of vernacular literature significant? Read one of the Canterbury Tales and describe what it reveals about medieval life.
5  Compare Romanesque and Gothic styles of building. Why do you think the new Gothic style was appropriate to the Church at the height of its power?
6  What conditions in the later Middle Ages made possible the flowering of medieval civilization?

## BIBLIOGRAPHY

*Which book might describe a variety of medieval heroes?*

HOFSTATTER, HANS H. *Art of the Late Middle Ages.* New York: Harry N. Abrams, 1968. *A beautifully illustrated volume that shows the stained glass, mosaics, illuminated manuscripts, and reliquaries that adorned the majestic cathedrals of the late Middle Ages.*

MCLANATHAN, RICHARD. *The Pageant of Medieval Art and Life.* Philadelphia: The Westminster Press, 1966. *An illustrated survey of the creative arts from medieval Europe, the Byzantine Empire, and the Islamic world. Examines the relationship of faith and artistic expression in cathedrals, paintings, and sculpture.*

HELEN M. MUSTARD and W. S. MERWIN, translators. *Medieval Epics.* New York: The Modern Library, 1963. *A collection of the major medieval epics, including* Beowulf, The Song of Roland, The Nibelungenlied, *and* The Poem of the Cid.

# THE MAYAS

*300–900*

Deep in the dense jungle of Central America, buried under plants, vines, and trees, lie massive stone temples and huge carvings that are evidence of an ancient civilization. These huge stone monuments and *stelae*, or stone pillars carved with pictures, tell the story of the Mayas, a people who lived in Central America as long ago as 2000 B.C. At the height of their civilization, the Mayas produced books and traded across a wide area, using cacao beans (from which chocolate is made) as money. They invented a sophisticated calendar that even today matches our own in accuracy. In terms of our calendar, the starting date for the Maya calendar is August 14, 3114 B.C.—a date that makes it over 5,000 years old.

## HISTORICAL OVERVIEW

The Mayas were a farming people who cleared the land and built their villages across a large part of Central America. The area settled by the Mayas includes the present-day regions of southern Mexico, Guatemala, Belize, Honduras, and El Salvador. At different times and at different places within this region, the Mayas developed flourishing cities and strong trading networks.

Maya history can be divided into three periods: the pre-classic, 1500 B.C.–300 A.D.; the classic, 300 A.D.–900 A.D.; and the post-classic, 900 A.D.–1517. During the pre-classic period, the first farming villages were built in the tropical highlands of present-day Guatemala. Maya farmers learned to domesticate a variety of plants, including maize, tomatoes, sweet potatoes, and avocados. They devised farm tools and made pottery. They built large stone buildings, the precursors of the vast religious ceremonial centers that would be so important in the classic period.

By the 1st century B.C., when Rome was expanding its control over the Mediterranean world, the Mayas were constructing irrigation systems to drain the swampy rainforests and were laying the foundations for the major cities that would control the busy trade of the highlands.

Maya civilization reached its peak during the 4th to the 10th centuries when western Europe was experiencing the turmoil and upheavals of the early Middle Ages. At a time when cities in Europe virtually disappeared, those in Central America thrived. For the Mayas, this 600-year period was an age of creativity in architecture and carving, and great advances in mathematics and astronomy. The spectacular achievements in building were made with stone tools and without

## MAYA CIVILIZATION
**To what country does the Yucatan belong today?**

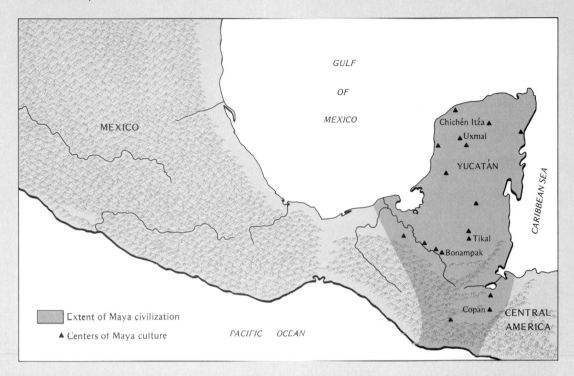

GULF

OF

MEXICO

MEXICO

Chichén Itza ▲
▲Uxmal

YUCATÁN

CARIBBEAN SEA

▲ Tikal
▲▲Bonampak

Copán ▲    CENTRAL
           AMERICA

▨ Extent of Maya civilization
▲ Centers of Maya culture

PACIFIC    OCEAN

the use of the wheel. For despite their many advances, neither the Mayas nor the other peoples of the Americas used the wheel until it was introduced by the Spanish at the time of the conquest.

About 900, Maya civilization declined. The populations of the great cities decreased; trade continued but on a reduced scale; and no new monuments were built. Scholars have yet to discover the reasons for the decline. Various theories have been proposed, including the disruption of trade by invasions, disease, or a major ecological disaster. When the Spanish reached Central America in the early 16th century, they came into contact with the descendants of the ancient Mayas. But by then, the cities and monuments were in ruins.

### CITIES
Settling the land, the Mayas developed an agricultural system based upon the domestication of maize, beans, and other plants. They utilized terracing and irrigation canals, and in addition constructed platforms of raised soil that enabled them to grow crops in lowland areas affected by seasonal flooding. As with other civilizations, the settled agricultural system of the Mayas produced a surplus that allowed some individuals to specialize in work and intellectual activity other than agriculture. As elsewhere, settled agricultural life produced villages, towns, and cities.

Maya cities were primarily religious centers, but the recent work of archaeologists and anthropologists has revealed that they were also centers of trade and other activities. Dominating each city and its surrounding land was a towering pyramid temple in the central plaza. The pyramid was built on top of a large stone platform. Nearby were other smaller temples and palaces. Like the great pyramids of Egypt, these monumental buildings were constructed by people who had only stone tools.

135

*The temple at Chichen Itza is one of the best examples of Maya pyramid architecture.*

At Maya sites, archaeologists have also uncovered "house mounds"—low dirt platforms that are surrounded by stone retaining walls. On these mounds, the poorer people built their houses of poles and thatched roofs. The earth platforms under the houses insured protection against flooding from summer rains. Even the towering temple buildings were built on platform bases, however, and these platforms served as gravesites for the wealthier people of the community.

With regard to the class structure, Maya society was divided into a number of layers. At the top were the rulers, probably divine kings. Next came a powerful noble class made up of priests and warriors. Only the priests and warriors were educated and knew the art of writing. Priests presided over the elaborate rituals that were part of daily Maya life. Warriors defended the cities, but, like the Vikings of northern Europe, they also apparently launched fierce raids on neighboring people. Supporting the ruling class were the artisans and merchants, as well as peasants and slaves who farmed the lands, built the huge stone structures, and carried the trade goods across great distances.

Because the Mayas had no draft animals, human porters transported all goods from cities in the highlands to those on the coastal lowlands. Burial objects in tombs and carvings on stelae in Tikal, an important Maya site in Guatemala, indicate that the Maya trading ventures reached as far away as Teotihuacán more than 600 miles to the west. The Tikal carvings show non-Maya people carrying weapons and ornaments that are associated with the people of central Mexico. Trade with Mexico was active and included salt from the Yucatan, honey, cotton, cacao beans, quetzal feathers, and slaves. Often, trade goods were carried by large canoes specially built by the coastal Mayas.

## RELIGION, SCIENCE, AND MATHEMATICS

The Mayas worshiped a variety of deities, most related to the forces of nature. Many were seen to have a two-sided nature—both good and evil. The rain god, for example, was highly regarded, for without rain the crops would wither. However, this same god could also send disastrous hailstorms and heavy floods. Besides the rain god, there were gods for the sun, moon, wind, sky, and death. Also, each social class and profession had its own god.

Maya life involved a continuous series of ceremonies in which the priests sought to please the gods and determine the will of the gods. The ceremonies conducted by priests were preceded by fasting and ritual purification. Sometimes, the ceremonies included animal and human sacrifices, although archaeologists believe that large-scale human sacrifice was a development of post-classic times. During times of emergency such as drought or famine, priests were likely to demand a greater number of sacrifices.

The Maya achievements in science and mathematics were closely tied to religion. Priests studied astronomy in order to learn the best time for certain religious rituals. To record events, the Mayas developed a form of writing that consisted of hieroglyphics with animals, faces, and abstract designs. To date, scientists have only a limited understanding of these "glyphs" despite the large number that have been found on sculptures, buildings, and other artifacts.

What scientists do know is that priests carefully recorded astronomical occurrences such as eclipses in books and used these records for their calculations. Maya priests developed a sophisticated form of mathematics that includes the number zero. Their method of computing in mathematics was based on 20—a "dot" equaled 1, a "bar" equaled 5, and a stylized shell equaled 0. Taken together, Maya astronomy and mathematics allowed the priests to produce a highly accurate calendar that used 18 months for a year of 365 days. With this calendar, they regulated the all-important events of the year, choosing the appropriate times for planting, harvesting, and processing crops.

Astronomical and historical records allowed the Mayas to predict lunar and solar eclipses, and with an error of only 14 seconds per year, they were able to calculate and plot the path of the planet Venus. These achievements, it should be noted, were made at a time when Europe was mired in the warfare of the early Middle Ages. In fact, Europeans did not have as accurate a calendar as the Mayas until the 18th century.

The dating of the decline of Maya civilization is well known because the Mayas included dates on many stelae. Fewer of these monuments were built in the 9th century than in earlier times. Also, new building platforms in some cities were left unfinished as were temples and palaces. Although the decline can be identified, scholars as yet have been unable to agree on why it occurred. According to one noted expert, the decline of Maya civilization may be linked to problems elsewhere in Mesoamerica.

*One may imagine a network of causes. The earlier decline of Teotihuacán and Monte Albán weakened the total fiber of Mesoamerica, but the Maya area took longer to die. Surely one of the factors was the rising of restless, aggressive people in central Mexico who came into the Southern and Northern areas and probably disrupted trade and the complex structure of Central Maya society. This Mexican influence may also have affected the Maya religion, as is suggested by the Mexican motifs in the art of the religious centers. At this time the Maya population was large and dependent for its support on trade and a well-organized social structure, and when its peripheral areas were affected by outside peoples and events the Central area probably collapsed slowly, like a be-*

*sieged fortress, its gods no longer effective, its economy destroyed. It has also been suggested that trade routes were changed, cutting off the Central areas, and possibly disease or crop disaster or some other ecological problems worsened the situation. Disasters rarely come singly.*

## INTRODUCTION TO THE DOCUMENTS

Archaeologists, anthropologists, linguists, and historians have searched through the jungles and coastlands of Central America to dig up the remains of the ancient Mayas, and they have found that the secrets are well guarded. Using aerial and satellite photographs of Central America, they have traced ancient irrigation canals, dikes, and manmade earth mounds that show the patterns of settlement. Meantime, others have used computers to help decode the books and writing of the Mayas.

Elizabeth P. Benson, *The Maya World* (New York: T. Y. Crowell, 1967), p. 131.

*In this Maya glyph, a scribe is shown writing in a codice. The sacred nature of this writing is indicated by the fact that it is bound in jaguar skin.*

The Maya religion was characterized by nature worship and human sacrifice. In this scene, a jaguar and a deer—each encircled by a serpent—look on as the man at center performs a ritual suicide.

While they had no apparent alphabet, the ancient Mayas coded their records by combining pictures, ideas, numbers, and sounds in a written language. These records are coded in "signs," called hieroglyphic script or glyphs. Hieroglyphic writing has been found on stelae, on the walls of temples, and on ceramic pottery buried in tombs. Many, but not all of these glyphs have been translated.

Many other Maya documents, however, were destroyed by the Spanish when they conquered the region. The Mayas recorded their history and learning in a number of books, or codices. Only three codices are known to have survived the Spanish conquest: the *Codex Paris*, *Codex Madrid*, and *Codex Dresden*. They are named for the cities in Europe where they are located. Most of the codices were burned in the 16th and 17th centuries by Spanish priests who wanted to eradicate the pagan practices that the Mayan insisted on clinging to. Many others may have perished in the rainforests.

## DOCUMENT 1   THE OLD GODS

*In Maya mythology, a serpent represents the sky, a deer represents the earth, and the jaguar represents the underworld. The deer and the jaguar may be a coded image for the Hero Twins—twin brothers who were sacrificed to the gods but revived themselves at the wish of the gods of the underworld.*

And they marveled,
    The lords.
    "And now sacrifice yourselves in turn.
    So we can see it.
    Truly our hearts are delighted with this dance of yours,"
        the lords repeated.
    "Very well, oh Lord," they said then.
    And so they sacrificed themselves. . . .

SOURCE: "Codex Fragment 1: The Codex of the Old Gods: Vessel 40," quoted in Francis Robicsek and Donald M. Hales, *The Maya Book of The Dead: The Ceramic Code* (Yale University Press, 1981), p. 118.

## DOCUMENT 2    PROPHECY OF THE SPANISH CONQUEST

*Foretelling the future was the function of a special branch of the priesthood called the* chilans. *Since many prophecies could be interpreted to have foretold the coming of the Spanish and the conversion of the Mayas to Christianity, the Spanish made extensive use of them to legitimize their rule.*

*This reading is taken from the* Books of Chilam Balam, *which were written down in Latin script in the 17th and 18th centuries. Because these books come from such a late date, they are not pure examples of ancient Maya literature. In this selection, Chilam Balam prophesizes the coming of strangers from the East, who will bring a new religion. Since he made this prophecy shortly before the Spanish arrived, it is thought that he foretold the "future" based on rumors that were reaching Central America from the West Indies, where the Spanish first landed.*

Then there shall be present the forceful one. . . . Like a jaguar is his head, long is his tooth, withered is his body, [like] a dog is his body. His heart is pierced with sorrow. Sweet is his food, sweet is his drink. Perchance he does not speak, perchance he will not hear. They say his speech is false and mad. No where do the younger sisters, native to the land, surrender themselves. They shall be taken away from the land here. So it shall always be with the maidens, the daughters whom they shall bear tomorrow and day after tomorrow. Give yourselves up, my younger brothers, my older brothers, submit to the unhappy destiny of the katun [a division of time] which is to come. If you do not submit, you shall be moved from where your feet are rooted. If you do not submit, you shall gnaw the trunks of trees and herbs. If you do not submit, it shall be as when the deer die, so that they go forth from your settlement. . . .

Then the judge . . . shall come, when he [who bears] the gold staff shall judge, when white wax [candles] shall be exchanged. It is to be white wax, when justice shall descend from Heaven, for Christian men to come up before the eye of justice. Then it shall shake heaven and earth. In sorrow shall end the katun of the Plumeria flower. No one shall fulfill his promises. The prop-roots of the trees shall be bent over. There shall be an earthquake all over the land. . . . If you surrender yourselves, you shall follow Christ, when he shall come. Then shall come to pass the shaking of the Plumeria flower. Then you shall understand.    shall Then it shall thunder from a dry sky. Then shall be spoken that which is written on the wall. . . . I hardly know what wise man among you will understand. He who understands will go into the forest to serve Christianity. Who will understand it?

SOURCE: Ralph L. Roys, ed., *The Book of Chilam Balam of Chumayel* (University of Oklahoma Press, 1967), pp. 120-23.

**How does the prophet believe Maya religion will be affected by the coming of the Spanish?**

## DOCUMENT 3   THE CREATION

*In the 16th century, not long after the Spanish conquered Mexico, a Quiché Maya from the highlands in Guatemala recorded the ancient history and legends of his people. The manuscript, known as the* **Popul Vah,** *included many oral traditions and relates some Maya ideas about the origin of the universe.*

This is the account of how all are in suspense, all calm, in silence: all motionless, still, and the expanse of the sky was empty.

This is the first account, the first narrative. There was neither man, nor animal, birds, fishes, crabs, trees, stones, caves, ravines, grasses, nor forests: there was only the sky. . . .

There was only immobility and silence in the darkness, in the night. Only the Creator, the Maker, Tepeu, Gucumatz, the Forefathers, were in the water surrounded with light. They were hidden under green and blue feathers, and were therefore called Gucumatz. By nature they were great sages and great thinkers. In this manner the sky existed and also the Heart of Heaven, which is the name of God and thus He is called.

Then came the word. Tepeu and Gucumatz came together in the darkness, in the night, and Tepeu and Gucumatz talked together. . . .

Then while they meditated, it became clear to them that when dawn would break, man must appear. Then they planned the creation, and the growth of trees and the thickets and the birth of life and the creation of man. Thus it was arranged in the darkness and in the night by the Heart of Heaven who is called Huracan. . . .

Thus let it be done! Let the emptiness be filled! Let the water recede and make a void, let the earth appear and become solid: let it be done. Thus they spoke. Let there be light, let there be dawn in the sky and on the earth! There shall be neither glory nor grandeur in our creation and formation until the human being is made, man is formed. So they spoke. . . .

SOURCE: Delia Goetz and Sylvanus G. Morley, eds., *Popol Vuh: The Sacred Book of the Ancient Quiche Maya* (University of Oklahoma Press, 1950), pp. 81-4.

**How does this Maya narrative compare with other Creation stories that you are familiar with?**

## TIME LINE FOR THE MAYAS AND WESTERN EUROPE

### THE MAYAS

**1500 B.C.** Pre-classic period: Mayas begin to domesticate maize, build towns and temples

**300 A.D.** Classic period begins: Maya cities thrive, carry on extensive trade with neighboring cultures; advances in science and mathematics

**900 A.D.** Post-classic period: Maya civilization declines; cities disappear, temples fall into ruins

**964 A.D.** New Mayan empire in Yucatan centered in Chichen Itza

**1200 A.D.** Beginning of Cocom dynasty in Mayapan

**1450 A.D.** Destruction of Mayapan

**1517 A.D.** Cortés begins conquest of Mexico

### WESTERN EUROPE

**1570 B.C.** Beginning of New Kingdom period in Egypt

**330 B.C.** Alexander the Great conquers the Persian Empire

**146 B.C.** Punic Wars end; Rome rules Carthaginian empire

**330 A.D.** Constantine I selects Constantinople as capital of Byzantine Empire

**476 A.D.** Collapse of Roman Empire; Germanic tribes divide up western Europe

**632 A.D.** Death of Mohammed. Islam is accepted by most people of Arabia and spreads to North Africa and western Europe

**840 A.D.** Viking, Magyar, and Moslem invasions of western Europe begin; Carolingian empire declines

**1066 A.D.** Norman conquest of England

**1096– 1099 A.D.** First Crusade

**1215 A.D.** Magna Carta signed

**1492 A.D.** Columbus sets sail from Spain; reaches the "New World"

UNIT III

# *Emergence of Nation States*

- *During all these shocks, there have been formed since the time of Charlemagne only two absolutely independent republics—that of Switzerland and that of Holland.*

  *What then have been the fruits of the blood of so many millions of men shed in battle, and the sacking of so many cities? Nothing great or considerable. The Christian powers have lost a great deal to the Turks, within these five centuries, and have gained scarcely anything from each other.*

  VOLTAIRE

- *An emperor is subject to no one but to God and justice.*

  FREDERICK BARBAROSSA

- *The pope is the only person whose feet are kissed by all princes. His title is unique in the world. He may depose emperors.*

  POPE GREGORY VII

# The Holy Roman Empire

In the 18th century, the French philosopher Voltaire made the famous judgment cited above on the Holy Roman Empire. By then, the empire had existed, in name at least, for more than 800 years, but it was far different from the political unit put together by Charlemagne's successor in the lands east of the Rhine River, the region that we know as Germany.

The Holy Roman Empire developed in the eastern kingdom that Charlemagne's grandson, Louis, had been granted by the Treaty of Verdun (Chapter 15). Although the area had been conquered by Charlemagne, the Germanic tribes who lived there were less influenced by Roman customs than the other peoples of Charlemagne's empire.

Louis and his descendants were generally ineffective rulers. By the time the last of them, Louis the Child, died in 911, the area had become fragmented into five large duchies, each ruled by a duke who was descended from Germanic chiefs. The dukes depended on the ties of tribal loyalty and their own skill to administer their territories. Besides these dukes, the bishops and archbishops of several larger cities exercised considerable power.

From the 10th century on, however, the European political scene slowly changed. Although feudalism remained strong and feudal nobles were carving out great estates for themselves and their heirs, feudal monarchs began to assert their power. Over centuries of struggle, they gradually combated the forces of decentralization by dominating or subduing rebellious nobles; seeking to control the power of the Church; establishing law and order; and inspiring loyalty first to a ruling house and much later to the still emerging concept of a nation. In Germany, England, and France, rulers pursued these goals with varying measures of success. In this chapter, you will study aims and achievements of the Holy Roman emperors.

**THE SAXONS** The five chief duchies of the area were Saxony, Franconia, Swabia, Bavaria, and Lorraine. On the death of the last Carolingian in 911, the dukes of these regions elected Conrad of Franconia, the weakest of the rulers, to be the king. Conrad held the title for eight years but did little more than rule Franconia. Like the Carolingians before him, Conrad was unable either to control the other dukes or defeat the Magyar invaders who threatened from the east. As he was dying, Conrad recommended that his rival, Henry, duke of Saxony, be elected as his successor.

### HENRY THE FOWLER (919-936)

Henry I, who became known as "the Fowler" because his favorite sport was hunting wildfowl, established the Saxon Dynasty. At first, his leadership was acknowledged only by Franconia and Saxony, but he soon forced Swabia and Bavaria to support him and assumed control of Lorraine, a duchy bordering Saxony in the west.

Besides gaining recognition of his authority, Henry moved firmly against the Vikings in the north and the Magyars and Slavs in the east. He built a line of forts along the eastern frontier to defend against attacks by the Slavs and Magyars. In several battles, he defeated these persistent invaders. As a result of these successes, Henry earned the respect of many people, who then turned to him, rather than to their feudal lords, for protection and leadership. When Henry named his son Otto as his successor, the nobles did not dispute the appointment.

### OTTO THE GREAT (936-973)

After Henry died in 936, Otto was crowned at Aachen, the capital of Charlemagne's empire. He strengthened his position by making an alliance with the Church, giving bishops control over vast holdings. In return, the bishops contributed money and soldiers to the king's army. Under the feudal system, the king appointed the bishops to their offices, and the bishops were bound to obey their feudal lord—the king. With the support of the Church, Otto was able to increase his power over the nobles. He seized the land of those who opposed him and either gave it to the Church or to a loyal relative.

Otto scored an impressive victory when he threw back a determined Magyar invasion. In 955, he thoroughly defeated the Magyars at the battle of Lechfeld. Otto followed

With the help of the Church, Otto the Great created a unified Germanic kingdom in the eastern part of Charlemagne's empire. This statue of Otto stood in a cathedral that he built at Magdeburg.

up his success by encouraging missionaries to go into Hungary to convert the Magyars to Christianity. At the same time, he pressed for German expansion to the east, persuading colonists to move into the lands of the Slavs and thereby control them.[1]

Like Charlemagne before him and like his own successors, Otto was drawn into the political battles of Italy. The Lombards who had controlled the north were divided among

---

[1] The idea of the "drive to the east" (*Drang nach Osten*) remained an important factor in German political decisions into the 20th century.

themselves, and their quarrels offered the pretext for interference. Also, the pope often faced difficulty controlling the Papal States in central Italy. In invading Italy, Otto followed the precedent that had been set by Charlemagne and sought to revive the glories of the old Roman empire.

In 951, Otto led his army across the Alps into Italy on the pretext of freeing Queen Adelaide, the widow of a Lombard king, who had been imprisoned by her enemies. He defeated her enemies, rescued her from prison, married her, and claimed the crown of Italy for himself. In 960, Pope John XII, whose lands were under attack, appealed to Otto for help. When Otto marched into Italy again, the grateful pope crowned him emperor in 962. To Otto, the pope's action placed him in the line of succession after the Roman emperors and Charlemagne. Not only was he the king of the German lands but also he was the supreme ruler of Christendom. Otto's coronation formally launched the Holy Roman Empire, as it was later called. It also bound up the fate of Germany with that of Italy for centuries to come.

### THE FRANCONIANS

Otto's successors neglected their lands in Germany while they attempted to strengthen their hold over Italy. The Slavs in the east and the Danes in the north exploited this neglect and attacked German strongholds, inflicting much damage. Despite their failings, the Saxon kings were the most powerful in Europe at the time, and the policies they laid down were followed by later German rulers. When the last Saxon king died in 1024, the German nobles elected Conrad II of Franconia (1024-1039) as king. The Franconian Dynasty ruled for only a century, but Conrad and his son Henry III (1039-1056) increased royal authority by centralizing power.

The Franconian rulers reduced the powers of the nobles by replacing as many of them as possible with *ministeriales* (from the Latin *minister* or servant), officials whose authority came directly from the king and whose children could not inherit their offices. The king did this to prevent any family from achieving enough power to challenge him. Conrad and Henry strengthened the royal treasury by collecting long-neglected taxes, making the nobles pay their feudal dues, and developing silver mines from which coins could be minted. The Franconian rulers appointed capable people who were loyal to them to positions of leadership in the Church and worked for much-needed reforms in the Church.

Henry III helped Leo IX become pope in 1049 and supported the new pope's efforts to correct the worst abuses of the clergy, including simony and the failure of priests to obey their vows of celibacy. When Henry III died in 1056, his six-year-old son, Henry IV, ascended the throne. During the boy's long minority, the nobles seized royal property and assumed many royal powers. As a result, when Henry began to rule in his own name, he was constantly struggling to assert royal authority over his unruly nobles.

### THE INVESTITURE CONTROVERSY

While Henry was busy recovering royal power, an ambitious new pope was chosen, and these two strong-minded men were destined to clash. In 1073, a monk named Hildebrand, who had been in the forefront of the Cluniac reform movement (Chapter 16), was elected to the papacy as Pope Gregory VII. Under him, the papacy reached new heights of power and prestige. Gregory was determined not only to end abuses among the clergy but also to free the Church from secular control by putting all members of the clergy under papal—not royal—control. Thus, he set out to end the practice of **lay investiture**, whereby monarchs invested, or installed ceremonially, bishops in office. To achieve this goal, Gregory issued a decree in 1075, forbidding lay investiture and threatening to excommunicate anyone who disobeyed it. The famous decree read in part:

••• [W]e decree that no one of the clergy shall receive investiture with a bishopric or abbey, or church, from the hand of an emperor, or king, or of any lay person, male or female. If he shall presume to do so, let him know that such investiture is void by apostolic authority, and that he himself shall lie under excommunication until fitting satisfaction shall be made.[2]

Although the pope's decree extended to all rulers, he did not enter into the battle with the kings of England or France. Instead, his action brought him into a decisive struggle with the emperor Henry IV, the most powerful ruler in Europe at the time.

With the nobles of the empire restless and resistant to his authority, Henry needed to be able to appoint bishops and archbishops who were loyal to him. His response to Gregory was immediate, forceful, and insulting. Addressing the pope as "Hildebrand, now no longer pope but false monk," Henry accused him of simony and other abuses. "By craft abhorrent to the profession of monk, thou hast acquired wealth; by wealth, influence; by influence, arms; by arms, a throne of peace; thou has turned subjects against their governors."[3]

Gregory then sent papal envoys to warn Henry that his insolence would not be tolerated. Henry, in turn, summoned a synod of German bishops loyal to him, and had them depose the pope. Gregory responded by excommunicating and deposing the em-

The humiliation of Henry IV at the hands of the pope became a celebrated episode in the struggle between church and state. In this illustration, the king begs an abbot and a countess to intercede with the pope on his behalf.

peror and releasing Henry's subjects from their oaths of allegiance to him.

The German nobles were delighted and invited the pope to Augsburg to preside over the election of a new emperor. Recognizing that he was threatened with the loss of his kingdom, Henry decided to seek forgiveness. In the winter of 1077, dressed as a humble pilgrim, he crossed the Alps to Canossa, in northern Italy, where he sought a meeting with the pope who had stopped there en route to Augsburg.

Under Church law, the pope had to pardon a penitent sinner, but he did not do so before Henry had suffered the humiliation of pleading for forgiveness:

••• Laying aside all the trappings of royalty, he stood in wretchedness, barefooted and clad in wool, for three days before the gate of

[2]"Decree of November 19, 1075," Gregorius Registrium, Book VI, in J. H. Robinson, ed., Readings in European History, vol. 1 (New York: Ginn, 1904), p. 275.

[3]"Henry IV's violent reply to Gregory," Monumenta Germaniae Historica Selecta, edited by Doebel, in Readings in European History, ed. Robinson, p. 280.

*the castle, and implored with profuse weeping the aid and consolation of apostolic mercy, until he had moved all who saw or heard of it to such pity and depth of compassion that they interceded for him with many prayers and tears.*[4]

After keeping Henry waiting in the snow for three days, the pope readmitted him to the Church. However, the events at Canossa did not end the struggle between the emperor and the pope. Henry at once began plotting his revenge. His chance came in 1083 when he captured Rome and set his own candidate on the papal throne. Supporters of Gregory appealed for help to the Normans, who controlled southern Italy. The Normans and their Moslem allies then marched on Rome, attacking and pillaging the city. When they withdrew, Gregory accompanied them because the Romans held him responsible for the looting of their city. He died in exile in 1085, worn out by his struggle to establish papal power. Henry, too, died alone after failing to regain his throne from his son who had rebelled against him.

### CONCORDAT OF WORMS

The conflict between emperors and popes continued until 1122, when the German nobles, weary of endless conflicts, forced the emperor Henry V to agree to a compromise with the pope. This compromise became known as the *Concordat of Worms* because it was signed in the German city of that name.

By the terms of that treaty, the emperor gave up his claim to invest the bishops with the symbols of their religious office (ring and staff), but he was still allowed to invest them with the sceptre that represented their temporal power. Also, the clergy's right to elect their bishops was recognized, but the election had to take place in the presence of the

emperor so that the emperor had at least some influence over the choice. While the pope agreed to give up his demand to govern religious estates in Germany, he got full control over the appointment of bishops in northern Italy. The Concordat was a compromise, but it weakened the Holy Roman Empire in both its German and Italian lands. The emperors would never again exert as much control over the Church in Germany as they had in the days of Otto.

### THE HOHENSTAUFENS

After the Franconian dynasty died out in 1125, Germany was torn by civil strife. The two most powerful noble families, the Welfs and Hohenstaufens, struggled for the title of emperor. When the German nobles chose a Hohenstaufen prince as Emperor Conrad III (1138-1152), warfare broke out between the families. After Conrad gained the throne, he set off on the Second Crusade but on his return to Germany found the nobles fighting each other and him. When Conrad III died without an heir, the nobles chose as emperor his nephew Frederick of Hohenstaufen, a compromise candidate because his mother had been a Welf.

---

[4]"Gregory's account of Henry's penance at Canossa," in *Readings in European History*, ed. Robinson, p. 283.

| RULERS OF THE HOLY ROMAN EMPIRE | |
| --- | --- |
| 911-918 | Conrad, duke of Franconia |
| 919-1024 | Saxon Dynasty |
| 919-936 | Henry I, the Fowler |
| 936-973 | Otto I, the Great |
| 1024-1125 | Franconian Dynasty |
| 1024-1039 | Conrad II |
| 1039-1056 | Henry III |
| 1056-1106 | Henry IV |
| 1125-1268 | Hohenstaufen Dynasty |
| 1138-1152 | Conrad III |
| 1152-1190 | Frederick Barbarossa |
| 1212-1250 | Frederick II |

## FREDERICK I (1152-1190)

Frederick I—called "Barbarossa" because of his red beard—was determined to centralize royal authority. To this end, he forced the nobles to reaffirm their feudal obligations, and attempted to assert control over appointments to Church offices. He suppressed a revolt led by a Welf cousin, and took steps to protect the northern and eastern boundaries of his empire from the Vikings.

As soon as Germany was under control, Frederick turned his attention to Italy where he looked on the cities of Venice, Genoa, Pisa, and Milan as sources of revenue for his empire. These great cities were profiting from the revival of trade that took place in the 12th century and were becoming the most powerful political forces within Italy. In each city, opposing groups struggled for leadership, and the weaker group frequently sought outside help, especially from the emperor.

Pope Adrian IV also sought Frederick's help to prevent the Norman king of Sicily, Roger II, from attacking Italy. At first, the pope was grateful for the emperor's assistance. But the cooperation did not last long, and war erupted between pope and emperor. The former was supported by the *Lombard League*, an association of northern Italian cities that resented the emperor's efforts to rule them. In 1168, Frederick defeated the pope and captured Rome, but he was forced to withdraw from the city when a disastrous epidemic broke out.

In 1176, the combined forces of the pope and the Lombard League defeated Frederick's army at Legnano and forced him to run for his life. However, Frederick recouped his fortunes quickly. The following year, he reconciled himself with the pope. In 1183, he signed the *Peace of Constance* with the Lombard League, in which he granted the cities the right of self-government in exchange for certain taxes. Although Frederick was forced to make some compromises, the terms of the treaty defended his claim as a feudal lord over the north of Italy and extended his direct rule over central Italy.

*After asserting the power of the Holy Roman Emperor with some success, Frederick Barbarossa embarked on the Third Crusade. He is shown here in the act of assaulting a Moslem fortress.*

*According to popular superstition, Frederick Barbarossa did not die during the Crusade, but fell asleep in a secret cave.*

Frederick strengthened his position further by marrying his son and heir, the future Henry VI, to Constance, the daughter of the Norman king of Sicily. By this marriage, Frederick posed a new threat to the papacy, whose lands were now enclosed by Hohenstaufen territories both in the north and in the south. When the news reached Europe that Saladin had captured Jerusalem, Frederick set out on the Third Crusade (Chapter 16), but he drowned while crossing a river in Asia Minor.

By sheer ambition and force of personality, Frederick had increased the power of the Holy Roman Empire. So great was his success that he became a German folk hero. For centuries, people believed that he was not really dead but merely asleep in a cave and that he would return to rescue them in a time of need.

Frederick had worked to establish strong feudal ties to himself, so that all feudal power derived from the emperor. However, several important duchies, such as Saxony and Bavaria, remained independent, and in time, German feudalism strengthened these rulers rather than the central government. In Italy, the growing wealth and prestige of the city-states made it possible for their leaders to challenge the control of the emperor.

### FREDERICK II (1220–1250)

Frederick Barbarossa's son, Henry VI, continued in his father's tradition, consolidating his power over Sicily and planning further conquests. But he died after a brief reign, leaving only an infant son, the future Frederick II. As a result, the Holy Roman Empire was torn by civil war as various nobles supported their own candidates to the imperial throne. During this period, the nobles became increasingly independent of the authority of the emperor. The pope, Innocent III, also took part in the struggle, supporting first one candidate for emperor and then the youthful Frederick from whom he extracted a promise to give up his claim to Sicily. Having no other choice, Frederick agreed to these terms and was proclaimed the Holy Roman emperor by Innocent.

Frederick turned at once to winning control of his German lands and gradually defeated the powerful forces in the field against him. Soon after Innocent died in 1216, Frederick retreated from his earlier agreement with the papacy and returned to Italy, where he was determined to expand his power over the Kingdom of the Two Sicilies (Sicily and Naples) to include all of the peninsula south of the Papal States.

Because Frederick II spent most of his life in Sicily, he had little interest in the northern part of his empire. To curry favor with the German princes and clergy, he transferred control of many royal estates in Germany to the local princes, bishops, and abbots, and

## THE HOLY ROMAN EMPIRE
*Why did the Holy Roman emperors have little real power over their German lands?*

DENMARK

LITHUANIA

POMERANIA

PRUSSIA

• Hamburg

SAXONY

BRANDENBURG

• Magdeburg

POLAND

Aachen •   • Cologne

LORRAINE

THURINGIA

FRANCONIA

• Worms

BOHEMIA

MORAVIA

FRANCE

SWABIA

AUSTRIA

• Vienna

HUNGARY

LOMBARDY   • Milan

Venice

CROATIA

Genoa

• Canossa

KINGDOM
OF
ITALY

SERBIA

*ADRIATIC SEA*

CORSICA

• Rome

Naples

SARDINIA

KINGDOM

OF SICILY

*MEDITERRANEAN SEA*

• Palermo

SICILY

| | Empire under Otto I, about 960 |
| --- | --- |
| | Empire under Frederick II, about 1250 |
| | Papal States |

**151**

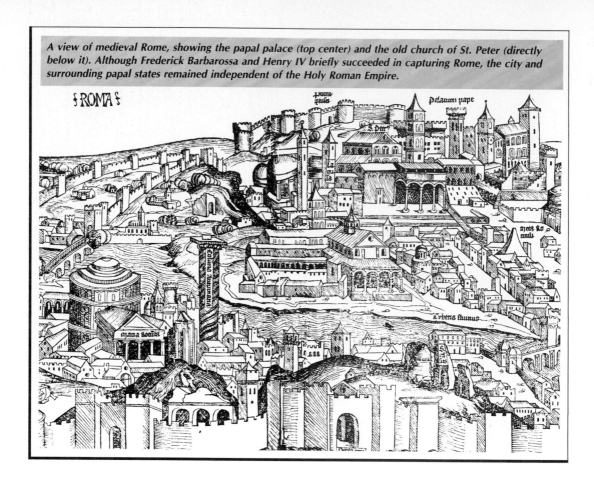

*A view of medieval Rome, showing the papal palace (top center) and the old church of St. Peter (directly below it). Although Frederick Barbarossa and Henry IV briefly succeeded in capturing Rome, the city and surrounding papal states remained independent of the Holy Roman Empire.*

exempted the churches from imperial jurisdiction. By allowing the clergy and nobles these privileges, Frederick gave up royal rights and set the stage for Germany to become a region of small independent states instead of a unified nation.

In Italy, Frederick first consolidated his power in Sicily, assuming direct control of the government. He then reorganized the army and navy as paid forces rather than feudal levies. He set up a more efficient treasury and established a university at Naples that would train students in Roman law. By these policies, Frederick set up a national monarchy more advanced than those of contemporary rulers in England and France. Yet Frederick's achievement was short-lived and

was overshadowed by his titanic conflict with the papacy.

When Gregory IX was elected pope in 1227, he became alarmed at Frederick's plans to unite Italy. In order to thwart such an undertaking, Gregory ordered Frederick to fulfill his earlier promise to lead a Crusade to the Holy Land. When Frederick failed to make plans for the Crusade, Gregory excommunicated him. To redeem himself, Frederick organized and departed on the Sixth Crusade in 1228. Through negotiation with the sultan of Egypt, Frederick gained control of Jerusalem, Bethlehem, and Nazareth—the three cities which were most holy to Christians—and won access to these cities through the port at Sidon.

Despite Frederick's success, his relations with the papacy worsened. Frederick returned from the Crusade to find his lands in southern Italy under attack by papal forces. From then on until his death in 1250, Frederick was at war with the papacy. To Pope Gregory IX and his successor, the emperor's attempt to extend his power over all of Italy was a deadly threat, while the emperor accused the pope of hypocrisy and attacked the clergy for their corruption and greed. Repeatedly deposed and excommunicated by the pope, Frederick fought on, and the bitter struggle raged not only in Italy but also in Germany. It would continue even after Frederick's death in 1250.

While Frederick did not have the political or military skills of his grandfather, he was better educated and more scholarly. Committed to intellectual pursuits, he became a patron of the arts and sciences and made his court in Sicily the cultural center of Europe. He composed one of the first poems ever written in Italian and wrote a treatise on falconry that is still regarded as an authoritative work on the subject. Not without good reason did Frederick's admirers call him *Stupor Mundi* ("the wonder of the world"), although his critics called him a "baptized sultan" because of his interest in and admiration for Islamic civilization. However, his constant conflict with the papacy and his neglect of his German possessions set the stage for the disintegration of the Holy Roman Empire.

### DECLINE OF THE HOLY ROMAN EMPIRE

After Frederick's death, the papacy renewed its offensive against his heirs. With the help of Charles of Anjou, brother of the French king Louis IX, the pope succeeded in overthrowing the Hohenstaufens in Sicily, and the last Hohenstaufen was captured and executed in 1268. A few years later in 1273, Rudolf of Hapsburg became emperor, establishing a new ruling dynasty that held power until 1806, when the Holy Roman Empire was finally swept away by the conquests of Napoleon Bonaparte.

In the century that followed Frederick's death, the princes and bishops of Germany gained more and more power at the expense of the emperor. In 1356, an effort was made to restore the prestige of the Holy Roman Empire by urging the stronger German princes to elect one of their number as emperor. The plan was described in a document known as the "Golden Bull." It established a council of seven electors, which was made up of the large archbishoprics of Germany—Mainz, Trier, and Cologne—and the secular rulers of four of the largest regions—the Palatine, Saxony, Brandenburg, and Bohemia. However, the system of electors prevented effective imperial rule. When a new emperor was to be chosen, the electors were able to demand concessions in exchange for their votes.

Without a strong central government, individual princely families came to the forefront of politics in Germany. Each controlled vast lands, and they were more interested in promoting their own interests than in the welfare of the empire as a whole—a situation known as particularism. In the late Middle Ages, several German cities declared their independence from the empire. Some of them, including Lübeck and Ulm, became major centers of industry, commerce, culture, and learning. The absence of a strong emperor also allowed regions on the border of the empire to develop into independent states, giving rise to the medieval states of Poland and Hungary (Chapter 22).

Despite the weakness of the Holy Roman Empire and the failure to centralize royal power, the emperor commanded a dominant position in European politics. The Hapsburg emperors rose to great prominence in the 16th century, ruling vast lands of their own in Austria, the Netherlands, and even Spain, as well as exercising at least nominal control over the states of the Holy Roman Empire.

## SUMMARY

*The Holy Roman Empire was put together in the eastern lands that were once part of Charlemagne's empire. In 962, Otto I, with papal support, assumed the imperial title and began to extend control over the empire. Otto's successors slowly strengthened their position against powerful dukes. However, the alliance that Otto had formed with the Church did not last as emperors and popes became embroiled in bitter power struggles. In the 11th century, the Holy Roman emperor Henry IV and Pope Gregory VII clashed in the investiture controversy. The struggle was not settled until 1122 with the Concordat of Worms, which gave the Church control over the selection of bishops.*

*The Hohenstaufen emperors became deeply involved in Italy, and their efforts to extend their control over the peninsula dragged them into wars with the cities of the north and with the papacy. Although Frederick II consolidated his power in southern Italy, he did so at the expense of his German lands. After his death, Germany was fragmented and remained so until the 19th century.*

## QUESTIONS

1 Describe the growth of the Holy Roman Empire from the 10th to the 13th centuries. Using a map of medieval Europe and a modern political map of Europe, name the present-day countries that were once part of the Holy Roman Empire.

2 How did the personalities of Henry IV and Gregory VII influence the investiture struggle? What were the central issues of this struggle? How was the struggle eventually resolved?

3 Why did Frederick Barbarossa and Frederick II each fail to develop a strong German state?

4 What reasons account for the decline of the Holy Roman Empire after 1250? Despite the decline, why do you think the empire continued to exist until the early 19th century?

5 Do you think that Voltaire's 18th century judgment of the Holy Roman Empire as "neither holy, Roman, nor an empire" was true in the 13th century? Explain.

## BIBLIOGRAPHY

### Which books might analyze Frederick II's conflict with the papacy?

BARRACLOUGH, GEOFFREY. *The Origins of Modern Germany.* New York: W. W. Norton, 1984. *A revised edition of a useful survey tracing the political, social, and economic forces that shaped Germany.*

BRYCE, JAMES. *The Holy Roman Empire.* New York: Schocken Books, 1961. *A 19th century history of the Holy Roman Empire that is still considered a classic.*

KANTOROWICZ, ERNST. *Frederick the Second, 1194-1250.* New York: Frederick Ungar, 1957. *A detailed, scholarly biography of this unorthodox and ambitious ruler. Explores the bitter rivalry between the papacy and the emperor.*

**9**

There is a saying known of yore,
What is a kingdom's treasury?
Cattle and beasts, corn stuffed in store,
Rich commons and wise clergy;
Merchants, squires, chivalry
That will be ready at need to rise;
And a chivalrous king, of wisdom high,
To lead in war and govern in peace.
ENGLISH POEM (1401)

# England in the Middle Ages

In the Middle Ages, Europe was a patchwork of many feudal territories that created a confusion of overlapping loyalties. A medieval monarch was not the supreme ruler of the land, but was rather one lord among many, and frequently ruled over nobles who had more land and even exercised more power than he. In legal matters, too, royal authority was limited since both the Church and the feudal lords had their own courts.

During the later Middle Ages, this situation changed dramatically as strong monarchs in different parts of Europe consolidated power. They gained control over the feudal lords and struggled for influence over the Church. In the process, they laid the foundations for the nation-states of today.

These early nation-states sometimes, but not always, welded together groups of people who shared a common language and common traditions, and lived in a clearly defined geographic area. To ensure royal power, strong monarchs established a central authority that kept order within the community; they resisted the efforts of decentralizing forces such as the Church and the feudal nobles; they expanded royal justice, making royal courts preferable to other courts; they set up a stable financial system; organized a royal bureaucracy to carry out royal commands; developed a standing army to replace uncertain feudal levies; and formed an alliance with the emerging middle class. In short, monarchs tried to establish the kind of ideal kingdom described in the English poem cited above. By doing so, they created the notion that the well-being of the state depended upon the ruler.

The establishment of a strong, centralized government did not follow the same pattern in all parts of Europe. As you have read, the struggles between emperors and popes distracted the rulers of the Holy Roman Empire and kept the area of present-day Germany from being united. On the western edge of Europe, however, England became one of the first countries to coalesce into a nation. Over the centuries, England was conquered by a succession of invaders, each of whom left their mark on the country's culture and institutions.

**THE BRITISH ISLES** The earliest inhabitants of England of whom we have substantial knowledge were the Celts, a group of Indo-European tribes

*155*

that the Greeks called *Keltoi*, and the Romans called *Gauls*. About 700 B.C., the Celts began to leave their original home, which is believed to have been the region between the upper Rhine and the Danube rivers. Some moved southward into the Italian peninsula, where they destroyed Etruscan cities and sacked Rome in 390 B.C. Others moved eastward into the Balkans, crossed the Hellespont into Asia Minor, and settled in an area that came to be called *Galatia*. Still others moved westward into present-day France and England. There, they defeated the native inhabitants and established their own culture.

The next invaders were the Romans. After conquering Gaul, Julius Caesar landed his legions in Britain and established relations with the inhabitants. Nearly a century later, in 43 A.D., the emperor Claudius conquered Britain and established Roman rule there. The Romans remained in Britain until shortly after 400 A.D. when their legions were withdrawn. But they left their mark on the islands, having brought Christianity to the Celts and built an excellent system of roads across the land. The Celts were left to maintain Roman ways and Christian beliefs against other invaders—the Angles, Saxons, and Jutes from northern Europe. Before long, the Latin language and Christianity disappeared almost completely from England.

Little is known about the 5th century invasions of the Angles, Saxons, and Jutes. These Germanic tribes ravaged the land, destroying the remains of Romano-British culture. According to legend, a Celtic leader named Artorius (or Arthur), who lived in the 6th century, fought heroically against the invaders and is credited with defending western England and Wales against the Saxons. For centuries, oral tales of Arthur's prowess circulated around Britain, and these tales gave rise to the Arthurian legends that were written down in the later Middle Ages. Recent archaeological explorations at Glastonbury in western England have provided scholars with intriguing evidence that there really was

According to legend, King Arthur and his men defended 6th-century Celtic settlements in western Britain against Saxon invaders. Later, other episodes—such as the search for the Holy Grail, and the romance of Lancelot and Guinevere—were added to the story.

a King Arthur, although many of the tales of knights and chivalry were inventions of later medieval minds.

### DEVELOPMENT OF CHRISTIANITY

Even while the Roman legions were leaving Britain in the early 5th century, the Church kept up its efforts to bring Christianity to the British Isles. Among the best-known missionaries was Saint Patrick, who carried Christianity to Ireland. As a result of his efforts, Ireland was a Christian stronghold in the early Middle Ages, and many Irish monks traveled to England and other parts of Europe to pursue their missionary activities. Irish monks preserved the scholarly traditions, learning Greek and Latin and producing splendid illuminated manuscripts such as the *Book of Kells*.

*During the 6th and 7th centuries. Irish monks traveled to Scotland and northern England to spread Christianity. They built monasteries at Iona, off the coast of Scotland, and at Lindisfarne ("Holy Island") in Northumbria, the ruins of which are shown here.*

In the 6th century, an Irish monk named Columba carried Christianity to the Picts, the people who inhabited Scotland. He traveled as far north as Inverness, preaching and baptizing the people. He also set up several monasteries, including one on the small island of Iona off the western coast of Scotland. During the invasions of the next few centuries, the monks of Iona preserved Christian traditions, and Iona eventually became the center of monasticism in Scotland.

As you have read, Pope Gregory the Great sent Augustine to England in 597 (Chapter 16). Augustine landed in Kent and walked to Canterbury, the site of a church dating back to Roman times. There, he established his "chair" and became the first archbishop of Canterbury. Through the work of Augustine and his successors, the Angles, Saxons, and Jutes were converted to Christianity.

### ANGLO-SAXON KINGDOMS

During the chaotic centuries of invasion, various tribal leaders set up a number of small kingdoms such as Sussex (kingdom of the South Saxons), Wessex (kingdom of the West Saxons), and Essex (kingdom of the East Saxons). Gradually, distinctions between Angles, Saxons, and Jutes became blurred, and the entire area became known as England, or Land of the Angles. By the 9th century, the kingdom of Wessex in south-central England emerged as the dominant power, and its ruler became the first English king.

**Alfred the Great.** Anglo-Saxon civilization reached its height under Alfred, king of Wessex (871-899). He was a man of great intelligence and ability, and he needed these qualities to meet the threat to his kingdom posed by the Danes, as the English called the Vikings who raided their shores. By the mid-9th century, the Danes had conquered all of England except Wessex and were readying an all-out assault on that stronghold. Early in his reign, Alfred purchased a truce from the Danes to give himself time to strengthen the defenses of his kingdom. He reorganized his army, had large fortifications constructed at strategic places, and ordered new ships built to defend the coast. These measures

*Beginning in 835, Danish Vikings carried out a full-scale invasion of England. In contrast to their earlier behavior, they did not merely raid the coastal areas, but conquered and settled the interior of the country.*

writing of the *Anglo-Saxon Chronicle*, an account of English history from Roman times to his own reign. Alfred decreed that a copy of the chronicle be placed in every cathedral and monastery so that events could be added as they occurred. The chronicle serves as our principal source of information about this period.

Alfred journeyed throughout his kingdom to see that local courts were dealing justly with the people, and he called on his officials to inform him of miscarriages of justice. For his many achievements, he earned the title *Alfred the Great.* After his death, the *Anglo-Saxon Chronicle* eulogized him.

• • • *[H]e exalted God's praise far and wide and loved God's law; and he improved the peace of the people more than the kings who were before him in the memory of man. . . . He came to be honored widely throughout the countries, because he zealously honoured God's name, and time and again meditated on God's law, and exalted God's praise far and wide, and continually and frequently directed all his people wisely in matters of Church and State.*[1]

**Government.** Alfred's successors continued to expand Anglo-Saxon power and unified the kingdom. By the mid-10th century, they had brought all of England under royal control. The Anglo-Saxon kings then developed new means of ruling the land. They divided the kingdom into areas called shires, or counties. Each shire was ruled by an *earl*, appointed by the king. In turn, each shire was subdivided into areas called *hundreds*; a *thegn* was appointed to rule each hundred. In every shire and hundred, a royal official, called a *reeve*, presided over the court system. At first, the shire-reeve (who later became known as the *sheriff*) only collected revenues for the king, but later he was given the duty of administering justice.

succeeded. In 878, Alfred defeated the Danes and set up a treaty under which the Danes were limited to settling in the *Danelaw*, a large area in northeastern England.

In addition to his military successes, Alfred proved his leadership in civil affairs. He collected all the written laws in England and fashioned them into a law code to be used throughout his kingdom. He invited scholars from all over Europe to his kingdom and asked them to recommend ways of reviving culture and learning, which had suffered during the long years of war. He supported education, encouraged the translation of Latin works into the vernacular, and was responsible for the

[1]D. Whitelock, ed., *The Anglo-Saxon Chronicle*, revised translation (New Brunswick: Rutgers University Press, 1961), pp. 74-75.

## ANGLO-SAXON KINGDOMS
*Which Anglo-Saxon kingdoms were most likely to be attacked by the Danes?*

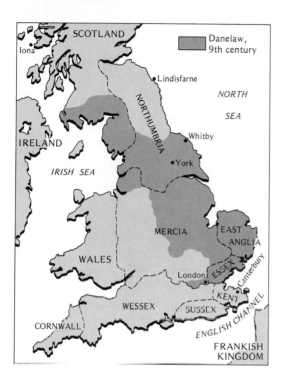

As the representative of the king, the shire-reeve brought wrongdoers before the local courts to answer for their misdeeds. A court was made up of the thegn who ruled the hundred where the accused lived, and a group of common people, called *doomsmen*. The accused could attempt to prove his or her innocence before the court by one of several methods: *compurgation*, persuading other people to swear to his or her good character; *wager of battle*, fighting the person bringing the complaint with fists or clubs to determine the winner; or *trial by ordeal*, undergoing a test, such as picking up hot metal (Chapter 17). While this system of justice may seem very harsh by today's standards, it formed the basis of the legal system that evolved in much of the Western world. The position of thegn ultimately developed into that of judge, the doomsmen eventually be-

came the jury, and compurgation evolved into the use of character witnesses.

Anglo-Saxon kings also sought the advice of a council known as the *Witan*, or *Witenagemot* (meaning "Council of Wise Men") made up of earls and thegns. The most important function of the Witan was electing a new monarch when the reigning one died.

### VIKING INVASIONS

In the late 10th century, the kingdom of Wessex faced a new threat when Vikings from Denmark again raided England. The king, Ethelred, was unable to curtail the growing power of his nobles or rally the people against the invaders. He then levied a heavy tax, called the *Danegeld*, on his subjects, and hoped to use the proceeds to bribe the Danes to stop their attacks. The money failed to accomplish its purpose, but Ethelred and his successors continued to use the Danegeld as a means of raising money. By 1013, Ethelred could no longer restrain the invaders, so he fled to Normandy, leaving his son Edmund to defend England. After Edmund died in 1016, the *Witan* named the Danish leader Canute to be the king of England.

Canute proved to be a wise choice. He eased the strife between the English and the Danes, married Ethelred's widow, Emma, and treated the Church generously. When he died in 1035, however, violence again broke out and lasted until the Witan chose another of Ethelred's sons, Edward, to be king of England.

Edward was devoutly religious and earned the nickname Edward the Confessor. He failed to unite the country, and the nobles steadily increased their powers at the expense of the king. When Edward died in 1066, there were three candidates for the throne of England: William, duke of Normandy; Harold Godwine, son of a prominent Anglo-Saxon noble; and Harold Hadrada, king of Norway. The Witan chose Harold Godwine to be king, but soon after he was crowned, the new ruler faced attacks from both his rivals.

**159**

Soon after Harold was crowned as the successor of Edward the Confessor, a luminous sphere—now known as Halley's comet—appeared in the sky. As this scene indicates, both the king and his subjects feared that the comet was an omen of disaster.

William of Normandy was one of the most powerful feudal lords in western Europe and an able administrator. In 1064, William had taken Harold Godwine captive and forced him to recognize William's claim to the English throne. So when Harold accepted the crown in 1066, William accused him of rejecting his oath and prepared to invade England. He convinced the pope to support the invasion by accusing Harold of the sin of perjury in breaking his oath.

**NORMAN CONQUEST** While William was organizing his expedition, Harold Hadrada of Norway landed in the north of England. Harold Godwine marched his army north to meet this threat. The armies of the two Harolds clashed at Stamford Bridge, near York, on September 28, 1066. Harold of Norway was killed, and his invasion was repulsed. But the king had barely left the battlefield when he heard that William of Normandy had set sail for England. Harold rushed south, giving his few

supporters no time to rest. On the way, he recruited whatever additional forces he could.

The two armies met at Hastings on the morning of October 14, 1066. In the ensuing battle, the Normans routed the Anglo-Saxons, and King Harold was killed. The battle of Hastings assured the Norman conquest of England. It stands as a major turning point in English history because it meant that the Normans rather than the Anglo-Saxons would rule England and shape its language and culture in the centuries ahead.

### WILLIAM I (1066-1087)

William of Normandy was crowned king of England on Christmas Day, 1066. He then set about subduing the country and consolidating his power. William was determined to keep the Norman knights who had crossed the English Channel and fought with him at Hastings from becoming powerful enough to challenge his authority. To protect his power, he gave them small, scattered fiefs and demanded their promise to recognize his supremacy. He limited the number and size of castles and forbade his Norman barons to build castles without his consent.

In 1086, William traveled to Salisbury where he demanded an oath of fealty, called the *Salisbury Oath*, from every vassal.

••• *[A]nd there his councillors came to him, and all the people occupying land who were of any account over all England whosoever's vassals they might be; and they all submitted to him, and swore oaths of allegiance to him that they would be faithful to him against all other men.*[2]

Under the Salisbury Oath, vassals owed their primary allegiance to William rather than to the lord from whom they had received their fiefs. This gave William and his successors an advantage over feudal monarchs on the continent who would spend centuries bringing the vassals of the great lords under their direct rule.

In government, William blended the political and social institutions of Anglo-Saxon England with Norman traditions. In the process, he laid the foundations for a strong, centralized government. William changed the Anglo-Saxon Witan into a Great Council that included the great lords of the kingdom. He also established a permanent council of royal advisers called the King's Council, or *Curia Regis*. These institutions would gradually evolve into the English Parliament. William kept the Anglo-Saxon system of local government with the shires, hundreds, and local courts, but he sent out royal commissioners to oversee the courts and sheriffs.

After ensuring his power, William began reforming the Church. He replaced Anglo-Saxon abbots and bishops with Norman clergy, allowed separate ecclesiastical courts to hear cases involving religious matters, enforced the rule of clerical celibacy, and decreed that no papal letter could be read in England without his consent. When Pope Gregory VII attempted to get William to swear allegiance to him and ordered the English bishops to appear in Rome, William rejected both demands. At the time, Gregory was deeply involved in his struggle with the Holy Roman emperor, Henry IV, so he did not contest William's action.

---

[2]Quoted in D. C. Douglas, *William the Conqueror* (Berkeley: University of California Press, 1964), p. 355.

William, duke of Normandy, invaded England with an army of well-trained cavalry troops.

In 1086, William ordered a survey of land ownership to be made throughout England. This survey became known as the *Doomsday Book* because information from it was used as the final *doom*, or judgment, in all disputes over land ownership. The Doomsday Book served an important function: it gave William a detailed record of the economic resources of his kingdom, so that he knew just how much financial and military support he could expect from his subjects. It included a record of all plows, forest land, cows, pigs, and other property in the land. As the *Anglo-Saxon Chronicle* noted, the survey was so complete "that there was not

In the decades following the conquest, Norman barons defended their holdings by building strongly fortified castles like this one.

one hide of land in England that he did not know who owned it, and what it was worth, and then set it down in his record."[3]

The Norman conquest brought many changes to England. Before 1066, England had been influenced by the culture of Scandinavia and northern Germany. After the Norman conquest, contact with Scandinavia decreased while contacts with other parts of western Europe increased. The new Norman lords of England encouraged artisans and traders from France to establish their businesses in England, and new cathedrals were built in the Norman style. William also introduced to England a centralized and efficient form of feudalism. As a result of the conquest, three languages were used in England: French was the language of the court

As king, William the Conquerer deposed the Anglo-Saxon barons of England and gave their lands and possessions to Normans. Here, he gives one of his followers the deed to Northumbria.

---

[3]*The Anglo-Saxon Chronicle*, ed. D. Whitelock, p. 164.

and the ruling class; Latin was the language of the Church; and Anglo-Saxon, or Old English, was the language of the common people. For some time, the distinction between Anglo-Saxon and Norman remained strong, but eventually, through intermarriage and assimilation, the two cultures were blended.

### WILLIAM'S SUCCESSORS

William's successors continued his policies of centralizing royal power. They developed a bureaucracy of paid royal officials who were responsible for administering the kingdom. Unlike the feudal lords, these men owed their positions to the king and could not hand them on to their sons. William's immediate successor was his son, William II (1087-1100), who was also called William Rufus. A harsh

and unpopular ruler, William was killed in a hunting accident and was not much mourned.

Another of William's sons, Henry I, then inherited the throne. Under his leadership, the administration of royal justice was strengthened. Henry sent itinerant judges to outlying areas to hear law cases, thereby diverting cases from the courts of feudal barons and the Church courts. During Henry's reign, vassals were encouraged to pay scutage, or "shield money," instead of performing military service. The royal officials who collected these and other taxes tallied their records on a checkered table resembling a chessboard. In time, the office where this work was done became known as the Exchequer. The Exchequer developed into an account-

*Westminster Abbey in London has been the scene of all royal coronations since the time of William the Conquerer. At right is the coronation chair.*

ing office and a court: the former collected rents, fees, fines, and taxes while the latter decided cases involving these payments.

### HENRY II

When Henry I died in 1135, controversy arose over a successor to the throne. Henry's only son, William, had drowned in a shipwreck, and his daughter, Mathilda, was married to the count of Anjou, the ruler of vast estates in France. The counts of Anjou were traditional enemies of the Normans. In 1154, after a long civil war, Mathilda's son became King Henry II and established a long line of rulers known as the *Plantagenet dynasty*.

By the time Henry II came to the throne of England, he had already inherited the French domains of Anjou and Maine. Through his marriage in 1152 to Eleanor of Aquitaine, he acquired control of Poitou, Gascony, and Aquitaine; thus Henry had authority over more than half of present-day France. He later made himself overlord of Scotland, Ireland, Wales, and Brittany as well.

Henry was a well-educated, intelligent, and able ruler. Soon after gaining the English throne, he set about reestablishing royal authority that had been eroded during the years of civil war. He ordered the destruction of all unlicensed castles and strengthened the royal treasury, dispatching officials to collect the taxes due to the crown. Most important, he broadened the scope of royal justice and extended the jurisdiction of royal courts. He did this through the use of itinerant judges who based their decisions on the common customs and traditions of the people. In doing so, he laid the foundations for the development of *common law*—law that is common to the entire land because it was carried out by royal courts. Gradually, common law came to refer to the body of legal principles based on the decisions of the royal courts. As people came to rely more and more on the royal courts, the importance of the competing Church and baronial courts declined.

Under Henry II, the early forms of a jury

Henry II, the first Plantagenet king, ruled much of modern France as well as England. His efforts to impose secular justice upon the clergy led to conflict with his friend Thomas à Becket.

system began to appear. There were two kinds of juries. One was assembled after a plaintiff purchased a royal *writ*, or order for a hearing before a royal official. At the hearing, the official asked a group of 12 people who were familiar with the case to present their information under oath. These 12 comprised a jury (from the French *juré*, meaning "sworn under oath"). This early kind of jury would eventually evolve into the trial jury of today.

A second kind of jury was established by the *Assize (Edict) of Clarendon* in 1166. It called for the sheriffs to assemble a group of 12 sworn men from each hundred to appear before the royal justices. They were "to reply truthfully to this question: whether anyone, within their hundred . . . has been accused, or publicly suspected of robbery, murder, or theft, or of harboring men guilty of such crimes, since the lord King's accession."[4] This jury became known as a jury of presentment because it presented the names of people suspected of crimes and was the forerunner of today's *grand jury*, which hears testimony concerning an alleged crime and hands down an indictment, or formal charge.

## STRUGGLE BETWEEN CHURCH AND STATE

Henry II's efforts to extend the activities of the royal courts led him into a bitter struggle with the Church courts. As you have read, Church courts had jurisdiction over many areas including cases that concerned the clergy (Chapter 16). Henry felt that Church courts dealt too leniently with members of the clergy when they were found guilty of serious crimes. Therefore, he issued the Constitution of Clarendon in 1164, which included a provision allowing a member of the clergy to be indicted by a royal court. The person could be tried in a Church court, but if convicted, could be returned to a royal court for punishment. Another provision forbade the clergy from appealing a sentence to the pope without the king's permission.

Henry's action was vigorously opposed by Thomas à Becket, a friend and adviser to the king, whom Henry had recently made archbishop of Canterbury. By this appointment, Henry had hoped to avoid conflict with the Church while he made the changes he wanted. To Henry's surprise, Becket did not acquiesce to the king's assertion of power but instead insisted that no cleric should be subject to the secular laws of England. When a dispute arose over whether royal authorities had the right to punish members of the clergy convicted in a bishop's court, Becket vowed to oppose the Constitution of Clarendon as long as he had breath in his body.

4"Assize of Clarendon," in J. J. Bagley and P. B. Rowley, *Documentary History of England*, vol. 1 (Baltimore: Penguin Books, 1966), pp. 54–55.

### NORMAN AND PLANTAGENET KINGS OF ENGLAND

| | The Normans |
|---|---|
| 1066–1087 | William I, the Conqueror |
| 1087–1100 | William II |
| 1100–1135 | Henry I |
| | |
| | The Plantagenets |
| 1154–1189 | Henry II |
| 1189–1199 | Richard I |
| 1199–1216 | John |
| 1216–1272 | Henry III |
| 1272–1307 | Edward I |
| 1307–1327 | Edward II |
| 1327–1377 | Edward III |
| 1377–1399 | Richard II |

In a fit of anger at his former friend's behavior, Henry is said to have asked, "Is there no one to rid me of this troublesome clerk?" Four of Henry's knights took these words as a command and murdered Becket as he was praying. Whether Henry was responsible for Becket's murder is still uncertain, but at the time people blamed him for it. As penance, Henry walked barefoot through the streets of Canterbury and submitted to flogging by the monks. Henry also agreed to recognize the authority of the pope in Church law and to exempt the clergy from punishment in civil courts. The martyred Becket was soon made a saint, and for centuries, pilgrims journeyed to Canterbury to visit his tomb.

Despite this tragedy, Henry's struggle to establish royal power won him the support of many people. Townspeople and peasants believed that they had a greater chance of obtaining justice in the king's courts than in those of their feudal lords. By setting up a royal bureaucracy of appointed officials who were loyal to the king, Henry II helped to build foundations of a stable government that would function even in the king's absence.

### RICHARD I

Richard I succeeded his father in 1189, but he was almost unknown to the people of England because he lived in his mother's lands of Aquitaine. During his 10-year reign, Richard spent fewer than 6 months in England.

Soon after he became king, Richard decided to take part in the Third Crusade (Chapter 16). Always short of money, he pressed his subjects to support his foreign adventures. Before leaving on the Crusade, he named Hubert Walter to be archbishop of Canterbury and justiciar, the highest positions in the Church and state. Hubert Walter governed England well during Richard's absence and even put down a rebellion fostered by Richard's younger brother, John.

On his way back from the Third Crusade, Richard was captured and held for ransom. The king's mother, Eleanor of Aquitaine, worked tirelessly to raise the ransom money and convinced the English people that their king was a great hero worthy of being called "the Lion-Hearted." The ransom cost workers in England almost a quarter of their annual wages, but it freed their king, who returned to England in 1194. After a few weeks, Richard left again to fight King Philip Augustus, who had seized several of his castles in France. He died in France in 1199.

Richard's wars nearly bankrupted England, and he failed either to defeat the Moslems in the Holy Land or protect his lands in France. Despite these setbacks, he later became a folk hero to the English people and was associated with Robin Hood, a legendary figure who defended the poor against the rich and powerful.

### KING JOHN AND THE MAGNA CARTA

Richard's successor was his younger brother, John, a clever but tyrannical ruler who fought and lost battles with the kings of France, the Church, and his nobles. He earned such a bad reputation that no future English monarch ever chose to take the name John. John

Although Richard I, "the Lion-Hearted," spent most of his time in France and imposed heavy taxes on his subjects, he was one of the most popular monarchs in English history. This statue stands in front of the Parliament buildings in London.

RICHARD·I· COEUR·DE·LION· 1189 · 1199·

*The Magna Carta defined the powers and responsibilities of the king in accordance with feudal tradition. Below are the opening lines of the charter; at bottom, the seal of King John, which was affixed to each copy.*

fought bitterly with Philip Augustus of France, who not only encouraged John's French vassals to revolt but also drove the English out of Normandy. John led a campaign to recover these lands, but when his allies were decisively beaten at Bouvines in 1214, John was forced to return to England with an empty treasury and shattered prestige.

John's position was further weakened by his struggle with Pope Innocent III. When the archbishop of Canterbury died in 1205, John named a successor. So, too, did the monks of Christ Church, who had the traditional right to elect the archbishop. The pope, who was determined to make the papacy supreme, rejected both choices and appointed the able and learned Stephen Langton to the office. When John refused to recognize Langton, Innocent retaliated by threatening John with excommunication and placing England under the interdict. The pope further threatened to depose John and encouraged

Philip Augustus to invade England. Realizing that he had no popular support, John submitted. In 1213, he accepted Langton as archbishop, agreed to recognize England and Ireland as fiefs of the pope, and paid homage to the pope as his vassal.

John's defeat at the hands of France and the papacy only worsened his standing with his English barons. Their quarrel with the king grew out of John's constant efforts to raise more money for the fighting in France. The king imposed illegal dues on his barons, and this practice ignored their traditional feudal rights. By 1215, their anger had caused them to join forces, and they drew up a list of demands, stating that they would make war on the king if he refused to accept their charter. On June 15, they confronted John at Runnymede and forced him to sign the *Magna Carta*, or Great Charter.

At the time, the Magna Carta was seen as an agreement between the king and his barons. It defined the rights and responsibilities of both in accordance with feudal traditions. For example, it protected the barons against the arbitrary exaction of feudal dues. Among its most important provisions was one stating that no unusual tax be levied without the consent of the king's Great Council. It also guaranteed the clergy the right to elect their own bishops and make appeals to Rome, and confirmed the charters of liberties for towns.

Although the provisions of the Magna Carta extended to freemen, the Charter did nothing for the serfs who made up the vast majority of the population. Yet eventually, the Magna Carta came to be seen as a vital step in the development of representative government. At its center was the principle that the monarch was subject to the law and must obey it just as everyone else. It provided for justice through the courts and protected some rights of free citizens. For example, if a freeman were arrested, the charter required that he be sent for trial before a court of his peers as quickly as possible. No freeman could be fined, imprisoned, or deprived of his property beyond the measure of the offense; no official could seize his property without immediate compensation; and no one could be tried more than once for the same offense.

Over time, the provisions of the Magna Carta were extended and interpreted to protect the rights of all citizens—not just the barons and Church leaders. And its influence spread. In the 17th century, the provision that the king could not raise taxes without the consent of the barons was interpreted to mean that no taxes could be levied without the consent of Parliament. In the 18th century, the personal liberties guaranteed by the Magna Carta were included in the Bill of Rights of the Constitution of the United States.

### ORIGINS OF THE PARLIAMENT

By the time King John died in 1216, two basic elements of English government were gaining acceptance: the use of common law in the system of justice and the concept that the king was subject to the law. By 1300, a third element was added: the practice of consulting Parliament.

Controversies over taxation had not ended with the signing of the Magna Carta. During the long reign of John's son, Henry III (1216-1272), the English were again called on to finance wars to regain royal holdings in France. Henry's frequent appeals for funds met the stubborn resistance of his barons. In 1263, civil war erupted with Simon de Montfort, earl of Leicester, leading the rebellious barons. Simon de Montfort succeeded in capturing the king and ruled in his name for 15 months. In 1265, he summoned an assembly of barons and clergy, and he also invited two knights from each shire and two burgesses (representatives) from each chartered town. Thus, for the first time, representatives of the middle-class were consulted. This assembly and its successors became known as Parliament (from the French *parler*, meaning "to speak"). Although Simon de Montfort was soon killed in battle and Henry III was restored to power, the king continued to con-

In an effort to gather support for their rebellion against Henry III, Simon de Montfort and other barons invited knights and burgesses to attend sessions of the king's Great Council. The new assembly came to be known as Parliament. This is a meeting of the higher and lesser clergy under Edward I.

and two burgesses from each chartered town. The barons and knights met in one group; the higher and lesser clergy in another; and the burgesses in a third. In time, the knights and burgesses found they had much in common, and during the 14th century, they joined together so that Parliament became divided into two houses: the House of Lords, consisting of bishops and nobles;[5] and the House of Commons, consisting of knights and burgesses representing the shires and towns, respectively. Although Parliament originated in the king's need to raise money, it would gradually gain additional responsibilities in the governing of the nation.

*HUNDRED YEARS'* By the 14th century, the
*WAR (1337-1453)* rulers of both England and France had established the foundations for strong national monarchies. However, the goals of English and French rulers were in fundamental conflict: while the English monarchs wanted to regain the vast lands that they had held in France under Henry II, the kings of France were determined to prevent this and to expand their power over other regions such as Flanders in the Lowlands. These conflicting goals resulted in a prolonged conflict known as the *Hundred Years' War.* In fact, the Hundred Years' War was a series of conflicts interrupted by periods of unstable peace.

Besides the clash over territory, the conflict grew out of economic rivalry. The English exported much raw wool to Flanders, the center of textile-making in northern Europe. This mutually beneficial relationship pleased the English and Flemish but not the French. Flanders was nominally under the control of French overlords, and efforts by the French king to assert his control over the region led

sult with these representatives whenever he needed more money.

### EDWARD I AND THE MODEL PARLIAMENT

Henry's son and successor, Edward I (1272-1307), continued to centralize royal power and consult with Parliament. Edward I fought to extend royal control over Wales, annexing that land in 1284 and later naming his son and heir the Prince of Wales, a title still used today. His efforts to conquer Scotland were less successful, and he died leading an army into that land.

Edward found that by summoning meetings of Parliament, he could raise taxes and deal with popular grievances more easily. In 1295, he summoned the "Model Parliament," so-called because it followed Simon de Montfort's model of including two representatives of the knights from each shire

[5]Gradually, the representatives of the lesser clergy stopped attending Parliament so that the clergy as a whole played a lesser role in political decisions in England than they did in the developing assemblies in France or Spain.

*To symbolize his claim to the throne of France, Edward III adopted a coat of arms which combined a French symbol, the fleur de lis, with English lions. His determination to rule France led to the outbreak of the 100 Years' War.*

to uprisings that the English were quick to encourage. Another issue underlying the conflict was the aid the French had provided to Scotland when England had tried to conquer that land. The immediate cause of the war, however, was a dispute over the succession to the French throne.

In 1328, the king of France died without a male heir (Chapter 21). King Edward III of England (1327-1377) laid claim to the throne through his mother, a sister of the last Capetian king. However, the French rejected Edward's claim because of the ancient Frankish tradition, known as the Salic Law, that said a woman could not inherit land. Instead, they chose Philip VI, a cousin of the last king. When Philip crushed a revolt of townspeople in Flanders, Edward pressed his claims to the French throne and prepared for war.

### THE FIRST PHASE (1337-1380)

When the war began, the English had several advantages over the French. The English army was well trained and regularly paid and had acquired battle experience in its recent wars against the Scots. The English knights were accustomed to dismounting during battle and fighting alongside the infantry, who were equipped with a relatively new weapon—the longbow. This bow proved to be a valuable asset because it could discharge steel-tipped arrows rapidly and accurately for distances up to 250 yards. Finally, the English had a secret ally in the duke of Burgundy, who wanted to expand his territory to control all of France.

By contrast, France was rather poorly prepared, although it was the wealthiest nation in Europe. Philip VI had only recently been crowned king of France, and his leadership ability was unknown. French knights wore heavy armor and generally remained mounted in combat. When they dismounted, they had trouble moving about in their armor, and they refused to fight alongside ordinary foot soldiers. French soldiers were equipped with heavy crossbows, which were far less efficient or effective than the English longbows.

As a result, the English won most of the

*At the battle of Crécy, English longbowmen won a decisive victory over French knights armed with crossbows. Crossbowmen (shown at left) had to reload their weapons with a crank mechanism, while longbowmen simply inserted a new arrow.*

*The "Black Prince," son of Edward III, won a notable victory over the French and even captured the French king. However, the prince fell ill soon afterwards, and Edward III eventually lost most of his French territories.*

The next year, the Black Death, a terrifying epidemic, swept through Europe, taking the lives of at least a third of the population (Chapter 23). Despite its catastrophic effects, the fighting resumed in 1356. At Poitiers, Edward's oldest son, known as the Black Prince because of the color of his armor, overwhelmed the French and captured their king, John II. Since the French failed to pay his ransom, John remained a prisoner in England until his death in 1364.

John's son, Charles V, took up the fighting again, but suffered several defeats that left France in ruins. Before his death in 1380, however, he had managed to regain control of much of France.

### CHANGES IN ENGLAND

During the war, Edward III had to ask Parliament repeatedly for funds to pursue his goals. As a result, Parliament was able to demand concessions from the king and to strengthen its role. During this period, the two houses began to meet separately.

The Black Death, official corruption, and heavy taxes to pay for the war caused peasant discontent to surface in England. In 1381, the peasants found two leaders in Wat Tyler and John Ball. An estimated 100,000 peasants marched on London where they demanded to speak to the king, Richard II. A 14th century chronicler, Jean Froissart described the events that followed:

● ● ● *They shouted much and said, that if the King would not come out to them, they would attack the Tower, storm it, and slay all who were within. The King, alarmed at these menaces, resolved to speak with the rabble; he therefore sent orders for them to retire to a handsome meadow at Mile-end, where in the summer time, people go to amuse themselves, at the same time signifying that he would meet them there and grant their demands. Proclamation to this effect was made in the King's name, and thither, accordingly, the commonalty of the different villages began to march; many, however, did not care to go, but stayed*

early battles of the war. In the first battle, Edward III won a great naval victory at Sluys (1340), which gave the English control of the Channel. Edward's next success came at the battle of Crécy in 1346 when some 10,000 English longbowmen defeated a force of 20,000 French knights. The battle was significant because it showed that the heavily armed knight could be routed by foot soldiers, and it forecast the eventual end of the mounted feudal warrior. Edward followed up this victory by besieging Calais until the inhabitants were starved into submission in 1347. Calais would remain in English hands for the next 200 years.

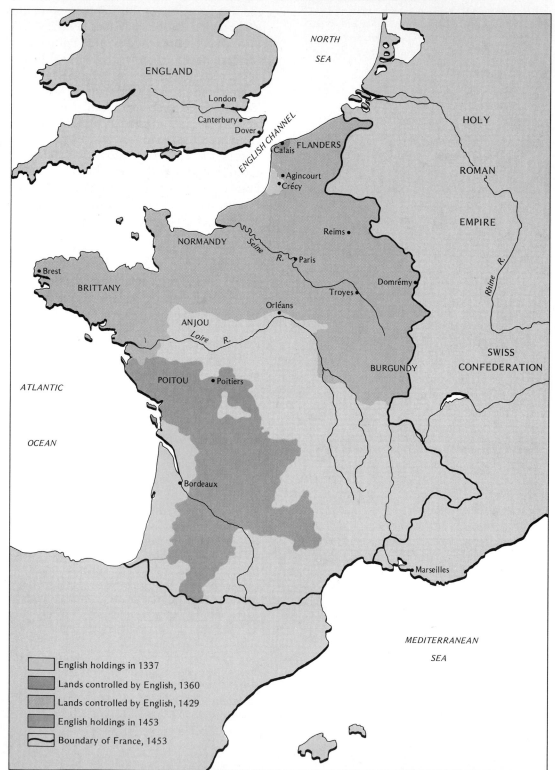

ENGLAND

London

Canterbury
Dover

ENGLISH CHANNEL

NORTH
SEA

FLANDERS

Calais

Agincourt
Crécy

HOLY

ROMAN

EMPIRE

NORMANDY

Seine R.

Reims

Paris

BRITTANY

Brest

Troyes

Domrémy

Rhine R.

ANJOU

Loire R.

Orléans

BURGUNDY

SWISS
CONFEDERATION

ATLANTIC

OCEAN

POITOU

Poitiers

Bordeaux

Marseilles

MEDITERRANEAN

SEA

English holdings in 1337

Lands controlled by English, 1360

Lands controlled by English, 1429

English holdings in 1453

Boundary of France, 1453

*The Peasants' Revolt. The ravages of the Black Death and the tax burdens of the 100 Years' War inspired the common people of England to desperate acts. In 1381, a large army of peasants entered London, murdered several officials, and demanded to speak to the king.*

behind in London, being more desirous of the riches of the nobles and the plunder of the city. . . . When the gates of the Tower were thrown open, and the King, attended by his two brothers and other nobles, had passed through, Wat Tyler, Jack Straw, and John Ball, with upward of 400 others, rushed in by force, and running from chamber to chamber, found the Archbishop of Canterbury, by name Simon, a valiant and wise man, whom the rascals seized and beheaded.[6]

[6]Jean Froissart, *Chronicles of England*, vol. 1, trans. Thomas Johnes (New York: Colonial Press, 1901), pp. 220-1.

In the end, the king tricked the peasants into disbanding and captured and executed Tyler and the other leaders. The *Peasant's Revolt* was then crushed with great brutality.

England changed in other ways during this period. By the late 1300s, the English language replaced French as the official language of the court, and English was being used by writers such as Geoffrey Chaucer in the *Canterbury Tales* (Chapter 18).

Dynastic upheavals also took place. Richard II was a harsh king whose unpopular rule ended in an uprising led by Henry Bolingbroke, the duke of Lancaster. Bolingbroke took power as Henry IV and established the House of Lancaster (1399-1461). During his reign, Henry was forced to give in to the demands of Parliament, allowing it to hold discussions about important matters and accepting the right of the House of Commons to initiate new taxes. Henry V, who succeeded his father in 1413, was a more forceful personality, and he renewed the war with France.

### FINAL PHASE (1415-1453)

In 1415, Henry V landed in France and met a strong French army at Agincourt. The English were aided in the battle by the powerful duke of Burgundy. As had happened at Crécy and Poitiers many years before, the English longbowmen took deadly aim at the French knights and won a stunning victory. Henry V then reconquered Normandy and forced King Charles VI of France to accept the Treaty of Troyes (1420). Under it, the French king recognized Henry's conquests, made Henry his heir, and allowed Henry to marry Catherine, Charles' daughter.

The king of England might well have ruled both England and France, but Henry V died of dysentery in 1422, leaving an infant son, the future Henry VI. When Charles VI died soon after, John, duke of Bedford, who ruled in Henry's name, claimed the crown of France for the child. The fighting erupted again as Charles VII, son of the late French king, attempted to win the throne. Charles and his

Henry V won a great victory over France at Agincourt in 1415, and reasserted English claims to the French throne. Here, he is shown wooing Catherine, daughter of Charles VI.

forces had little hope of victory until they were inspired by the visions of a young peasant woman, Joan of Arc (Chapter 21). In 1429, a French army led by Joan of Arc defeated the English at Orléans. Although Joan was later captured by the Burgundians, then tried and executed by the English, her martyrdom revitalized the French. The war dragged on, but the Burgundians later withdrew their support, after signing a separate peace treaty with Charles VII.

The French king reorganized his forces and gradually drove the English out of Normandy and Aquitaine. By 1453, when the Hundred Years' War finally ended, only Calais remained under English control. Although England's loss of its continental holdings ended a tradition dating back to the conquest, it allowed the English people and their rulers to concentrate on developing their resources at home.

By the end of the Hundred Years' War, the authority of the kings of England and France was much greater—each in his own land—than it had been at the beginning. Many feudal nobles who had opposed the centralization of royal powers had been killed in the fighting. During the long conflict, both England and France had begun to establish permanent, paid armies so that the kings no longer had to depend on their vassals for feudal levies. During this period, too, cities expanded and the money economy grew (Chapter 23), giving monarchs another source of taxable wealth besides the feudal dues levied on nobles. The importance of the feudal nobility declined for other reasons. For example, new technologies such as the longbow and the introduction of gunpowder led to new methods of fighting that would make mounted knights obsolete.

## WARS OF THE ROSES (1455-1485)

Even before the Hundred Years' War ended, England was torn by dynastic disputes that led to a 30-year struggle known as the *Wars of the Roses*. The dispute pitted two families, the House of Lancaster and the House of York, against each other. Both were descended from the Plantagenet king, Edward III. During their struggle, the Lancastrians used a red rose as their symbol while the Yorkists chose a white rose.

As you have read, Henry Bolingbroke seized power from Richard II in 1399 and established the House of Lancaster. Although he and his successor, Henry V, faced social and religious discontent, they managed to retain power. During the reign of Henry VI, however, troubles arose. Not only were the English defeated in France but also the king began to show signs of mental instability. With a weak king on the throne, corruption grew. Quarrels developed among the various factions vying for control of the government, and royal officials were appointed to office in exchange for their support of one noble faction or another. The crisis broke into the open when Richard, duke of York, gained the backing of Parliament against Henry and his supporters. Although Richard died before he could be crowned king, the ambitious earl of Warwick helped Richard's son take the throne as Edward IV.

Edward established the House of York, but his reign was marked by warfare as his supporters battled the nobles who backed the House of Lancaster. During these battles, many nobles were killed.

Edward IV died in 1483, leaving two young sons. One was briefly named Edward V, but his uncle, Richard of Gloucester, persuaded Parliament to declare the boys illegitimate. The boys were imprisoned in the Tower of London and secretly murdered. Although Richard was suspected of the murder of the "little princes in the Tower," there is much controversy over his guilt or innocence. Richard was then crowned king, and as Richard III, he tried to restore order but with little success because the death of the princes and factional disputes led to new fighting.

The forces opposed to Richard found a leader in Henry Tudor, a Lancastrian who later married Elizabeth of York. In 1405, Henry returned from exile in France and raised an army that defeated Richard III on Bosworth Field. Richard was killed in the fighting, and Henry was named king. As Henry VII, he set out to assure the future of the new dynasty, the House of Tudor.

Although Henry had a vague hereditary claim to the throne, he owed his crown in large part to the acceptance of Parliament.

Henry VII, the first Tudor king, defeated Richard III at Bosworth field. He restored the prestige and power of the monarchy, and won the support of the increasingly powerful middle classes.

**KINGS OF ENGLAND IN THE LATE MIDDLE AGES**

| | |
|---|---|
| **House of Lancaster** | |
| 1399–1413 | **Henry IV** |
| 1413–1422 | **Henry V** |
| 1422–1461 | **Henry VI** |
| **House of York** | |
| 1461–1483 | **Edward IV** |
| 1483 | **Edward V** |
| 1483–1485 | **Richard III** |

With the death on the battlefield of large numbers of nobles, Henry had an opportunity to increase royal power. An able and determined ruler, he worked tirelessly to increase royal revenues, end abuses of justice, and reestablish law and order. Henry also restored the prestige of the monarchy and thereby enhanced royal power. However, although Henry VII and his successors were forceful rulers, they did not have absolute power. During the Wars of the Roses, Parliament had strengthened its hand, and both Henry and his Tudor successors carefully avoided confrontations with Parliament that might lead to further limits on royal power.

## SUMMARY

*After the Romans withdrew their legions from England, the land was invaded by Germanic tribes, including the Angles, Saxons, and Jutes. The Anglo-Saxon kingdoms that emerged were later overwhelmed by the Viking invasions. In 1066, William of Normandy conquered England. William and his successors asserted their authority over rival feudal lords and created a system of royal justice.*

*The increase of royal power did not go unchallenged. When Henry II pressed his claim of jurisdiction over the clergy, his friend, Thomas à Becket, archbishop of Canterbury, refused to submit. King John's failure on the battlefield and violation of feudal rights of his nobles led to the signing of the Magna Carta. In the 13th century, Parliament began to take shape as an assembly with representatives from the clergy, nobility, and middle class. In time, Parliament would gain greater power, especially when it won the "power of the purse."*

*During the Hundred Years' War, England lost its holdings in France, and Parliament increased its power. The power of the feudal nobles was greatly reduced during the Wars of the Roses when many nobles were killed. In 1485, with the accession of the Tudor king, Henry VII, England regained stability and entered on a period of development as a strong nation-state.*

## QUESTIONS

1  How did Anglo-Saxon traditions influence later developments in England?
2  What advantages did William's conquest of England give him over feudal monarchs elsewhere in Europe? How did William ensure royal supremacy?
3  Compare the quarrel between Henry II and Thomas à Becket in England to the struggle between the Holy Roman emperor, Henry IV, and Pope Gregory VII.
4  Study the origins and content of the Magna Carta in England and the Bill of Rights in the Constitution of the United States. How were they similar and how different?
5  What were the causes of the Hundred Years' War? Why were the English victorious in the first phase of the war? What changes took place in England during the war?

## BIBLIOGRAPHY

### Which books might describe the Norman conquest of 1066?

**DAHMUS, JOSEPH.** *Seven Medieval Queens.* New York: Doubleday, 1972. *A useful book that discusses the lives of seven medieval women who played decisive roles in history.*

**DOBSON, R. B.**, ed. *The Peasants' Revolt of 1381.* New York: St. Martin's Press, 1970. *A valuable exploration of the various, and often contradictory, accounts of the peasant uprising in England. Uses such documents as trial records, contemporary poems, chronicles, and archives.*

**GILES, ST. AUBYN.** *The Year of the Three Kings, 1483.* New York: Athenaeum, 1983. *A balanced narrative of the power struggles among the noble families who were determined to control the English throne. Author presents the crimes with which Richard III is usually charged—conspiracy, child-murder and tyranny—and stimulates readers to form their own conclusions.*

**KNOWLES, DAVID.** *Thomas Becket.* Stanford University Press, 1971. *An excellent biography that traces Becket's complicated career from his friendship with Henry II to his murder in the cathedral in 1170.*

**TETLOW, EDWIN.** *The Enigma of Hastings.* New York: St. Martin's Press, 1974. *A careful examination of the events leading up to the Battle of Hastings and the battle itself.*

**10**

This is that house, the glory of the Franks, whose
Praises the eternal centuries will sing.
This is that house which holds in its power
Gaul might in war, Flanders magnificent in wealth.
This is that house whose sceptre the Burgundian,
Whose mandate the Norman, and whose arms the
Britons fear.

GUY OF BAZOCHES (12TH CENTURY)

# France in the Middle Ages

In the glowing description above of the palace of King Louis IX of France, the chronicler captures the sense of royal power that was emerging in France in the late 12th century. During the period from about 1100 to 1500, the rulers of France, like their counterparts in England, consolidated their power. Unlike William the Conqueror, however, who took control of England within his lifetime, the kings of France faced an array of competing feudal principalities and had to pursue a painstaking policy of expanding the royal domain.

Like Henry II and Edward I of England, a number of capable rulers helped to weld the fiefs and duchies of medieval France into a nation-state with an efficient royal bureaucracy and a strong standing army. As in England, too, the Church represented a challenge to royal authority and became the center of controversy. But in France, there was no document like the Magna Carta to support evolving ideas about representation. Although the French kings convened an assembly of representatives from the clergy, nobility, and townspeople, this assembly never gained the power that the English Parliament did.

**FRANCE AFTER CHARLEMAGNE** In 843, you will recall, Charlemagne's grandsons agreed to the Treaty of Verdun that divided up his empire. Charles the Bald received the western portion, which he and his successors ruled until 987.

The weakness of the Carolingian rulers led to political fragmentation. When it became clear that the king could not defend the land against attack, strong independent nobles organized the defense of their own territories. In 887, after Odo, count of Paris, valiantly defended his city against the Vikings, the French nobles chose him king. Following his death, however, they restored the Carolingians to the throne. But by the 10th century, the descendants of Charlemagne held the title of king in little more than name. They could not control the powerful nobles who ruled a patchwork of counties and duchies as separate, independent kingdoms. When the last Carolingian died in 987 without a direct heir, the French nobles had to choose between two leading candidates: Charles, duke of Lorraine, and Hugh Capet, duke of Franconia and count of Paris. The archbishop of Rheims addressed the assem-

177

bled feudal lords and clearly stated his preference:

*● ● ● Make a choice, therefore, that shall insure the welfare of the state instead of being its ruin. If you wish ill to your country, choose Charles; if you wish to see it prosperous, make Hugh, the glorious Duke, king. . . . Choose the duke, therefore; he is the most illustrious among us by reason of his exploits, his nobility and his military following. Not only the state, but every individual interest, will find in him a protector.*[1]

The nobles took the bishop's advice and chose Hugh Capet, a descendant of the famous Count Odo. Hugh established the Capetian dynasty that ruled France for 300 years.

### THE EARLY CAPETIANS

Some scholars believe that the French nobles chose Hugh Capet because he was not a strong ruler and therefore posed little threat to their power. And in fact, he controlled only a small territory that stretched for about 25 miles around Paris and was known as the Ile de France. Although Hugh's domain was strategically located near the center of France, it was surrounded by the large territories of Flanders, Brittany, Normany, Burgundy, Anjou, and Poitou, whose powerful lords could command larger armies than the king.

Despite this situation, Hugh Capet and his successors slowly increased royal power and influence. First, Hugh was crowned by the Church, a ceremony which legitimized his rule. Then, with the support of the Church, he arranged for the coronation of his eldest son, thus eliminating the nobles' role in electing the new king and firmly establishing the right of primogeniture—the exclusive claim to inheritance of the eldest son. This practice ended quarrels over succession and

ensured a peaceful succession. Fortunately for the Capetians, they continued to have sons who lived to maturity and inherited the throne from 987 to 1328.

Hugh's successors used their base of the Ile de France, their alliance with the Church, and their own wits to extend their holdings. They also enjoyed long reigns that helped to ensure stability. By the 11th century, while William of Normandy was conquering all of England, Philip I (1060-1108) of France still ruled a relatively small domain extending from Paris to Orléans, an area about 150 miles north-south by 50 miles east-west, or about the size of the state of Vermont. Like other medieval rulers, Philip had no permanent capital but moved his court from one fortified stronghold to another while he fought an unending series of wars against his more powerful neighbors.

In the 12th century, French monarchs gradually increased the royal domain and consolidated royal power. Louis VI, who succeeded Philip I, came to be known as Louis the Fat because of an illness that caused him to become overweight in his later years. A more fitting name for him was Louis the Wide Awake because he traveled continually throughout his kingdom, seeking to control his feudal lords. He made Abbot Suger of St. Denis his chief minister, and with his assistance, moved against unruly nobles. He established several new towns and encouraged his subjects to seek protection from him rather than from the local feudal lords. In doing so, he built up a good relationship with the small but growing middle class of townspeople.

Louis VI increased the royal revenues substantially by imposing tolls on those who traveled on the Seine River, an important trade artery. He also tried to make travel safer by severely punishing anyone who attacked travelers. Even more important, he enhanced the prestige of the monarchy to such an extent that he was able to arrange an advantageous marriage between his son, the future

---

[1]"Adalbero's Plea to Elect Hugh Capet, 987," in Milton Viorst, ed., *The Great Documents of Western Civilization* (Philadelphia: Chilton Books, 1965), p. 66.

Louis VII, and Eleanor, the heiress to Aquitaine, a large, powerful duchy in southern France.

## LOUIS VII

In 1137, Louis VII succeeded to the throne and married Eleanor. Raised in the wealthy court of Aquitaine, which placed great emphasis on elegant dress, gracious manner, and stimulating conversation, Eleanor became one of the most influential women in the Middle Ages. During her long life, she negotiated with popes, kings, and emperors, and was a

*With her husband, Henry II of England, Eleanor of Aquitaine ruled more than half of France. Her inheritance of these vast territories limited the growth of the French monarchy during her lifetime.*

patron of troubadours, the wandering poet-musicians who composed and sang songs extolling chivalry and courtly love.

As queen of France, Eleanor accompanied Louis to the Holy Land on the Second Crusade. She bore Louis two daughters but no son, so in 1152 he secured from the pope an annulment of the marriage. Through this unwise action, he lost much of the territory that his father had won for him. Soon afterward, Eleanor married Henry, duke of Normandy, count of Anjou, and heir to the English throne. Eleanor's vast possessions were joined with those of her new husband so that when Henry II became king of England in 1154, he ruled more of France than Louis did. In addition to Aquitaine, Poitou, and Gascony, which he acquired through his marriage to Eleanor, Henry held Normandy, Anjou, Brittany, and Maine.

English control of extensive lands in France fueled a bitter rivalry between the French and English monarchs that lasted for 300 years (see Chapter 20). Louis and his successors struggled at length against the English threat. Through plotting, marriage, and warfare, French kings slowly ousted the English and cemented a strong nation.

## GROWTH OF ROYAL POWER

Between 1180 and 1314, the later Capetians expanded their control over more and more of France so that by the early 14th century the king of France was the most powerful ruler in Europe. The three shrewd monarchs who were largely responsible for this success were Philip II (1180-1223), Louis IX (1226-1270), and Philip IV (1285-1314).

*Philip II.* The wily ruler Philip II, who became known as Philip Augustus, pursued the two major goals of medieval monarchs —the expansion of the royal domain and the consolidation of royal power—with marked success. Through his marriage to Isabella of Haiment, Philip acquired control of Artois, which gave him access to the English Channel. During his reign, he plotted tirelessly

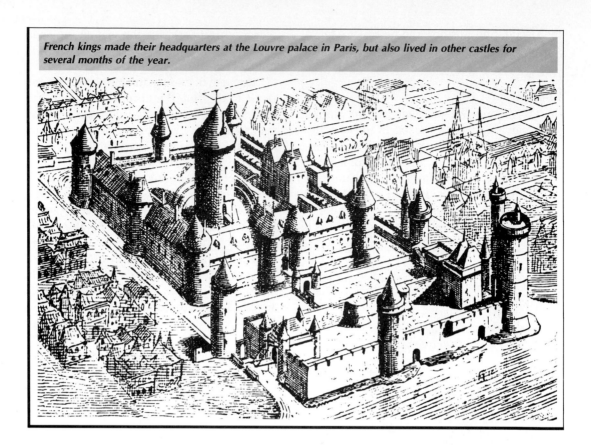

*French kings made their headquarters at the Louvre palace in Paris, but also lived in other castles for several months of the year.*

against the Plantagenet rulers of England. He tricked Henry II's sons, Richard and John, into rebelling against their father. Then, after Henry's death, he encouraged John to plot against Richard. As you have read, Philip joined the ill-fated Third Crusade in 1190 along with Frederick Barbarossa, the Holy Roman emperor, and Richard the Lion-Hearted, heir to the English throne (Chapter 16). The rivalry between Philip and Richard, however, led to bitter quarrels, so that the French king left his army in Palestine and returned home. After Richard died and his brother John became king of England, Philip continued his fight against John. When Philip seized Normandy and Anjou, John made an alliance with the feudal rulers of Flanders and Toulouse and with the Holy Roman emperor, Otto IV. Philip defeated this powerful alliance at the battle of Bouvines in 1214,

## RULERS OF MEDIEVAL FRANCE

| | Capetian Dynasty |
|---|---|
| 987–996 | Hugh Capet |
| 996–1031 | Robert II |
| 1031–1060 | Henry I |
| 1060–1108 | Philip I |
| 1108–1137 | Louis VI (the Fat) |
| 1137–1180 | Louis VII |
| 1180–1223 | Philip II (Augustus) |
| 1223–1226 | Louis VIII |
| 1226–1270 | Louis IX (Saint Louis) |
| 1270–1285 | Philip III |
| 1285–1314 | Philip IV (the Fair) |
| 1314–1316 | Louis X |
| 1316 | John I |
| 1317–1322 | Philip V |
| 1322–1328 | Charles IV |

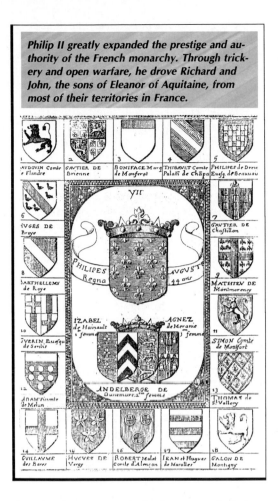

*Philip II greatly expanded the prestige and authority of the French monarchy. Through trickery and open warfare, he drove Richard and John, the sons of Eleanor of Aquitaine, from most of their territories in France.*

thereby gaining control of Normandy, Flanders, and Anjou, and becoming more powerful than any of his vassals.

Philip did far more than increase the size of his kingdom, for he also greatly improved its administration. He appointed new officials, many of them from the middle class, and made them directly responsible to him. Unlike the feudal nobles, the new officials owed their paid positions to him and thus formed a corps of loyal and professional administrators. They were charged with collecting revenues, administering justice in the royal courts, and keeping watch on the local nobles. In northern France, these officials were called *baillis* (bailiffs); in southern France, *seneschals*. In setting up this system of royal

officials, Philip laid the groundwork for a bureaucracy of capable professional civil servants.

Philip amassed a sizable treasury, which he used to pave the muddy streets of Paris and to begin construction on the cathedral of Notre Dame. In 1200, he offered students immunity from certain laws if they would remain in Paris to study, a move that led to the establishment of the University of Paris.

Philip maintained fairly good relations with the Church. When Pope Innocent III called for a crusade against the Albigensians in 1208, Philip was not enthusiastic but he did allow his vassals to participate. When Philip's successor, Louis VIII (1223-1226), personally led an attack against the Albigensians, he acquired control of Languedoc, in southern France, thereby gaining access to the Mediterranean Sea.

Philip Augustus died in 1223, leaving a kingdom much larger and stronger than the one he had inherited. He had reduced the power of the feudal lords, broken the English hold on much of France, and set up an efficient administrative system. He had extended royal justice by making the *curia regis* (king's court) the highest court in the land. In time, this court became known as Parlement. By having nobles convert their feudal services into money payments and by levying a new tax, Philip had also acquired the resources to keep his own standing army.

***Louis IX.*** Although Louis IX was only three years old when he inherited the throne, he later continued Philip's policies of strengthening royal power. Louis was raised by his mother, Blanche of Castile, a devout Christian who is reported to have said of her son, "I would rather see him dead at my feet, than guilty of one mortal sin." As an adult, Louis' piety and humility earned him the name Saint Louis, and less than 30 years after his death, he was canonized by the Roman Catholic Church. Louis established hospitals, asylums, orphanages, and homes for reformed prostitutes; he fed the poor at public expense

Louis IX, later known as Saint Louis, participated in the Sixth and Seventh Crusades. He became famous for the fairness and impartiality of his royal courts, and was even called upon to arbitrate disputes in other countries.

• • • *Many a time it happened that in summer time he would go and sit down in the wood at Vincennes, with his back to an oak, and make us take our seats around him. And all those who had complaints to make came to him without hinderance from ushers or other folk. Then he asked them with his own lips: "Is there any one here who has a cause?" Those who had a cause stood up, then he would say to them: "Silence all, and you shall be dispatched one after the other."*[2]

Louis became so renowned for his fairness that he was often called on to mediate disputes between the monarchs of Europe. Within his own lands, he forbade feudal warfare, and even though he defeated the English in battle, he signed a generous treaty with Henry III in 1259 that permitted the English king to retain control of Guienne and Aquitaine. In return for these lands, the English king renounced his claims to Normandy, Anjou, and Poitou. In 1270, Louis IX died of the plague while he was on a Crusade in North Africa.

*Philip IV.* The third monarch to increase royal power was Philip IV, a grandson of Saint Louis, who was nicknamed "the Fair" because he was so handsome. Unlike his grandfather who was renowned for his devotion to justice and saintliness, Philip was a crafty and cruel ruler who was ruthless in his push for power. His wars with England were so costly that Philip was constantly looking for ways to raise money. When his attempts to gain control of Flanders and Aquitaine severely strained his resources, he borrowed vast sums of money from Jewish and Italian moneylenders as well as from the Templars, who had become leading international bankers. He later arrested the moneylenders and cancelled his own indebtedness. When he found himself unable to pay his debts to the Templars, he abol-

and often waited on them in person. In Paris, he built a beautiful little chapel, called Sainte Chapelle, near the cathedral of Notre Dame to house the religious relics he had acquired on his Crusade against the Moslems in 1248.

Louis IX expanded the administration of royal justice, requiring certain cases, such as treason, to be tried in royal courts. He established a supreme court of justice (*Parlement*), which was composed of trained lawyers, nobles, and members of the clergy. Common people were encouraged to bring complaints before the king's courts, and royal officials were given a maximum of 40 days to render judgment on each complaint. In the more difficult cases, Louis often sat as a judge himself. A contemporary chronicler described Louis' interest in dispensing justice.

[2]Joinville, "Memoirs of St. Louis," in J. F. Scott, A. Hyma, and A. H. Noyes, eds. *Readings in Medieval History* (New York: Crofts, 1946), p.464.

## GROWTH OF THE FRENCH ROYAL DOMAIN, 1180–1337
How did the expansion of the royal domain increase the king's prestige and power?

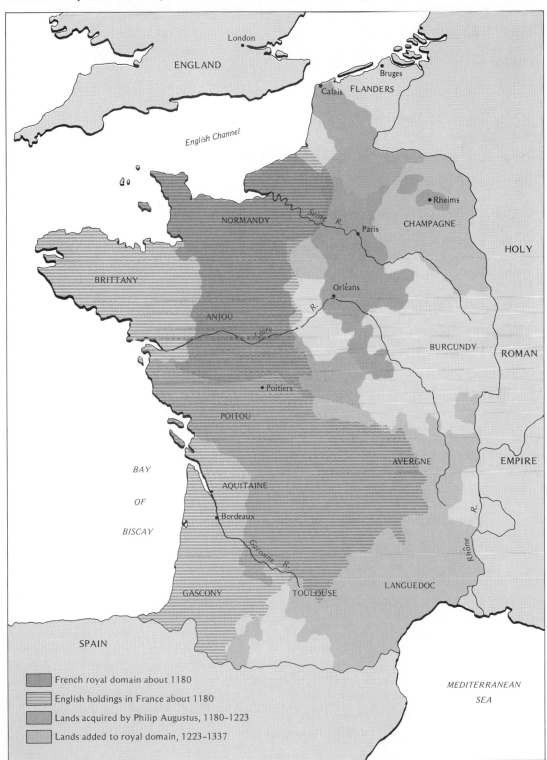

ENGLAND

London

Bruges

FLANDERS

Calais

English Channel

NORMANDY

Seine R.

Paris

CHAMPAGNE

Rheims

HOLY

BRITTANY

Orléans

R.

ANJOU

Loire R.

BURGUNDY

ROMAN

Poitiers

POITOU

AVERGNE

EMPIRE

BAY

OF

BISCAY

AQUITAINE

Bordeaux

Garonne R.

GASCONY

TOULOUSE

LANGUEDOC

Rhône R.

SPAIN

French royal domain about 1180

English holdings in France about 1180

Lands acquired by Philip Augustus, 1180–1223

Lands added to royal domain, 1223–1337

MEDITERRANEAN
SEA

**183**

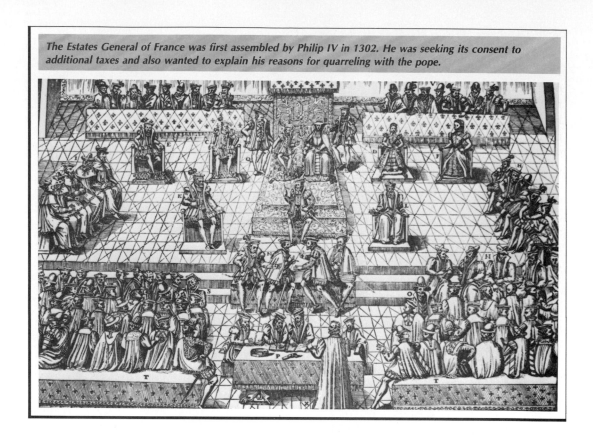

The Estates General of France was first assembled by Philip IV in 1302. He was seeking its consent to additional taxes and also wanted to explain his reasons for quarreling with the pope.

ished the order, had its leaders tortured and murdered, and seized its funds.

During his reign, Philip made several improvements in government organization. He expanded the royal bureaucracy, setting up a treasury department to supervise the collection of taxes and keep accurate records of royal income and expenditure. Like his predecessors, he came to rely on middle-class professionals, many of them trained lawyers, to staff the burgeoning civil service. Increasingly, Paris became the center of the French monarchy, and the Parlement of Paris emerged as the chief court of justice.

To gain support in his efforts to increase royal revenues, Philip called for an assembly made up of representatives from the clergy, nobility, and townspeople. The assembly became known as the *Estates General*. (In France, an estate was a social class, with so-

ciety made up of three estates: the first, the clergy; the second, the nobility; and the third, the common people.) Although Philip and later rulers consulted with the Estates General and sought its backing for their efforts to raise taxes, this representative body never acquired the same power as the Parliament in England. A major reason was that it failed to get the right to approve all taxes, as the Parliament eventually did. As a result, the Estates General remained a tool in the hands of the increasingly powerful monarchy rather than an independent institution with the power to challenge royal authority.

***Clash with the Papacy.*** Philip's need for money led him into a long-running controversy with Pope Boniface VIII. In 1296, in an effort to help finance his wars with England, Philip levied a tax on the French clergy. The pope insisted that the clergy could not be taxed without his permission and forbade the French clergy from paying. In response, Philip placed an embargo on the shipment of all gold, silver and jewels, which greatly reduced the papal revenues received from France. The pope was then forced to back down, and in 1297 he recognized the right of the French king to tax the clergy in an emergency.

The conflict between Philip and Boniface erupted anew in 1301 when Philip imprisoned a French bishop and defied the pope's order to release the man at once. In 1302, Philip assembled the Estates General to gain its support in his quarrel with the pope.

At the same time, the pope was declaring that all monarchs owed allegiance and homage to the pope in both spiritual and temporal matters. In a famous document, the *Unam Sanctam*, he claimed papal supremacy over all secular rulers.

● ● ● *Both swords, therefore, the spiritual and the temporal, are in the power of the church. The former is to be used by the Church, the latter for the Church; the one by the hand of the priest, the other by the hand of kings and knights, but at the command and permission of the priest. Moreover, it is necessary for one sword to be under the other, and the temporal authority to be subjected to the spiritual; for the apostle says, "For there is no power but of God; and the powers that are ordained of God; but they would not be ordained unless one were subjected to the other, and, as it were, the lower made higher by the other."*[3]

The controversy heated up when Philip charged Boniface with immorality, and the pope excommunicated the French king. In 1303, Philip sent soldiers to arrest Boniface and bring him to France for trial. When the soldiers arrived at Anagni, the pope's summer palace in northern Italy, they found him

resting from the summer heat with a crucifix on his chest. The French troops seized Boniface, but a contingent of Italian soldiers rescued him. Weakened by these struggles and ill health, the pope died soon after.

*"Babylonian Captivity."* Philip's effort to control the papacy did not end with the pope's death. Benedict XI, successor to Boniface VIII, chose not to continue the quarrel with Philip. When Benedict died in 1305, Philip maneuvered to have a French cardinal elected pope. Philip then insisted that the new pope, Clement V, move the papal headquarters to Avignon in southern France, giving the French king great influence over Church policies.

From 1305 to 1378, the papacy remained in Avignon, a period that became known as the second "Babylonian Captivity"—the first being the time that the Jews were in captivity in Babylon, almost 2000 years earlier. During this time, the popes appeared to be under the direct control of the French kings, and, therefore, the Avignon papacy became an object of contempt outside of France. Although Philip's victory over the papacy increased the prestige of the French king at home, it greatly reduced the influence of the pope in England and the rest of Europe.

The "Babylonian Captivity" was followed by an even greater disaster for the Church. In 1377, Pope Gregory XI returned the papacy to Rome. When he died the next year, the people of Rome forced the cardinals to choose an Italian to be pope. However, most of the cardinals were French, and once they left Rome and returned to Avignon, they met again to declare their earlier election invalid and choose a French pope. Since the Italian pope refused to resign, there were then two popes: one in Rome and one in Avignon.

During the *Great Schism* (1377-1417), as this split in the papacy was called, each pope tried to depose the other, selected his own bishops and cardinals, and claimed that he alone was the rightful head of the Church. European monarchs lined up in support of

---

[3]"The Unam Sanctam of Pope Boniface VIII, 1302," in Viorst, *The Great Documents of Western Civilization*, p. 72.

one pope or the other, depending on their individual interests. The schism caused great dismay to many devout Christians. The Great Schism only furthered the trend toward corruption in the Church since neither pope had the authority to command all of Christendom. Calls for reform multiplied, and heretical movements spread.

This chaotic situation was made worse when a Church council met in 1409 and tried to get the two popes to step down. It chose a new pope, but when the other two refused to abdicate, Christians faced the disgraceful scene of three contending pontiffs. This Great Schism finally was ended in 1417 by the Council of Constance. This council deposed all three popes and elected Martin V, who reestablished the papal court in Rome.

The new pope and his successors could not undo all of the damage to Church power and prestige that had been brought on by the Babylonian Captivity and the Great Schism. Moreover, by the early 15th century, the emergence of strong monarchies in England, France, Spain, and elsewhere had effectively limited the secular power once wielded by the Church. Although some rulers continued to work in alliance with the papacy, no pope would ever again claim supremacy over secular rulers as Innocent III and Boniface VIII had done.

### 14th- AND 15th-CENTURY FRENCH KINGS

|  | House of Valois |
| --- | --- |
| 1328–1350 | Philip VI |
| 1350–1364 | John II |
| 1364–1380 | Charles V (the Wise) |
| 1380–1422 | Charles VI |
| 1422–1461 | Charles VII |
| 1461–1483 | Louis XI (the Spider king) |
| 1483–1498 | Charles VIII |

## HUNDRED YEARS' WAR

The consolidation of royal power in France suffered a severe setback not long after the reign of Philip IV. On Philip's death in 1314, the throne passed in turn to each of his three sons, but none of them had a legitimate male heir. In 1328, the Capetian dynasty ended. The French nobles, you will recall, rejected the claim of King Edward III of England (Chapter 20) and chose Philip VI, head of the House of Valois and a cousin of the last Capetian king. Edward's rejected claim gave him an added incentive to challenge the new French monarch on the battlefield.

For the French, the opening phase of the Hundred Years' War brought devastation to the country, huge losses of territory, and severe social unrest. As you have read, the English won stunning victories at Crécy (1346) and Poitiers (1356) and captured the French king, John II (1350-1364). While the king was held captive, his son, the future Charles V, ruled France.

Early in the war, the French king imposed a salt tax on the people, which not only caused hardship but also led to increased discontent. The pillaging of much of France by bands of English and even French soldiers and the miseries caused by the Black Death also contributed to a peasant uprising in 1358. This revolt became known as the *Jacquerie* after Jacques Bonhomme (Jack Goodfellow), the French nickname for all peasants. During the uprising, peasants burned the manor houses of the nobles, attacked tax collectors, and roamed the countryside in mobs. A popular uprising in Paris led by a merchant named Etienne Marcel also threatened the monarchy. However, Charles V (1364-1380) managed to rally his forces, crush the peasant rebellion, and suppress the uprising in Paris. The struggle led to brutal reprisals in which an estimated 20,000 peasants were killed.

Despite his harshness, Charles V earned a reputation as an effective ruler and was known as Charles the Wise. He called meetings of the Estates General, and although this

*Charles VII had little success in claiming the French throne until Joan of Arc came to his aid. Under her leadership, French armies defeated the English and brought the 100 Years' War to an end.*

of Agincourt (1415). In the next few years, France suffered more setbacks, culminating in the Treaty of Troyes (1420), in which Charles VI was forced to disinherit the dauphin, as his son was called, and make King Henry V of England his heir. When both kings died suddenly in 1422, the dauphin—the future Charles VII—tried to go to Rheims to claim the throne, but he was unable to rally his demoralized forces against the English, who were besieging the city.

### JOAN OF ARC

Within a few years, however, the tide began to turn when France found a savior in a young peasant woman named Joan of Arc (1412-1431). Joan lived in the small town of Domrémy, about 175 miles east of Paris. As a young girl, she began to hear "voices," which she believed to be those of saints and angels. The voices ordered her to help the dauphin claim his crown and lead the French army against the English forces in Orléans.

Because the French situation was so desperate, when Joan sought an audience with the dauphin, she was admitted and eventually convinced him of the validity of her vision. Her leadership so inspired the French soldiers that they recaptured Orléans and ended the English siege of Rheims so that the dauphin could be crowned Charles VII of France in 1429. Soon afterward, Joan was captured by the Burgundians, who sold her to their English allies.

In 1431, Joan was tried on charges of witchcraft and heresy before an ecclesiastical court and was sentenced to death by burning. During the trial, the examiners questioned her closely about her visions.

• • • *Asked if God ordered her to wear a man's dress, she answered that the dress is a small, nay, the least thing. Nor did she put on a man's dress by the advice of any man whatsoever; she did not put it on, nor did she do aught but by the command of God and the angels. . . .*

assembly might have taken advantage of the war emergencies to expand its power at the expense of the king, it did not. Instead, Charles managed to play on the distrust among the three estates to gain his own ends.

The Jacquerie led Charles V to accept the Treaty of Bretigny in 1360 in which the French recognized Edward's control over Calais and Aquitaine in exchange for his renunciation of his claim to the French throne. In 1369, however, the fighting was renewed, and before his death in 1380, Charles had forced the English to retreat from many regions that they had won earlier.

Charles' successor, Charles VI (1380-1422), was a weak ruler subject to periods of insanity. During his reign, the powerful dukes of Burgundy and Armagnac carried out a violent and destructive quarrel. The Burgundians finally allied themselves with the English and helped them to win the battle

In these portraits, the two aspects of Joan of Arc's life are commemorated. Left: Joan as a pious country maid from the town of Domremy. Right: As the soldier who inspired French armies to victory during the darkest years of the 100 Years' War.

*Asked whether, when she saw the voice coming to her, there was light, she answered that there was a great deal of light on all sides, as was most fitting. She added to the examiner that not all the light came to him alone!*

*Asked whether there was an angel over her king's head, when she saw him for the first time, she answered: "By Our Lady! if there was, I do not know and did not see it."*[4]

Charles VII, who owed his crown to the *Maid of Orleans*, as Joan was later called,

remained indifferent to her plight and made no attempt to help her. But Joan of Arc became a symbol of French pride and patriotism, and her martyrdom proved to be a turning point in the struggle against the English. (Later, the Church overturned Joan of Arc's conviction of heresy, and she was declared a saint in 1920.)

### CHARLES VII

When Charles VII was crowned at Rheims in 1429, he was faced with overwhelming problems. The English still controlled Flanders, Brittany, Anjou, and Aquitaine; many villages had been destroyed or deserted; arable land lay uncultivated; and wolves prowled

---

[4]Quichert, "The Trial of Jeanne D'Arc," in *Readings in Medieval History*, ed. Scott, Hyma, and Noyes, p. 508.

the streets of Paris. Commerce had come to a standstill because the roads and canals had fallen into disrepair. Bands of robbers called "flayers" roamed the countryside. Impoverished nobles attempted to ease their financial difficulties by charging tolls for the right to cross their estates.

With the advice and support of able counselors, Charles VII turned the tide. He enlisted the aid of Jacques Coeur, an astute French banker, to improve the methods of handling the royal finances. In harmony with the spirit of unity generated by Joan of Arc, the Estates General allowed the king to levy taxes to hire soldiers whenever he needed an army, without seeking its approval. The king thus could establish a permanent standing army without relying on his nobles. With this new force, he was able to push the English out of Normandy and Aquitaine so that by 1453, when the Hundred Years' War ended, they held only the port of Calais.

By 1453, Charles had gained great popularity among the French people because of his victory over the English, and he took advantage of this success to reassert royal power. He resisted attempts by the nobles to regain their influence over the government, and he sought advice from merchants and manufacturers. He used his army to seek out and destroy the lawless bands of brigands. Roads and harbors were repaired, and wastelands were brought under cultivation. He enforced laws prohibiting the maintenance of private armies and the collection of tolls by individuals. By the end of the Hundred Years' War, therefore, the king was in a strong position. The Estates General had given him important powers of taxation, and he had limited the power of the Church and the nobles.

**THE FRENCH NATION-STATE** Louis XI (1461-1483) continued the process of centralizing royal power and expanding the areas under royal control. By the end of his reign, the process of welding a patchwork of rival feudal territories into a nation-state was virtually complete, and France was ready for new adventures.

Louis earned the nickname of the Spider because he wove a web of intrigue throughout Europe. Well educated, with a shrewd mind and a ruthless lust for power, Louis schemed and plotted to achieve his unscrupulous ends. While Louis XI was personally objectionable, the list of his accomplishments is impressive. He destroyed the power of the dukes of Burgundy and built a professional army that was considered the best in Europe. He chose ambitious and talented men to serve as advisers and he imposed more controls on the feudal nobility. He strengthened royal finances and kept the Church in line. He encouraged industry and commerce, further improved the roads and harbors, established a postal system, and invited foreign artisans to settle in France.

The chief rival of Louis XI was Charles the Bold, duke of Burgundy (1467-1477), who ruled the rich agricultural region of southeastern France. Charles also controlled Flan-

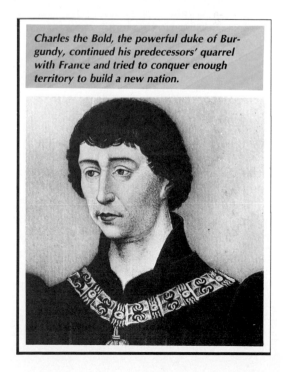

*Charles the Bold, the powerful duke of Burgundy, continued his predecessors' quarrel with France and tried to conquer enough territory to build a new nation.*

Louis XI, the Spider King, prevented Charles the Bold from seizing Alsace and Lorraine. As a result, Burgundy was incorporated into France rather than becoming the center of a separate kingdom.

ders and the Lowlands, and he was eager to gain control of Alsace and Lorraine, the regions extending along the eastern border of France.

To foil Charles' ambitions, Louis incited the leaders of the Swiss Confederation and the princes of the various states of the Holy Roman Empire located along the Rhine River to resist Charles when he marched into Lorraine in 1473. Charles died in battle a few years later, and Louis eventually gained control of Burgundy, Artois, and Picardy. At this point, all of present-day France except Brittany was united under one ruler.

In 1483, Charles VIII succeeded Louis XI as king of France, and eight years later he married Anne, the heiress to the duchy of Brittany, thereby uniting this province to France. Political unity encouraged economic development, but the growing prosperity of France led Charles VIII into ventures beyond his own borders. Like other ambitious monarchs, Charles dreamed of uniting Europe into one nation and even of liberating Constantinople from the Ottoman Turks. His dreams embroiled him and his successors in a series of struggles known as the *Italian Wars*, which lasted from 1494 to 1559.

## SUMMARY

*In France, as in England, the period from about 1100 to 1500 was one in which monarchs set out to centralize their authority. From a small domain centered on the Ile de France, French rulers gradually gained control over a vast kingdom. They achieved this expansion of territory through war, diplomacy, and marriage. The major figures in the emergence of the French state were Philip II, who organized the early government bureaucracy that would become a mainstay of royal power; Louis IX, who brought dignity and honor to the monarchy; and Philip IV, who built on the successes of his predecessors and triumphed over the papacy.*

*During the Hundred Years' War, many of these gains were lost, and for a time, France was torn apart by warfare and the rival ambitions of powerful feudal nobles. The appearance on the scene of Joan of Arc, who inspired the French to renew their struggle against the English, helped set Charles VII and his successors on the road to restoring royal authority.*

*During the reign of Louis XI, the Spider king, France became a unified nation with the machinery of a centralized government in place. Unlike the Parliament in England, which won the right to approve taxes, the Estates General in France did not win similar authority and instead became subject to royal power.*

## QUESTIONS

1 Describe the domain of the early Capetian kings. Compare it to the Carolingian Empire in 800 and to France in 1483.

2 Why were the rulers of France and England rivals throughout the Middle Ages? How did Philip Augustus use this rivalry for his own ends?

3 What was the cause of the struggle between Philip IV and the Church? How did Philip strengthen royal power in this struggle?

4 In what ways did the Babylonian Captivity and the Great Schism hurt the Church? How do you think it opened the way for the Protestant Reformation that began in the 16th century?

5 What role did Joan of Arc play in the Hundred Years' War? Why is she credited with helping to build the French nation-state?

## BIBLIOGRAPHY

### Which books might describe the growth of the French nation-state?

DENEUIL-CORMIER, ANNE. *The Wise and Foolish Kings.* New York: Doubleday, 1980. *An interesting account of the Valois kings who ruled France from 1328 to 1498 and helped transform France from a fragmented medieval kingdom into a modern nation-state.*

FOWLER, KENNETH. *The Age of the Plantagenets and the Valois.* New York: Putnam, 1967. *A survey of the origin of the Hundred Years' War and the structure of the late medieval society. It discusses the social and economic impact of the war on the civilian population and on the intellectual climate.*

PERNOUD, REGINE. *Blanche of Castile.* New York: Coward, McCann, & Geoghegan, 1975. *A sympathetic biography of the wise and capable ruler who dominated Europe during the first half of the 13th century. Blanche, the granddaughter of Eleanor of Aquitaine and wife of Louis VIII, was determined to unify the dissident factions in France during her successful regency for her son, the future Louis IX.*

## 11

> The fame of him resounds in every direction;
> more flock to My Cid, you may know, than go from him
> and his wealth increases. . . .
> My Cid Don Rodrigo did not wish to delay;
> he set out for Valencia and will attack them.
> My Cid besieges it closely; there was no escape.
> He permits no one to enter or depart. . . .
> Great is the rejoicing in that place
> When My Cid took Valencia and entered the city. . . .
> My Cid rejoiced, and all who were with him
> when his flag flew from the top of the Moorish palace.
>
> POEM OF EL CID

# Nation-Building on the Periphery

By the late Middle Ages, changes were taking place all over Europe. Trade was reviving, and cities were expanding. Monarchs in England and France were extending their power over feudal nobles. The process of nation-building was affecting other parts of Europe, too. In Spain, feudal monarchs faced a unique situation because their chief rivals were the Moslems, who had conquered the land in the 8th century. The development of royal power, therefore, was often cloaked in the language of a holy crusade against the Moslems. Among the heroes of this Crusade was the Cid, a Christian knight whose capture of the Moslem stronghold of Valencia is described above. The Cid became a symbol of the emerging sense of national pride in Spain.

Other nations on the fringes of Europe emerged in the late Middle Ages, including Portugal, the Swiss Confederation, and the powerful states of Poland and Hungary in eastern Europe. Still further to the east, Russia was a latecomer to the nation-making process. After being conquered by the Mongols in 1223, Russia was isolated from the West and evolved a separate culture based on Byzantine and other ancient traditions.

**SPAIN** In the early Middle Ages, Spain, like other parts of western Europe, suffered from the Germanic invasions. Early in the 5th century, the Vandals and later the Visigoths conquered the Iberian peninsula. The Visigoths established a unified kingdom with codified laws and a system of tax collection. But since the Visigoths practiced the Arian form of Christianity and most of the people they ruled were Roman Catholic, civil wars often broke out. In 589, however, the Visigoth king Reccared accepted baptism into the Roman Catholic faith, and Spain came under the protection of the Roman Catholic Church.

Despite the support that the Church gave to the Visigothic monarchy, Christianity was almost destroyed in Spain in the 8th century. As you have read (Chapter 14), Tarik, an energetic Moslem leader, crossed from North Africa to Spain in 711 and swept north at the head of a Moslem army. He easily defeated the Visigoths, whose land had become divided into several rival kingdoms. By 721, the Moslems had conquered all of the Iberian peninsula except the mountainous regions of the northwest.

## MOSLEM SPAIN

In the next decades, the Moslems consolidated their control over Spain, and in 756, Abd-al-Rahman established an independent caliphate with its capital at Cordoba (Chapter 14). During the Cordoba caliphate, which lasted until 1031, Spain enjoyed a "golden age": the government was ably administered, the economy thrived, and culture flourished. The Moslems were, in general, tolerant of both the Christian and Jewish communities under their rule. Jewish communities benefited from these tolerant policies and had one of the most prosperous and culturally creative periods in their history.

Cordoba itself was a bustling, wealthy city. At a time when the population of Paris numbered barely 15,000 people and London was even smaller, Cordoba had a population of 500,000. In Cordoba, Granada, and other Spanish cities, merchants sold products from all over the world, including such delicacies as dates, olives, lemons, and peaches. Christian travelers were amazed at the goods they saw in the marketplaces, the beautiful gardens, and the splendid palaces of Cordoba.

Moslem Spain, you will recall, was also a thriving center of culture and scholarship. Arabic civilization was cosmopolitan, and Spanish cities were united to other major Islamic centers in North Africa and the Middle East. Fortunately for western Europe, peaceful contacts took place in Spain between Moslem, Jewish, and Christian scholars. Moslem scholars preserved Greek and Roman texts and translated many of them into Arabic. Later, when Christian scholars translated these works into Latin, Europe was able to recover at least some of the learning of the ancient world.

## THE RECONQUEST

In the 8th century, Moslems ruled all of Spain except some tiny Christian kingdoms in the north. In time, these kingdoms became the focus of Christian efforts to conquer Spain. The first campaigns against the Moors, as Christians called the Moslems in Spain, were

## SPAIN AND PORTUGAL

*In what ways can the reconquest of Spain be compared to the Crusades to win the Holy Land?*

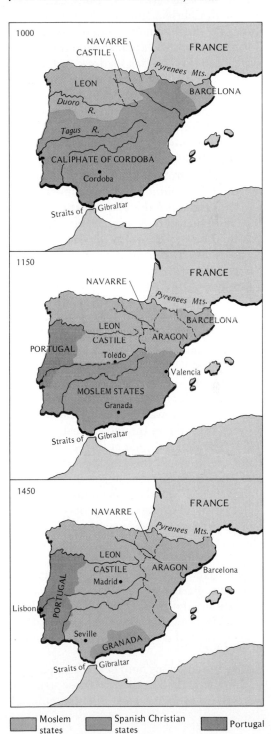

Moslem states | Spanish Christian states | Portugal

**193**

led by Charlemagne (Chapter 15). As you read, he crossed the Pyrenees Mountains and advanced on Saragossa (present-day Zaragoza). Although Charlemagne was forced to withdraw, he did conquer a small area in the north known as the *Spanish March*. This region became a Christian border kingdom that served as a buffer between the Franks and the Moslems. Unlike the rest of Spain, the Spanish March was influenced by the Christian and Frankish traditions.

The heroic deeds of the Frankish knight Roland during Charlemagne's campaign against Moslem Spain were immortalized in the *Song of Roland*, and this famous epic may have shaped the antagonistic attitude that Christian Europeans continued to hold toward Moslem Spain in the later Middle Ages. After the breakup of the Carolingian Empire, the Spanish March was divided into a number of tiny kingdoms: Catalonia, Galicia, the Asturias, Leon, and Navarre.

Slowly, these small Christian states in the north pushed south. The struggle by Christians to regain Spain became known as the *Reconquista* and went on for more than 500 years. By the late 10th century, the kingdom of Castile, which had grown out of the Asturias and Leon, was beginning to emerge as a powerful force in the reconquest.

In 1031, quarrels among the Moslems led to the overthrow of the caliphate of Cordoba, and Moslem Spain was broken up into more than 20 rival Moorish kingdoms. This disunity gave the Christian kingdoms in Spain an opportunity to make new conquests. Sancho the Great (1000-1035), who ruled Castile, united the local governments north of the Tagus River and led his army against the Moslems. In 1063, the pope proclaimed a crusade for the reconquest of Spain. Many knights from northern Europe answered the pope's call and traveled to Spain to fight the Moslems.

The most famous hero of the *Reconquista* was Rodrigo Díaz de Bivar, whose exploits were recalled in the great Spanish epic, *El Cid*. Although the poem romanticizes the Cid as the perfect Christian knight, in reality Díaz was an adventurer who fought for hire and battled both Christians and Moslems. He led the siege against the Moslem stronghold at Valencia and was made the ruler of that city after it was taken.

*The Crusading Spirit.* Like the Crusades to the Holy Land, the *Reconquista* was seen as a holy war. It continued for many centuries with periods of fierce struggle and times of relative peace between Christian and Moslem states. Like the earlier Moslem rulers, Christian rulers were generally tolerant of their non-Christian subjects. They allowed Moslem artisans and traders to conduct their businesses, which contributed to the prosperity of their kingdoms.

In Spain, the rallying point for the crusading fervor was the great cathedral of Santiago de Compostela, in northwestern Spain. According to tradition, Saint James, one of the 12 apostles, went to Spain after the death of Jesus. Although he later returned to Palestine and was possibly martyred, the Spanish Christians believed that his body had been miraculously transported back to Spain. According to legend, his burial place was revealed to a shepherd boy in about 900. When the boy reported his vision to the priests, they built a cathedral at Santiago de Compostela, where they enshrined the remains of the saint. During the Middle Ages, thousands of Christians from all over Europe made pilgrimages to this shrine, and the slogan "Santiago!" became the rallying cry for the crusade to drive the Moslems out of Spain.

*Early Governments.* Gradually, the Christian kingdoms of Spain pushed the Moslems further south. Within each kingdom, feudal monarchs faced problems similar to those of their contemporaries elsewhere in Europe as they tried to establish their authority. Moreover, each kingdom had assemblies known as *Cortés* made up of representatives of the clergy, nobility, and townspeople. The Cortés had the power to vote taxes, monitor finances, and petition the ruler to make new laws or reform existing ones. A ruler had to assemble the Cortés at least once a year and cooperate with it in order to win approval for any new taxes.

The rulers of these Christian kingdoms were unable to establish strong, central governments for several reasons. First, local nobles had assumed many political and military powers during the long struggle with the Moslems. Second, crusading knights from other lands had formed powerful, independent organizations, similar to the Templars and Hospitalers, that defied the local authorities. Third, the Church had been given vast estates and many privileges in exchange for its help in the reconquest, so that it was even more influential in Spain than elsewhere in Europe.

In 1212, three Christian kingdoms—Castile, Aragon, and Navarre—joined in a new drive against the Moslems and defeated them at the battle of Las Navas de Tolosa. Not long afterward, they captured Cordoba and Seville, leaving only the Argave (the southern part of present-day Portugal) and the kingdom of Granada in Moslem control.

During the next 200 years, the momentum of the *Reconquista* slowed, until it was revitalized by the forceful personalities of Ferdinand of Aragon and Isabella of Castile.

### FERDINAND AND ISABELLA

By the mid-15th century, the Iberian peninsula was divided among three Christian kingdoms: Aragon in the northeast, Castile in the center, and Portugal along the Atlantic coast. In 1469, Ferdinand, heir to the throne of Aragon, married Queen Isabella of Castile. Through this marriage, they united most of Spain. At the time, royal power was weak in both kingdoms, but Ferdinand and Isabella moved forcefully to centralize and consolidate their authority—each in his or her own kingdom.

To centralize power, they allied themselves with the towns against the nobles. They

Queen Isabella of Castile. Her marriage to Ferdinand of Aragon united the two largest provinces in Spain.

gained the support of townspeople by granting them charters that spelled out the privileges and responsibilities of each town, and appeased lesser nobles by giving them honorary positions in the royal court and exempting them from certain taxes. They destroyed the castles of uncooperative nobles, seized vast amounts of treasures, and appointed royal officials loyal to the crown to positions of responsibility. They seized the property of the powerful crusading orders and established a strong standing army. They seldom consulted with the Cortés of either Aragon or Castile.

Ferdinand and Isabella strengthened the economy by establishing a uniform system of weights and measures for their united kingdoms and replacing the many kinds of money then in use with newly minted coins stamped with their likenesses. They im-

*Ferdinand and Isabella receive a delegation of Jews, as a zealous monk gestures at right. During their reign, Ferdinand and Isabella expelled thousands of Jews and Moslems from Spain.*

proved roads and harbors, built bridges, and organized trade fairs that attracted merchants from all over the Mediterranean world. They encouraged learning by exempting printers from certain taxes, establishing a new university, and sponsoring translations of classical Greek and Roman writings into Spanish.

Queen Isabella decided that if Spain were to become a strong nation it must enforce religious as well as political unity. To achieve this, the two monarchs made the Church a staunch ally. They thereby avoided the confrontation between Church and state that took place in other emerging nation-states. The Spanish rulers persuaded the pope to give them the authority to appoint bishops and abbots, and they introduced to Spain the *In-quisition*, a Church court responsible for locating and suppressing heresy.

The Inquisition had been established by the pope in the early 13th century. People accused of heresy were assumed to be guilty by the Inquisition and had to prove their innocence. They were not allowed to question their accusers and were often tortured into making confessions. In Spain, the Inquisition was organized and led by Father Tomás de Torquemada. Anyone found guilty of heresy by the tribunal of the Inquisition was burned at the stake.

By using the Inquisition to enforce religious unity, Ferdinand and Isabella increased royal power. Fear of the Inquisition made the Spanish profess their loyalty to the crown and the Church. The Inquisition di-

In the hope of finding a sea route to India, Ferdinand and Isabella subsidized the westward voyage of Columbus in 1492. His discoveries enabled Spanish monarchs to claim a large portion of the New World.

rected many of its activities against the two religious minorities of Spain: the Moslems and Jews. Although both groups had enjoyed tolerance under many earlier rulers, Christian townspeople had often attacked them, forcing some to convert to Christianity. The Inquisition ruthlessly persecuted those Moslems and Jews who had converted to Christianity but were suspected of clinging to their former beliefs.

In 1492, Spanish Jews were given a choice: convert to Christianity or leave the country at once without taking any of their property. Tens of thousands went into exile. These Jews, called *Sephardim*, settled mostly in North Africa and the Middle East. Ten years later, the Moslems were given no choice: they had to accept baptism and became known as

*Moriscoes*. Historians estimate that between 120,000 and 250,000 people fled from Spain to escape from the Inquisition and its persecution—most of them Moslems or Jews. Spain never recovered from this loss of its most skilled and learned citizens.

By 1492, Ferdinand and Isabella had achieved another victory in their drive toward centralizing royal power. That year, Christian knights conquered Granada, the last Moslem stronghold in Spain. Territorial unity was at last achieved. At the same time, Queen Isabella sponsored the voyage of Christopher Columbus across the Atlantic Ocean in the hope of finding a sea route to India. The voyages of Columbus and later explorers would enable Spain to acquire a vast empire in Central and South America.

Ferdinand and Isabella achieved national unity, established the basis for absolute royal power, and paved the way for Spain to become the most powerful nation in Europe. However, their successes were achieved at great cost. Many of the most talented people in Spain were forced to leave the country because of their policy of intolerance.

## PORTUGAL

The unified kingdom of Ferdinand and Isabella included all of the Iberian peninsula except Navarre, in the far north, and Portugal, lying along the western coast. During the early Middle Ages, Portugal was not a separate state and had the same political experience as the rest of the peninsula. For centuries, it was part of the Cordoba caliphate. Then, during the *reconquista*, it was incorporated into the Christian kingdom of Castile.

Portugal remained a province of Castile until 1095, when Alfonso VI, king of Castile, gratefully gave his daughter, Theresa, in marriage to Henry of Burgundy, a Crusader who had helped Alfonso turn back a Moslem assault. For her dowry, Theresa received Portucali and Coimbra, two counties located on the Atlantic coast between the Douro and Minho rivers. This dowry became the foundations of a new kingdom—Portugal.

Henry and Theresa were determined to convert their fiefs into an independent kingdom. After the death of her husband, Theresa continued to struggle for independence from Castile. She fortified the important towns and personally led troops on campaigns to consolidate her control. Her son, Alfonso Henriques, extracted a promise from the king of Castile to let him rule any territory south of the Douro River that he seized from the Moors.

Alfonso Henriques defeated the Moors at Ourique in 1139, but the king of Castile refused to honor his promise. Four years later, Pope Innocent III was asked to mediate the dispute between the two rulers. Although Innocent decided in favor of the king of Castile, Alfonso Henriques continued the struggle.

He offered his kingdom as a fief to Pope Alexander III, successor to Innocent III, if the pope would recognize him as the king of Portugal. In 1143, Alexander III declared Portugal to be a sovereign kingdom under the rule of Alfonso I.

### EXPANSION

Since the kingdom of Portugal was bounded to the west by the Atlantic Ocean and to the north and east by the powerful kingdom of Castile, the only route toward expansion lay to the south. During the Second Crusade (1146-1149), a group of knights from northern Europe helped Alfonso free the cities of Lisbon and Santarem from the Moors. The capital of Portugal eventually was moved from Coimbra to Lisbon.[1]

Sancho I (1185-1211), son of Alfonso I, earned the nickname "the Colonizer" (*O Povoador*) because he encouraged Christians to settle in the areas that his father had seized from the Moors. Like other medieval monarchs, he and his immediate successors worked to consolidate royal power by controlling the decentralizing forces of the Church and the nobles. They set up royal commissions charged with recovering lands that they believed the Church had gained illegally. They also expanded royal territory, and in 1249, Alfonso III (1248-1279) captured the last Moslem stronghold in the Algarve region of Portugal.

### DINIS

The most important ruler of medieval Portugal was Dinis (1279-1325), known as "the Farmer King" (*O Lavrador*) because he both encouraged his nobles to cultivate their lands and distributed uncultivated tracts to the

---

[1]According to tradition, Lisbon had been founded by the legendary Greek hero, Ulysses, during his wanderings after the fall of Troy. On several medieval maps, the city that is now called Lisbon appears as *Ollissibona* (meaning "Ulysses the Good").

peasants. Dinis founded a school of agriculture to teach farmers better methods of growing crops, raising animals, and controlling soil erosion. As a result of these efforts, the farmers were able to satisfy local needs and developed a surplus that could be sold abroad. To transport this surplus to foreign countries, Dinis organized a merchant marine and encouraged mariners from other lands to settle in Portugal and teach the Portuguese the most modern techniques of navigation.

Dinis required that all official documents be written in the vernacular rather than in Latin, thereby stimulating the use of Portuguese. In 1278, he limited the Church to its existing holdings. He supported poets and scholars and founded a university in Lisbon. During his reign, Portugal achieved political and territorial unity, and its borders have remained unchanged since then.

As in Spain, the Cortés in Portugal at times tried to assume an important role. But the makeup of the Cortés in Portugal was even less representative than the ones in Spain because only the clergy and nobles—and not townspeople—could send official representatives. The Cortés did not develop into a powerful institution, however, since it met only when called into session by the monarch and did not have the right to enact laws.

## HOUSE OF AVIZ

In 1385, Portugal faced a serious threat when the king of Castile launched an all-out offensive to regain this former province. Portugal preserved its independence under the successful leadership of John I, who established the Aviz dynasty. The House of Aviz set Portugal on a course of expansion that would bring it to the height of its power in the 15th and 16th centuries.

In 1386, John concluded the Treaty of Windsor with England, gaining its support against Moslem and Spanish threats. This treaty is still in effect, making it the oldest political alliance in Europe. John also continued the offensive against the Moors, attacking Moslem strongholds in North Africa.

John's youngest son, Henry (1394-1460), known as Prince Henry the Navigator, followed his example. Prince Henry was driven

Prince Henry the Navigator, although not a sailor himself, encouraged and subsidized voyages to unknown lands. His ventures marked the beginning of the Age of Exploration.

| IMPORTANT MONARCHS OF PORTUGAL | |
|---|---|
| 1139–1185 | Alfonso Henriques |
| 1185–1211 | Sancho I |
| 1245–1279 | Alfonso III |
| 1279–1325 | Dinis |
| | *House of Aviz* |
| 1385–1433 | John I |
| 1438–1481 | Alfonso V |
| 1481–1495 | John II |
| 1495–1521 | Manuel |

In 1498, Vasco de Gama reached India with the help of Arab pilots from Africa. The valuable cargo of spices he brought back demonstrated the profitability of such expeditions.

In the 15th century, the Portuguese planted trading outposts on the coast of Africa, paving the way for their future empire. Under King John II (1481-1495), the Portuguese sailor, Bartholomeu Dias, rounded the tip of southern Africa (1488), which he named the Cape of Storms. The king renamed it the Cape of Good Hope because it offered the chance of fulfilling a dream: the discovery of an all-water route to the riches of the East. Such a route would break the trade monopoly long held by the northern Italian city-states and give Portugal access to the spices and other trade goods of the East.

When Vasco da Gama reached India in 1498, he opened a sea route to the East. Other navigators followed, and within a few years Portugal controlled a rich commercial empire in India and the Far East.

## THE SWISS CONFEDERATION

While Spain and Portugal were cementing their respective frameworks for strong, unified nation-states, other states were emerging elsewhere in Europe. In the Holy Roman Empire, you will recall, the pattern of political development had fallen away from centralization with the emergence of numerous small, virtually independent duchies, counties, and baronies (Chapter 19). Although these states and even some "free cities" such as Lübeck and Ulm owed nominal allegiance to the Holy Roman emperor, most went their own ways. The disunity of the empire enabled several small *cantons*, or states, to emerge on the western frontier. These cantons formed the nucleus of the Swiss Confederation.

### EARLY HISTORY

Around 500, the Franks made Helvetica part of the Frankish kingdom. Three centuries later, Charlemagne introduced Christianity into the region now called Switzerland. Several monasteries were established, the most important of which was Saint Galen, which still exists. After the division of Charle-

by religious and economic motives to encourage Portugal to look outside its borders for new opportunities. A devout man, he pursued the Crusade against the infidels by seizing Arab towns along the coast of North Africa, where he dreamed of establishing a Christian kingdom. Because Portugal was poor in land and resources, expansion overseas offered the promise of wealth and power.

Early in the 15th century, Henry set up a center for the study of navigation that would enable Portugal to push its explorations out into the Atlantic and cautiously move south along the coast of West Africa. In 1419, Portuguese sailors reached the Madeira Islands; in 1427, the Azores; and in 1445, the Cape Verde Islands.

magne's empire, most of the area came under the rule of the Holy Roman Empire.

Although feudalism developed in this mountainous region, it did not take hold as firmly as elsewhere, and the peasants enjoyed more freedom than their counterparts in other parts of Europe. Free peasants began to govern themselves through local assemblies. In time, some of the towns that were located on important trade routes—such as Basel, Lucerne, and Zurich—developed into major cities.

In 1231, the Holy Roman emperor, Frederick II, granted the canton of Uri, on Lake Lucerne, a charter guaranteeing it certain freedoms from local feudal lords in exchange for its pledge of loyalty. Soon after, the canton of Schwyz (from which the name Switzerland is derived) received a similar charter.

In 1291, the cantons of Uri, Schwyz, and Unterwalden took the first step toward breaking away from the Holy Roman Empire. That year, they drew up a treaty in which they agreed to defy their feudal obligations to the Holy Roman emperor, render mutual assistance if any one of them was attacked, and settle their internal disputes by arbitration. This union was first known as the *League of Upper Germany*, then as the Swiss Confederation, and in the 19th century as Switzerland.

### STRUGGLE FOR FREEDOM

The succeeding centuries saw the Swiss Confederation meet numerous challenges to its independence. Many stories emerged of heroic defenders repulsing powerful invaders. In 1315, Duke Leopold I of Austria invaded Schwyz. As his army marched through the narrow pass at Morgarten, the Swiss peasants, who had assembled on the mountainside above the pass, rolled huge boulders and logs down onto the invaders. They then attacked and defeated the trapped Austrians. Between 1332 and 1335, five more cantons, including Zurich and Lucerne, joined the confederation.

In 1386, Duke Leopold III attempted to invade Switzerland, but the Swiss again defeated the Hapsburgs of Austria and won recognition of their independence. In the 15th century, a dispute that arose between the townspeople of Zurich and the peasants of Schwyz led to another invasion and a Hapsburg alliance with the citizens of Zurich. However, the armed forces of the other cantons inflicted a decisive defeat on the combined armies of Zurich and Austria. Zurich renounced its alliance with Austria and rejoined the confederation. Louis XI of France, who had provided mercenary troops to help Austria, was so impressed with the fighting abilities of the Swiss that he attempted to recruit them to fight for him. The pope, too, recruited Swiss fighting men, an arrangement that still exists in the Swiss Guards who protect the Vatican City.

Although the Swiss Confederation represented a small and not very powerful force, it did influence events in Europe. For example, in 1476, it decisively defeated the ambitious duke of Burgundy, Charles the Bold, greatly reducing the forces of this once powerful ruler. Unfortunately, the victory produced a rift among the cantons when they attempted to divide the spoils. Since the confederation did not have a strong central government to enforce its decisions, there were often disputes between the larger urbanized cantons and the smaller rural ones. Early in the 16th century, the Swiss entered into their only expansionist enterprise. France, you will recall, had become involved in the Italian Wars under Charles VIII and seized parts of northern Italy. The Swiss, who were determined to control the Alpine passes leading into Italy, successfully attacked the French in 1512 and 1513 but were later defeated by them. The Swiss Confederation then retreated from its policy of expansion.

The Swiss Confederation differed markedly from the other emergent nation-states of western Europe. Although its borders were gradually defined and it won independence from the Holy Roman Empire, it did not have a strong centralized government. Instead, it was a union of many states with a weak federal government. Each canton preserved its own character and culture, choosing its own language and religion. The remarkable feature of this small landlocked nation is that it preserved its independence and unique government system even while revolutionary upheavals transformed the powerful states on its borders.

## EASTERN EUROPE

During the Middle Ages, eastern Europe was culturally very different from western Europe. Most of it had not been ruled by Rome or influenced by Roman civilization. Christianity was not brought to the peoples of eastern Europe until much later than the West, and even then, two churches—Roman Catholic and Eastern Orthodox—competed for victory in converting the Slavs, Magyars, and other peoples of the area. Feudalism did develop in eastern Europe, but it evolved later than in the West and differed in significant ways. The process of nation-building was also different in eastern Europe and was interrupted in the 13th and 16th centuries by Mongol and Turkish invasions.

During the Middle Ages, various groups of migrating people settled along the eastern shores of the Baltic, were conquered, uprooted, and forced to move again. Among those who would leave their mark on the region were Germans, Prussians, Poles, and Lithuanians. In the 10th century, Otto the Great encouraged Germans to colonize the Slavic lands to the east, initiating a policy of expansion that would continue for 1000 years. In the 13th century, the Teutonic Knights, whose crusading order had been founded a century earlier, descended on the pagan Slavs in Prussia to force them to convert. In time, the Teutonic Knights carved out their own states that later were absorbed into the kingdom of Prussia.

## POLAND

To the south of Prussia lay the exposed, flat plains of north-central Europe inhabited by the West Slavs. In the late 10th century, the West Slavs, who lived between the Oder and Vistula rivers, were united under a powerful tribe known as the Polanians, or dwellers of the plains. Their chieftain, Miesko, signed a treaty with Otto I, in which the Holy Roman emperor promised not to invade Poland in his "drive to the east."

In 965, Miesko married Dubravka, a Roman Catholic princess of Bohemia, and was baptized a Christian. Within a short time, the Catholic Church became one of the most important institutions in Poland, and so it remains. In 1000, Miesko's son and successor, Bolesaw I, became the first Polish ruler to bear the title king.

From the 11th to 13th centuries, dynastic struggles left Poland weak and divided into many small, independent duchies. Invasions by the Prussians from the north and the Mongols from the east created further chaos. In 1241, the Mongols swept into Poland from the steppes of southern Russia. They burned towns, looted churches, and massacred people. They invaded again in 1259 and 1287. The Teutonic Knights also defeated the Poles and expanded their power in the Baltic region.

In the 14th century, Poland had several rulers who strengthened royal power. Wladislaw I (1320-1333) arranged alliances with Hungary and Lithuania that ensured peace with these neighbors. His son and successor, Casimir III, moved to establish a strong central government. He reorganized the administration of the royal courts, and ordered a comprehensive code of laws to be compiled so that a uniform system of law could be set up for the entire kingdom. Casimir also enacted many measures to improve the economy of his kingdom. He pursued a program of draining marshes and clearing forests to create new farmland, and stimulated trade by improving roads, building bridges, and

## CENTRAL AND EASTERN EUROPE
*What methods did Polish kings use to expand their territory?*

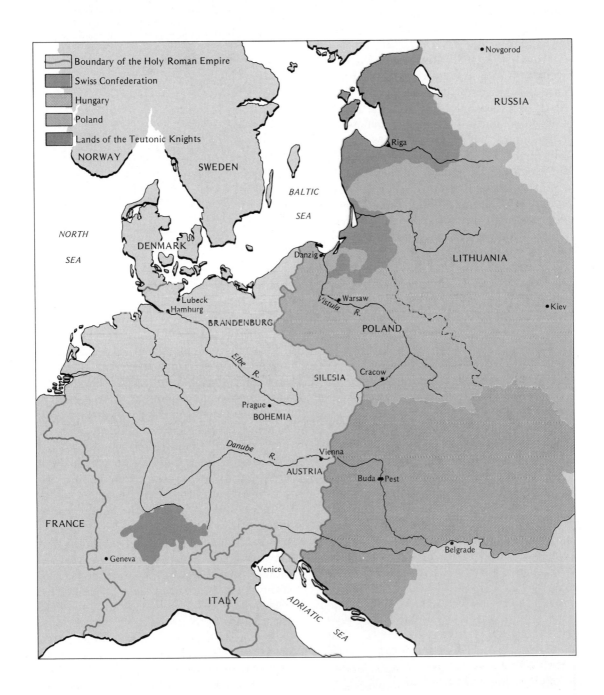

203

strengthening the monetary system. He supported the development of new towns and of cultural centers such as the University of Cracow. He invited Jews, victims of religious persecution in other parts of Europe, to settle in Poland.

Later in the 14th century, the Polish throne went to Casimir's daughter, who became Queen Jadwiga and married Jagello, grandduke of Lithuania in 1384. The marriage merged Poland and Lithuania into the largest kingdom in Europe. In 1410, the kingdom was further expanded when Jagello crushed the Teutonic Knights in the battle of Tannenberg. Under the terms of the treaty that ended the fighting, Poland gained western Prussia; east Prussia (Pomerania), although ruled by the Teutonic Knights, became a vassal state of Poland.

*Copernicus' view of the universe involved concepts that were not generally accepted for more than 150 years: that the earth rotates, even though it appears to stand still; and that the earth is not the central focus of the system.*

*Nicolaus Copernicus was one of Poland's most famous native sons. His theory that the sun, not the earth, was the center of the universe contradicted Ptolemy's geocentric theory and was rejected by the Church.*

The descendants of Jadwiga and Jagello ruled the united kingdom of Poland–Lithuania for 200 years until 1572. Although the kingdom was large and had great potential, it faced constant threats from Russia as well as from powerful nobles within. As a result, the Jagellonian dynasty was not able to continue the progress that Casimir had made in developing towns and strengthening the power of the central government.

In 1493, the first national Diet, or parliament, was established, consisting of an upper house that included clergy, nobles, and royal officials, and a lower house that included townspeople. The lower house had little power and had to defer to the nobles. The nobles also controlled the army and held the top positions in the royal bureaucracy. They jealously guarded their powers and enacted laws that reduced the free peasants to serfdom. Although their purpose was to exploit peasant labor on their lands, another effect of their policy was to cripple the economy of the towns so that a middle class could not develop.

Despite the political problems, the two centuries of rule by the Jagellonian dynasty has been called the "Golden Age of Poland." Printing was introduced at an early date, and an almanac was published in Latin in 1473. During this time, Poland produced its most famous scientist—Nicolaus Copernicus (1473-1543). He proclaimed a revolutionary theory in astronomy that shattered beliefs held throughout the Middle Ages. In this theory, he held that the earth and other planets revolved around the sun. In the 16th century, too, the Polish court flourished as a center of Renaissance culture.

### HUNGARY

Another state that emerged in eastern Europe during the Middle Ages was the kingdom of Hungary. It was settled by the Magyars after their defeat at the hands of Otto the Great (Chapter 19). Late in the 10th century, the Magyars converted to Christianity. According to tradition, on Christmas Day of the year 1000, Stephen was crowned the first king of Hungary by Pope Sylvester II. Stephen is considered one of the greatest rulers of Hungary, for he set up a system of royal administration, protected the boundaries, and made the Roman Catholic faith the official religion of the kingdom.

Although Stephen laid the foundations for a strong monarchy, his successors were ineffective rulers. Because Hungary had no recognized rule of succession, dynastic struggles frequently erupted, weakening royal power. Without a strong monarchy, feudal nobles competed for control, and the lesser nobles suffered under the tyranny of the higher ones. In the 13th century, a group of nobles forced King Andrew II (1205-1235) to grant the *Golden Bull*, which provided remedies for many of the abuses that had occurred. It prohibited any noble from holding more than one important position in the government, and guaranteed that nobles could not be brought to trial, except before the king. Military obligations were defined, and a noble was allowed to dispose of his fief as he pleased unless he died without an heir, in which case the land would revert to the king. Finally, the Golden Bull granted nobles the right to resist actions of the king that violated any of its provisions. Although there were no provisions for enforcing the bull, feudal nobles asserted their rights and remained strong in Hungary.

In the 13th century, Hungary, too, felt the impact of the Mongol invasions. In 1241, the Mongols devastated the countryside and slaughtered half the population, then withdrew the next year when their leader died. Bela IV, the king of Hungary, tried to ensure against another assault by reorganizing the army and building a chain of fortresses along the borders. The king also encouraged economic growth by inviting colonists to settle in Hungary and granting liberal charters to the towns. However, Bela and his successors struggled unsuccessfully to dominate the powerful feudal nobles.

In the 14th century, Hungary reached its greatest territorial extent. A new ruling house established by Charles Robert of Anjou ushered in a new age. Charles was unable to suppress the feudal nobles, but he did impose some regulations on them. His son and successor Louis (the Great) established his capital at Buda, on the Danube River, and became a great patron of learning. During his long reign (1342-1382), he expanded Hungarian power into the Balkans. In 1370, Louis became the king of Poland as well as of Hungary, but he spent little time or effort on ruling that land, concentrating instead on bringing the feudal nobles of Hungary under royal control.

After the death of Louis, royal power suffered a decline. Sigismund (1387-1447) not only was king of Hungary but also Holy Roman emperor and king of Bohemia. Because he spent much of his time in his Germanic lands, he was unable to supervise the great lords of Hungary.

In the 15th century, the Hungarians launched several crusades against the Turks who were steadily advancing into Europe. Under Osman (1290-1326), the founder of the Ottoman dynasty, the Turks had begun a series of conquests that would eventually lead them to the gates of Vienna. In 1437, John Hunyadi, a Hungarian noble, defeated the Turks and temporarily halted their advance. In the next few years, he repeatedly fought the Turks and ended the Turkish siege of Belgrade. After Hunyadi's death in 1456, his son Mathias (1458-1490) was elected king of Hungary.

Mathias was one of Hungary's greatest kings. He reestablished royal power, codified the laws, and won the title "Mathias the Just," for his efforts to end corruption and ensure justice. He was a distinguished patron of the arts and learning, and founded a university and a library.

Mathias was not only an able administrator but also a brilliant military tactician. He formed a standing army, called the Magyar Hussars, that was the best disciplined army in Europe at the time. With it, he won victories over the Czechs, whom he expelled from northern Hungary, and over the Hapsburgs, whom he forced out of western Hungary. He annexed Moravia, Lusitia, and Silesia. In 1485, he laid siege to Vienna and forced the Holy Roman emperor to cede to him Austria, Styria, and Carunthia.

When Mathias died in 1490, Hungary was the dominant power in central Europe. However, his successors were ineffectual rulers who were forced to give up the lands Mathias had conquered and were unable to control the nobles. During this time, serfdom became more deeply entrenched in Hungary even while it was declining in western Europe. Mathias' successors also faced new threats from the Turks, who seized Belgrade in 1521

and advanced into Hungary. In 1540, the Turks conquered central Hungary, captured Buda, and set up their own government. Large parts of Hungary remained under Turkish rule until the late 17th century.

***RUSSIA*** To the east of Hungary and Poland lay the lands of European Russia. In the early Middle Ages, from about the 5th to 8th centuries, these lands were settled by the eastern Slavs. In the next two centuries, Vikings from Sweden, called Varangians, pushed south, raiding and trading along the river routes that lead from the Baltic to the Black Sea. They extended their control over the Slavic communities and set up their own rulers in two major centers, Novgorod in the north and Kiev in the south. According to legend, a Varangian leader named Rurik became prince of Novgorod about 863, and his successors expanded their power to Kiev, which became the center of the early Russian state.

### KIEVAN RUSSIA

Kiev was at the center of a loose association of city-states that thrived on trade. In the 10th century, aggressive Varangians launched raids on the Byzantine Empire, including Constantinople, and forced the Byzantines to grant them trading privileges. In the end, the Byzantine emperors not only granted them such privileges, but also began hiring Varangian mercenaries to defend their empire.

The busy trade that developed between the Byzantine Empire and the Russian city-states led to increasing cultural contacts. In 989, Vladimir, prince of Kiev, converted to the Eastern Orthodox faith and married the daughter of the Byzantine emperor. This event tied the emerging Kievan state closer to the Byzantine Empire. Orthodox priests went to Kiev and presided over the mass conversion of the Russian people. They also set up the Russian Church under the guidance of the patriarch of Constantinople.

# THE GROWTH OF MEDIEVAL RUSSIA
In which directions was Russia likely to expand in the 16th and 17th centuries?

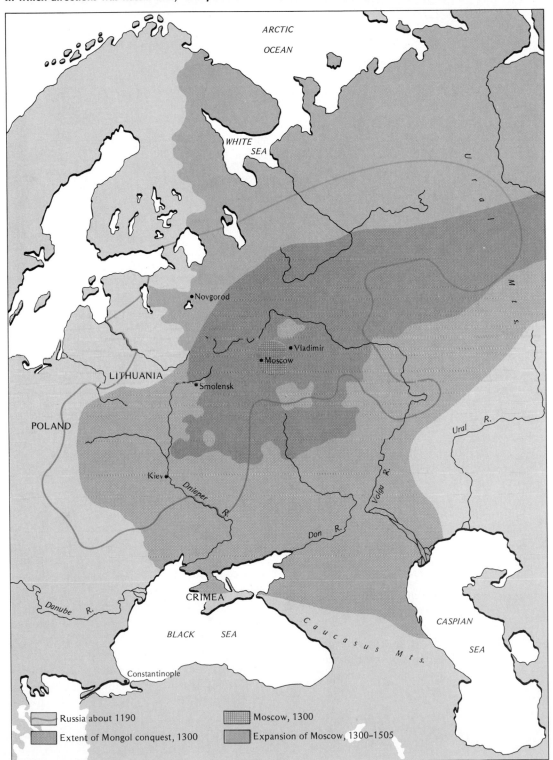

ARCTIC OCEAN

WHITE SEA

U r a l   M t s.

•Novgorod

•Vladimir
•Moscow

LITHUANIA

•Smolensk

POLAND

Ural R.

Kiev•

Dnieper R.

Volga R.

Don R.

CRIMEA

Danube R.

BLACK SEA

C a u c a s u s   M t s.

CASPIAN SEA

Constantinople

| | |
|---|---|
| Russia about 1190 | Moscow, 1300 |
| Extent of Mongol conquest, 1300 | Expansion of Moscow, 1300–1505 |

In early medieval Russian cities, log buildings mingled with European-style structures.

Vladimir weighed his options carefully before choosing the Eastern Orthodox Church. He looked at Islam but rejected it because Moslems were forbidden pork and wine. He turned down Judaism because he felt that the God of the Jews had failed to protect them. Roman Catholicism, he said, required too much fasting, and he was suspicious of papal claims to supremacy in secular matters. So he was left with the Byzantine Church. The fact that the Byzantine Church was ruled by the emperor probably added to its appeal.

Kievan Russia reached its height under Yaroslav the Wise (1019-1054). A scholarly and able ruler, he promoted education, codified the law, and protected his lands from invaders. During his reign, many beautiful churches were built in Kiev, including the cathedral of Saint Sophia. About this time, Russia was probably in advance of western Europe, but while the West emerged from the chaos of the early Middle Ages and revived after 1000, Russia suffered setbacks in its development. After Yaroslav's death, Kiev slowly declined under pressure from nomadic invaders and internal power struggles. In the next 200 years, other centers including the towns of Vladimir and its nearby neighbor, Moscow, began to gain prominence.

During the 14th century, Moscow became the leading city of Russia, succeeding Kiev and Novgorod. Shown are the government buildings of the Kremlin.

## MONGOL INVASION

In the 13th century, Russia was overrun by the Mongols. Under their leader Genghis Khan (1155-1227), these central Asian people had embarked on a course of conquest that would give them an empire stretching from Korea in the East to Poland and Hungary in the West. The Mongols swept into the lands that they conquered with huge numbers of well-mounted horsemen. The Mongol conquest of Russia was achieved in stages, but in 1240, they captured and totally destroyed Kiev. For the next 250 years, they dominated Russia.

The "Golden Horde," or Tartars, as the Mongols in Russia were called, ruthlessly annihilated resistance, leaving terror in their wake. Once they had brought Russia under their control, however, they were relatively tolerant rulers. They let the Russians govern themselves but required them to pay a huge annual tribute in money and men to serve in the khan's army.

The Mongol conquest had profound effects on Russia. It largely cut Russia off from contacts with the rest of Europe. At a time when the intellectual and commercial life of the West was quickening, Russia was forced to submit to its overlords from the East. Although the Mongols established excellent trade routes across their Asian empire, the Russians did not benefit greatly from this commerce. Russian trade and industry declined. The Russian peasants were heavily taxed for the tribute payments to the Mongols. The Russian Church, which was not taxed, urged the peasants to submit to the

*The Church of the Holy Trinity in Moscow. The distinctive architecture draws upon both Byzantine and Moslem traditions.*

over Vladimir, near Moscow, and after his death, his son, Daniel, founded the grand duchy of Moscow that would become the focal point of the future Russian state.

### RISE OF MOSCOW

Daniel's descendants in Moscow slowly rose to prominence. Ivan I (1325-1341) earned the nickname "Moneybags" both for his miserly habits and his role as collector of the Mongol tribute from the other Russian princes. He used his carefully acquired wealth to increase his influence with the Mongols, and later princes of Moscow continued this policy. They gained the title grand prince, putting them above their rivals. The position of Moscow was further enhanced when it replaced Kiev as the headquarters of the Russian Church.

In the mid-14th century, Prince Dmitri Dinski (1359-1389) embarked on the long struggle to overthrow the Mongols. Although Mongol power was already declining, the conflict would drag on for the next century. The final defeat of the Mongols was achieved by Ivan III (1462-1505).

Ivan the Great, as he was later called, is often regarded as the founder of the modern Russian nation. A patient but shrewd ruler, he expanded the territory controlled by Moscow. In 1480, he refused to acknowledge Mongol overlordship any longer and gradually drove the Mongols out of Russia. He also renewed contacts with Europe by establishing diplomatic relations with various countries.

In 1472, Ivan married Sophia Paleologus, the niece of the last Byzantine emperor. (Constantinople, you will recall, had fallen to the Turks in 1453.) He thereby claimed to be the successor to the Byzantine and Roman emperors. Ivan proclaimed Moscow the Third Rome and adopted the Byzantine title "autocrat." Many other Byzantine practices, especially court ceremonies, as well as the concept of royal supremacy over Church and state held sway in Russia.

"Tartar yoke." Many Mongols intermarried with the Russians, and some of their traditions, including the low status in which they held women, were absorbed by the Russians. Politically, Russia remained a feudal state, and individual Russian princes battled one another to preserve control over their own territories.

One such prince was the Russian hero Alexander Nevski (1236-1263), prince of Novgorod. He accepted Mongol domination, seeing a greater threat in the encroaching forces from the West. He fought and won several decisive battles against invaders from the West. In 1240, he crushed the Swedes; two years later, he destroyed an army of Teutonic Knights. In 1252, he extended his rule

## SUMMARY

*During the Middle Ages, the process of nation-building influenced events on the periphery of Europe. As elsewhere in Europe, strong rulers tried to consolidate royal power, but the pattern of development varied greatly. In Spain, the* Reconquista *occupied the attention of Christian rulers for many centuries. Once the land was united under Ferdinand and Isabella, Spain was on its way to becoming the dominant power in Europe.*

*Portugal, Spain's neighbor to the west, developed its own distinctive government and found its greatness through the conquest of a vast overseas empire. On the western frontier of the Holy Roman Empire, the Swiss cantons offered still another pattern of nation-building. Unlike the nations of western Europe that were united under the strong centralized authority of a monarch, the Swiss Confederation was based on a loosely organized group of states.*

*The plains of central and eastern Europe were the setting for power struggles first among various migrating people and later among medieval monarchs eager to expand their territories. Poland and Hungary each emerged as powerful states that competed for dominance with the Holy Roman Empire. Further east, the Russian state developed, first centered on Kiev and later on Moscow. Unlike the civilization of western Europe, which was shaped by Roman traditions and the Roman Catholic faith, Russia was influenced by Byzantine traditions and the Eastern Orthodox Church. For more than 200 years after the Mongol conquest, Russia was virtually cut off from the West. During the reign of Ivan the Great, however, Russia inherited the mantle of the fallen Byzantine Empire and renewed its contacts with the West.*

## QUESTIONS

1 Describe the major steps in the Reconquista. *How did Ferdinand and Isabella ensure unity in Spain?*
2 Explain how geography and the policies of Prince Henry the Navigator helped set Portugal on a course toward winning an overseas empire.
3 In what ways was the Swiss Confederation different from other states of medieval Europe?
4 Why was eastern Europe a battleground for much of the Middle Ages? How did problems over royal succession hurt the development of both Poland and Hungary?
5 How was medieval Russia influenced by Byzantine civilization? By the Mongol invasions?

## BIBLIOGRAPHY

*Which book might discuss Switzerland's unique form of government?*

HALECKI, O. *History of Poland.* New York: McKay, 1976. *A comprehensive history of Poland from its emergence as a Christian state in the 10th century to modern times.*

JACKSON, GABRIEL. *The Making of Medieval Spain.* New York: Harcourt Brace Jovanovich, 1972. *An excellent account of Spain from the 8th to the 16th century.*

PARES, BERNARD. *A History of Russia.* New York: Knopf, 1968. *The classic survey of the rise of the Russian people from the prehistoric Slavs to the present.*

SINOR, DENIS. *History of Hungary.* New York: Praeger, 1959. *A narrative history of Hungary that examines the impact of outstanding figures on its history and sets them in the cultural, political, social, and economic perspective of their times.*

THURER, GEORGE. *Free and Swiss.* University of Florida Press, 1971. *A fast-moving account of the development of Switzerland from earliest times through the 20th century.*

# WEST AFRICA

750–1600

Africa is the second largest continent. Within its boundaries, one can fit both the United States and China. This great landmass contains a variety of climates, ranging from the desert environments of the Sahara in the north and the smaller Kalahari in the south to the belts of steppe and savanna climates that stretch across much of the continent. Only ten percent or less of the continent is rainforest, and a small fringe of land on the northern and southern coasts of Africa has a balmy Mediterranean climate.

## GEOGRAPHICAL SETTING

Africa is so large that it is often divided into geographical regions. Of the two main parts—North Africa and sub-Sahara Africa—the latter has been further divided into West Africa, East Africa, and Southern Africa. North Africa is often included in discussions as part of the Middle East because it was conquered by the armies of Islam in the 7th and 8th centuries and its subsequent history and culture were closely tied to developments in the Islamic world. As a result, North Africa has generally been portrayed by Western scholars as Arabic (semitic), Islamic, and "civilized," whereas sub-Sahara Africa has been portrayed as Black (Negro), "tribal,"

and separate from the Judeo-Christian and Islamic heritage of North Africa. In the past, this division has encouraged the mistaken notion that North Africa was culturally distinct and historically separate from sub-Sahara Africa. Recent scholarship has revealed the long and continuous commercial relationship between sub-Sahara Africa—in particular the regions surrounding the Niger River—and the Mediterranean coast of Africa as well as Asia and Europe. These commercial contacts dated back to the ancient Egyptians and Phoenicians. Furthermore, as you will read, from the 8th through the 16th centuries A.D., West Africa was an important and vital link in international trade.

The first great civilizations of Africa, Egypt and Kush, were located along the Nile River—a region that provided an ample supply of fertile soil and water. The ancient Egyptians and Kushites created unique African cultures, and their achievements also had a significant impact on later European and Asian history. You are familiar with the outlines of Egyptian civilization and with the later civilizations—Phoenician, Roman, and Islamic—that flourished in North Africa. What we will focus on here are three major trading empires that emerged in West Africa.

The Arabs called the area south of the

The nomadic "people of the veil" of the western Sudan still ply some of the ancient caravan routes established by their ancestors. These nomads are watering their camels with the use of a leather bag and a trough made from a log.

Trade in Africa using camels dates to the era of Roman rule, and Carthage carried on a large trade using chariots before that. Between 750 A.D. and 1500 A.D., three major trading kingdoms emerged in West Africa: Ghana, Mali, and Songhai. Each owed its power and success to its control over trade. Well before the 8th century, when the first of these kingdoms was emerging, the basic lines of the long and extremely hazardous trans-Saharan trade had been established. After the conquest of North Africa by Islamic armies, Arab and Berber traders set up outposts in the north from which they sent their caravans south, putting themselves into this trading system. For a thousand years until the late 1800s, camel caravans traveled this dangerous two-month desert crossing. Although the risks were great, the profits were equally high.

From the north, merchants sent steel, copper, glass beads, horses, and slaves. On their way south, the caravans stopped at Taghaza, an oasis that stood above a vast salt mine. The salt that was so plentiful at Taghaza was worth its weight in gold just 500 miles to the south in the Sudan. Loading up on huge blocks of salt, the caravans plodded on to busy trading centers that grew up at the southern terminus of the desert. For the return journey, caravans carried back leather goods, cotton cloth, malaquetta pepper, acacia gum, kola nuts, and slaves. Most important, however, they stocked up on gold.

Gold and salt were the two essential commodities of the trans-Saharan trade. Whereas plentiful supplies of gold were found in West Africa, salt was rare and highly prized. The gold-salt exchange not only affected merchants in West Africa and North Africa but also had an impact on the trade of three continents: Africa, Europe, and Asia.

Before Europeans gained access to the gold of the Americas, they had no substantial gold supplies of their own. Instead, it was the gold mined in West Africa that eventually became the basis of international currencies. By the late Middle Ages, the emerging nation-states of Europe were desperate for gold. Monarchs needed money to pay their armies and civil servants as well as to finance the growing expenses of their courts. Also, as trade with the East expanded,

Sahara *Bilad el-Sudan*, or land of the blacks. In the western Sudan, the area immediately south of the Sahara and west of Lake Chad, the Niger, Senegal, and other rivers slice through the open savanna. Since ancient times, small settled populations had farmed the land, raising cereals, millet, and sorghum as well as a variety of fruits and vegetables. Because of limited rainfall and infertile soils, farming was hazardous, and villages faced frequent famines. Yet farmers did produce regular surpluses in most years until the twentieth century that were used to trade at local and regional markets. In fact, these small local exchanges formed part of a more complex trading network that linked up all parts of West Africa and carried goods to the edge of the Sahara.

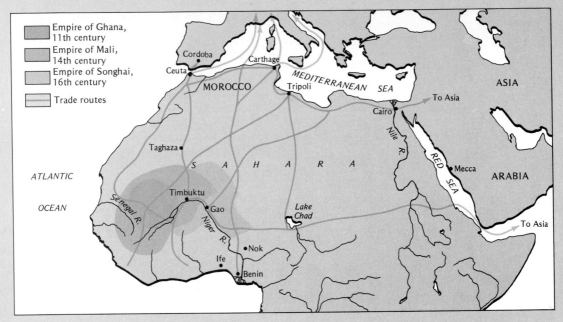

much gold was being sent overseas to buy the goods of India and China. The gold shortage was, therefore, a major concern of medieval monarchs. The influence of West African gold was evident in the English coin called a "guinea," as direct reference to its West African source. The need for gold and the desire to tap West African sources of this precious metal motivated Prince Henry the Navigator's support for voyages of exploration along the coast of West Africa.

## EMPIRE OF GHANA

Gold was the foundation of the kingdom of Ghana that emerged in the 8th century and controlled the area between the Senegal and Niger rivers. Originally called Wagadu by its rulers, the name Ghana came into use because one of the king's titles was *ghana*, or "war chief." The rise of Ghana to political and economic domination over neighboring regions was achieved through its control of gold and other valuable resources. Beginning as a trading center, Ghana served as a go-between between the merchants of North Africa and the gold- and ivory-pro-

ducing land to the south. The rulers of Ghana accumulated wealth by taxing all merchants who passed through their lands. Further, the kings of Ghana established a monopoly in gold, allowing only limited quantities to leave the kingdom. In this way, they maintained a high market value for gold.

In the 9th century, Ghana reached the peak of its power, exerting influence over a large region and enjoying the outward trappings of its prosperity. The ruler of Ghana held public audiences dressed in the finest cloth and adorned with spectacular gold ornaments. With riches from gold, the ruler maintained a strong army, which he used to collect taxes and preserve order. While the king and most of his subjects were not Moslem, many of his advisers and officials were. Islam had been brought to West Africa by the trade caravans, and Moslem communities were set up in all the major trading centers.

In the 11th century, Ghana suffered a series of reversals from which it never recovered. The Almoravids, Moslems from North Africa, were inspired to fight a holy war that extended from southern Spain to West Africa. One group marched across the desert and attacked Ghana. In 1055, the Almoravids captured the important trading city of Awdaghost, and Ghana's economy was seriously weakened as a result. Smaller states controlled by Ghana took advantage of the war to revolt, further weakening the empire. Although the Almoravid movement soon collapsed, Ghana was unable to recover its former power. Slowly, it lost control of the gold trade when the states it had dominated broke away and set up their own empires. By the early 13th century, the merchants of Kumbi, capital of the old empire, abandoned the city in favor of other trading centers.

## EMPIRE OF MALI

Out of the ruins of Ghana, the small subject state of Kangaba on the upper reaches of the Niger River put together the foundations of a new empire. The Malinke people lived in this region, where they practiced farming. According to tradition, a ruler named Sundiata defeated rival rulers around 1235 and expanded his base of power to include the regions formerly ruled by ancient Ghana. Sundiata took control of the rich gold bearing region of Wangara and within a few years greatly increased his power. The new empire became known as *Mali*.

By the 13th century, the kings of Mali were Moslem, and they were supported in power by Moslem officials and merchants. The majority of the people were pagan, but the rulers of Mali permitted them to practice their ancient traditions with toleration. Like its predecessor, the empire of Mali was built on farming villages but gained wealth and power from its control of the gold-salt trade. During this time, Timbuktu became a great trading center and developed into a city renowned for its learning.

The best known ruler of Mali was Mansa Musa (1312–1337), who achieved fame for his fabulous pilgrimage to Mecca in 1324. At the head of the vast caravan, he led an estimated 60,000 people on the journey across Africa. In Cairo, Moslem chroniclers counted some 500 slaves, each carrying a staff of gold. They commented on the camels laden with gold and other riches and applauded the ruler's decision to

Islam was introduced into West Africa by Arab traders during the 7th century. Shown is a group of Moslems in front of a mosque in present-day Mali—all traffic has ceased during the time of prayer.

carry home Moslem scholars, poets, and architects to improve his empire. During this pilgrimage, Mansa Musa was said to have given away so much gold that the general value of gold was depreciated for the next 12 years.

The empire of Mali flourished until the late 14th century. But then struggles over succession weakened royal power, and in the 15th century attacks by desert nomads and revolts from within further undermined its foundations.

## EMPIRE OF SONGHAI

Among the subject states that broke away from Mali was the trading city of Gao. About 1464, Gao and the surrounding Songhai lands were ruled by an especially able king, Sunni Ali, also known as Ali Ber or Shi. He spent much of his reign in battle and conquered a large empire across West Africa. He recaptured Timbuktu from desert nomads and annexed other trading centers that had once been part of the empire of Mali. In addition to battling his enemies, he also built the framework for an imperial government. Sunni Ali died in 1492, the year Christopher Columbus set sail from Spain.

Songhai reached its greatest extent under the reign of Muhammad Toure, better known as Askia Muhammed (1493–1528). A devout Moslem, Askia won the support of the leading merchants and Islamic religious leaders. During his reign, Islam became the official religion of Songhai, and he made all state laws conform to Islamic law. In addition, he established a government bureaucracy in which promotions were based upon merit to run the day-to-day operations of the empire. Further, he continued to expand the borders of the empire, making Songhai the largest empire ever seen in West Africa.

Although Askia put together this vast empire, neither he nor the rulers that followed him were able to ensure a peaceful line of succession. By the late 16th century, the pattern of decline again developed as disunity within and attacks from without weakened the great trading empire. In 1591, the ruler of Morocco launched an attack on Songhai from across the desert, hoping to gain access to the gold country of West Africa. The Moroccans were far outnumbered by the forces of Songhai, but they had the advantage of weapons, being armed with muskets that sent terror through the ranks of the Songhai soldiers. After its defeat at the hands of these invaders, Songhai quickly collapsed. No large successor state emerged as in the past; instead small kingdoms struggled to survive the constant attacks of desert raiders. Despite the uncertainties and dangers, camel caravans continued the ancient gold-salt exchange across the desert and into West Africa.

The age of the great West African trading kingdoms ended in the late 16th century at a time when the newly emergent nation-states of Europe were taking to the seas, ushering in an era of overseas exploration. The urgent need for gold had been somewhat allayed by the discovery of vast gold and silver resources in the Americas. To many Europeans, however, West Africa still meant gold, and it was to the "Gold Coast" that they continued to look for new riches. For the next several centuries, West African rulers held the newcomers in check and determined the terms of the trade. Only in the late 19th century did both internal and external forces create the conditions that would lead for the first time to the conquest of West Africa by European powers.

## INTRODUCTION TO THE DOCUMENTS

Until relatively recently, Western scholars knew little about African history except in the regions occupied by the Nile River valley civilizations and Ethiopia. Slowly, however, they have pieced together a knowledge of the people who developed their own distinct cultures in other parts of Africa. In West Africa, for example, the art and artifacts of the Nok culture have provided useful information about the early Iron Age in this region.

In addition to archaeology, much information about West Africa was provided by the oral traditions of the people. In West Africa, as elsewhere on this vast continent, oral history was preserved and passed along from one generation to the next. Such oral histories might record events that took place hundreds of years earlier. The most important written sources for West African history after about 1000 A.D. are writings of Africans. The Tarikh al Sudan and Tarikh al Fattash, chronicles written in Timbuktu, are the most important sources for Mali and Songhai. Yet another source of information, especially after 1000 A.D., are the written works of Moslem scholars, who based their accounts on the reports of Arab travelers to West Africa. With the growth of the trans-Saharan trade came an influx of Moslem scholars and religious leaders into West Africa, and they also added to the record of the great West African kingdoms.

## DOCUMENT 1    WEST AFRICAN PROVERBS

*Every group of people that has a long history also has a set of proverbs and moral tales associated with its experiences. Many of the communities of Africa have rich oral histories and tales which present religious as well as moral lessons. The selections that follow include proverbs from a variety of West African people, including the Asante of Central Ghana.*

Rain beats a leopard's skin, but it does not wash out the spots. [Asante]

Wood already touched by fire is not hard to set alight. [Asante]

One falsehood spoils a thousand truths. [Asante]

When a man is wealthy, he may wear an old cloth. [Asante]

Hunger is felt by a slave and hunger is felt by a king. [Asante]

The ruin of a nation begins in the homes of its people. [Asante]

When a king has good counselors, his reign is peaceful. [Asante]

By the time a fool has learned the game, the players have dispersed. [Asante]

When you are rich, you are hated; when you are poor, you are despised.
    [Asante]

A crab does not beget a bird. [Ghana]

If you find no fish, you have to eat bread. [Ghana]

One camel does not make fun of the other camel's hump. [Guinea]

To make preparations does not spoil the trip. [Guinea]

Knowledge is like a garden: if it is not cultivated, it cannot be harvested.
    [Guinea]

A wise man who knows his proverbs can reconcile difficulties. [Niger]

Ashes fly back into the face of him who throws them. [Niger]

Familiarity breeds contempt; distance breeds respect. [Niger]

Proverbs are the daughters of experience. [Sierra Leone]

---

*SOURCE:* Charlotte and Wolf Leslau, eds., *African Proverbs* (Mt. Vernon, N. Y.: Peter Pauper Press, 1962), pp. 7-42.

**Compare one of these proverbs to a proverb of a Western civilization.**

## DOCUMENT 2    TIMBUKTU

*Timbuktu was founded in about the 12th century and became one of the richest and most distinguished centers of learning in West Africa during the empire of Mali. In the early 16th century, a Moroccan traveler named Leo Africanus visited Timbuktu and left this description.*

Here are many shops of artificers and merchants, and especially of such as weave linen and cotton cloth. And hither do the Barbary [North African] merchants bring the cloth of Europe. All the women of this region except the maidservants go with their faces covered, and sell all necessary victuals. The inhabitants, and especially strangers . . . are exceedingly rich. . . . Here are many wells containing most sweet water; and so often as the river Niger overflows they convey the water thereof by certain sluices into the town. Corn, cattle, milk, and butter this region yields in great abundance. . . . The inhabitants are people of a gentle and cheerful disposition, and spend a great part of the night singing and dancing through all the streets of the city. Here [in Timbuktu] are great store of doctors, judges, priests, and other learned men, that are bountifully maintained at the king's cost and charges. And hither are brought diverse manuscripts or written books out of Barbary, which are sold for more than any other merchandise.

SOURCE: Richard W. Hull, African Cities and Towns Before the European Conquest (New York: Norton, 1976), pp. 13-14.

*How did geography contribute to the importance of Timbuktu?*

The legendary city of Timbuktu prospered from the trade across the Sahara Desert.

## TIME LINE FOR WEST AFRICA AND EUROPE

| WEST AFRICA | | EUROPE | |
|---|---|---|---|
| 640 | Islamic armies capture Egypt; Moslem traders begin to visit West Africa | | |
| 750 | Empire of Ghana controls gold trade of West Africa | 750 | Islamic armies under Omayyad Dynasty conquer all of North Africa and Spain |
| 1055 | Decline of Ghana; Almoravids (Moslems from North Africa) capture Awdaghost | 1066 | Norman conquest of England |
| 1235 | Sundiata creates empire of Mali | 1180–1223 | Philip Augustus strengthens French monarchy |
| 1324 | Mansa Musa's pilgrimage to Mecca; empire of Mali at its height | 1337–1453 | Hundred Years' War |
| 1400 | Decline of Mali | | |
| 1464 | Sunni Ali unites empire of Songhai, largest kingdom in West Africa | 1453 | Fall of Constantinople to the Turks |
| 1493–1528 | Askia Mohammed strengthens empire of Songhai; adapts Islamic law | 1492 | Columbus sets sail from Spain; reaches "New World" |
| 1591 | Moroccans invade Songhai; empire collapses | | |

UNIT  **IV**

# Europe in Transition

- *All things that are exchanged must be somehow comparable. It is for this end that money has been introduced, and it becomes in a sense an intermediate; for it measures all things.*

  **ARISTOTLE**

- *Of couse the Renaissance culture was an aristocratic superstructure raised upon the backs of the laboring poor; but, alas, what culture has not been?...We shall not defend the despots... but neither shall we apologize for Cosimo and his grandson Lorenzo, whom the Florentines obviously preferred to a chaotic plutocracy. As for the moral laxity, it was the price of intellectual liberation; and heavy as the price was, that liberation is a valuable birthright of the modern world, the very breath of our spirits today.*

  **WILL DURANT**

- *There are two ways of contesting, the one by the law, the other by force; the first method is proper to men, the second to beasts; but because the first is frequently not sufficient, it is necessary to have recourse to the second.*

  **MACHIEVELLI**

- *The arts of painting, sculpture, modeling and architecture had degenerated for so long and so greatly that they almost died with letters themselves, but in this age they have been aroused and come to life again.*

  **LORENZO VALLA**

*A merchant wishing that his worth be great
Must always act according as is right;
And let him be a man of long foresight,
And never fail his promise to keep. . . .
He will be worthier if he goes to church,
Gives for the love of God, clinches his deals
Without haggle, and wholly repeals
Usury taking. Further, he must write
Accounts well-kept and free from oversight.*
DINO COMPAGNI

# Economic Development in the Late Middle Ages

Between about 1050 and 1300, western Europe made enormous economic progress. This progress was so striking that historians consider it one of the most impressive achievements in European history. For three centuries before the year 1000, Europe had been ravaged by Viking, Moslem, and Magyar invasions. Most of the people had lived and died on the manors where they were born, their energies consumed by the struggle to survive. Diets were poor; trade was negligible; money had virtually disappeared; the few towns of any size that had survived the fall of Rome were stagnant.

By 1300, this bleak picture had been completely transformed. More and better food was being produced. Trade was booming, both within Europe and between Europe and the East. Under the impetus of trade, old cities were expanding, and new towns were springing up. Luxury goods were being imported from the East. Money had become an important medium of exchange, facilitating the exchange of goods and services. This chapter will explore the reasons for this remarkable economic development and the far-reaching changes that accompanied it.

**AGRICULTURAL REVOLUTION** The major force behind the economic progress of the later Middle Ages was an agricultural revolution that began in the 11th century. The revolution almost completely transformed the way Europeans grew their food. As a result, peasants produced more to eat. More food meant that the European population could expand: by 1300, there were three times as many people living in western Europe as there had been in the year 1000. In turn, the production of surplus food and the growing population allowed people to become involved in activities outside the manor and thereby encouraged the growth of trade and cities.

The agricultural revolution was the result of several factors, including the political stability that developed after the mid-11th century and changes in the climate of western Europe, which became somewhat warmer and drier from the 8th to 13th centuries. With the decline in feudal warfare and the emergence of national monarchies came an atmosphere of political security that encouraged new ventures such as the clearing of land for farming. The more favorable climate also fa-

222

*The heavy plow included a deep blade and a curved iron to turn over the sod. Because the plow was difficult to turn, fields were made as long as possible.*

vored farming, and peasants began to cultivate land in northern France, England, the Low Countries, and Germany.

Political stability also enabled Europeans to take advantage of important inventions in agricultural technology that were made about this time. Among the most useful of these was the development of the heavy plow. With it, peasants could till the heavy soils of northern Europe. New harnesses were invented, including a tandem harness which allowed farmers to use more than one team of animals. As a result, peasants could yoke horses and oxen together to pull heavier loads. The use of iron horseshoes gave horses better footing on rough terrain.

By the 8th century, European peasants had discovered the value of the three-field system of crop rotation (Chapter 17). Before modern fertilizers, part of a farmer's land had to lie fallow each year to avoid exhausting the soil. The Romans had left half of their

arable land uncultivated each year. Medieval farmers reduced this to one-third by dividing their plots of land into three parts. Each year, one part would lie fallow, and one part would be sown with grain in the fall that was harvested in the early summer. The third part would be sown in the spring with a different crop, usually beans or oats, that was harvested in the late summer. Thus, while Roman farmers had only been able to have one harvest a year, medieval farmers had two.

Moreover, the widespread growing and eating of beans made for a much healthier diet, since in combination with bread, the mainstay of the peasant diet, beans make up a complete protein.

With the increased grain supply that these methods provided, peasants could increase their livestock. More pigs, cattle, sheep, goats, and poultry meant more meat, milk, cheese, butter, and eggs for Europeans to eat or sell to townspeople.

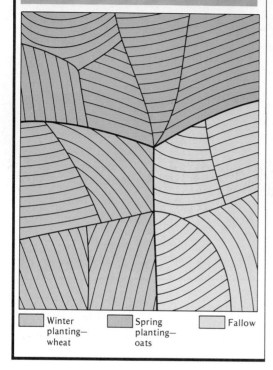

In the three-field system of agriculture, one field was left uncultivated each year, while the others were planted with different crops in the fall and spring. Peasants were allotted strips of land in each of the three fields.

Winter planting— wheat    Spring planting— oats    Fallow

**TECHNOLOGY** There were important technological advances made at this time that would influence European life profoundly. Soap, for example, was invented in the late 12th century. The Greeks and Romans had cleaned themselves with oil, usually olive oil, that had to be laboriously scraped off afterward. Soap was much easier to use and store. Like many new products, soap at first was a luxury available only to the rich, but it gradually fell in price and became accessible to the poorer classes.

During the Middle Ages, a variety of mechanical devices were invented to convert running water into a source of power. With the use of gears, cams, and pulleys, engineers were able to convert the circular motion of a water wheel into up-and-down motion, or into the faster motion of a smaller wheel. Water-powered mills soon dotted the landscape and allowed people to perform a multitude of tasks—such as grinding grain, tanning leather, forging iron, or even brewing beer—much more efficiently than before. Windmills, invented in Holland around 1170, enabled regions without rivers to utilize wind power for these tasks.

The 13th century saw both the invention of the spinning wheel, which would revolutionize the making of cloth, and the start of commercial coal mining. We do not know when Europeans discovered that coal would burn, but by the 13th century it was being extensively mined near Liege, in what is now Belgium. The use of coal as fuel in the later Middle Ages was made necessary by the deforestation of large parts of northern Europe. As more and more land was cleared for agriculture to feed the growing population, peasants and townspeople could no longer rely on the forests for fuel.

In the late 15th century, new mining tech-

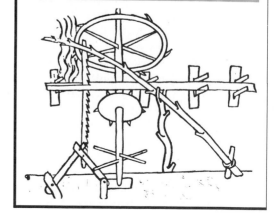

Medieval engineers harnessed water and wind power for many tasks. Shown is a water-powered saw: circular movement is converted to the up-and-down motion of the saw by means of the cams on the wheel shaft. The diagonal twig serves as an automatic feed device, keeping the saw pressed against the wood.

A medieval mining operation. Water and wind power were used to extract ores, to operate the bellows that heated blast furnaces, and to drive the hammers used in forging.

The design of the three-masted carrack, with triangular sails, made navigation of open seas much more feasible. Older ships had just one mast and a square sail.

niques made it possible to extract ores more effectively than before. Horizontal and vertical shafts were braced with timbers, and water-powered or horse-powered devices were developed to pump water from mines. Large power-operated bellows were devised to increase the temperature of fires used for smelting ores and producing cast iron. In turn, the increased availability of cast iron meant more iron tools for farmers and artisans.

Technological advances also made ocean travel more safe and efficient. The magnetic compass and astrolabe, which reached Europe from China during the 13th century, and charts of shorelines and harbors made navigation safer. Also in the 13th century, shipbuilders developed a caravel, a three-masted ship with a rounded bottom that could be operated in shallow water and could be steered in a cross wind. Larger three-masted ships, called *carracks* or *galleons*, were built to carry heavier cargoes. As cargoes became more valuable, many merchant ships carried soldiers and, increasingly after 1400, cannons, for defense against pirates.

### TRADE AND COMMERCE

On the foundation of the agricultural revolution, trade expanded. As manors produced more food than they needed, the lords began to trade some of it for luxuries or other goods that the manor did not produce. This trade expanded swiftly within Europe and was also directed toward the East after the Crusades increased the growing taste among nobles for luxuries such as silks and spices.

During the Crusades, merchants from Venice, Genoa, and Pisa set up a highly profitable trading enterprise. They purchased luxury goods in the Levant[1] and carried them by ship to ports in Italy and southern France. (These luxury goods had been brought to the Levant by caravans from Persia, India, and China as well as from Moslem lands in North Africa.)

The main French port for the eastern trade was Marseilles. From there, merchants transported the goods up the Rhône valley to the interior of France. At the same time, merchants from cities in Germany and other countries of northern Europe bought goods at Venice or Genoa and carried them across the Alps and along the Rhine valley. Goods that were taken by land into northern Europe were then shipped by water to Britain and Scandinavia. The merchants from the south traded their wares for grain, leather, and especially wool, the principal products of northern Europe.

As trade expanded, the region along the North Sea—known as the *Lowlands* (or Netherlands) because it was low, flat, marshy terrain—came to prominence. In the western part of the Lowlands, called *Flanders*, the Flemish found raising sheep was more profitable than growing grain because sheep thrived on the abundant marsh grasses of the region. As early as Charlemagne's day, the Flemish were renowned for the fine woolen cloth that they produced, and Flemish cloth became a medium of exchange in the commerce between Europe and the East. Since the finest wool available was that produced by English sheepherders, merchants began

A woolweaver and his tools. The textile industry was central to the economies of both England and Flanders.

to import wool from England. As a result, sheepraising expanded in England, and the English and Flemish wool industries became interdependent.

Early in the 14th century, Venetian merchants created what came to be known as the "Flanders Fleet"—ships that traveled 2500 miles along the coast of western Europe from Flanders to Venice. The sea route was easier and less expensive than the 400-mile overland route because ships did not have to pay tolls, climb mountains, ford rivers, or pass through hostile countries. Since Venetian merchants also controlled many trade routes to the East, Venice became a thriving marketplace for goods from every part of the world. It was the most cosmopolitan European city, and also profited from its own distinctive industries such as glass-making and printing.

As trade expanded in the 12th and 13th centuries, towns along the major European trade routes began to set up trade fairs. There, the merchants from various regions met to

---

[1]The eastern coastline of the Mediterranean Sea—present-day Syria, Lebanon, and Israel—was long known as the *Levant*.

226

International trade fairs enabled merchants to expand their businesses and to exchange ideas and opinions with people from other countries.

settle accounts for past shipments and arrange for future trade.

Fairs came to be held annually at such places as Champagne, Ghent, Leipzig, and Winchester. The nobles on whose lands the fairs were held found it profitable to provide services such as special courts to settle disputes, guards to protect the merchants and their goods, clerks to keep track of transactions, and even sheds in which people could meet.

Fairs served as useful centers not only for the exchange of goods but also for the diffusion of ideas. Unlike the markets in towns and villages, which were local affairs, these trade fairs were international. In time, these fairs helped to break down the isolated world of the manor and introduced peasants and nobles to a wider world.

*GROWTH OF GUILDS* As towns grew, merchants and artisans began to unite in mutual-aid associations known as *guilds*. In time, guilds acquired considerable power: they regulated the quantity and quality of the goods that were produced; set the price for goods; and protected the interests of guild members.

During the Middle Ages, two kinds of guilds emerged: merchant and craft guilds. The merchant guilds were the first to appear, and their goal was to control trade within a certain area. All the merchants in a town would join together to supervise trade, see that foreign merchants paid certain taxes, and regulate weights and measures. If disputes arose, they were settled at the guild courts. Guilds helped to protect merchants on their travels and negotiated with guilds in other towns on issues such as the payment of debts.

Guilds also served religious, social, and charitable functions. They held festivals to honor the patron saint of the guild. At guild meetings, members enjoyed fine dinners with the best food and entertainment in the town. The guild paid the burial expenses of a member who died and contributed to the family of a member who became incapacitated. One guild, for example, made this provision for its members:

• • • [I]f by chance any of the said trade shall fall into poverty, whether through old age or because he cannot labor or work, and shall have nothing with which to keep himself, he shall have every week from the said [offering] box seven pence for his support, if he be a man of good repute. And after he decease, if he have a wife, a woman of good repute, she shall have weekly for her support seven pence from the said box, so long as she shall behave herself well and keep single.[2]

### CRAFT GUILDS

In the 11th century, the growth of trade and the specialization of labor within the towns led to the emergence of craft guilds that eventually superseded the merchant guilds. Workers in each trade such as weaving, leatherworking, goldworking, baking, and so on organized themselves into guilds and allowed only people practicing the same craft to join. Like merchant guilds, the craft guilds supervised the production of goods, and each guild had a monopoly over its own product. By controlling the quality of articles they produced, the guilds protected consumers against shoddy goods. The use of poor ma-

The seal of the Flemish city of Ypres, showing the great hall of the textile guild. Guilds played an important role in the governments of many towns.

terials or the sale of badly made goods could lead to a fine or expulsion from the guild.

Each craft guild limited its membership by establishing a system for admitting newcomers. To become a guild member, a worker had to pass through three stages from apprentice to journeyman to master craftsman. Boys who were accepted for training as apprentices received no pay but were given food and shelter. After anywhere from 3 to 12 years, an apprentice was examined on the skills he had learned. If he passed the examination, he was admitted to the guild as a *journeyman* (from the French *journée*, meaning "a day's work") and could be paid for his work. When he reached the age of 23 years, a journeyman was eligible to submit a *masterpiece*, a complete work to prove his skill in his craft. If his masterpiece were accepted by the guild, he became a master craftsman, was admitted to the guild, and could open his own shop.

As guilds grew in power, they assumed leading roles in the government of the towns. In Florence, for example, the Wool Guild,

---

[2]"Rules of the Guild of White-Tawyers," quoted in J. H. Robinson, ed., *Readings in European History*, vol. 1 (New York: Ginn, 1904), p. 411.

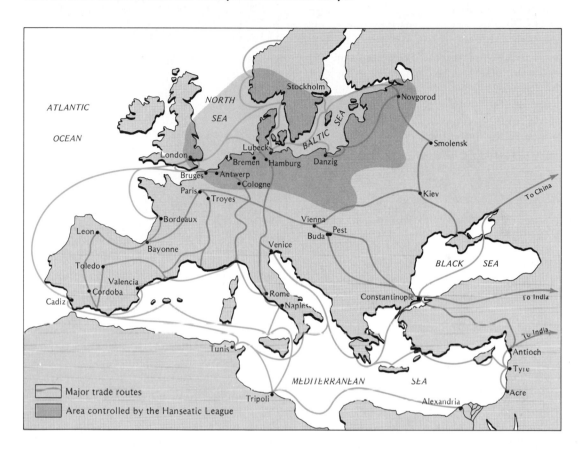

ATLANTIC

OCEAN

NORTH

SEA

Stockholm

Novgorod

BALTIC SEA

Smolensk

Lubeck
Bremen Hamburg Danzig
London
Bruges Antwerp
Paris Cologne
Troyes

Kiev

To China

Bordeaux

Vienna
Buda Pest

Leon

Bayonne

Venice

BLACK SEA

Toledo

Valencia
Cordoba

Rome

Constantinople

To India

Cadiz

Naples

To India

Tunis

Antioch

Tyre

MEDITERRANEAN     SEA

Acre

Tripoli

Alexandria

Major trade routes

Area controlled by the Hanseatic League

Silk Guild, and Guild of Bankers and Moneylenders dominated the government. Guilds hired watchmen to patrol the streets, contributed to the building of churches and cathedrals, and set up schools and hospitals.

By the end of the Middle Ages, the guild system had become rigid and restrictive. Often, membership was limited to sons of members. As a result, many young men were forced to remain journeymen, or day-wage laborers, without the hope of being admitted to the guild. The earlier ties of loyalty and trust between journeyman and master craftsman were replaced by frustration and bitterness. In some cities, the discontent of journeymen led to riots, especially during times of economic depression.

## THE HANSEATIC LEAGUE

Early in the 14th century, the merchants from several major coastal towns on the Baltic and North seas formed a guild to secure trading privileges for its members in foreign ports. As the guild succeeded in this objective, it attracted the attention of merchants in other ports, and it grew to include members from almost 200 cities. This guild grew into the powerful *Hanseatic League* that dominated the trade of northern Europe for almost 300 years.

In time, the league achieved a virtual monopoly on trade in northern Europe. It gained control of many business operations from England to Russia. It established its own navy to protect the ships and ports of member cities and developed its own system of weights and measures to standardize transactions among the members.

The league was governed by merchant representatives from each of the member cities, but the governing body seldom met unless an emergency threatened. Nevertheless, the league had great political influence because of its wealth and economic domination of the region. When that control was broken in the 16th century, the power of the league rapidly declined.

**MONEY ECONOMY** In the early Middle Ages, as you have read, most people lived on self-contained manors. The few goods that they needed from the world outside the manor were acquired by barter. In the 11th century, however, the economic climate began to change. Slowly, money transactions began to replace barter as trade revived, and for the first time since the fall of Rome in the 5th century, coins were used as a medium of exchange.

By the 13th century, the use of coins was widespread in Europe. Medieval monarchs and the city-states of northern Italy issued their own coins and established their own monetary systems. As the demand for coins grew, nobles mortgaged or sold their lands to raise the cash they needed. Townspeople also began to use cash, and money came into use at the trade fairs. Of all the coins in use during the late Middle Ages, the ducats of Venice and the florins of Florence were the most widely accepted.

To prevent the counterfeiting of money, individual rulers ordered that gold and silver coins in their lands be minted, or stamped, to a standard size, weight, and design. By this means, they tried to ensure its value by preventing the substitution of less valuable metals, such as tin or copper, for the gold or silver in the coin. Certain Italian merchants began to specialize in the evaluation of coins. Because they weighed and analyzed coins on

As coins became a common medium of exchange, certain merchants began to specialize in moneychanging and lending. They usually worked on a banc, or bench.

benches, or *bancs*, their business operations became known as "banks."

*CHANGING ATTITUDES TOWARD WEALTH*
The revival of trade and the increased economic activity meant that some people had a surplus of cash, while other people wanted to borrow: monarchs needed money to wage war, merchants to finance trade, nobles to buy luxuries. However, the Church prohibited Christians from practicing usury—that is, charging interest on money.

In the 4th century, Augustine had condemned usury in these words:

• • • *I will not have you be money lenders, and for this reason, that God would not have you so. . . . If you have lent your money, that is to say, advanced a loan to someone from whom you expect to receive interest, and not only in money, but in whatever you gave, whether wheat or wine or oil or anything else; if, as I said you expect to receive back more than you gave, you are a usurer, and in this respect you deserve blame and not praise.[3]*

[3]*St. Augustine on the Psalms*, vol. 2, trans. Scholastica Hebgen and Felicitas Corrigan (London: Longman, 1961), p. 110.

Therefore, during much of the Middle Ages, some Christians chose to lend their money through Jewish middlemen, who were not restricted by the prohibitions of the Church. Moreover, money lending was one of the few occupations permitted to Jews in medieval society. Most states and cities forbade Jews to own land, practice a profession, or join a guild.

In the later Middle Ages, however, the Jews were overshadowed as money lenders by the Italian merchant-bankers. As commerce and manufacturing expanded, entrepreneurs found it necessary not only to borrow money occasionally, but also to have standardized coins, and to secure places to store money and a safe way of transporting money over long distances. The Italians specialized in these activities. When the importance of such transactions became apparent, the Church removed some of its restrictions on making loans by approving of "reasonable" rates of interest. After this, usury came to mean "the charging of excessive rates of interest."

The quickening economic pace of the late medieval period affected other ideas about acquiring wealth. When the guilds first appeared, they established what was called a "just price" for the goods they produced. In accordance with Church teachings, which condemned making large profits at the expense of others, the *just price* for an article would include the cost of the material plus a justifiable (small) profit. After setting a just price, the guild was not supposed to change it. As the money economy expanded, however, the attitude of merchants and entrepreneurs changed so that it became possible to charge high prices—or whatever customers would pay—and the making of large profits was no longer condemned as severely.

Enterprising people studied the best ways to do business, and in the 15th century, books began appearing that offered advice on how to operate a successful business. The advice given in the excerpt below might well appear in a business textbook today:

• • • *Do not exercise any trade or business in which you have no experience. Do what you are able to do and beware of everything else, for [otherwise] you would be cheated. And if you want to become experienced in anything, practise it as a child, be in shops . . . and in banks with others, go abroad, frequent merchants and merchandise, see with [your own] eyes the places and countries where you have in mind to do business. Try a friend—or rather the man whom you believe to be a friend—a hundred times before you rely upon him a single time, and never rely on anyone so deeply that he may ruin you.*[4]

### RISE OF BANKING

In the late Middle Ages, merchants and other people handling large sums of money developed a form of banking. They learned that the safest way to move money was by accounting entries: that is, coins were deposited at one point—in Milan, for example—and other coins of the same value were picked up at a distant point such as London. The receipt for a deposit made in 1248 demonstrates how this system operated.

• • • *March twenty-eighth, in the year of the Incarnation of the Lord, 1248. I, Giraud Alaman, money-changer, citizen of Marseilles, confess and admit to you, Peter Mazele of Baza, that I have had and received from you by way of deposit ten pounds of mixed money now current in Marseilles . . . I have promised to give and pay to you these ten pounds or to a known messenger of yours or to any one whom you command to receive it, whenever it shall please you. Pledging my goods, etc.; renouncing all delays of the law, etc.*[5]

Because the city-states of northern Italy were at the center of the growing money

---

[4]Written in Florence in 1393, quoted in R. S. Lopez and I. W. Raymond, *Medieval Trade in the Mediterranean World* (New York: Norton, 1955), pp. 422 and 375.

[5]Roy C. Cave and Herbert H. Coulson, eds., *Medieval Economic History* (Milwaukee: Bruce Publ. Co., 1936), p. 144.

economy, it was in this region that several families set up the first banking businesses. The Peruzzi family, for example, made a business arrangement with the pope to collect taxes in England for the Church. With profits from this activity, the Peruzzis developed a network of banks in 16 cities across Europe and loaned money to the kings of Naples and England. Their enterprise, however, collapsed when the king of Naples repudiated his debt, and warfare bankrupted the English treasury.

The Medici family of Florence established many independent banks throughout Europe and set up a system to ensure against collapse. The manager of each branch was made responsible for any loans he made and could not expect the debts that he incurred to be assumed by other branches or by the parent bank in Florence. If one Medici bank failed, there would thus be no serious effect on the others. The Medici family became so wealthy that they not only dominated the government of Florence (Chapter 24) but also won control of the papacy and married into the ruling dynasties of Europe.

In France, the most prominent banker was Jacques Coeur (1395–1456), the son of a fur merchant of Bourges. When his father died, Coeur inherited the business, which he and his associates developed into a company that dealt "in every class of merchandise . . . in which they could make a profit."[6] The company established warehouses in several cities, developed mines, and carried on trade with the Middle East.

In 1437, the king of France chose Coeur to organize the mint, and two years later, appointed him treasurer-steward of the royal household. Coeur lent money to rulers, nobles, popes, and in exchange arranged prosperous marriages and high ecclesiastical positions for his children. When jealous no-

bles spread accusations against Coeur, the wealthy banker was imprisoned and tortured, and his property was confiscated. Fortunately for Coeur, the pope intervened to prevent his execution. Coeur escaped from prison in 1454 and fled to an island in the Aegean Sea, where he died two years later.

A leading German bank was established by Jacob Fugger (1459-1525), who was born in Augsburg. Fugger studied to become a monk but later left the monastery to work in the textile industry. He accumulated wealth and became an important moneylender. He loaned vast sums to popes and to the Holy Roman emperor, Maximilian I. His son, Jacob "the Rich," loaned 500,000 gulden to bribe the electors of the Holy Roman Empire to choose Maximilian's grandson as Emperor

Jacob Fugger was one of the most prosperous medieval bankers. He had branch offices in Nuremberg, Venice, Lisbon, Rome, and many other cities.

[6]Kenneth Setton and National Geographic Society staff, *Age of Chivalry* (Washington, D. C.: National Geographic Society, 1969), p. 303.

Charles V. In return for these loans, the Fuggers gained the right to exploit gold and silver mines in Hungary and Spain. The Fuggers had branches in all the chief cities of Europe. Before the family abandoned banking in the 17th century, they had been granted the title of prince by the emperor.

## BUBONIC PLAGUE

In the mid-14th century, economic progress came to a temporary halt. The chief cause was an epidemic of bubonic plague, which had originated in Asia and struck Europe in 1348.[7] It is estimated that by the time the plague, which became known as the Black Death, had run its course, it had killed from a third to a half of the population of Europe. Giovanni Boccaccio, a prominent writer of the 14th century, described attempts to thwart the disease:

• • • *[In] spite of all means that art and human foresight could suggest, such as keeping the city clear from filth, the exclusion of all suspected persons, and the publication of copious instructions for the preservation of health; and notwithstanding manifold humble supplications offered to God in processions and otherwise; it began to show itself in the spring of the aforesaid year [1348], in a sad and wonderful manner. Unlike what had been seen in the east, where bleeding from the nose is the fatal prognostic, here there appeared certain tumours in the groin or under the armpits, some as big as a small apple, others as an egg; and afterwards purple spots in most parts of the body; in some cases large and but few in number, in others smaller and more numerous, both sorts the usual messengers of death. To cure this malady,*

*The bubonic plague, or Black Death, swept through 14th-century Europe with devastating force, killing one-third of the population and permanently altering the basic values and beliefs of the survivors.*

*neither medical knowledge nor the power of drugs was of any effect.*[8]

### ECONOMIC AND SOCIAL DECLINE

The plague killed so many people that there was a critical shortage of labor in agriculture and industry; fields lay fallow, and sheep roamed untended over the pastures. Survivors were stunned by the devastations caused in the three years from 1348 to 1351. Many people wandered homeless through the countryside. Others turned to robbery. Because of the labor shortage, able-bodied workers could charge high wages. In England, King Edward III issued the Statute of Laborers in 1351 to regulate wages and prices and stop the growth of vagrancy.

---

[7]Outbreaks of the bubonic plague had occurred before. In the 5th century B.C., the plague had struck Athens during the Peloponnesian War. An outbreak occurred in the 3rd century A.D. in the Roman Empire. The plague swept through Europe twice in the 14th century, appeared in England in the 17th century, and took huge tolls in India in the late 19th century.

[8]Giovanni Boccaccio, *The Decameron*, in J. F. Scott, A. Hyma, and A. H. Noyes, eds., *Readings in Medieval History* (New York: Crofts, 1946), p. 495.

*Medieval physicians did not know how the plague was spread, but took various precautions to avoid contagion. In this satiric portrait, a doctor's protective clothing includes a bird mask.*

causing prices to rise rapidly. Sharp price increases in turn led to further social unrest.

For the rest of the 14th century and well beyond, Europe suffered from the damage of the plague. A second outbreak in the same century caused new panic but took a smaller toll, and the populations of nations such as England or France did not reach their pre-plague levels for 100 years. The economic dislocations were matched by a sense of demoralization. People had seen their families, friends, and neighbors die in a matter of days; they had suffered from the looting, burning, and lawlessness that the breakdown in order had brought.

The plague was not the only factor in the economic decline of the 14th century. The economies of France and England were greatly disrupted by the Hundred Years' War (1337-1453) that wasted enormous resources in both countries and produced widespread social unrest. Thus, the peasants of France rose up in the Jacquerie Rebellion of 1358, and the English peasants revolted in 1381. The uprisings were crushed with brutal measures, but they further contributed to the economic depression of the century.

### LASTING CHANGES

The 14th century was a time when unsettling currents were undermining the fabric of medieval society. As you have read, the power of the Church declined in the later Middle Ages. In the 14th century, monarchs in England and France consolidated their power and clashed with the Church in disputes over taxes and jurisdiction in legal matters.

The rise of national monarchies and the shift to a money economy changed the way of life of feudal nobles. Monarchs tried to limit the feudal warfare that had marked the medieval world. As a result, nobles no longer had to defend their domains against invaders, and they raised money by requiring payments of feudal obligations in cash instead of military services. With money, they transformed their cold and drafty manors and cas-

*• • • And because many strong beggars as they may live by begging, do refuse to labor, giving themselves to idleness and vice, and sometimes to theft and other abominations; none upon the said pain of imprisonment, shall, under the color of pity or alms, give anything to such, who are able to labor, or presume to favor them in their idleness, so that thereby they may be compelled to labor for their necessary living.[9]*

The effects of the plague were felt everywhere. In government, experienced officials who died from the plague were replaced with men who were often incompetent and sometimes unscrupulous. Economic activity declined everywhere. Goods became scarce,

---

[9]"The Ordinance of Laborers of Edward III," in David Herlihy, ed., *Medieval Culture and Society* (New York: Walker, 1968), p. 361.

As a result of the bubonic plague, the rise of mercantilism, and other factors, the underlying assumptions of medieval society came to be questioned. In the Dance of Death, one scene of which is illustrated here, Death mocks an emperor, an archbishop, a rich merchant, and other symbols of power and vanity, but shows compassion for the poor laborer in the field.

tles into luxurious palaces and bought splendid clothes and jewelry in which to attend the king at court.

Life changed for the peasants, too, as serfdom declined in western Europe. Many serfs sold the surplus food they produced and used the money to buy their freedom. Some lords began to rent out their land to serfs for money instead of payment through labor so that in time these serfs became tenant farmers—or even earned enough to buy their own farms.

By the mid-15th century, the economy of Europe regained the momentum that it had lost in the 14th century. In the wake of the plague, populations increased again. Commerce revived, and the growing populations of cities provided markets for an increasing volume of agricultural produce and manufactured goods. When the demand for manufactured goods exceeded the supply that the guilds could produce, enterprising businessmen began to finance independent manufacturing facilities. They developed two ways of creating more, high-quality products. A few set up primitive factories, or large buildings in which hired workers with various skills produced goods in one place. Others sent materials out to workers who produced goods in their own homes. This "putting out" system, or cottage industry, gradually began to replace the craft guilds in the 15th and 16th centuries.

## SUMMARY

*Between 1050 and 1300, Europe made enormous economic progress based on political stability and technological advances. An agricultural revolution transformed the way crops were grown and greatly increased the amount and quality of food that was grown. As a result, the population of Europe tripled between the years 1000 and 1300. Important technological advances were also made during these centuries.*

*Commerce, both within Europe and between Europe and the East, also revived. Skilled artisans organized themselves into guilds that controlled the quality and price of the goods of their members. The guilds also acted as social welfare organizations for their members.*

*For the first time since the fall of Rome, Europe returned to a money economy. Gold and silver coins that were minted by cities and states became the medium of exchange, replacing the barter economy of the early Middle Ages. The money economy gave rise to money lending and banks.*

*In the mid-14th century, the Black Death and the Hundred Years' War caused widespread misery and social upheavals. But the resulting economic decline was only temporary, and Europe recovered its prosperity and self-confidence during the 15th century.*

## QUESTIONS

1 Explain how the agricultural revolution and other technological developments led to the expansion of the European economy in the late Middle Ages.
2 Describe how a person became a master craftsman. How did the merchant and craft guilds control the economy of medieval towns? Compare medieval guilds to today's labor unions.
3 How did the Hanseatic League become so powerful?
4 Why was banking necessary for increased commerce? How were banking methods of the late Middle Ages similar to or different from those of today?
5 What were the causes of the economic decline in the 14th century?
6 Why did feudalism decline in western Europe during the late Middle Ages?

## BIBLIOGRAPHY

#### Which books might discuss agriculture in the late Middle Ages?

GIES, JOSEPH and FRANCES C. *Life in a Medieval City.* New York: Crowell, 1969. *A very human account of life in Troyes, France, from Roman times to 1250, when it became the capital of Champagne and the site of annual fairs.*

GOTTFRIED, ROBERT S. *The Black Death: Natural and Human Disaster in Medieval Europe.* New York: Free Press, 1983. *A detailed study of the immediate and long-term impact of the Black Death on Europe. Uses Church and tax records as well as the writings of medieval poets, historians, and physicians to describe the epidemic.*

WHITE, JR., LYNN. *Medieval Technology and Social Change.* London: Oxford University Press, 1962. *A brief look at the impact of new technologies on land use, food production, and other aspects of medieval life.*

# 13

● *In order to represent in some degree the adored image of Our Lord, it is not enough that a master should be great and able. I maintain that he must also be a man of good conduct and morals, if possible a saint, in order that the holy ghost may rain down inspiration on his understanding.*

MICHELANGELO

# The Renaissance

The word "renaissance" ("rinascenza" in Italian) is French for rebirth. It was first used by 16th-century Italians, who believed that the civilizations of ancient Greece and Rome had been reborn in Italy after the long, dark night of the Middle Ages. In the 19th century, this view was strongly supported by the famous Swiss historian Jacob Burckhardt. In a famous study, *Civilization of the Renaissance in Italy*, published in 1867, Burckhardt argued that the Renaissance marked the birth of the modern world. According to Burckhardt, the revival of ancient learning allowed Renaissance Italians to replace the medieval outlook, which had been based on religion, with a rational, realistic view of the world.

Burckhardt overstated his case. Many of the changes that he believed had started in the Renaissance had in fact begun in the late Middle Ages. Today, most historians consider the Renaissance to be an era of transition between medieval and modern times. Thus, religion remained extremely important in the Renaissance just as it had been in the Middle Ages, but the difference was that secular values also became important. Whereas in the Middle Ages salvation in the next world was stressed, in the Renaissance the emphasis was on "humanism," or the need for each person to realize his or her potential as an individual in this world. The combination of religious and secular values is evident in the words and works of Renaissance artists such as Michelangelo, who is quoted above.

Changes also took place in the political and economic structure of Europe during the Renaissance. Medieval Europe had been a feudal society with weak central governments and an economy based on agriculture. Renaissance Europe was marked by political centralization and an increasingly urban economy based on large-scale commerce and capitalism. Centralization took different forms: in Italy, powerful city-states presided over political and economic affairs; in France and England, national monarchies triumphed over the decentralizing forces of feudalism.

In this chapter, we will concentrate on the Renaissance in Italy between the 14th and 16th centuries. The Renaissance began in northern Italy, which saw its most distinctive and striking achievements, but it soon spread north of the Alps to France, England, and Germany and other parts of Europe.

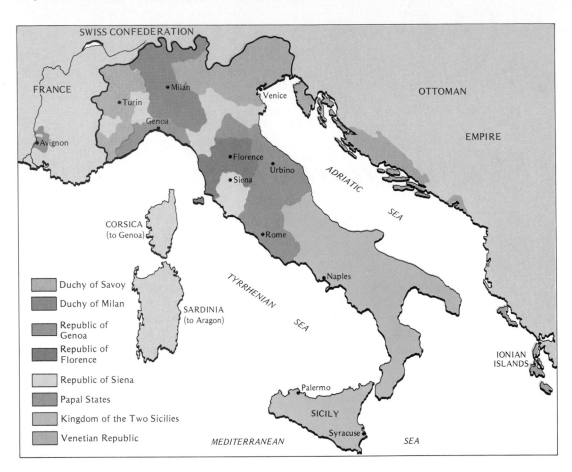

SWISS CONFEDERATION

FRANCE

• Milan

• Turin

Genoa

• Avignon

Venice

OTTOMAN

EMPIRE

• Florence

Urbino

ADRIATIC

• Siena

SEA

CORSICA
(to Genoa)

TYRRHENIAN

• Rome

SARDINIA
(to Aragon)

SEA

Naples •

IONIAN
ISLANDS

Palermo •

SICILY

Syracuse •

MEDITERRANEAN

SEA

- Duchy of Savoy
- Duchy of Milan
- Republic of Genoa
- Republic of Florence
- Republic of Siena
- Papal States
- Kingdom of the Two Sicilies
- Venetian Republic

**ITALY IN 1350** Geography gave Italy a certain advantage over northern Europe because it jutted into the Mediterranean, a natural artery along which both trade goods and ideas flowed between Europe and the East. Throughout the Middle Ages, the cities of northern Italy prospered from trade, bringing luxury goods from the Byzantine Empire and the Moslem world to the rest of Europe. In the 14th century, the greatest of these cities—Venice, Florence, and Milan—became powerful states ruling large areas of the countryside around them.

During the Middle Ages, feudalism did not achieve the importance in northern Italy that it attained elsewhere in Europe. This was due in part to the survival of trade and a money economy there. And Italy did not develop a centralized monarchy along the lines of those in France and England. By the mid-14th century, the attempts of the Holy Roman emperors to impose their rule on Italy had failed, and Italy was divided into a number of states. Later, another obstacle to unity was the competition between the city-states in the north and the papacy, which ruled a large territory in the center of Italy known as the Papal States. Yet these rival centers of power and wealth became the cradle of the Renaissance.

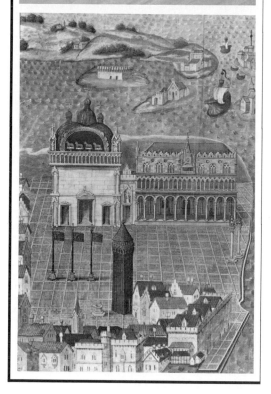

The magnificent cathedrals and private palaces of Venice reflected the city's prosperity and international importance. Shown is the Plaza of Saint Mark.

## VENICE

The city of Venice was founded by people fleeing from Attila's invasions during the 5th century. It was located on a group of islands at the northern end of the Adriatic Sea, close to the foothills of the Alps. From the start, its economy was tied to the sea, and it traded with the Byzantine Empire and the Moslem world. During the Crusades, its power and influence grew, especially because it provided transportation to people bound for the Holy Land. By the late 13th century, it was the most prosperous city in Europe. During the 14th century, Venetian ships carried goods to ports all over Europe from England and Flanders to the Black Sea. At the peak of its power, it had 36,000 sailors operating 3300 ships, giving it domination over the commerce of the Mediterranean.

The government of Venice reflected its commercial interests. In 1297, the leading merchants of the city took charge of its affairs. They prepared the *Golden Book*, listing the names of the most influential families of the city. Thereafter, only people listed in this book were eligible to serve on the Great Council, the body that appointed all public officials and enacted all laws. Each year, the Great Council elected from its members the Council of Ten to serve as administrators of the city. The Great Council also selected one of its members to be doge (duke) of Venice, the ceremonial head of the city. The doge served for life but had little power.

The city itself owned all the merchant ships and leased them to individual merchants for particular voyages. It also collected duties, or taxes, on all merchandise brought into the harbor. Venice built warships to protect the valuable cargoes of its merchant ships from pirate raids. The city also controlled the passes through the Alps and collected tolls from merchants of northern Europe who came to Venice to trade. With the vast wealth from trade, the leading families of Venice vied with one another to build the finest palaces or support the work of the greatest artists.

## FLORENCE

Florence, the "city of flowers," was located in the hill country of north-central Italy. It became an independent city in 1250. During the Middle Ages, Florence had a much more turbulent history than Venice, for it was the center of the struggle between popes and emperors. In Florence, a deep division arose between the Guelfs (those who favored the pope) and the Ghibellines (those who favored the emperor). Other struggles disrupted the city as workers fought the wealthy, and nobles fought the bourgeoisie. Street fighting was so common that the expression "going to the public square" came to mean "going to a riot." Despite the turmoil, the city

*Rivalries between noble families as well as conflicts between the Guelfs and the Ghibellines led to constant street violence in Florence and other Renaissance city-states. Assassinations such as the one depicted here were a common occurrence, and most people surrounded their houses with defensive walls.*

The people of Renaissance Florence were divided into four social levels. The nobles owned much of the land, lived in splendid castles on large estates outside the city walls, behaved according to the rules of chivalry, and disdained the newly rich merchants. The wealthy merchants, who formed the class called the "fat people," sought to protect their wealth by controlling the government and tried to enhance their social status by marrying into the nobility. To curry public favor and gain recognition, they became great patrons of the arts. The middle class was made up of shopkeepers and professionals, who were called the "little people."

At the lowest level were almost 30,000 workers, most of whom lived under the domination of the wool merchants. Working long hours for low wages, they were dependent on their employers for most aspects of life. Workers who violated rules could have their wages withheld or be discharged from their

prospered because it had set up a profitable wool industry. Sheep were raised in the rocky hill country of central Italy, and Florence was a center of wool processing.

During most of the Renaissance, the political power of Florence was concentrated in the hands of a few wealthy merchants, who dominated the wool industry. Like the rich families of Venice, these merchants competed with one another in building the grandest palaces for themselves in the city and villas in the country. They contributed in many ways to the beautification of the entire city. They believed that people who prospered should show their appreciation for their success by financing the construction of churches in which God could be glorified. To carry out these ambitions, they hired the most talented artists and artisans and encouraged them to produce their best work.

*Although the government of Florence was nominally a democracy, Cosimo de Medici was recognized as its real governor. His liberal endowment of public monuments won him the title "father of his city."*

*Lorenzo "the Magnificent" was a central figure of the Florentine Renaissance. Due to his generous patronage, many of the most talented artists in Italy made their homes in Florence.*

works of Plato and appointed Marsilio Ficino (1433-1499), a priest, as its first director. The scholars who were invited to join this elite group lived in gracious villas near the city, and the only requirement placed on them, besides pursuing their studies, was to dine with Cosimo once a week.

When Cosimo died in 1464, his son, Piero (1464-1469), and grandson, Lorenzo (1469-1492), continued his policies. The Medici maintained the stability of the city by exiling people who disagreed with them and encouraging other cities in Italy to join with Florence in shifting alliances to maintain the balance of power.

Under the leadership of Lorenzo, the economy of the city expanded greatly, and the workers, although still poorly paid, were protected from fluctuations in the economy. During this period, Florence became the most important city-state in Italy and the most beautiful in Europe. Because of his extensive

*Savonarola, a fanatical priest, was opposed to everything the Medici stood for. His sermons won him enough popular support to seize control of the government of Florence.*

jobs. As difficult as their lives were, however, these urban workers were better off than the rural peasants.

*The Medici.* In the 15th century when neighboring city-states posed growing threats to Florence, the influential people of the city came to the realization that they needed a strong leader. They chose Cosimo de Medici, a wealthy banker, to head the government and by 1434 he had consolidated power in his own hands. He maintained the appearance of the republican form of government that Florence had had but appointed his relatives and people he could control to important positions.

Cosimo commissioned works of art to beautify the city and encouraged architects to construct new churches. In 1438, he established an academy for the study of the

*Within a few years, the Florentines tired of Savonarola's apocalyptic teachings, and he and his supporters were executed in a public square.*

patronage of the arts, Lorenzo became known as "the Magnificent."

**Savonarola.** In 1494, two years after Lorenzo's death, a popular uprising forced the Medici to flee Florence. The uprising was inspired by a fiery Dominican priest, Girolamo Savonarola (1452-1495). Since 1491, when he had been elected prior of the Convent of San Marco in Florence, Savonarola's passionate sermons, condemning the worldliness of the papacy and the paganism of the Renaissance, had attracted enthusiastic crowds. He called for a return to the simple faith of the early Christians and warned of the spiritual corruption caused by wealth and power.

● ● ● *These wicked princes are sent as punishment for the sins of their subjects; they are truly a great snare for souls; their palaces and halls are the refuge of all the beasts and monsters of the earth, and are a shelter . . . for every kind of wickedness. Such men resort to their courts because there they find the means and the excitements to give vent to all their evil passions. There we find the wicked counsellors who devise new burdens and new imposts for sucking the blood of the people. There we find the flat-*

*tering philosophers and poets, who, by a thousand stories and lies, trace the genealogy of those wicked princes from the Gods; and, what is still worse, there we find priests who adopt the same language. That, my brethren, is the city of Babylon, the city of the foolish and the impious, the city which the Lord will destroy.*[1]

When Savonarola assumed the leadership of Florence after the Medici had been expelled, he drafted a constitution, based on that of Venice, reorganized the collection of taxes, and reformed the system of justice. He was determined to convert the pleasure-loving city of Florence into an example of medieval piety for all Christendom. He exiled many scholars and patrons of the arts. He encouraged people to gather up what he considered immoral books, frivolous objects, and pagan artwork and burn these symbols of corruption in huge bonfires. In this manner, many valuable works of art were destroyed.

In 1495, Pope Alexander VI ordered Savonarola to stop preaching and threatened to put Florence under the interdict. In reply, Savonarola issued a call for a general council to depose the pope. By this time, however, the Florentines had turned against the fiery reformer. In the political intrigues that followed, Savonarola was proclaimed a heretic, tortured, and burned at the stake.

After the death of Savonarola, the Medici returned to Florence and resumed their leadership of the city, but Florence never again regained its position of preeminence in Italy. In 1494, you will recall, Charles VIII of France invaded Italy, and during the next 50 years, the monarchs of France and Spain would struggle for control of Italy. Despite this turmoil and political disorder, however, the Renaissance spirit continued to flourish in Florence.

[1]Quoted in Pasquale Villari, *The History of Girolamo Savonarola and His Times*, trans. Leonard Horner (London: Longman, Green, 1863), p. 171.

## MILAN

Milan, near the center of the broad, fertile plain of Lombardy, came to dominate much of the Po River valley. Although it was situated on a major trade route connecting Genoa to northern Europe, Milan developed greater military than economic importance. Because of its strategic location and the need for a strong military leader, Milan became a monarchy under a succession of dukes, rather than a republic like Venice or Florence.

The Visconti family ruled Milan as dukes almost continuously from 1317 to 1447. At the height of their power, they controlled much of northern Italy. After the last Visconti died in 1447, the Milanese tried to replace the monarchy with a republic, but this form of government failed to provide the military discipline needed to protect the city's vulnerable position. In 1450, Francesco Sforza, a mercenary soldier who had been hired by the Visconti to defend Milan, seized control of the government. He and his successors ruled Milan until France and Spain gained control of northern Italy in the late 15th century.

*Francesco Sforza, a professional solider, seized control of Milan in 1450. Leonardo da Vinci sketched this plan for an equestrian statue in his honor.*

*The fortified palace of the Sforza family in Milan. The Sforzas were renowned for their cruelty and ruthlessness, and their wealth rivaled that of the pope. Like the Medici, they displayed their wealth in lavish public pageants and commissioned many great works of art.*

**HUMANISM** During the Renaissance, the attitudes of the people in western Europe changed, especially among the better educated middle class. People wanted to understand the nature of how things worked. They became interested in individual achievement and emphasized life in this world rather than looking to that of the next world. The interest in learning and the importance of the individual were reflected in education as well as in the arts. Renaissance scholars rejected much of medieval civilization, which they considered backward and unenlightened. Instead, they looked further back in history to the ancient Greeks and Romans. In the works of the ancients, they found a spirit similar to theirs that valued the individual in the world.

In the 15th century, many Greek scholars left Constantinople, which was coming under increasing pressure from the Ottoman Turks, and took refuge in the Italian city-states. When Constantinople fell in 1453, the exodus turned into a flight, and the newcomers brought to the West not only the treasures of the Byzantine Empire but also their knowledge of ancient Greek civilization. The arrival of so many Greeks in the West caused some people to remark that "Athens has migrated to Florence." In Florence and elsewhere, the Greeks contributed to the growing interest in the learning of the ancient world.

Renaissance scholars stressed the *studia humanitatis*, or the study of the humanities, that included such subjects as grammar, rhetoric, poetry, and history. People who studied these subjects became known as **humanists**. Renaissance humanists believed strongly in the potential for achievement of human beings whether in the arts, literature, politics, or simply in one's personal life. The word "humanism," meaning a stress on human dignity as the most valuable of God's creatures, sums up the Renaissance intellectual ideal.

## PETRARCH

One of the first writers to express the humanist spirit of the Renaissance was Francesco Petrarch (1304-1374), often called the "founder of humanism." Petrarch believed that the only true models of eloquence and ethical wisdom were to be found in the works of the ancient Roman authors, especially Virgil and Cicero. He traveled throughout France, Germany, and Italy, searching the libraries of monasteries and cathedrals for ancient manuscripts to copy for his own study. It is said that by the time of his death, Petrarch had one of the finest libraries in Europe.

*Petrarch's major writings expressed his deep religious conviction and admiration of Latin literature. He was best known, however, for his love sonnets to Laura, which were written in Italian.*

Petrarch's enthusiasm and reverence for classical literature led him to imitate its style, content, and form. He wrote epic poems, biographies of historical figures, and letters in polished and eloquent Ciceronian Latin. One of his most popular letters, "The Ascent of Mount Vertoux," was written to explain his feelings as he climbed Mount Vertoux. The story it tells represents more than a desire to see the view from the top of a mountain. Rather, it is an allegory in which Petrarch compares the hardships involved in climbing a mountain to the struggles that are necessary to achieve Christian virtue:

● ● ● *The life that we call blessed is situated on a high place; and narrow, we are told, is the way that leads to it; and many hills stand in the way, and we must advance from virtue to virtue up shining steps. The summit is the ultimate goal, the terminus of the road on which we journey. Everyone wishes to arrive there, but, as Ovid says, "To wish is not enough; to gain your end you must ardently yearn." . . . What then holds you back? Surely nothing but the level road that seems at first sight easier, amid base earthly pleasures. But after much wandering you will either have to climb upward eventually, with labors long shirked, to the heights of the blessed life, or lie sluggishly in the valley of your sins. And if—I shudder at the thought! —the darkness and shade of death find you there, you will spend an eternal night in perpetual torture.[2]*

Like many Renaissance intellectuals, Petrarch had two sides to his personality. While he felt comfortable in the seclusion of a monastery, he loved to travel; while he believed in the medieval ideal of self-denial, he enjoyed the pleasures of the world; while he loved learning, he feared that worldly knowledge might prevent him from achieving salvation.

Although Petrarch aspired to equal the

[2]*Letters from Petrarch*, trans. Morris Bishop (Bloomington: Indiana University Press, 1966), p. 47.

245

achievements of the great authors of ancient Rome, he won fame during his lifetime mainly for the love poems that he wrote in vernacular Italian to honor Laura, a beautiful woman whom he admired. These poems consist of 14 lines, rhymed according to a certain pattern, that became known as the *Petrarchan sonnet*. The pattern was later adopted by the great poet of the English Renaissance, William Shakespeare.

## THE EARLY RENAISSANCE

The humanists who followed Petrarch agreed with the need for eloquence and the study of classical literature, but they also stressed the need for an active life. To fulfill their natures, they believed, people had to achieve in as many fields as possible—in politics, in the quest for material possessions, in art and literature, and in the appreciation of beauty.

This concept eventually developed into the ideal of the "Renaissance man," a polished, well-rounded individual who was comfortable with every expression of human activity. The Renaissance ideal was best expressed by Baldassare Castiglione (1478-1529) in his work, *The Book of the Courtier*, published in 1518. The book depicts the ideal courtier as intelligent, charming, chivalrous, honorable, and skillful in sports; all these talents were expressed with seemingly little effort. The ideal courtier should also be knowledgeable about the classics, appreciative of the arts, and a connoisseur of beauty.

Castiglione's ideal was reflected in the goals of Renaissance education, at least for the upper classes. While the universities retained much of their medieval structure and curriculum, particularly in theology, medicine, and law, it became fashionable in the Renaissance for the sons of nobles to attend a university, as their medieval counterparts had not. At the university, young nobles were expected to learn the accomplishments that they needed to display in polite society. They learned to read and write Latin (and perhaps even Greek), speak well, and know something of the classical authors.

### PAINTING

The arts—particularly painting, sculpture, and architecture—changed significantly during the 15th century. In keeping with the spirit of humanism, artists created lifelike people dressed in contemporary clothes set against backgrounds of Italian scenery. They experimented with new techniques and materials, developed formulas to guide them in showing the human body in correct proportion, and set standards for judging the merits of works of art. They developed techniques of shading and perspective in paintings that gave scenes and objects a three-dimensional appearance, very different from the flat and stiff works of medieval artists. They observed flora and fauna and studied the anatomy of animals and humans to achieve more perfect representations of natural objects.

While medieval artists usually belonged to a guild and remained largely anonymous, Renaissance artists tended to work in schools, signed their works, and enjoyed the fame and glory of their success. When a master artist received a commission for a major work of art, he usually painted or carved the most prominent features of the work and assigned his students to complete the rest. In this way, aspiring artists learned the techniques from their masters and then went on to produce works on their own. The competition among wealthy individuals for the services of the best artists led some artists to feel that their talents entitled them to special privileges and consideration.

*Giotto.* The first important painter of the early Italian Renaissance was Giotto di Bondone (1266-1337), who broke away from the rigid forms of medieval Gothic and Byzantine art and inspired his successors to study nature so that they could depict the real world. As a youth, Giotto studied with a prominent Florentine painter named Cimabue. On one occasion, Cimabue tried to brush a fly from a

*Giotto's paintings had a great influence upon Renaissance artists. This is his Adoration of the Magi.*

canvas that Giotto was painting only to discover that his target was a picture of the insect. Giotto set the stage for later artists, who refined and developed many of his techniques. As one art historian has explained, "Giotto . . . discovered, to a certain extent, the necessity of foreshortening the figure, and began to give some intimation of the passions and affections, so that fear, hope, anger, and love were in some sort, expressed by his faces."[3]

In 1334, Giotto was appointed chief ar-

[3]Giorgio Vasari, *The Lives of the Most Eminent Painters, Sculptors, and Architects*, trans. Mrs. Jonathan Foster, in J. F. Scott, A. Hyma, and A. H. Noyes, eds. *Readings in Medieval History* (New York: Crofts, 1946), pp. 604-605.

chitect in Florence and was placed in charge of civic and military construction. During this period, he designed the bell tower (*campanile*) for the cathedral of that city. As his reputation grew, rulers of other Italian cities tried to lure him away to beautify their palaces and churches.

**Masaccio.** Giotto's foreshortening of figures was the first step in the development of the techniques of perspective that gave paintings a three-dimensional look. A later painter, Tommaso Guidi (1401-1428), developed rules of perspective. He was given the nickname Masaccio (Messy Tom) because of his disheveled appearance, and in time this nickname replaced his real name. He is credited with mastering the techniques of perspective and is believed to have been the first Renaissance artist to paint human figures in the nude and to model figures through the use of light and shadow (*chiaroscuro*) rather than by means of sharp lines.

Masaccio's best known work is *The Tribute Money*, an excellent example of the use of the principle of "continuous narration" because three separate episodes are united into one harmonious composition. Like many Renaissance paintings, it portrays scenes from the Bible. In another work, *Expulsion From Paradise*, he shows Adam and Eve as they leave the Garden of Eden, covering their faces to hide their shame and grief. Masaccio died in 1428 at the age of 27.

**Botticelli.** Among the outstanding artists of the late 15th century was Sandro Botticelli (1444-1510). Botticelli became a member of the circle of artists and scholars sponsored by the Medici in Florence, and he was greatly influenced by the mysticism of *Neoplatonism*, a philosophy that sought to blend the teachings of Christianity with the ideas of Plato. Botticelli's most famous work, the *Birth of Venus*, shows the goddess of love rising from the sea on a conch shell, and clearly expresses the spirit of Neoplatonism. As one art historian has commented, "a modern scholar sees, beyond the simple depiction of

a myth of the birth of Venus, an allegory of the innocence and truth of the human soul naked to the winds of passion and about to be clothed in the robe of reason."[4]

As a resident of Florence in the late 1490s, Botticelli was inspired by the teachings of Savonarola and burned many of his paintings with pagan themes. Thereafter, he devoted himself exclusively to the painting of religious themes.

## SCULPTURE AND ARCHITECTURE

Renaissance artists turned their talents to many fields. Often, they were painters, sculptors, and architects, and applied the rules of perspective that they developed in one endeavor to their work in another. In architecture, Renaissance artists attempted to achieve the symmetry and harmony of Greek and Roman buildings, the remains of which they studied in great detail. They were encouraged in their pursuit of perfection by wealthy patrons who commissioned them to design palaces that were more beautiful in grace and proportion than those of their neighbors.

As city officials, these same wealthy patrons planned the finest possible public buildings and churches. They invited architects and sculptors to compete for commissions by submitting innovative plans and designs. In the early 15th century, the most prominent architects and sculptors were Lorenzo Ghiberti, Filippo Brunelleschi, and Donato di Niccolo di Betto Bardi—better known as Donatello. For a time, one of these three won almost every major commission.

**Ghiberti.** In 1401, a competition was announced in Florence to choose the artist to design and sculpt a pair of bronze doors for the north side of the Baptistry, a church dedicated to Saint John the Baptist. Each contestant was required to submit a sample panel,

---

[4]Helen Gardner, *Art Through the Ages*, 7th ed., rev. Horst de la Croix and R. G. Tansey (New York: Harcourt Brace Jovanovich, 1980), p. 518.

*One of the greatest treasures of Florence is the pair of bronze doors sculpted by Ghiberti. This panel from one of the doors illustrates the Biblical story of the sacrifice of Isaac.*

the subject of which was the sacrifice of Isaac, to be set within a *quatrefoil* (a Gothic framework with four foils, or lobes). Lorenzo Ghiberti (1378-1455) and Filippo Brunelleschi (1377-1446), the two most respected artists in Florence, entered the contest. Ghiberti was declared the winner, but even with the help of his assistants, it took him 28 years to complete the panels.

In the panels, Ghiberti developed the techniques of three-dimensional sculpture, with the figures closest to the viewer in high relief and the figures in the background in low relief. Later, he designed other panels for the east doors. Many years later when Michelangelo saw these doors, he reportedly exclaimed, "These doors are worthy to decorate the gates of Paradise." The Florentine authorities were so impressed with Ghiberti's work that they made him a city magistrate.

**Brunelleschi.** After losing to Ghiberti, Brunelleschi traveled to Rome. There, he studied the ancient Roman statues scattered about the city and sketched the remains of Roman buildings. Brunelleschi took measurements of many ruins, and became convinced that the beauty of an impressive building is based on certain mathematical relationships among its various dimensions.

In 1417, he again competed for a commission with Ghiberti; this time, to design the dome for the still unfinished cathedral of Florence. Brunelleschi was awarded the commission for his design of a great octagonal dome, which was inspired by the domes seen in late Roman architecture. The dome, constructed of two separate shells that rein-

*Donatello's portrait of a famous condottiere (mercenary soldier) was the first equestrian statue to be created since classical times.*

*Brunelleschi's great dome for the cathedral of Florence was inspired by the architecture of the Romans and Byzantines, but its design was more daring than those of earlier domes.*

force each other, rises 133 feet above the supporting walls of the cathedral. It still dominates the skyline of Florence.

**Donatello.** Donatello (1386-1466), the greatest sculptor of the early Renaissance, was born in Florence and worked in the studio of Ghiberti. He accompanied Brunelleschi to Rome, and like him, was inspired by the classical sculpture and architecture he saw there. Donatello created several masterpieces for his patron, Cosimo de Medici, the most important of which is the statue of *David*. This work was unique at the time because Donatello portrayed the ancient Hebrew hero, King David, in the classical tradition as a Greek god. More importantly, Donatello's *David* was the first free-standing nude figure sculpted since the Roman era.

In 1443, Donatello cast the first bronze statue of the Renaissance. It shows a soldier on horseback, and the figure is so realistic that it appears ready to move.

In his portraits and caricatures, as in his other activities, Leonardo Da Vinci demonstrated his versatility. Shown are a self-portrait, the head of a young woman, and caricatures or "grotesques" of elderly subjects.

## THE HIGH RENAISSANCE

Artists of the early Renaissance (1350-1450) broke away from the rigidity of Byzantine and Gothic conventions by using the laws of perspective and representing humans and animals in a naturalistic manner. Artists of the High Renaissance (1450-1550) went beyond these advances to create works of beauty that would evoke emotional responses in their viewers. Florence produced more great artists in the early period than in the later period, but the works of Florentine artists of the High Renaissance are more widely known. The best known of these artists are Leonardo da Vinci, Michelangelo, Raphael, and Titian. Each was considered to have been divinely inspired, and wealthy patrons were anxious to secure their services.

### LEONARDO DA VINCI

Leonardo da Vinci (1452-1519) epitomized the Renaissance ideal: he was a talented painter and sculptor; he was fascinated by technology, and his interests and curiosity were limitless. Born in a small town near Florence, Leonardo exhibited his artistic talent at a young age and was apprenticed to a leading Florentine painter and craftsman.

In 1482, Lorenzo de Medici learned that Leonardo had created a silver lyre in the shape of a horse's head. Lorenzo purchased this masterpiece to present to Lodovico Sforza, the duke of Milan, in the hopes of winning his favor. Leonardo begged permission to deliver the lyre in person, and when Lodovico saw it, he asked Leonardo to stay in Milan. While there, Leonardo painted the *Last Supper* on the wall of a monastery.

When the French captured Milan in 1499, Leonardo returned to Florence. There, he took on the position of chief military engineer, designing fortifications and weapons for the city. In 1513, Leonardo went to Rome, hoping to secure a commission from Pope Leo X, a son of Lorenzo de Medici, but the pope preferred the work of Raphael, a younger artist. When he left Rome two years later, Leonardo was reported to have said, "The Medici made me and broke me." In 1516, he was appointed court painter and chief engineer to King Francis I of France, and he remained in that position until his death in 1519.

Leonardo felt impelled to explore the mysteries of the universe. He always carried notebooks, which he filled with sketches, notes, and excerpts from books. Perhaps to make his notes harder for others to read, he wrote from right to left, which meant that the notes could be read easily only if held up to a mirror. This unusual style of writing caused his enemies to accuse him of witchcraft. His notebooks that have recently been published include ideas for such varied devices as a scaling ladder, rotating bridge, machine to mint coins, breach-loading cannon, submarine, armored vehicle, and flying machine.

Leonardo was a keen observer of nature because he felt that he could draw more accurately if he understood how things worked. He analyzed the anatomy, behavior, and flight of birds and predicted that humans would someday fly. He studied the structures and sexual characteristics of plants, noted the arrangements of leaves on stems, and concluded that the rings in a cross-section of a tree indicate its age. He examined fossils and developed a theory of the origin of the earth; he watched the flow of streams around rocks and deduced the cause of whirlpools. He expanded his knowledge of human anatomy by dissecting cadavers, sketched the chambers of a human heart, and detected the problem known as double curvature of the spine. He was, in sum, the first medical illustrator.

While painting the *Last Supper* as a fresco in Milan, Leonardo experimented with an oil-tempera medium on the plaster wall; unfortunately, the mural began to disintegrate a few years after completion. (It is currently being restored.) In showing the moment when Jesus announced to his apostles, "One of you will betray me," Leonardo interpreted each apostle's reactions so vividly that the viewer

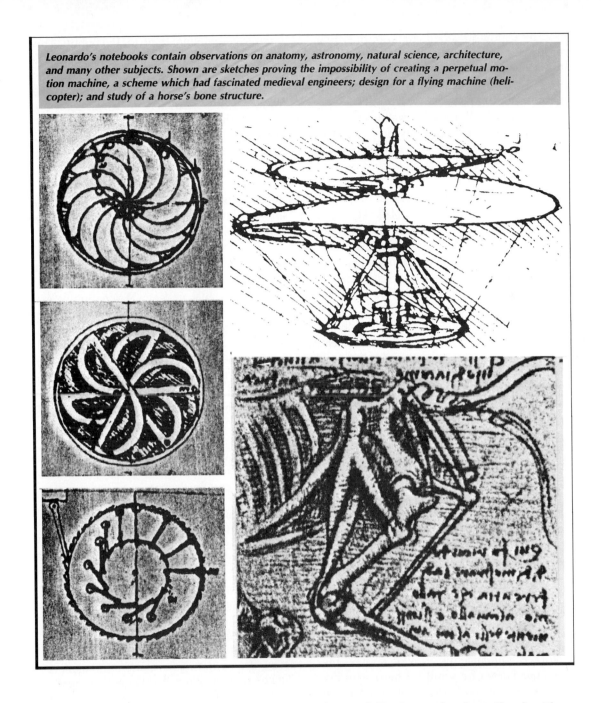

Leonardo's notebooks contain observations on anatomy, astronomy, natural science, architecture, and many other subjects. Shown are sketches proving the impossibility of creating a perpetual motion machine, a scheme which had fascinated medieval engineers; design for a flying machine (helicopter); and study of a horse's bone structure.

can speculate what each is thinking. When King Louis XII of France saw this painting in 1499, he wanted to have it moved to Paris.

In addition to the *Last Supper*, his best known painting is the *Mona Lisa*, a portrait of Lisa della Giaconda, the wife of a Florentine merchant. Her enigmatic smile has fascinated viewers from the time it was painted. The remote, dream-like quality of the portrait results from a technique devel-

253

oped by Leonardo called *sfumato*, in which very delicate gradations of light and shade are used in modeling the figure. In his later years, Leonardo painted less frequently and devoted his time almost exclusively to scientific studies. While his notebooks reveal that he planned many projects, he completed very few of them, perhaps because he did not have the necessary tools or resources.

## MICHELANGELO

Michelangelo Buonarroti (1475-1564)—sculptor, painter, architect, and poet—has come to represent the genius of the High Renaissance. At the age of 13, Michelangelo enrolled in the school for sculptors established by Lorenzo de Medici, and before long, his work attracted the personal attention of Lorenzo. For several years he lived in the Medici palace in Florence as a member of the family, and he was strongly influenced by the concepts of humanism and Neoplatonism that flourished under the Medici's patronage. While seemingly preoccupied with the classical Greek and Roman concepts of beauty, Michelangelo never wavered from his deep Christian faith or sense of divine mission as expressed in the quotation cited at the beginning of this chapter.

When the Medici were driven from Florence in 1494, Michelangelo fled to Bologna. Later, he traveled to Rome, where, at the age of 23, he carved the *Pietà* on commission from a French cardinal. The idealized beauty of the Madonna and the sensitivity of her expression brought him instant recognition as an important sculptor. When he returned to Florence in 1501, he was commissioned to carve a statue of the Hebrew hero-king David. Michelangelo's *David* shows the muscular body of a youthful hero who appears to be filled with a sense of purpose and power. To many, *David* came to symbolize the city of Florence itself, and it can still be admired there.

Michelangelo was summoned to Rome in 1505 by Pope Julius II and commissioned to build a monumental tomb for the pontiff. This assignment was never completed, because Michelangelo interrupted his work on the tomb to decorate the Sistine Chapel in the Vatican. When Michelangelo began this work in 1508, the chapel was a long, unadorned, rectangular room—44 feet wide and 132 feet long. Its vaulted ceiling reaches 68 feet above the floor. Michelangelo decorated the walls and ceiling with scenes from Genesis illustrating Biblical events from the Creation of the world through the Flood. The scenes were peopled with over 300 human figures.

The project was enormously difficult. Working alone, Michelangelo had to lie on his back atop high scaffolding while he painted the vast ceiling. When finally exposed to view, the huge frescoes met with both praise and criticism. Seeing the many figures that the artist had drawn, Cardinal Biagio do Cesena noted that such a crowd would be more appropriate in a wineshop than in the papal chapel. In response to this criticism, Michelangelo added a portrait of Biagio among the figures of the damned in the scene of the Last Judgment.

While painting the Sistine Chapel, Michelangelo composed these verses to express his agony and frustration:

*I've got myself a goiter from this strain,*
*As water gives the cats in Lombardy*
*Or maybe it is some other country;*
*My belly's pushed by force beneath my chin.*
*My beard toward Heaven, I feel the back of*
*    my brain*
*Upon my neck, I grow the breast of a Harpy;*
*My brush, above my face continually,*
*Makes it a splendid floor by dripping down. . . .*
*John, come to the rescue*
*Of my dead painting now, and of my honor;*
*I'm not in a good place, and I'm not a painter.*[5]

---

[5]Michelangelo, *Sonnet to John Pistolo on the Sistine Ceiling*, in *Complete Poems and Selected Letters of Michelangelo*, 3rd. ed., trans. with Foreword and notes by Creighton Gilbert (Princeton University Press, 1980), pp. 5-6.

*Michelangelo preferred to work as a sculptor or architect, but was persuaded to paint the ceiling of the Sistine Chapel. Shown is his rendering of the moment of man's creation.*

During the last years of his life, Michelangelo worked almost exclusively as an architect. He was chosen to complete the basilica of St. Peter's that had originally been designed by another artist. The immense dome designed by Michelangelo is 138 feet in diameter and rises 400 feet above the floor of the sanctuary. While Michelangelo was inspired by Byzantine architecture, his work would later inspire both Christopher Wren, architect of Saint Paul's Cathedral in London, and Charles Bulfinch, architect of the Capitol in Washington, D.C., in designing domes for these famous buildings.

### RAPHAEL

Raphael (1483-1520), the leading painter of the High Renaissance, was born Raffaello Santi in Urbino. In 1504, Raphael moved to Florence to study the principles of anatomy, drawing, and perspective under Leonardo. He was so talented that in 1508, at the age of 25, he was summoned to Rome by Pope Julius II to decorate the papal apartments in the Vatican. On the walls of the pope's private library, he painted four frescoes depicting what he considered to be the four most important fields of study: philosophy, theology, the arts, and law. The most widely

*The Venetian artist Titian became court painter to the Holy Roman emperor Charles V. This is Titian's portrait of his patron.*

ziana Vecellio in the Italian Alps, he later moved to Venice to study painting. Prior to 1518, Titian painted frescoes and murals, including the famous *Sacred and Profane Love*, an allegorical work showing the two aspects of Christian love, love of God and of neighbor. Between 1518 and 1532, he served as a court painter in the city-states of Ferrara, Mantua, and Urbino, before becoming official painter to the Holy Roman emperor, Charles V. During this period, he specialized in portraiture, and his clients included Francis I of France and Philip II of Spain as well as the emperor.

Titian ignored the traditional rules of painting by using bright colors, bold brush strokes, and the technique of *impasto*, by which repeated layers of opaque pigment are used to give colors greater subtlety and depth.

### CELLINI

Benvenuto Cellini (1500-1571) was an outstanding Florentine sculptor and goldsmith whose services were sought by princes and popes. His autobiography, the *Life of Benvenuto Cellini*, gives us a picture of the adventures, determination, and talents of this

*Cellini's gold-plated saltcellar symbolized the meeting of sea and land.*

known of these paintings, the *School of Athens*, is an imaginary assembly of famous philosophers, including Plato and Aristotle, discussing their ideas in a huge basilica. Not one to be modest, Raphael painted himself as an observer among these scholars.

Raphael held many other commissions from the pope. Although he died at the early age of 37, he was so renowned that he was buried in the Pantheon in Rome.

### TITIAN

The greatest Venetian artist of the High Renaissance was Titian (1485-1576). Born Ti-

gifted Renaissance figure. In 1540, Cellini was invited by King Francis I of France to set up his workshop in Paris. There, he served as consultant on royal fortifications and fashioned exquisite works for the king. Among them was a silver and gold saltcellar with Neptune, god of the sea, holding table salt, while the goddess of earth rests beside a small Greek temple holding pepper. This saltcellar is Cellini's only work in a precious metal to have survived. In 1545, he returned to Florence where he remained until his death in 1571.

**INVENTION OF PRINTING** During the Renaissance, a large number of scholars and writers produced a rich array of works on subjects ranging from history

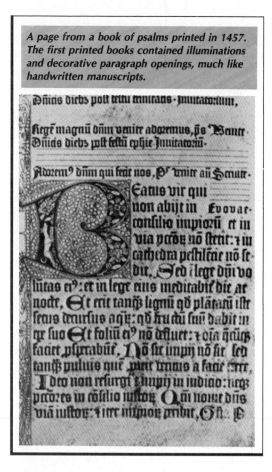

A page from a book of psalms printed in 1457. The first printed books contained illuminations and decorative paragraph openings, much like handwritten manuscripts.

The first printed book, a Bible, was produced in the shop of Johann Gutenberg in 1454.

and science to technology and religion. Their writings reached larger audiences than ever before, not only because more people were learning to read and write but also because books were becoming cheaper and easier to obtain. This latter development was due to the invention of printing in Europe in the mid-15th century.

The invention of printing was based on earlier techniques, including printing from wood blocks. The Chinese were the first people to invent movable type that allowed the printer to use and reuse pieces of metal engraved with letters and words. Whether Europeans knew of the Chinese printing processes that had been developed in the 11th century is subject to debate, although by the 15th century a number of Europeans had visited China and written about other Chinese inventions. From the Moslems, Europeans had learned to make paper, an important ingredient for producing printed books.

The first European to use movable type to produce a printed book was Johann Gutenberg of Mainz, Germany. In 1454, he published the famous *Gutenberg Bible*, and this event ushered in the age of printed books. Before long, printing presses had spread all over Europe and were pouring out a wealth of new works. The new technology brought the price of books tumbling so that many more authors could be published and read.

### LITERATURE

**Boccaccio.** In literature as in painting and sculpture, writers explored both secular and religious themes. Among the outstanding figures of the early Renaissance was Giovanni

*Giovanni Boccaccio is best known for his series of stories called the* Decameron *in which medieval fables, morality tales, and romances were updated for a Renaissance audience.*

Boccaccio (1313-1375), a Florentine writer whose most famous work is the *Decameron* (meaning "ten days"). The *Decameron* is a collection of 100 stories written in the Italian vernacular and set in Florence during the Black Death that struck the city in 1348. In the story, three men and seven women seek refuge from the plague in a country villa and pass the time telling stories. The tales are based on humor, folklore, fables, moral examples, and romance. They reflect the traditions and values of various social classes, including the urban middle class, the clergy, and the peasantry.

**Pico.** Other Renaissance writers dealt with themes reminiscent of the scholastics. Their conclusions, however, differed from those of medieval writers, who had emphasized faith above all things. Among the Renaissance writers who studied the works of Aristotle and the ancient Greeks was Giovanni Pico della Mirandola (1431-1494). In 1484, Pico became a member of the Platonic academy in Florence, the literary and intellectual circle sponsored by the Medici. While living in Florence, Pico learned Hebrew and Aramaic. He studied the Talmud under Jewish scholars and struggled to reconcile the teachings of Judaism, Christianity, and Islam. In 1486, he published a collection of 900 philosophical treatises dealing with all aspects of human knowledge. Like the scholastics, he tried to reconcile his ideas with doctrines of the Roman Catholic Church, but his conclusions often differed from theirs.

In his best known work, the "Oration on the Dignity of Man," Pico explained that God created people "to know the laws of the universe, to love its beauty, to admire its greatness. He bound him to no fixed place, to no prescribed form of work, and by no iron necessity, but gave him freedom to will and to move."[6] Pico's oration pointed to a major dif-

[6]Quoted in Jacob Burckhardt, *Civilization and the Renaissance* (New York: Harper & Row, 1958), p. 352.

ference between the teachings of the Church and the ideals of the Italian humanists. Contrary to Church dogma, Pico believed that people possessed free will, enabling them to make decisions, and that the study of philosophy prepared people to recognize the truth. He further believed that any individual could commune directly with God, an idea that would become central to Protestant thought during the Reformation. Not surprisingly, the Church condemned Pico's writings and declared him a heretic. Forced to flee, Pico was saved by Lorenzo de Medici, who intervened on Pico's behalf so that he could return to Florence.

**Machiavelli.** One of the most influential writers of the Renaissance was Niccolo Machiavelli (1469-1527), who was born in Florence to an impoverished noble family. When the French invaded northern Italy in 1494, the ruling council of Florence appointed Machiavelli to be an ambassador. On a mission to France, Machiavelli realized that the relatively small Italian city-states would be no match for French military strength. He decided that Italy could be saved only if it were united under a respected and powerful ruler.

After 10 years' involvement in the endless wars and intrigues of the various city-states of Italy, Machiavelli retired to a small farm to write *The Prince* (1513), which may have been intended as a guidebook for the leader whom he hoped would unite Italy. Machiavelli was convinced that Christianity was an inadequate basis for government and that a ruthless patriotic citizen-soldier was the best kind of ruler to defend the state.

A political realist, Machiavelli believed that a ruler's job was to succeed by any means necessary. In *The Prince*, he advised rulers to be benevolent only if it suited their purposes. Otherwise, he warned, it was better to be feared than loved. This handbook for rulers had a great impact on European political life as rulers attempted to follow Machiavelli's recommendations and came to accept views such as this:

*Macchievelli's work* The Prince *set forth a program of action for creating a unified Italian state, based upon the methods that the Medicis, Sforzas and others had used to achieve power.*

● ● ● You must know, then, that there are two methods of fighting, the one by law, the other by force; the first method is of men, the second of beasts; but as the first method is often insufficient, one must have recourse to the second. It is therefore necessary for a prince to know well how to use both the beast and the man. . . .

A prince being thus obliged to know well how to act as a beast must imitate the fox and the lion, for the lion cannot protect himself from traps, and the fox cannot defend himself from wolves. One must therefore be a fox to recognize traps, and a lion to frighten wolves. Those that wish to be only lions do not understand this. Therefore, a prudent ruler ought not to keep faith when by so doing it would be against his interests, and when the reasons which made him bind himself no longer exist.[7]

[7]Niccolo Machiavelli, *The Prince*, with analysis by J. P. Barricelli (Woodbury, N.Y.: Barron's, 1975), pp. 105-106.

During the Renaissance, scholars developed new methods of analyzing the past and examined historical documents in the light of their new learning. Two high-ranking clergymen, Lorenzo Valla (1407-1457), a secretary to the pope, and Nicholas of Cusa (1400-1464), a cardinal, introduced a research technique that became known as "textual criticism." In this type of study, a written document is analyzed to determine both internal and external consistency. Are the words, spellings, and references, for example, consistent with the time that the document was written?

The use of this technique led to astonishing results. For example, the Roman Catholic Church had long claimed that the emperor Constantine had bestowed control of Italy on Pope Sylvester I when he had moved the capital of the Byzantine Empire to Constantinople. The Church's claim was based on a document called "The Donation of Constantine." Valla and Nicholas of Cusa proved that the document was a forgery that had been written about 400 years after the death of Constantine. By examining the document, they found that it used words such as "fief" that were unknown in Constantine's time. This spirit of inquiry inspired later thinkers who were willing to put aside accepted notions and discover new ideas. The Church, however, frowned on Valla's work since it led people to question long-accepted truths.

## WOMEN IN THE RENAISSANCE

For most women, life in the Renaissance remained much as it had been during the Middle Ages. They were expected to be wives and mothers; subject to their parents before marriage, to their husbands after it. Peasant women worked in the fields alongside their husbands. In the cities, women ran households and helped with their husbands' work. Women who did not marry either lived in the households of their male relatives or entered convents.

*Lucretia Borgia (top), once portrayed as a monster of cruelty and deceit, is now considered to have been merely the pawn of her ambitious father, Pope Alexander VI (below).*

A few wealthy women from the aristocracy, however, were able to break out of this mold. Two of the most famous and accomplished of these women were Lucrezia Borgia (1480-1519) and her sister-in-law Isabella d'Este (1474-1539).

Lucrezia Borgia was the daughter of Rodrigo Borgia, who became Pope Alexander VI (1492-1503). As pope, he decided to further his political ambitions by arranging an advantageous marriage for Lucrezia. Accordingly, she was married at the age of 13 to a member of the Sforza family, which ruled Milan. Four years later, when Alexander no longer needed support from that city, he annulled the marriage. He then arranged for Lucrezia to marry an illegitimate son of the king of Naples, by whom she bore a son. According to tradition, this husband was murdered by Lucrezia's brother Cesare. In 1502, when Lucrezia was 22, Alexander married her to the duke of Ferrara, Alfonso d'Este. The trousseau for this third marriage was so vast that 150 mules were required to carry it. Until her death in 1519, Lucrezia remained in Ferrara, a devoted wife and mother and a noted patron of the arts.

Isabella d'Este, Lucrezia's sister-in-law, was a brilliant woman who mastered Greek and Latin and memorized the writings of Virgil and Terence. She frequently gave performances in which she displayed her talents in singing, dancing, and playing musical instruments. In 1490, she was married to the duke of Mantua, Francesco Gonzaga, who approached Castiglione's version of the ideal courtier. Under the guidance of Isabella d'Este, the court of Mantua became renowned as a center of wit, elegance, and artistic genius. She promoted the textile and clothing industries so that the manufacture of velvet, satin, and damask became the chief source of income for the inhabitants of the city.

When her husband was captured in battle, Isabella ruled Mantua and the small duchy of Romagna. Her successful reign in Romagna gained her the respect of the people.

Isabella D'Este was noted for her patronage of the arts and capable management of Mantua. This portrait was sketched by Leonardo da Vinci.

As a generous patron of the arts, she assembled an outstanding collection of paintings, sculpture, manuscripts, and musical instruments.

## INFLUENCE OF THE RENAISSANCE

By 1500, the independence of the Italian city-states was diminishing as they became prizes sought by ambitious rulers of the emerging nation-states of northern Europe. After 1500, the culture of the Renaissance began to move northward to France, Germany, England, and other parts of Europe as scholars, students, and soldiers from these lands carried the achievements of the Italians to their homes. As a result, the Renaissance became less Italian and more European in scope.

## SUMMARY

*The Renaissance continued the political, economic, and social changes that were already underway in the late Middle Ages. It began in Italy, which had a long tradition of commercial and cultural ties to the East and a vigorous urban society. By the mid-13th century, Venice, Florence, and Milan had become rich and powerful city-states. Their wealthy upper classes vied with one another in support of the arts and humanities.*

*Early Renaissance artists developed new techniques that paved the way for the masterpieces of the High Renaissance. The invention of printing and the increase in education spread the ideas of Renaissance humanists, who believed in human dignity and individual potential for achievement. Renaissance humanism fostered a creative outburst in literature and the arts that was best expressed in the works of writers such as Petrarch and Boccaccio and the artists Leonardo, Michelangelo, and Raphael.*

## QUESTIONS

1 What are some possible explanations why the city of Florence presided over so many achievements of the Renaissance?

2 Compare the attitudes of Renaissance humanists to those of medieval scholastics. Why do you think these attitudes developed first in the city-states of northern Italy?

3 What contributions did painters and sculptors of the early Renaissance make? Who were the outstanding artists of the High Renaissance? Describe one achievement of each.

4 Why was Leonardo da Vinci regarded as the ideal Renaissance person? Would it be possible for someone today to match his achievements? Explain your answer.

5 Explain how the art and literature of the Renaissance reflected society in the 14th and 15th centuries. What do modern art and literature tell us about our own society?

6 What impact did the invention of printing have on Europe?

## BIBLIOGRAPHY

### Which books might tell you about life in Renaissance Florence?

COUGHLIN, ROBERT. *The World of Machiavelli, 1475-1564.* New York: Time-Life, 1966. *An examination of the works of Machiavelli and of the outstanding artists of the Renaissance from Giotto to Raphael.*

KETCHUM, RICHARD M., ed. *The Horizon Book of the Renaissance.* New York: American Heritage Publishing, 1961. *A finely illustrated review of the ideas and institutions of the Renaissance that shows how the Renaissance developed gradually and was nurtured by the circumstances of the 14th century.*

LUCAS-DUBRETON, J. *Daily Life in Florence in the Time of the Medici.* New York: Macmillan, 1961. *A reconstruction of the habits and customs of the Florentine people during the years of Medici rule. Based on contemporary diaries and historical accounts, the book describes fashions, food, and the ceremonies of daily life.*

STRAGE, MARK. *Women of Power.* New York: Harcourt Brace Jovanovich, 1976. *A careful study of the lives of three powerful Renaissance women: Catherine de Medici, who dominated France for three decades; Diane de Poitiers, who exerted great political influence on Henry II; and Marguerite, queen of Navarre, who presided over a brilliant court.*

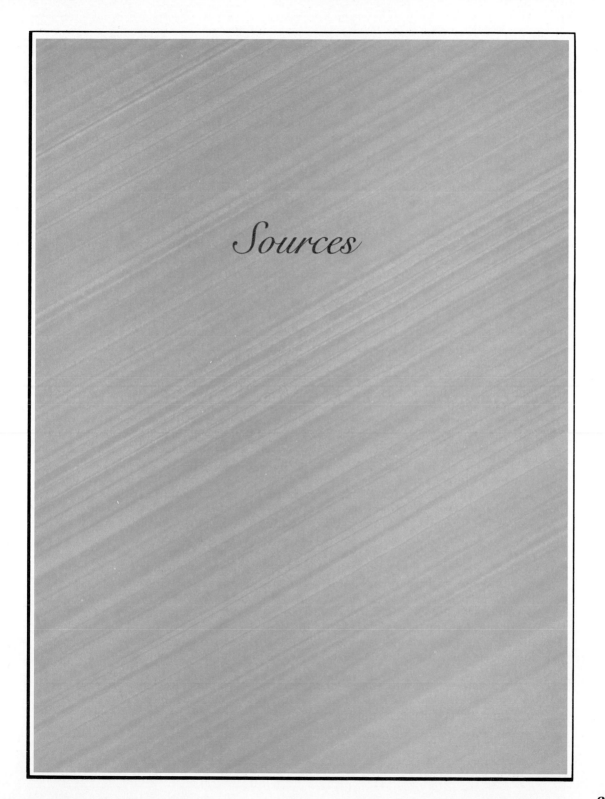

*Sources*

## THE EMPEROR CHARLES

*Einhard was one of the renowned scholars whom Charlemagne invited to his court. He became a close friend of the emperor and served as his ambassador to Rome. Einhard was with Charlemagne when the pope crowned him emperor on Christmas Day of the year 800. Later, Einhard wrote* The Life of the Emperor Charles *to honor the man who had been his patron.*

He took constant exercise in riding and hunting, which was natural for a Frank, since scarcely any nation can be found to equal them in these pursuits. He also delighted in the natural warm baths, frequently exercising himself by swimming, in which he was very skillful, no one being able to outstrip him. It was on account of the warm baths at Aix-La-Chapelle [Aachen] that he built his palace there and lived there constantly during the last years of his life. . . .

He wore the dress of his native country, that is, the Frankish; next his body a linen shirt and linen drawers; then a tunic with a silken border, and stockings. He bound his legs with garters and wore shoes on his feet. In the winter he protected his shoulders and chest with a vest made of the skins of otters and sable. He wore a blue cloak, and was always girt with his sword, the hilt and belt being of gold and silver. Sometimes he wore a jewelled sword, but he did so only on great festivals or when receiving foreign ambassadors. . . .

In his eating and drinking he was temperate; more particularly so in his drinking, for he had the greatest abhorrence of drunkenness in anybody, but more especially in himself and his companions. He was unable to abstain from food for any length of time, and often complained that fasting was injurious to him. On the other hand, he very rarely feasted, only on great festive occasions, when there were very large gatherings. The daily service of his table consisted of only four dishes in addition to the roast meat, which the hunters used to bring in on spits, and which he partook more freely than any other food.

While he was dining, he listened to music or reading. History and the deeds of men of old were most often read. He derived much pleasure from the works of St. Augustine, especially from his book called *The City of God*. He partook very sparingly of wine and other drinks, rarely taking at meals more than three draughts. In summer, after the midday repast, he would take some fruit and one draught, and then, throwing aside his clothes and shoes as at night, he would repose for two or three hours. He slept at night so lightly that he would break his rest four or five times, not merely by waking, but even getting up.

While he was dressing and binding on his sandals, he would receive his friends; and also, if the count of the palace announced that there was any case which could only be settled by his decision, the suitors were immediately ordered into his presence, and he heard the case and gave judgement as if sitting in court. And this was not the only business that he used to arrange at that time, for he also gave orders for whatever had to be done on that day by any officer or servant.

He was ready and fluent in speaking, and able to express himself with great clearness. He did not confine himself to his native tongue, but took pains to learn foreign languages, acquiring such knowledge of Latin that he could make an address in that language as well as his own. Greek he could better understand than speak. Indeed, he was so polished in speech that he might have passed for a learned man.

SOURCE: Einhard, *Life of the Emperor Charles*. In *Readings in European History*, Vol. 1, ed. J.H. Robinson (New York: Ginn, 1904), pp. 126-8.

**1. *What evidence does Einhard provide of Charlemagne's character and contribution to the Carolingian Renaissance?***
**2. *Despite Einhard's biases, why is his work valuable to historians?***

## BENEDICT'S RULE

*Benedict's Rule, written during the 6th century, became the standard code of conduct for most western European monastic orders. The Rule contains 73 chapters governing such aspects of daily life as the recitation of prayers, care of the sick, responsibilities of the abbot, and the amount and type of food to be distributed to each monk.*

### Chapter 34   WHETHER ALL SHOULD RECEIVE NECESSARIES IN LIKE MEASURE

Let us follow the scripture: *Distribution was made to every man according as he had need.* By this we do not mean that there should be respect of persons (God forbid), but consideration for infirmities. He that needeth less, let him thank God and not be discontented; he that needeth more, let him be humbled for his infirmity and not made proud by the mercy shown to him: so will all the members be at peace. Above all, let not the vice of murmuring show itself in any word or sign, for any reason whatever. But if a brother be found guilty of it, let him undergo strict punishment.

### Chapter 57   THE CRAFTSMEN OF THE MONASTERY

If there be craftsmen in the monastery, let them practice their crafts with all humility, provided the abbot give permission. But if one of them be puffed up because of his skill in his craft, supposing that he is conferring a benefit on the monastery, let him be removed from his work and not return to it, unless he have humbled himself and the abbot entrust it to him again. . . . And, as regards the price, let not the sin of avarice creep in; but let the goods always be sold a little cheaper than they are sold by people of the world, *that in all things God may be glorified.*

SOURCE: Benedict, *The Rule of Saint Benedict*, trans. Abbot Justin McCann (London: Broadwater Press Ltd., 1952), pp. 87, 129.

**1. *In what ways might the rules cited above help to promote the ideals of obedience and humility?***

## WALDO OF LYONS

*In 1176, Peter Waldo, a wealthy merchant of Lyons, renounced his possessions and established a religious order called the Poor Men of Lyons. The order that became known as the Waldensians believed that lay people could preach the gospel and condemned the worldliness of the Church. The following passage, written by an unidentified person in 1218, describes Peter Waldo's decision to change his life.*

And during the same year, that is the 1173rd since the Lord's Incarnation, there was at Lyons in France a certain citizen, Waldo by name, who had made himself much money by wicked usury. One Sunday, when he had joined a crowd which he saw gathered about a troubadour, he was smitten by his words and, taking him to his house, he took care to hear him at length. The passage he was reciting was how the holy Alexis died a blessed death in his father's house. When morning had come, the prudent citizen hurried to the schools of theology to seek counsel for his soul, and when he was taught many ways of going to God, he asked the master what way was more certain and more perfect than all others. The master answered him with this text: "If thou wilt be perfect, go and sell all that thou hast," etc.

Then Waldo went to his wife and gave her the choice of keeping his personal property or his real estate. . . . She was much displeased at having to make this choice, but she kept the real estate. From his personal property he made retribution to those whom he had treated unjustly.

At the Assumption of the blessed Virgin, casting some money among the village poor, he cried, "No man can serve two masters, God and mammon." Then his fellow-citizens ran up, thinking he had lost his mind. But going on to a higher place, he said: "My fellow-citizens and friends, I am not insane, as you think, but I am avenging myself on my enemies, who made me a slave, so that I was always more careful of money than of God, and served the creature rather than the Creator."

On the next day, coming from the church, he asked a certain citizen, once his comrade, to give him something to eat, for God's sake. His friend, leading him to his house, said, "I will give you whatever you need as long as you live." When this came to the ears of his wife, she was not a little troubled, and as though she had lost her mind, she ran to the archbishop of the city and implored him not to let her husband beg bread from anyone but her. . . .

[Waldo was accordingly conducted into the presence of the archbishop.] And the woman, seizing her husband by the coat, said, "Is it not better, husband, that I should redeem my sins by giving you alms than that strangers should do so?" And from that time he was not allowed to take food from anyone in that city except from his wife.

SOURCE: "Waldo of Lyons, the founder of the Waldensians," by a writer of about 1218. In *Readings in European History*, Vol. 1, ed. J.H. Robinson (New York: Ginn, 1904), pp. 380-1.

1. *Is the author of this passage sympathetic to Waldo?*
2. *What evidence suggests that the Church did not approve of Waldo's actions?*
3. *Find out more about Waldo and his followers. Why did the Church declare his teachings to be heresy?*

## FRANCIS OF ASSISI

*As a young man, Francis of Assisi renounced personal comfort and wealth to live a simple life of poverty and service to others. He soon attracted a group of followers, who became known as Franciscans. The Franciscans chose to live and preach among the poor rather than to cloister themselves in monasteries. The excerpt below was written in 1228, two years after the death of Saint Francis at the age of 44.*

The father of the blessed Francis, when he learned that his son was ridiculed in the open streets, first strove by abuse to turn him from his chosen way. When he could not thus prevail over him, he desired the servant of God to renounce all his inheritance. That this might be done, he brought the blessed Francis before the bishop of Assisi. At this Francis did greatly rejoice and hastened with a willing heart to fulfill his father's demands.

When he had come before the bishop he did not delay, nor did he suffer others to hinder him. Indeed, he waited not to be told what he should do, but straightway did take off his garments and cast them away and gave them back to his father; and he stood all naked before the people. But the bishop took heed of his spirit and was filled with exceeding great wonder at his zeal and steadfastness; so he gathered him in his arms and covered him with the cloak that he wore. Behold now had he cast aside all things which are of this world.

The holy one, lover of all humility, did then betake himself to the lepers and abode with them most tenderly for the love of God. He washed away all the putrid matter from them, and even cleansed the blood and all that came forth from the ulcers, as he himself spake in his will: "When I was yet in my sins it did seem to me too bitter to look upon the lepers, but the Lord himself did lead me among them and I had compassion upon them."

Now upon a certain day, in the church of Santa Maria Portiuncula the gospel was read—how that the Lord sent forth his disciples to preach. It was while they did celebrate the solemn mystery of the mass, and the blessed one of God stood by and would fain understand the sacred words. So he did humbly ask the priest that the gospel might be expounded unto him. Then the priest set forth plainly to him, and the blessed Francis heard how the disciples were to have neither gold nor silver, nor money, nor purse, nor script, nor bread, not to carry any staff upon the road, not to have shoes nor two coats, but to preach repentance and the spirit of God, rejoicing always in the spirit of God.

Then said the blessed Francis, "This is what I long for, this is what I seek, this is what I desire to do from the bottom of my heart."

SOURCE: Thomas of Celano, *Life of St. Francis*. In *Readings in European History*, Vol. 1, ed. J.H. Robinson (New York: Ginn, 1904), pp. 390-1.

**1.** *Look up the words* leper *and* leprosy. *Why was the behavior of Francis toward the lepers courageous?*

**2.** *What opinion does Thomas of Celano, the author of this excerpt, have of Francis of Assisi?*

**3.** *Why do you think the Franciscans were accepted by the Church while the Waldensians were declared heretical?*

## DICTATUS, POPE GREGORY VII

*Soon after he became pope in 1073, Gregory VII issued the* Dictatus, *in which he stated his views on the Church and the role of the pope. A portion of the document is given below. The Holy Roman emperor Henry IV attempted to challenge Gregory's authority, but was forced to yield to the pope's demands during their meeting at Canossa in 1076.*

The Roman church was founded by God alone.

The Roman bishop alone is properly called universal.

He alone may depose bishops and reinstate them.

His legate, though of inferior grade, takes precedence, in a council, of all bishops and may render a decision of deposition against them.

He alone may use the insignia of empire.

The pope is the only person whose feet are kissed by all princes.

His title is unique in the world.

He may depose emperors.

No council may be regarded as a general one without his consent.

No book or chapter may be regarded as canonical without his authority.

A decree of his may be annulled by no one; he alone may annul the decrees of all.

He may be judged by no one.

No one shall dare to condemn one who appeals to the papal see.

The Roman church has never erred, nor ever, by the witness of the Scripture, shall err to all eternity.

He may not be considered Catholic who does not agree with the Roman church.

The pope may absolve the subjects of the unjust from their allegiance.

SOURCE: Pope Gregory VII, *Dictatus* (1075). In *Readings in European History*, Vol. 1, ed. J.H. Robinson (New York: Ginn, 1904), pp. 274-5.

**1.** *Make a list of words that have the same root as "dictatus." What connotation do these words have in common?*

**2.** *Which of the powers claimed by Gregory conflicted with those claimed by the Holy Roman emperor?*

**3.** *Compare the Church of Gregory's time to the early church described in Chapter 12.*

## STATUTE OF LABORERS

*Between 1348 and 1351, the Black Death ravaged the population of Europe. In an attempt to alleviate the economic and social disruptions caused by the plague in England, Edward III (reigned 1327–1399) issued the Statute of Laborers. In this document, he forbade laborers to profit from the fact that their services were in much greater demand than they had been before the plague struck.*

Because a great part of the people and especially of the workmen and servants has now died in that pestilence, some, seeing the straights of the masters and the scarcity of servants, are not willing to serve unless they receive excessive wages, and others, rather than through labor to gain their living, prefer to beg in idleness: We, considering the grave inconveniences which might come from the lack especially of ploughmen and such laborers, have held deliberation and treaty concerning this with the prelates and nobles and other learned men sitting by us; by whose consentient counsel we have seen fit to ordain: that every man and woman of our kingdom of England, of whatever condition, whether bond or free, who is able bodied and below the age of sixty years, not living from trade nor carrying on a fixed craft, nor having of his own the means of living, or land of his own with regard to the cultivation of which he might occupy himself, and not serving another—if he, considering his station, be sought after to serve in a suitable service, he shall be bound to serve him who has seen fit so to seek after him; and he shall take only the wages, liveries, meed or salary which, in the places where he sought to serve, were accustomed to be paid in the 20th year of our reign of England, or the five or six common years next preceding.

And if a reaper or mower, or other workman or servant, of whatever standing or condition he be, who is retained in the service of any one, do depart from the said service before the end of the term agreed, without permission or reasonable cause, he shall undergo the penalty of imprisonment, and let no one, under the same penalty, presume to receive or retain such a one in his service. Let no one, moreover, pay or permit to be paid to any one more wages, livery, meed or salary than was customary as has been said. . . .

SOURCE: Edward III, *Statute of Laborers*. In *Select Historical Documents of the Middle Ages*, ed. Ernest F. Henderson (New York: Biblo and Tannen, 1965), pp. 165–6.

1. *To what category of laborers is Edward's decree directed?*
2. *How does Edward view the efforts of laborers to profit from increased demand for their services, and the willingness of employers to pay higher wages?*

## EFFECTS OF THE PLAGUE IN FLORENCE

*In 1348, the Bubonic plague swept over Europe. At least one third of the population died within three years, and outbreaks reoccurred several times during the following century. Giovanni Boccaccio, one of the great writers of the early Renaissance, described the effects of the plague on Florence in the stories of the* **Decameron.**

My own eyes, as I said a little while ago, saw one day (and other times besides) this occurrence. The rags of a poor man dead from this disease had been thrown in a public street. Two pigs came to them and they, in their accustomed manner, first rooted among them with their snouts, and then seized them with their teeth and tossed them about with their jaws. A short hour later, after some staggering, as if the poison was taking effect, both of them fell dead to earth upon the rags which they had unhappily dragged.

Such events and many others similar to them or even worse conjured up in those who remained healthy diverse fears and imaginings. Almost all were inclined to a very cruel purpose, that is, to shun and to flee the sick and their belongings. By so behaving each believed that he would gain safety for himself. Some persons advised that a moderate manner of living, and the avoidance of all excesses, greatly strengthened resistance to this danger. Seeking out companions, such persons lived apart from other men. They closed and locked themselves in houses where no sick person was found. To live better they consumed in modest quantities the most delicate foods and the best wines, and avoided all sexual activity. They did not let themselves speak to anyone, nor did they wish to hear any news from the outside, concerning death or the sick. They lived amid music and those pleasures which they were able to obtain.

Others were of a contrary opinion. They affirmed that heavy drinking and enjoyment, making the rounds with singing and good cheer, the satisfaction of the appetite with everything one could, and the laughing and joking which derived from this, were the most effective medicine for this great evil. As they recommended, so they put into practice, according to their ability. Night and day, they went now to that tavern and now to another, drinking without moderation or measure. . . . This they could easily do, since everyone, as if he was destined to live no more, had abandoned all care of his possessions and of himself. Thus most houses had become open to all, and strangers used them as they happened upon them, as their proper owner might have done. With this inhuman intent, they continuously avoided the sick with all their power.

In this great affliction and misery of our city, the revered authority of both divine and human laws was left to fall and decay by those who administered and executed them. They too, just as other men, were all either dead or sick or so destitute of their families, that they were unable to fulfill any office. As a result, everyone could do just as he pleased.

*SOURCE:* Giovanni Boccaccio, *The Decameron,* trans. David and Patricia Herlihy. In *Medieval Culture and Society* (New York: Walker and Co., 1967), pp. 353-4

1. *In light of today's medical knowledge, explain the merits of the two plans people used to avoid the plague.*
2. *What were the most devastating effects of the plague on the lives of the survivors?*

*In the late 14th century, Geoffrey Chaucer produced one of the greatest works in vernacular English.* **The Canterbury Tales** *includes a prologue in which Chaucer introduces the reader to each of the 29 pilgrims traveling to the shrine of Thomas à Becket at Canterbury. Two of these introductions are reproduced below. The language in these excerpts has been updated; it is not the language of Chaucer's time.*

### THE WIFE FROM BATH

A Good Wife was there from beside the city
Of Bath—a little deaf—which was a pity.
Such a great skill on making cloth she spent
That she surpassed the folk of Ypres and Ghent.
No parish wife would dream of such a thing
As going before her with an offering,
And if one did, so angry would she be
It put her wholly out of charity. . . .

Bold was her face, and fair and red of hue.
She was a worthy woman all her life;
Five times at church door had she been a wife,
Not counting other company in youth—
But this we need not mention here, in truth.
Thrice at Jerusalem this dame had been,
And many a foreign river she had seen,
And she had gone to Rome and to Boulogne,
To St. James' in Galicia, and Cologne.
Much lore she had from wandering by the way;
Still, she was gap-toothed, I regret to say. . . .
No tongue was readier with a jest than hers.
Perhaps she knew love remedies, for she
Had danced the old game long and cunningly.

### THE KNIGHT

A Knight there was, and that a noble man,
Who from the earliest time when he began
To ride forth, loved the way of chivalry,
Honor and faith and generosity.
Nobly he bare himself in his lord's war,
And he had ridden abroad (no man so far),
In many a Christian and a heathen land,
Well honored for his worth on every hand.
He was at Alexandria when that town
Was won, and many times had sat him down
Foremost among the knights at feast in Prussia.
And everywhere he went his fame was high.
And though renowned, he bore him prudently;
Meek was he in his manner as a maid.
In all his life to no man had he said
A word but what was courteous and right;
He was a very perfect noble knight.
But now to tell you what array he had—
His steeds were good, but he himself was clad
Plainly . . .

SOURCE: Geoffrey Chaucer, *The Canterbury Tales*, trans. Frank E. Hill (London: Longman, Green & Co., 1945), pp. 4-5, 18-19.

**1. List the places the woman of Bath had visited. What was the importance of each in medieval Europe?**
**2. Analyze Chaucer's attitude toward each of these two pilgrims.**

## THE MAGNA CARTA

*In 1215, the barons of England forced King John to sign the Magna Carta, a document which defined the rights of the king and the feudal privileges of the nobility. Although the articles of the charter addressed the specific issues of the time, many of them became the foundation for new freedoms which eventually extended to all British people. For example, paragraph 12 addressed the fact that King John had repeatedly imposed burdensome feudal taxes upon his free subjects. In time, the language of this paragraph led to the concept that no taxes can be levied without the consent of the governed. Another important article of the charter is paragraph 39, which eventually led to the right of all subjects to a trial by a jury of their peers.*

2. If any earl, baron, or other person that holds lands directly of the Crown, for military service, shall die, and at his death his heir shall be of full age and owe a "relief," the heir shall have his inheritance on payment of the ancient scale of "relief." That is to say, the heir or heirs of an earl shall pay 100 pounds for the entire earl's barony, the heir or heirs of a knight 100 shillings at most for the entire knight's "fee," and any man that owes less shall pay less, in accordance with the ancient usage of "fees."

8. No widow shall be compelled to marry, so long as she wishes to remain without a husband. But she must give security that she will not marry without royal consent, if she holds her lands of the Crown, or without the consent of whatever other lord she may hold them of.

12. No "scutage" or "aid" may be levied in our kingdom without its general consent, unless it is for the ransom of our person, to make our eldest son a knight, and (once) to marry our eldest daughter. For these purposes only a reasonable "aid" may be levied. "Aids" from the city of London are to be treated similarly.

13. The city of London shall enjoy all its ancient liberties and free customs, both by land and by water. We also will and grant that all other cities, boroughs, towns, and ports shall enjoy all their liberties and free customs.

17. Ordinary lawsuits shall not follow the royal court around, but shall be held in a fixed place.

20. For a trivial offence, a free man shall be fined only in proportion to the degree of his offence, and for a serious offence correspondingly, but not so heavily as to deprive him of his livelihood. In the same way, a merchant shall be spared his merchandise, and a husbandman the implements of his husbandry, if they fall upon the mercy of a royal court. None of these fines shall be imposed except by the assessment on oath of reputable men of the neighborhood.

23. No town or person shall be forced to build bridges over rivers except those with an ancient obligation to do so.

28. No constable or other royal official shall take corn or other movable goods from any man without immediate payment, unless the seller voluntarily offers postponement of this.

35. There shall be standard measures of wine, ale, and corn . . . throughout the kingdom. There shall also be a standard width of dyed cloth, russett, and haberject, a type of cloth, namely two ells within the selvedges. Weights are to be standardised similarly.

39. No free man shall be seized or imprisoned, or stripped of his rights or possessions, or outlawed or exiled, or deprived of his standing in any other way, nor will we proceed with force against him, or send others to do so, except by the lawful judgment of his equals or by the law of the land.

40. To no one will we sell, to no one deny or delay rights or justice.

41. All merchants may enter or leave England unharmed and without fear, and may stay or travel within it, by land or water, for purposes of trade, free from all illegal exactions, in accordance with ancient and lawful customs. This, however, does not apply in time of war to merchants from a country that is at war with us.

45. We will appoint as justices, constables, sheriffs, or other officials, only men that know the law of the realm and are minded to keep it well.

48. All evil customs relating to forests and warrens, foresters, warreners, sheriffs and their servants, or river-banks and their wardens, are at once to be investigated in every county by 12 sworn knights of the county, and within 40 days of their enquiry the evil customs are to be abolished completely and irrevocably. But we, or our chief justice if we are not in England, are first to be informed.

52. To any man whom we have deprived or dispossessed of lands, castles, liberties, or rights, without the lawful judgment of his equals, we will at once restore these. In cases of dispute the matter shall be resolved by the judgment of the 25 barons referred to below in the clause for securing peace (61). In cases, however, where a man was deprived or dispossessed of something without the lawful judgment of his equals by our father King Henry or our brother King Richard, and it remains in our hands or is held by others under our warranty, we shall have respite for the period commonly allowed to Crusaders. . . . On our return from the Crusade, or if we abandon it, we will at once render justice in full.

61. Since we have granted all these things for God, for the better ordering of our kingdom, and to allay the discord that has arisen between us and our barons, and since we desire that they shall be enjoyed in their entirety, with lasting strength, for ever, we give and grant to the barons the following security:

The barons shall elect 25 of their number to keep, and cause to be observed with all their might, the peace and liberties granted and confirmed to them by this charter. . . .

---

SOURCE: The Magna Carta. In *British Documents of Liberty* by Henry Marsh (Rutherford, N.J.: Fairleigh Dickinson University Press, 1971), pp. 41-6.

1. *What were the major concerns of the barons who forced John to sign the Magna Carta?*
2. *Compare the articles cited above to the American Bill of Rights (the first ten amendments to the Constitution of the United States). Which articles in the two documents are comparable? What are the similarities and differences?*

## THE PRINCE

*Niccolo Machiavelli presented his book* The Prince *as a handbook for a medieval ruler who wanted to stay in power. The methods he advocates seem cynical to modern readers, and some have even suggested that the book is a parody.*

Laying aside, therefore, all imaginary notions of a prince, and discoursing of nothing but what is actually true, I say that all men when they are spoken of, and especially princes, who are in a higher and more eminent station, are remarkable for some quality or other that makes them either honorable or contemptible. Hence it is that some are counted liberal, others miserable . . . some munificent, others rapacious; some cruel, others merciful; some faithless, others precise; one poor-spirited and effeminate, another fierce and ambitious; one sincere, another cunning; one rugged and morose, another accessible and easy; one grave, another giddy; one devout, another an atheist.

No man, I am sure, will deny but that it would be an admirable thing and highly to be commended to have a prince endowed with all the good qualities aforesaid; but because it is impossible to have, much less to exercise, them all by reason of the frailty and grossness of our nature, it is convenient that he be so well instructed as to know how to avoid the scandal of those vices which may deprive him of his state, and be very cautious of the rest, though their consequences be not so pernicious, so that where they are unavoidable he need trouble himself the less.

To come now to the other qualities proposed, I say that every prince should desire to be esteemed merciful rather than cruel, but with great caution that his mercy be not abused. Caesar Borgia was counted cruel, yet that cruelty reduced Romagna, united it, settled it in peace, and rendered it faithful. . . .

And from hence arises a new question, Whether it is better to be beloved than feared, or feared than beloved? It is answered both would be convenient, but because that is hard to attain, it is better and more secure, if one must be wanting, to be feared rather than beloved; for, in general, men are ungrateful, inconstant, hypocritical, fearful of danger, and covetous of gain. Whilst they receive any benefit by you, and the danger is at a distance, they are absolutely yours; their blood, their estates, their lives, and their children, as I said before, are all at your service. But when mischief is at hand, and you have present need of their help, they make no scruple to revolt; and that prince who leaves himself naked of other preparations, and relies wholly upon their professions, is sure to be ruined; for amity contracted by price, and not by greatness and generosity of the mind, may seem a good pennyworth, yet when you have occasion to make use of it, you will find it of no account.

---

*SOURCE:* Machiavelli, *The Prince.* In *Readings in European History*, Vol. 1, ed. J.H. Robinson (New York: Ginn, 1904), pp. 518-20.

**1.** *How does Machiavelli justify his statement that it is better for a ruler to be feared than loved?*

**2.** *Machiavelli is well known for his stated belief that "the ends justify the means." What are the "means" that he advocates here, and what is the "end" that justifies them?*

## A STREET FIGHT IN MILAN

*Benvenuto Cellini, a talented Renaissance sculptor and goldsmith, lived an extraordinarily full and adventurous life. His fiery temper led him to engage in many exploits such as the one recounted below.*

In the meanwhile my enemies had proceeded slowly toward Chiavica, as the place was called, and had arrived at the crossing of several roads, going in different directions; but the street in which Pompeo's house stood was the one which leads straight to the Campo di Fiore. Some business or other made him enter the apothecary's shop which stood at the corner of Chiavica, and there he stayed a while transacting it. I had just been told that he had boasted of the insult which he fancied he had put upon me; but be that as it may, it was to his misfortune; for precisely when I came up to the corner, he was leaving the shop, and his bravi [guards] had opened their ranks and received him in their midst. I drew a little dagger with a sharpened edge, and breaking the line of his defenders, laid my hands upon his breast so quickly and coolly, that none of them were able to prevent me. Then I aimed to strike him in the face; but fright made him turn his head around; and I stabbed him just beneath the ear. I gave only two blows, for he fell stone dead at the second. I had not meant to kill him; but, as the saying goes, knocks are not dealt by measure. With my left hand I plucked back the dagger and with my right hand drew my sword to defend my life. However, all those bravi ran up to the corpse and took no action against me; so I went back alone through Strada Giulia, considering how best to put myself in safety.

. . . A few days afterwards the Cardinal Farnese was elected Pope.

After he had put affairs of greater consequence in order, the new Pope sent for me, saying that he did not wish anyone else to strike [design and make] his coins. To these words of his Holiness a gentleman very privately acquainted with him, named Messer Latino Juvinale, made answer that I was in hiding for a murder committed on the person of one Pompeo of Milan, and set forth what could be argued for my justification in the most favorable terms. The Pope replied: 'I knew nothing of Pompeo's death, but plenty of Benvenuto's provocation; so let a safe conduct be at once made out for him, in order that he may be placed in perfect security.' A great friend of Pompeo's, who was also intimate with the Pope, happened to be there; he was a Milanese, called Messer Ambrogio. This man said: 'In the first days of your papacy it were not well to grant pardons of this kind.' The Pope turned to him and answered: 'You know less about such matters than I do. Know then that men like Benvenuto, unique in their profession, stand above the law; and how far more he, then, who received the provocation I have heard of?' When my safe conduct had been drawn out, I began at once to serve him, and was treated with the utmost favor.

---

SOURCE: Benvenuto Cellini, *The Life of Benvenuto Cellini* (Garden City, N.Y.: Phaidon, 1960), pp. 136-8.

1. *What did Cellini mean by the phrase "knocks are not dealt by measure"?*
2. *What does this excerpt reveal about Cellini's character and about the society in which he lived?*
3. *What do you think of the pope's statement that "men like Benvenuto stand above the law"?*

# Index

Attila the Hun, 67
Augustine, Saint (354–430), of Hippo, 15–16, 230
Augustine, Saint (d. 604), archbishop of
    Canterbury, 87, 157
Augustus, Philip. *See* Philip II (king of France)
Averroes (Moslem philosopher), 51, 122
Avicenna (Moslem physician), 44, 45
Avignon papacy, 185. *See also* Roman Catholic
    Church (Middle Ages)

Babylonian captivity
    of Jews, 2
    as term for Avignon papacy, 185
Bacon, Roger, 122, 123
Baghdad, in Moslem world, 43
*Baillis*, 181
Ball, John, and Peasants' Revolt, 171, 173
Banking, rise of, 231–3
Barbarossa, Frederick. *See* Frederick I (Holy
    Roman emperor)
Barrel vaulting, in architecture, 130
Barter, and medieval economy, 230
Basil II (Byzantine emperor), 25
Bavaria, in Holy Roman Empire, 144
Becket, Thomas à, 165
Bede, Venerable, 87, 117
Bedouins, 32, 33
Bela IV (king of Hungary), 205
Belisarius (Byzantine general), 20
Benedict, Saint, 86–7
Benedict XI (pope), 185
Benedictines, 86–7
*Beowulf*, 80, 126
Berbers, 41
Bernard of Clairvaux, 88–9, 97
Bezant (coin), 28
*Bible*, 15
Bill of Rights (U.S.), 168
Bishop, in Christian churches, 13–14, 15
Bishop of Rome (pope), 14
Black Death. *See* Bubonic plague
Black Prince, in England, 171
Black Stone, of Mecca, 33, 36, 37
Blanche of Castile, 181
Bloodletting, in medieval medicine, 123, 124
Boccaccio, Giovanni, 233, 258, 298
Bolesaw I (Polish king), 202
Bolingbroke, Henry. *See* Henry IV (king of
    England)
Bologna, university at, 118–19
Boniface VIII (pope), 184–5
*Book of Kells*, 156
*Book of the Courtier* (Castiglione), 246
*Book of the Secret of Secrets* (Rhazes), 47
Books, in Middle Ages, 117. *See also* Printing
Borgia, Lucretia, 260, 261

Botticelli, Sandro, 248
Bouvines, battle of, 180
Brunelleschi, Filippo, and Renaissance
    architecture, 250
Bubonic plague
    economic effects of, 233–4, 235
    in England, 171
Buddhism, in Japan, 54–5
    Mahayana Buddhism, 58–9
    Zen Buddhism, 55, 57, 58
Buonarroti, Michelangelo. *See* Michelangelo
Burckhardt, Jacob (historian), 237
Burgundians, and division of Gaul, 68
Buttresses, in architecture, 130, 131
Byzantine Church. *See* Orthodox Church
Byzantine Empire, 18–31
    agriculture in, 28–9
    architecture in, 29–30
    art in, 29–30
    citizenship in, 22
    civilization in, 28–30
    commerce in, 28–9
    decline of, 25–6
    and dynasty of Heraclius, 23–4
    education in, 29
    extent of, during Justinian's reign, 20–1
    and fall of Constantinople, 25–6, 99–100
    influences of, 29, 30
    invasions of, 23
    under Justinian, 19–23
    and Leo III, 24–5, 26–7, 42
    and Macedonian dynasty, 25
    and Roman legal traditions, 22
    rulers of, 22
    theological controversies in, 26–7
    and spread of Islam, 40
    and Viking raids, 79
    and wars with Persia, 23
Byzantium, 18–19. *See also* Constantinople
Byzas, and Byzantium, 18

*Caesaropapism*, 22–3
Cairo, in Moslem world, 43
Calendar
    Gregorian, 5
    Islamic, 35
    of the Mayas, 137
*Caliph*, 39
Calligraphy, Moslem, 49
*Canon of Medicine* (Avicenna), 45
Canossa, 147–8
Canterbury, first archbishop of, 157
*Canterbury Tales* (Chaucer), 127–8, 173
Cantons, Swiss, 200
Canute (Danish king), 78, 159

277

278